CQ GUIDE TO

CURRENT AMERICAN
GOVERNMENT

Fall 2006

CQ PRESS

A Division of Congressional Quarterly Inc.

Washington, D.C.

i

Congressional Quarterly Inc.

Congressional Quarterly Inc., a publishing and information services company, is the recognized national leader in political journalism. CQ Inc. serves clients in the fields of business, government, news and education with complete, timely and nonpartisan information on Congress, politics and national issues. CQ Press is a division of Congressional Quarterly Inc. The Library Reference imprint of CQ Press publishes this work and hundreds of others on the institutions, processes and policies of government to serve the needs of librarians, researchers, students, scholars and interested citizens. Other titles include the *Guide to the Presidency,* the *Guide to Congress,* the *Guide to the U.S. Supreme Court,* the *Guide to U.S. Elections* and *Politics in America.* CQ Press's American Government A to Z Series is a reference collection that provides essential information about the U.S. Constitution, Congress, the presidency, the Supreme Court and the electoral process. *Congress and the Nation,* a record of government for each presidential term, is published every four years. CQ Press also publishes the *CQ Researcher,* a weekly print periodical and online reference database covering today's most debated social and political issues. Visit www.cqpress.com to learn more about these and other publications of CQ Press.

CQ Press
1255 22nd Street, NW, Suite 400
Washington, DC 20037

Phone: 202-729-1900; toll-free, 1-866-4CQ-PRESS (1-866-427-7737)

Web: www.cqpress.com

Cover photos: Scott J. Ferrell and Patsy Lynch, Congressional Quarterly
Cover design: Paul P. Pressau

♾ The paper used in this publication exceeds the requirements of the American National Standard for Information Sciences—Permanence of Paper for Printed Library Materials, ANSI Z39.48-1992.

Printed and bound in the United States of America
10   09   08   07   06   1   2   3   4   5

ISBN 0-87289-345-6
ISSN 0196-612-X

Contents

Introduction v

Foundations of American Government • 1

Mr. Sam Comes to Washington • 2
After a few miscues, Wal-Mart is building a powerful Washington lobby shop and toting up a stack of wins as it confronts rising opposition from its critics
By Michael R. Crittenden and Rebecca Adams

Toward a More Perfect Definition of 'Citizen' • 12
Some in Congress say it's time for another look at how the 14th Amendment applies to illegal immigration
By Michael Sandler

Privacy Erosion: A 'Net Loss • 14
As government snooping on the Web increases, lawmakers are under pressure to find a cyber-age definition of 'unreasonable searches and seizures'
By Joelle Tessler

Imbalance of Power • 20
Lawmakers have offered little resistance to White House claims of authority to write rules in the war on terrorism. Now the NSA surveillance case has many pushing back
By Keith Perine

Federalism

The Perils of a Low Profile • 27
Lacking clout and Hill defenders, smaller social programs are the easiest victims when the GOP decides to curtail spending
By David Nather

Washington's Rules Put the Squeeze on States • 32
White House liability protections for industry prompts concern among conservatives and local officials
By Rebecca Adams

Political Participation • 35

Playing Defense • 36
The Republicans face newer and thornier obstacles as they strive for a continuing majority in 2006
By Bob Benenson

Scrutiny on Tribes Keeps Stakes High • 42
American Indian leaders urged to press on with Hill agenda despite flak from Abramoff lobbying scandal
By John Cochran

The End of the Republican Revolution • 45
It's still the majority party, but the potent mix of vision and will that won it control of the Capitol has all but evaporated
By John Cochran

A New Medium for the Message • 53
Grass-roots advocacy has exploded on the Internet, giving business and interest groups a powerful tool for rallying troops to their cause. But will an e-mail to your congressman be heard above the electronic din?
By John Cochran

Government Institutions • 61

Congress

Focusing on a Fresh Start • 62
Having seen their legislative blueprint crumpled last year by a mix of hard losses and victories that failed to inspire the party base, Republicans are eager to get 2006 rolling
By Amol Sharma

Learning to Stick Together • 66
House Democrats reached record unity in 2005, as the Senate GOP's loyalties swayed slightly
By Martin Kady II

The Presidency

Taking 'As Long As It Takes' No Longer • 70
Congress is saying 'enough' to the president it has always backed on Iraq, demanding realistic goals and a timely drawdown of U.S. troops
By Jonathan Broder

Bold, Sweeping Agenda: Not This Time • 76
Bush defends war, wiretapping but ratchets down big plans
By Martin Kady II

Supreme Court and the Judiciary

Precedent Heeded, but Not Revered • 80
While respect for settled law is Topic A in nomination hearings, the high court has a history of reversing itself
By Keith Perine

CONTENTS

A Risky Strategy for Judging Judges • 82

Democrats, by sowing the wind with ideological opposition to Alito, risk reaping the whirlwind

By Seth Stern

Politics and Public Policy • 85

Food Industry

Obesity on the Docket • 86

Industry is bracing for a tough battle in the 'food court' as the rising cost of obesity has states looking for relief in litigation

By Adriel Bettelheim

Foreign Investment

Defining 'Ours' in a New World • 93

Foreign investment in U.S. industry and infrastructure worries many, but proponents say capital without borders is key to the global economy—and America's prosperity

By John Cranford

Health Care

A Nation of Health Shoppers • 100

Bush sketches a 'consumer driven' plan to fight rising health care costs, but critics question the savings and say key problems are unaddressed

By Rebecca Adams

Immigration

A Parting of Ways at the Border • 107

The rift in the GOP over Bush's immigration policy reflects the nation's mixed signals on an issue roiled by security fears, regional biases and hard economic realities

By Michael Sandler

Taxation

The Power of Status Quo • 114

Overhauling the tax code has been a popular idea for years. But fundamental reform will involve disrupting some deeply rooted social and corporate policies

By Joseph J. Schatz

Appendixes • 119

The Legislative Process in Brief • 120

The Budget Process in Brief • 124

Glossary of Congressional Terms • 125

Congressional Information on the Internet • 148

Index • 150

Introduction

The *Guide to Current American Government* is a collection of articles from *CQ Weekly*, a trusted source for in-depth, nonpartisan reporting on and analyses of congressional action, presidential activities, policy debates and other news and developments in Washington, D.C. *CQ Weekly* broadened its editorial focus in January 2005 to cover more closely the intersection of government and commerce; several of the articles included in this collection involve this relationship, which reflects much of the dynamic in American government today. The articles, selected to complement introductory American government texts with up-to-date examinations of current issues and controversies, are divided into four sections: Foundations of American Government, Political Participation, Government Institutions, and Politics and Public Policy.

Foundations of American Government. This section examines issues and events involving interpretation of the U.S. Constitution, such foundational principles as federalism and democracy, and political ideologies and political culture in the United States. This edition of the *Guide* includes a look at how indispensable lobbying at the national level has become to big business, a profile of a group in Congress trying to establish a constitutional basis for denying citizenship to the children of illegal immigrants, an examination of constitutional issues raised by recent NSA wiretapping, a glimpse into how small social programs fall victim to budget cuts and an exploration of how President George W. Bush's efforts on behalf of liability protection for industry have disappointed states' rights proponents.

Political Participation. The articles in this section examine current issues in electoral and party politics, voting behavior and public opinion. Those selected for this edition examine the outlook for the Republican Party in the 2006 midterm elections, ways in which the Abramoff lobbying scandal has affected Indian tribes' participation in the political process, the departure of former House majority leader Tom DeLay and why companies and interest groups are turning to the Internet as a lobbying tool.

Government Institutions. This section explores the inner workings of Congress, the presidency and the federal courts. The articles included analyze the legislative records of the two major parties in Congress as they gear up for the 2006 midterm elections and President Bush's scaled-back vision for domestic policy and the U.S. commitment in Iraq. Two articles look at ways in which ideological issues affect the composition of the Supreme Court.

Politics and Public Policy. This section profiles major policy issues on the national agenda. This edition features articles on the potential for obesity litigation against the food industry, arguments over medical savings accounts, the port security controversy as it relates to the global economy, the immigration reform debate and prospects for tax code reform.

Foundations of American Government

This section highlights current issues in American politics that involve the core principles of democracy—individual rights and liberties, the role of government, the limits of federalism, and American political ideologies and political culture. These foundations frame the attitudes, interests, and institutions that dictate political choices and outcomes.

In light of the scandal involving high-profile lobbyist Jack Abramoff, the relationship between lobbyists and Washington policymakers is coming under increased scrutiny. The first article provides a glimpse into just how entrenched that relationship is in American political culture. Faced with a determined opposition made up of union organizers and liberal activists bent on thwarting its efforts at expansion and consolidation, Wal-Mart, the nation's largest retailer, has discovered what other mega-corporations have long known—effective lobbying at the federal level is simply one of the costs of doing business.

Easily overlooked in the debate over immigration reform are the constitutional underpinnings of immigration law. One reason for this oversight is that the language in the 14th Amendment guaranteeing citizenship to all persons born or naturalized in the United States has been settled law for more than a hundred years. But, as the second article reveals, some conservative Republicans in Congress are drifting from their usual strict constructionist interpretation of the Constitution to consider legislative intent as they push for legislation that would deny "birthright citizenship" to the children of illegal aliens. The Fourth Amendment's restriction on unreasonable searches and seizures of "persons, houses, papers, and effects" is the foundation of privacy laws, but the framers could not have anticipated an era in which people commonly warehouse electronic versions of their most intimate records with private companies. The third article details how Congress's inability to keep pace with technology has allowed government agencies to find new ways to snoop on private individuals and examines the legislative efforts being made to counteract this trend.

Since the attacks on September 11, 2001, the Bush administration has demonstrated a willingness to assert for itself an expanded executive authority in prosecuting the war on terror. The fourth article explores how the National Security Administration's program of warrantless surveillance relates to the Constitution's war powers provisions and has created a showdown between Congress and the executive branch. How this controversy is resolved will determine what limits, if any, President Bush and future presidents will have in gathering wartime intelligence.

The first article in this section explores how powerful interest groups wield tremendous political clout to achieve their goals. The fifth article looks at a different aspect of political culture, one in which smaller social programs—even those with proven track records of providing assistance to the most needy—are frequently the first to fall victim to budget cuts.

The final article examines how President Bush's vision of a more limited role for the federal government in local affairs contrasts with his administration's attempts to limit individuals' ability to sue corporations. The administration's efforts in this direction have frustrated certain states' efforts to regulate business and have drawn the ire of some conservatives who depend on the president to advance a consistent states' rights philosophy.

NEW CREW IN TOWN:
Newly hired Wal-Mart lobbyist Lee Culpepper, seated, is assembling a staff to handle the company's Washington issues that he hopes will number at least 12 by the end of this year.

Mr. Sam Comes to Washington

After a few miscues, Wal-Mart is building a powerful Washington lobby shop and toting up a stack of wins as it confronts rising opposition from its critics

BROKEN ARROW is a little town on the outskirts of Tulsa, Oklahoma, just the sort of place where the world's largest retailer can operate two of its superstores and do quite well. It's hardly the place to have an epiphany about how not to conduct business.

But when Wal-Mart Stores Inc. was blocked six years ago from buying a bank in Broken Arrow by actions taken 1,200 miles away on Capitol Hill, the company was forced to accept belatedly what most of corporate America learned long ago: A significant presence in Washington is indispensable to any major company's business plan.

Wal-Mart was and still is an unconventional company. Founder Sam Walton decided that he and his managers could do things differently than other retailers and succeed. Running its global business from a headquarters in remote Bentonville, Arkansas, Walton's hometown, is just one manifestation of that attitude.

It was also a company that had no full-time representative in Washington, so there was no one to warn people at the top that its bid to get into banking was bound for trouble. Nor was

there anyone to sell its side of the story.

Wal-Mart learned that lesson the hard way. But since the Broken Arrow debacle, and particularly in the past year, Wal-Mart has built an influential lobbying operation that befits the company that sits atop the Fortune 500. It is now capable of currying favor with lawmakers and inserting its agenda into policy debates ranging from banking to Medicare prescription drug payments. And Wal-Mart notched victories earlier this year on such issues as civil liability law, Labor Department investigations and trucking regulations.

Contributions from the company's political action committee surged to $2.2 million in 2004 from $148,250 in 1998, while in-house lobbying expenses amounted to $1.2 million last year, up from zero in 1998. Wal-Mart's government affairs office is in the midst of a hiring binge, beefing up its in-house staff to as many as 12 by year's end from four in January.

"They have become very sophisticated," said Ron Ence, vice president of congressional relations for the Independent Community Bankers of America, one group that vigorously opposes Wal-Mart's banking venture. "They have a substantial PAC, a substantial lobbying staff, they are seen at every PAC event and they

are walking the halls," he said.

Closely tied to Wal-Mart's lobbying enterprise is its stepped-up public relations effort. Confronted with accusations from a host of critics that it underpays workers, hurts local economies and is generally a cold-blooded colossus intent only on the size of its profit, Wal-Mart has gone on the offensive.

In Bentonville, the company assembled political campaign veterans to set up a public relations "war room" and respond to a salvo of attacks, the latest being an independent film, "Wal-Mart: The High Cost of Low Price," that premiered Nov. 1 in New York.

The company's critics — union workers, environmentalists and liberal activists — want to transform their concerns into a political crusade that will galvanize state legislatures across the country and Congress. These critics portray the fight as a struggle over the future of America's economy, and charge that Wal-Mart is the embodiment of corporate evils condoned by the Bush administration. They plan more than 1,000 religious events, community rallies and academic conferences in November to draw attention to what they identify as Wal-Mart's disdain for its 1.3 million U.S. workers.

3

How Wal-Mart's Spending on Lobbying, Politics Stacks Up

Wal-Mart's Washington presence has grown, but the company's spending to lobby at the federal level is still below that of the country's remaining top 10 companies, many of whom face greater regulatory scrutiny. Wal-Mart spends far more on lobbying than any other retailer.

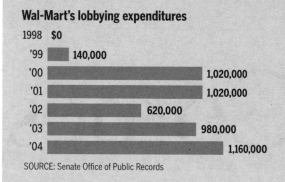

Wal-Mart's lobbying expenditures

1998	$0
'99	140,000
'00	1,020,000
'01	1,020,000
'02	620,000
'03	980,000
'04	1,160,000

SOURCE: Senate Office of Public Records

Lobbying by largest U.S. companies
Ranked by revenue, 2004

Wal-Mart	$1.2 million
Exxon Mobil	7.7 million
General Motors	8.5 million
Ford Motor	7.2 million
General Electric	17.2 million
Chevron Texaco	5.2 million
ConocoPhillips	2.7 million
Citigroup	7.2 million
AIG	8.1 million
IBM	6.5 million

Lobbying by largest U.S. retailers
Ranked by revenue, 2004

Wal-Mart	$1.2 million
Target	200,000
Sears Roebuck	700,000
J.C. Penney	82,000
Kmart	110,000
Federated Department Stores	None
Kohl's	None
Dillard's	77,000
Dollar General	None
Nordstrom	None

SOURCES: Senate Office of Public Records, Center for Public Integrity, Fortune Magazine 500

"We will make this the most important political fight in the country," said Chris Kofinis, a spokesman for Wake Up Wal-Mart, a group run from the Washington offices of the United Food and Commercial Workers International Union. "This debate is about what kind of America we want to live in."

As a result, Wal-Mart's Washington lobbyists say they spend more than half of their time defending the company's reputation.

"The attacks have grown bigger and bigger, and so the stakes have become bigger and bigger," said George W. Koch, a lobbyist with the Washington office of the Kirkpatrick & Lockhart law firm. Koch, a longtime Washington hand who has personal ties to President Bush, has been retained by Wal-Mart to lobby on banking issues.

Wal-Mart was highly visible in response to hurricanes Katrina and Rita, donating products, workers and money to relief efforts along the Gulf Coast. Chief Executive Officer H. Lee Scott Jr. has undertaken a charm offensive on behalf of the retailer, suggesting that Congress should raise the minimum wage to help the company's customers and promising to enforce environmental and labor standards at its overseas suppliers. *(Aiming at Wal-Mart in China, p. 6)*

The growing influence is paying off. The company's recent record shows that it rarely loses when it is the principal advocate on an issue. And there is little chance Wal-Mart will be caught off guard in Washington ever again.

A CULTURE CHANGE

Before 1999, Wal-Mart had little interest in involving itself in Washington politics. Longtime Arkansas Sen. Dale Bumpers, a Democrat, says he was a friend of patriarch Sam Walton, who died in 1992, and the rest of the Walton family. But with 24 years in the Senate, Bumpers has "no recollection" of the company lobbying him on legislation.

"They were simply not tuned into what was going on in Washington," he said. "They had a culture there that just didn't include lobbying and directing the way legislation was handled."

Blanche Lincoln, another Arkansas Democrat who served in the House for four years and replaced Bumpers in the Senate in 1999, said lawmakers would occasionally have to call Wal-Mart's Bentonville offices to alert them to legislation that might affect the company.

Even when Wal-Mart had a direct interest in a legislative issue, its representatives sometimes failed to take basic steps to notify its allies of its concerns. Four years ago, Lincoln voted against a floor amendment that would have allowed businesses to selectively bar certain solicitations on their premises. Wal-Mart wanted the amendment, which would have allowed the company to permit Salvation Army kettles by the front door and block union organizers.

She voted no because the company hadn't told her of its position, or warned her it would be debated on the floor, and the amendment failed. That and other slip-ups motivated Lincoln to prod the company to pay closer attention.

"I encouraged that they have some sort of Washington presence just because I thought it was important for them to be able to tell their story to more than just me and the rest of the Arkansas delegation," Lincoln said.

She wasn't alone. Trent Lott, a Mississippi Republican and former Senate majority leader, and Tom DeLay, the Texas Republican who recently stepped down as House majority leader, also told Wal-Mart to open its own lobbying shop rather than rely on consultants.

The company avoided Washington in large part at the insistence of Sam Walton, who eschewed spending to keep the company's overhead costs — and its prices — low.

"Mr. Sam's reputation was that he really didn't care what the government did as long as it left him alone," said Marion Berry, an Arkansas Democrat who represents the state in the House.

That position became untenable for Wal-Mart executives in the late 1990s. Not only had it been shut out of its bank acquisition, but other mega-corporations were becoming targets for regulatory and congressional scrutiny. The federal government was investigating computer giant Microsoft Corp. as a predatory monopoly. The tobacco industry had been accused of conspiracy to defraud consumers. Gun manufacturers were under attack, as were health care insurers.

Bumpers said the company's absence inside the Washington Beltway was a source of conversation among lawmakers, especially in light of its legislative loss. At the time, Wal-Mart was alone among the top five U.S. corporations by revenue that didn't have its own lobbyist.

"When a major company doesn't have an office here, it's viewed more as arrogance than as being naïve," said Erik Winborn, who was hired as Wal-Mart's second lobbyist in 2000 and left the company earlier this year.

The thrifty nature of Wal-Mart's business carried over to the character of its earliest forays into lobbying. Retired Air Force Lt. Gen. Norm Lezy, who was the company's first Washington representative, was asked to work from his home. There was no lavish party marking the Washington debut. Lezy was instructed to take lawmakers out for breakfast, not expensive dinners, Winborn recalled.

Even today, Wal-Mart lobbyists aren't reimbursed if they serve alcohol at fundraisers and big events on Capitol Hill. Its Washington

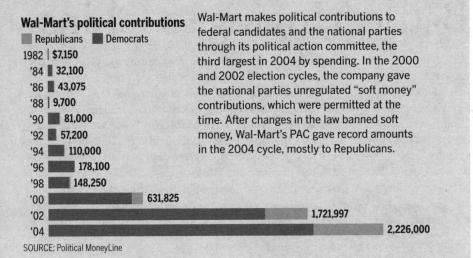

Wal-Mart's political contributions

Republicans ■ Democrats

1982	$7,150
'84	32,100
'86	43,075
'88	9,700
'90	81,000
'92	57,200
'94	110,000
'96	178,100
'98	148,250
'00	631,825
'02	1,721,997
'04	2,226,000

SOURCE: Political MoneyLine

Wal-Mart makes political contributions to federal candidates and the national parties through its political action committee, the third largest in 2004 by spending. In the 2000 and 2002 election cycles, the company gave the national parties unregulated "soft money" contributions, which were permitted at the time. After changes in the law banned soft money, Wal-Mart's PAC gave record amounts in the 2004 cycle, mostly to Republicans.

hibits commercial companies from owning banks, but made an exception for stand-alone savings and loans like the one in Broken Arrow.

It was a savvy move — to a point. And the company might have succeeded, except that it bungled the timing. Just as Wal-Mart was applying to purchase the thrift, Congress was debating an overhaul of banking laws, and the company's actions handed banking industry lobbyists the ammunition they needed to convince lawmakers that its plans were a threat to ordinary banks.

Wal-Mart wasn't prepared to defend itself and lawmakers pulled the loophole closed.

This time, the company's development into a lobbying powerhouse may turn the tables on its banking industry opponents.

Once again, Wal-Mart is attempting to take advantage of a loophole in the law. In July, the company filed with the Federal Deposit Insurance Corporation and with Utah banking regulators to purchase a so-called industrial loan company — a type of bank that, under Utah and federal laws, a commercial company can control.

Wal-Mart says it wants this bank merely to save money in the processing of checks, and credit card and debit card transactions. But its opponents in the banking industry are convinced the company's long-term goal is to run its own bank, with branches in every store,

offices are restrained in their decoration and avoid the opulent, wood-paneled look of many lobbying shops.

Wal-Mart's current legislative affairs chief, Lee Culpepper, said this isn't an accident, that it continues to reflect the corporatewide effort to spend as little as necessary. Still, he said the company has accepted the fact that lobbying, like research and development, is a normal cost of doing business.

Culpepper, the former top lobbyist at the National Restaurant Association, was hired by Wal-Mart earlier this year, and has been rapidly expanding his staff of lobbyists, support personnel and people focused on the firm's political action committee.

"I think they came to the realization that we really need to invest some money in Washington to be successful," Culpepper said.

BANK FIGHT RENEWED

The biggest focal point for Wal-Mart's lobbying forces right now is making sure the company will be allowed to own a bank. While the fight is an echo of the Oklahoma defeat of six years ago, the outcome may well be different.

Back then, Wal-Mart was hoping to exploit a loophole in federal law that generally pro-

Standing Behind Its Interests

Wal-Mart's lobbying interests run the gamut from banking to pharmaceuticals to taxes. As the country's largest private employer and the largest freight-hauler, its Washington-based concerns aren't confined to Capitol Hill, but also reach to regulatory agencies.

BANKING
Wal-Mart wants to charter an industrial loan company, a special type of bank that commercial firms can own. The company filed applications with Utah banking regulators and the FDIC in July. Neither regulator has made a decision.

TRADE
Wal-Mart is a strong supporter of free trade and promoted the Central America Free Trade Agreement, which passed this summer.

HEALTH CARE
Wal-Mart supported passage of the 2003 Medicare prescription drug law and is offering drug plans created under the law to seniors. Wal-Mart also supports legislation that would require other companies to follow its practice of putting products, such as cold medicines, that can be used to make methamphetamines behind the counter. And the company opposes Medicaid cuts to pharmacies that Congress is debating as part of pending deficit-reduction bills. The retailer also is playing defense, trying to calm criticism that some of its workers have to rely on Medicaid to pay for health care services.

TRANSPORTATION
Wal-Mart favored a proposal by Rep. John Boozman, R-Ark., to let truck drivers work 16 hours a day. Boozman failed to add the language to a five-year highway bill this summer, but the Federal Motor Carrier Administration approved a rule allowing short-haul drivers, such as those working for Wal-Mart, to work 16-hour days twice a week.

TAXES
Wal-Mart wants depreciation allowances and other tax relief for the rebuilding of stores and businesses in areas ravaged by this fall's hurricanes. Also, Wal-Mart favors a permanent extension of the work opportunity and welfare-to-work tax credits, which are aimed at encouraging employers to hire economically disadvantaged workers. The credit can reduce an employer's tax liability by as much as $8,500 per new hire.

CIVIL LAW LIABILITY
Wal-Mart supported a law enacted earlier this year designed to shift many class action lawsuits to federal courts.

AGRICULTURE
The company backed a delay in country of origin food labeling that passed this year.

DIGITAL TV
Wal-Mart supports provisions in the House and Senate deficit-reduction bills that set a specific deadline for television broadcasters to switch from analog to digital programming.

Unions See Battle Moving to China

OF ALL ITS CRITICS, none is tougher on Wal-Mart Stores Inc. than union organizers — the activists who claim to speak for the very working people the world's largest retailer says it is out to serve with low, low prices. But the company has had one great advantage over the unions: Wal-Mart's reach is global. The labor movement's is not.

In fact, U.S. union leaders have for years largely refused to engage with China, which is Wal-Mart's No. 1 supplier today — the single biggest source of the cheap labor that helps make the company's low prices possible. U.S. union officials have viewed Chinese labor as a threat to jobs. Moreover, they have objected that China's only trade federation isn't a real union at all, but part of the state apparatus of an undemocratic regime.

That's beginning to change. Just as Wal-Mart is developing new public relations strategies for defending itself at home against its antagonists and building its lobbying muscle to protect its turf in Washington, union organizers and scholars have begun, tentatively, to reach out to Chinese labor, including its state union. Their ultimate hope is to organize workers from one end of the global supply chain to the other and check the power of multinational companies such as Wal-Mart to set the terms and standards of what is fast becoming a worldwide economy.

Andrew J. Stern, president of the Service Employees International Union and one of the most prominent and aggressive figures within the U.S. labor movement, has traveled to China four times since 2002. Stern has met both with independent activists and the state-sanctioned All China Federation of Trade Unions (ACFTU). He has offered to share information and organizing expertise — and pledged to help with any efforts to unionize Wal-Mart's giant retail stores in China, which now number 49. Joining him on one of those trips, about a year ago, was Barbara Shailor, director of international affairs for the AFL-CIO.

At the same time, many labor academics have been telling U.S. unions that refusing to engage with Chinese labor groups, including ACFTU, just plays into the hands of global companies such as Wal-Mart, which are able to take advantage of divisions and com-

OPENING DOORS: With 49 Wal-Mart stores in China today, the company presents a target for unions as both importer and employer.

petition among workers to drive down wages and benefits in the relentless pursuit of lower costs and higher profits.

"If Chinese and American workers decide, 'We're not going to let ourselves be pitted against each other,' that kind of cooperative spirit across borders can be a powerful bond," says Katie Quan of the Center for Labor Research and Education at the University of California-Berkeley, an expert on Chinese labor who has provided information to both Stern and Shailor.

Stern and others are just beginning to think through the difficulties and complexities of engaging with their counterparts in a country that has a long history of suppressing dissent and resisting scrutiny by outsiders. Late last year, Chinese officials agreed to a meeting in Beijing with international labor and business leaders to discuss the regulation of multinational companies doing business in China, but then they abruptly canceled it. The government yanked the visas of participants — including Shailor and AFL-CIO President John J. Sweeney — a few days before.

Stern, Shailor and others won't divulge details of their conversations with independent labor groups in China for fear, they say, of getting those activists into serious trouble with the authorities.

And even as U.S. activists talk about renewing the old dream of global worker solidarity, the American labor movement itself is fractured. Stern leads a group of unions that earlier this year broke with Sweeney and the AFL-CIO over how best to revive the movement's flagging fortunes. So far, U.S. labor groups have failed to unionize any Wal-Mart stores at home, although their efforts continue.

But Stern, in particular, insists the time is ripe for reaching out to China, the world's most populous country and a giant in the global marketplace. The country's economy is booming, life there is changing rapidly, and workers are learning what a hard and demanding master a company such as Wal-Mart can be, Stern says.

"The truth is," he says, "multinationals are drawing us together."

And there are some ideas circulating for turning such solidarity against Wal-Mart. A sociologist and labor researcher at the Univer-

taking deposits and making loans.

They fear Wal-Mart will do to small-town and suburban banking what it has done to grocery and pharmacy stores — swamp them.

"What they are trying to do now is essentially camouflage their long-term intent to launch a nationwide banking empire through this very limited application," Ence said.

The issue engenders strong opinions both from critics and friends of the company. On the opposing side is Jim Leach, an Iowa Repub-

lican and former chairman of the House Banking Committee, who is among a group of lawmakers that vigorously opposes the idea of a retailer owning any sort of banking operation. Leach has pushed to limit Wal-Mart's ability to proceed with its plan.

Working on the company's behalf is Robert F. Bennett, a Utah Republican and member of the Senate Banking Committee. Bennett has no intention of letting Congress restrict his home state's banking rules.

Until now, Wal-Mart's critics have succeeded in blocking the company's every effort. In addition to the Broken Arrow thrift, Wal-Mart made two other failed attempts at starting a banking operation. In 2001, it tried to join with a U.S. subsidiary of Canada's Toronto-Dominion Bank, but that bid was nixed by the federal Office of Thrift Supervision, which regulates savings and loans acquisitions. The following year, Wal-Mart made its first attempt at acquiring an industrial loan charter, this time

sity of California-Riverside, Edna Bonacich, and a graduate student at the school have proposed organizing "logistics workers" around the world who move Wal-Mart's goods from factory to store and then threatening to choke off the flow at key points — warehouses or ports — to force concessions from the company.

"Wal-Mart is a global company and must be attacked as such," they write. "This is the only way to bring the big gorilla down."

What Wal-Mart Says

Wal-Mart estimates that it imported about $15 billion worth of goods from China last year — about as much as was imported from China by the United Kingdom, and more than France. Wal-Mart's purchases amounted to 12 percent of all U.S. imports from China, and if the company were a nation, it would tie the U.K. as the seventh biggest buyer of Chinese goods.

Wal-Mart says its connections with Chinese producers and its role in the global economy is good for workers and for consumers, who get quality items at the lowest possible cost. The company says it works hard in a competitive environment to see that its suppliers abide by local laws and don't mistreat their workers.

"It's an area we pay great attention to," says a Wal-Mart spokeswoman, Beth Keck.

A team of 200 company employees, along with independent auditors hired by Wal-Mart, inspect factories around the world, Keck says. They inspected roughly 7,600 suppliers last year, and stopped doing business with 108 — in one case because of forced labor and the others because of "serious child labor violations," according to an annual company report on supplier standards. Keck says the child labor violations were mostly instances where workers were a few months shy of legal age. The company doesn't disclose the locations of the factories it inspected or identify the ones that failed.

Wal-Mart stores themselves also provide Chinese workers with sought-after jobs — which is why no Wal-Mart store in China has organized a branch of the ACFTU, Keck says. She pointed to a BusinessWeek interview from August with a leader of the official union, Li Jianming, in which he is quoted saying the jobs in Wal-Mart's stores across China "in reality are quite good."

But the full quote in that BusinessWeek interview cuts both ways for the company: The union leader goes on to say that workers in

Top importers from China
Value of 2004 imports, in billions

United States:	$124.9
Hong Kong:	100.9
Japan:	73.5
South Korea:	27.8
Germany:	23.8
Netherlands:	18.5
Wal-Mart:	15.0
United Kingdom:	15.0
Taiwan:	13.5
Singapore:	12.7
France:	9.9

SOURCE: U.S. China Business Council

Chinese Wal-Mart retail outlets are afraid the company will fire them if they try to form a union.

Keck says Li is wrong. Some Wal-Mart workers overseas — in Argentina, Brazil, Mexico and Germany — do belong to unions, she says. But labor leaders say Wal-Mart has bitterly fought efforts to organize its workers around the world. In Mexico, unionized workers came with stores that Wal-Mart purchased, and some countries impose rules that require companies to recognize worker groups. Earlier this year, Wal-Mart closed a store in Quebec where workers had organized, saying the location wasn't making money. Labor leaders said the company's action was clearly intended to keep unions out.

Unions also say that companies such as Wal-Mart cannot police themselves or their suppliers. The global economy needs minimum standards to protect workers everywhere, they say.

For a labor movement trying to serve as a counterweight to Wal-Mart's global influence, the stakes in China are particularly high, since that country supplies a quarter of the world's workers. Southern China, Shailor says, is dotted with grimy factory towns serving Wal-Mart and other Western corporations.

Wal-Mart won't disclose how many suppliers it has in China, but Shailor estimates that more than 6 million Chinese workers labor to keep Wal-Mart's shelves stocked with toys, clothing and other goods. "What happens to Wal-Mart in China is important first to workers in China, but also for workers everywhere who are producing for multinational corporations like Wal-Mart," she says.

At its convention earlier this year, the AFL-CIO called for global labor solidarity and a campaign against Wal-Mart's "anti-union business model." Shailor says the best way to engage with workers in China is through independent groups and activists, although if there are opportunities to work with the ACFTU, the AFL-CIO would consider them. Stern says the bottom line for U.S. labor organizers is that the Chinese government will never allow the ACFTU to be supplanted, so they need to do everything they can to convince the existing leadership to become more independent, more active and outward-looking. Labor analysts say that some within its ranks are open to change and dialogue with the outside.

Stern says he's so far gotten no answer to his offer to help the ACFTU organize at Wal-Mart stores. But "the door," he says, "was left open."

---

in California. That attempt was blocked when state legislators passed a law barring commercial firms from buying a state-chartered bank.

The company's critics hope Congress will take a similar approach and block Wal-Mart's latest attempt to get into banking. And if Congress does act, it will probably close the door on the company's last, best chance.

Wal-Mart's strategy is to play defense, making sure its opponents in Congress aren't successful in limiting their opportunity while the

company's application is being considered by federal and state bank regulators.

Lobbyist Koch said he and other company representatives regularly talk with members of the Senate Banking and House Financial Services committees, and other interested lawmakers. It doesn't hurt his appeal that Wal-Mart has 3,702 retail locations with more than 1 million workers across the country, with stores in almost every House district.

The company's message is simple: It is inter-

ested only in cutting the cost of processing roughly 140 million credit card, debit card and check transactions made by its customers each month. Culpepper said the company estimates that by not having to contract that work to other banks, it will save $5 million to $10 million a year.

"Basically, it would be a back office transaction center," Culpepper said. "It wouldn't be related to anything a customer would see."

The Utah industrial loan company (ILC) charter that Wal-Mart wants perfectly suits

Trying to Hold On for Charity

THE LATE SAM WALTON, founder of Wal-Mart Stores Inc., eschewed politics, asserting that hard work was all that was necessary to succeed. That may have worked for Dad, but not for wife and kids.

The Walton family, wealthier than Bill Gates and Warren Buffet combined, finds itself in a peculiar predicament. Sam's wife, Helen, and her children own an unusually large 40 percent stake in Wal-Mart, currently worth about $79 billion. And like many ultra-wealthy families in America, they have set up sophisticated family trusts, partnerships and foundations to shield their wealth from estate taxes, currently levied at 47 percent of inherited assets over $2 million.

Ideally, the family would like to shift some of their Wal-Mart stock to the tax-exempt Walton Family Foundation, whose mission is to make grants to other nonprofits of the family's choosing, such as educational and religious groups.

Current federal rules would require them to sell the stock over 10 years, but it appears the family would like to retain control of the company: One of Sam and Helen Walton's surviving sons, Rob, is chairman of the Wal-Mart board.

Even the Gates and the Buffets don't have this problem. The Gates Foundation, for example, sold its stock years ago and has its assets in U.S. Treasury securities.

So the Waltons have launched a high-priced Washington public relations offensive, pointing out all the things their foundation does.

ALL IN THE FAMILY: The Waltons — sons, Jim, John (deceased) and Rob, with mother, Helen — want to find a way to retain their shares.

"In Washington, the family's attention has been directed at promoting funding for K-12 education initiatives and reforms that would create new incentives for private charitable giving," according to a statement from Lance Morgan, the Walton family's Washington spokesman, who was hired more than a year ago. Morgan is president of Powell Tate, a public relations boutique founded by Jody Powell, President Jimmy Carter's former spokesman, and Sheila Tate, the former spokeswoman for first lady Nancy Reagan.

But the family also has paid a top Washington tax lobbyist, Aubrey Rothrock III of Patton Boggs, at least $1 million since 1999, mostly to change the tax rules affecting private family foundations.

At the moment, the family's Wal-Mart shares are held by Walton Enterprises, a family partnership set up by Sam Walton before he died to avoid estate taxes. His children, Rob, John, Jim and Alice, each were allotted one-fifth of the partnership — or about 8 percent of the family's Wal-Mart's shares each. Sam and Helen each got a tenth, and when Sam died in 1992, Helen inherited his stake tax-free.

The Waltons have said they plan to give Helen's Wal-Mart stock to the Walton Family Foundation at some point, perhaps after her death. Helen is now in her 80s and frail.

Many affluent families used to use family foundations as a way

of keeping control of their companies while avoiding taxes. But in 1969, Congress passed a law to forbid a foundation and its family members from owning more than 20 percent of any company.

"The point of the rule is that individuals shouldn't be able to use private foundations as a device to control the business," said Janne Gallagher, general counsel of the Council on Foundations, a Washington-based trade association for these charitable organizations.

But Congress also gave family foundations an escape hatch, saying they don't have to worry that a family's collective holdings exceed the limit, as long as the foundation itself doesn't own more than 2 percent. But Helen's 8 percent holdings far exceed the cap. So, the Waltons have asked lawmakers to lift the limit to 5 percent.

CHARITABLE GIVING BILL

In making their case on Capitol Hill, the Waltons deny trying to cling onto the family business, instead saying they want to maximize their donations to charity. They argue that if they had to liquidate such a large number of shares in a hurry, or during a period of declining stock prices, their return would be depressed. Ultimately, that would mean less money for charity.

In 2003, the most recent year records are available, the foundation gave $107 million, largely to support programs such as charter schools and school vouchers.

Son John, who was killed in a small plane accident in June, had led the family's philanthropic efforts. There has been no public disclosures of what happened to his shares, but his wife can inherit them tax-free and keep them with the family partnership.

"The code doesn't require a fire sale," said Gallagher. The law not only gives five years to sell the excess stock, it also gives an additional five-year extension for a total of 10 years to dispose of the shares.

The Council of Foundations doesn't lobby for or against the Walton's proposal, but Gallagher said she is unaware of any other family in America that is pressing for the same privilege.

Despite the family's formidable political donations, it hasn't yet had much luck convincing Congress. A charitable giving bill — the most obvious vehicle for the family provision — is dead, due to unrelated disputes among senators over nonprofit activities. The last time similar legislation almost became law in 2003, the Waltons had no provisions in one chamber's version and were disappointed with what the other chamber included.

This fight is different from the preoccupation of other rich families: whether to keep or abolish the estate tax. The Waltons refuse to say what their position is on inheritance taxes, but they probably were aware that Rothrock, their Washington lobbyist, represents a coalition of other powerful families, including the Marses and the Gallos, in the anti-estate tax movement.

And the family foundation has donated tens of thousands of dollars to conservative policy groups, such as Americans for Tax Reform, the Cato Institute and the Heritage Foundation, who have lead the ideological charge to eradicate the estate tax.

the company's needs. Created to provide blue-collar workers with loans they couldn't get elsewhere, these state-chartered banks have evolved in recent years into niche financial institutions used to conduct larger and more complex financial transactions, particularly credit cards and mortgage loans.

Under current laws, these institutions are about the only means for commercial companies to conduct certain banking operations. That is why half of the six ILC charters the FDIC approved in 2004 were controlled by commercial companies, including Wal-Mart rival Target Corp.

These special charters are most common in three states — Utah, California and Nevada — which gives Wal-Mart a powerful ally in Utah's Bennett. He supports the special place of industrial loan charters in his state's economy, and is loath to limit them, making it difficult for any bill restricting Wal-Mart's ILC acquisition to progress in the Senate.

But opponents are still trying. Leach, the most outspoken critic of what Wal-Mart wants to accomplish, has introduced a bill that would prevent commercial firms from purchasing industrial loan companies. He has tried unsuccessfully to add similar language to other legislation. "I've taken the approach that I'll try and attach it to anything," he said.

Leach isn't alone, especially in the House. A bill that chamber passed in May contains a provision that would prevent banks owned by commercial companies from offering interest-bearing accounts to businesses. And Massachusetts Rep. Barney Frank, the senior Democrat on the Financial Services panel, said he would support legislation specifically aimed at stopping Wal-Mart's application.

"If Wal-Mart persists with its application, I think you are likely to see a bill filed that will deal with that," he said.

Capitol Hill isn't the only target of banking groups' efforts. Ence of the Community Bankers of America said Wal-Mart's opponents have also flooded the FDIC with more than 1,400 comment letters from community banks and banking groups across the country, requesting the agency deny Wal-Mart's application. A typical application for federal deposit insurance garners about half a dozen comment letters.

The regulators aren't expected to rule on Wal-Mart's bid until sometime next spring.

FIGHTING FOR THE BOTTOM LINE

The proposed bank acquisition is just one instance of many where Wal-Mart has directly engaged its critics because it was concerned

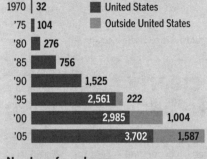

Global Growth

Wal-Mart is by far the world's largest retailer. The company is currently expanding most rapidly overseas, but it estimates it can more than double its 3,702 locations in the United States.

Number of stores

	United States	Outside United States
1970	32	
'75	104	
'80	276	
'85	756	
'90	1,525	
'95	2,561	222
'00	2,985	1,004
'05	3,702	1,587

Number of employees

1970	1,500
'75	5,800
'80	21,000
'85	81,000
'90	275,000
'95	622,000
'00	1.14 million
'05	1.6 million

Sales
In millions of dollars

1970	30.9
'75	236.2
'80	1,248.2
'85	6,400.9
'90	25,810.7
'95	82,494
'00	165,013
'05	285,222

SOURCE: Wal-Mart Stores Inc.; totals by fiscal year

that government action might cut its profit.

In June, company allies successfully thwarted Rep. Rosa DeLauro, a Connecticut Democrat and one of Wal-Mart's sharpest critics. DeLauro had wanted to derail a Labor Department ruling that benefited the company, offering a floor amendment to the department's fiscal 2006 spending bill that would have effectively barred the government from enforcing the ruling. The amendment was soundly rejected, when 22 mostly Southern Democrats joined all but three Republicans in voting for the company's position.

"One of the biggest successes has been fending off any kind of congressional investigation" into employment practices, said Win-

born, the former Wal-Mart lobbyist.

From Wal-Mart's perspective, even seemingly minor bills can be important. Missouri Republican Roy Blunt, a company ally and currently House majority leader, introduced a bill this year at the company's request that would pre-empt states from writing laws that govern the sale of certain over-the-counter cold remedies, and instead set a national standard. Wal-Mart has hopes of winning on this issue before the year is out.

Wal-Mart is promoting the national standard to avoid having to comply with a patchwork of ever-changing state laws. "It makes it that much more confusing to them," said Berry, who is cosponsor of a related bill that goes beyond what Wal-Mart wants and would allow states to enact stiffer rules than federal law. "That's the sort of thing that they lobby us about," he said.

The company has won other, similar battles in recent years. In 2001, it joined with several business groups and overturned a Clinton administration Labor Department regulation that would have required the company to adopt new ergonomics policies and educate workers about ways to prevent injuries from repetitive motions, such as sorting or lifting heavy loads.

If a worker reported an injury, employers would have had to reconfigure the workplace to prevent recurrences and give workers with long-lasting injuries up to 90 percent of their salaries for as long as 90 days while they were unable to work.

Lincoln and other Wal-Mart-friendly Democrats sided with Republicans to reverse the regulation through the rare use of the Congressional Review Act, which uses expedited procedures to allow Congress to undo actions of federal agencies.

The retailer also played an important role on a bill that would have given patients additional leverage over their health care insurance providers, including the right to sue. Wal-Mart became a player in the fight in 2001, three years after the debate began, winning inclusion of language that would have allowed big companies that self-insure their workers — of which Wal-Mart is one — the right to defend lawsuits in federal courts, considered a more business-friendly forum, than in state courts.

A year later, as the number of uninsured Americans began to rise and concerns mounted over health care costs, Wal-Mart and other business interests privately congratulated themselves when the measure died.

Earlier this year, Congress cleared a bill that

is expected to curb class action lawsuits nationwide because it strips plaintiffs of the right to sue in state courts in certain circumstances. The legislation was important to Wal-Mart, which is the target of several high-profile class action cases, including allegations of gender discrimination that involve more than 1.5 million current and former female employees, and denial of overtime pay.

Wal-Mart lobbyists worked with House Republican leaders to quietly push for changes in the measure and bankrolled the lobbying campaign for the bill that the U.S. Chamber of Commerce led, industry lobbyists say.

Sometimes, the company has to avoid getting involved in issues — immigration, for instance — where its reputation would diminish its influence.

The company favors an open immigration policy because it sees immigrants as a valuable pool of potential customers and it values the inexpensive labor that newcomers are willing to provide. But an $11 million fine that the company paid to settle federal allegations that it used illegal immigrants to clean its stores keeps Wal-Mart from vocalizing its interest often.

WORKING REGULATORY LEVERS

When Wal-Mart doesn't win on Capitol Hill, it finds other avenues to press its case. During debate this year on a five-year highway authorization bill, the company almost succeeded in winning an expansion of the number of consecutive hours truckers may drive to 16 from 11. The company operates the biggest fleet of freight-haulers in the country. And it particularly wanted an exemption from the time restrictions on short-haul drivers, who load goods at a regional distribution center and deliver them to stores.

The prospects in Congress looked good until James L. Oberstar of Minnesota, the senior Democrat on the House Transportation and Infrastructure Committee, said he wouldn't go along with the change. Oberstar's refusal denied the company needed bipartisan support, but the company proved its ability to pivot by appealing to the Federal Motor Carrier Safety Administration, an agency of the Transportation Department.

The agency accepted at least part of Wal-Mart's plea, and in August published a regulation expanding the number of hours that a trucker can drive. The rule didn't completely exempt short-haul drivers from the limits, as Wal-Mart had hoped, or give them a consistent 16-hour day. But it did allow short-haul drivers to work 16-hour days twice a week, including loading time. It also exempted them from keeping a logbook that officials could review to enforce the time limit. Wal-Mart lobbyists applauded the direction of the rules change and said they will keep working to mold the regulations to their liking.

The company also frequently has received a sympathetic ear at the Labor Department. Wal-Mart has faced many allegations of labor violations in the past few years and critics say that the department goes out of its way to accommodate the company's requests.

One example is the agreement that DeLauro and other congressional Democrats tried to block this summer. Wal-Mart's critics were angry the department had agreed to give the company extra warning of planned investigations into its scheduling and pay practices. The department's Wage and Hour Division had decided to give the company a 15-day notice before investigating a complaint, more than most companies receive. In addition, the company was allowed extra time to change its behavior and avoid penalties for violations.

The department's inspector general found in an Oct. 31 report that the agreement with the company "gave significant concessions to Wal-Mart" and represented "serious breakdowns" in the department's rules.

THE PR FRONT

While the retail giant can claim a string of legislative victories in recent years, labor unions and their allies have also succeeded in putting the company on the defensive. And Wal-Mart's ability to become an indomitable lobbying force on Capitol Hill will depend on the company's ability to counter its critics.

A growing number of outside groups are rallying against the company's workplace policies and business practices. They include: Wake Up Wal-Mart, the grass-roots organization run by organized labor; Wal-Mart Watch, a coalition founded by the Service Employees International Union that includes the National Partnership for Women & Families, Common Cause, and the Sierra Club; and Wal-Mart vs. Women, a group led by the 1992 Miss America, Carolyn Sapp, which protests "sexist policies" that it says Wal-Mart follows.

Many of these groups are led by one-time political operatives, such as Andrew Grossman, who was executive director of the Democratic Senatorial Campaign Committee and now heads Wal-Mart Watch, and Paul Blank, a former official in the 2004 presidential campaign of current Democratic National Committee Chairman Howard Dean, who helps run Wake Up Wal-Mart. They are treating their anti-Wal-Mart efforts much as they would run a grass-roots election challenge.

About 46 percent of the children of Wal-Mart employees either lack health insurance or rely on public health programs, such as Medicaid. The company's critics encourage state and federal lawmakers to introduce legislation aimed at forcing the company to offer affordable health care to its workers and move them off public assistance. They call for boycotts of Wal-Mart's stores. And they get their message out through e-mail and paid advertising campaigns. Wal-Mart critics say at least 120,000 activists stand ready to hold rallies or fundraisers on short notice.

Wal-Mart's opponents say they have to be large and well-organized because the company is so powerful. "I'm not aware of any other company that is as omnipresent," said Tracy Sefl, communications director for Wal-Mart Watch. "They have developed a pretty centralized and pretty ingrained presence here in Washington with some powerful people."

While many of the company's most vocal critics have a liberal cast, Wal-Mart Watch is among those that takes pains to invigorate opposition to Wal-Mart from all corners, including those that don't always align politically with labor unions and their often Democratic allies. Wal-Mart Watch hired a director of interfaith outreach to enlist churches and religious groups to oppose the company. And it is trying to build alliances with small-business owners to fight against the domination of Wal-Mart in small-town America.

And some left-leaning groups are so active in attacking the company that Wal-Mart lobbyists complain privately and occasionally publicly that the groups are violating rules governing the political activities of nonprofit organizations, which are limited in their right to lobby. The groups deny that they are breaking the law and so far the IRS hasn't found them in violation.

The good news for Wal-Mart is that its critics don't always coordinate efforts and occasionally appear to compete for attention.

> ## "There is clearly a threat here."
>
> — **Ron Ence**, vice president of congressional relations, Independent Community Bankers of America

But despite the splintered approach by labor and its allies, the war between liberal activists and Wal-Mart may determine how far the company's influence will reach in Washington. If Wal-Mart continues to spend much of its time fending off complaints that it undercuts the American way of life, it will be difficult for it to focus on its legislative goals.

Labor unions are leading the effort to invest millions into the campaigns because Wal-Mart threatens their dwindling relevance. Union workers now account for less than 9 percent of the private American workforce. The organizations would love to add Wal-Mart workers to their fold, but Wal-Mart has gone as far as to close a store rather than allow workers to organize. More and more the company is dominating markets, such as grocery stores, that once were stocked with union workers.

Wal-Mart Watch was the initial source of an internal company memo The New York Times published Oct. 25, The memo, which Wal-Mart also eventually gave to the newspaper, outlined options for employee rules changes. It recommended adding physical labor to all job descriptions to discourage unhealthy people from working for the company and running up high medical bills. The memo also called for lowering retirement contributions and cutting health care benefits in other ways.

The memo was released just as the company was engaged in a high-profile effort to burnish its image through calls for a higher minimum wage and other pro-worker initiatives.

Wake Up Wal-Mart worked with DeLauro and other congressional Democrats on bills introduced in the House and Senate in June that would force Wal-Mart to reveal how many of its workers receive public health assistance instead of employer-sponsored insurance. The Maryland Legislature is expected to vote when it reconvenes in January to override the veto by that state's Republican governor of a similar health care bill aimed at Wal-Mart.

But the reality of the marketplace may be the deciding force in this battle between the company and its antagonists. If the anti-Wal-Mart groups succeed in motivating consumers to abandon shopping at Wal-Mart stores, the company's investors will take notice and that will probably have more of an influence on its actions than anything that happens in Washington or in state capitals.

Wal-Mart's stock price has fallen about 13 percent in the last 12 months, and damage to the company's image may have a direct effect in further depressing its profit and share price.

Company executives estimate that between 2 percent and 8 percent of shoppers may avoid the store because of the adverse publicity.

A BANKING BEHEMOTH

To both supporters and critics, Wal-Mart's business practices demonstrate a forceful, and sometimes ruthless, determination to keep costs low so that the company will dominate markets. The company is only now beginning to show the same type of determination in the political world.

Whether Wal-Mart eventually faces pressure from Capitol Hill to change its practices — or whether Washington accommodates this corporate giant, which is likely to grow even larger — remains to be seen.

Either way, the questions involved in Wal-Mart's rise in Washington and the marketplace will affect the nation's competitive edge, the strength of labor, the role of government in providing for workers and corporate responsibility.

For the company's most vigorous opponents, Wal-Mart's increasing clout has far-reaching implications. "There is clearly a threat here," Ence said. "One of the things they are good at is destabilizing communities."

There is no clearer place where that battle may be fought than over the company's appeal for a bank charter. And assurances from the company that its aspirations are limited don't convince its opponents.

Banking industry groups say that once Wal-Mart has a Utah bank charter and is eligible for federal deposit insurance, the company would be positioned to start banking operations in the future and little could deter it. Under existing agreements, a Utah-chartered bank would be allowed to open branches in 22 other states. Given Wal-Mart's history with mom-and-pop retailers and local grocery chains, Ence said this could doom local banks.

"Clearly, if they wanted to engage in predatory pricing to drive out local establishments . . . they have the resources to do it," Ence said.

The company insists that its banking goals are restrained, noting that it currently has agreements and leases with more than 300 banks that have installed branches in about 1,100 Wal-Mart stores. Some of these leases run through 2024. "We're committed to this, and I don't know how else we can commit to it to any greater degree unless maybe we write it in blood," Koch said.

Still, Wal-Mart has already made limited forays into financial services. The company has an agreement with General Electric Capital Corp. to offer a Wal-Mart credit card. In certain localities, customers can obtain a Wal-Mart debit/ATM card, and from its Web site the company offers access to credit reports and check printing services. In its stores, Wal-Mart will allow customers to cash their paychecks, pay major bills, purchase money orders and transfer money both domestically and internationally. Typically, these services are offered at prices well below what a bank or check cashing service would charge.

At the moment, Wal-Mart appears to be in an advantageous position to win its bank charter. That would be a big victory. And Wal-Mart's business decisions clearly demonstrate that it takes a long view.

For Culpepper, that means putting off such simple things as taking the time to hang pictures of his family on the noticeably bare walls of his office. At the moment, he says, he has more pressing matters to attend to.

"After the next presidential election, I should have the time. I'll make an appointment for Dec. 1, 2008, to do it," Culpepper laughed. ∎

Toward a More Perfect Definition of 'Citizen'

Some in Congress says it's time for another look at how the 14th Amendment applies to illegal immigration

"ALL PERSONS BORN or naturalized in the United States and subject to the jurisdiction thereof are citizens of the United States."

Those words, the first sentence of the 14th Amendment, embody a birthright that millions of Americans have enjoyed. At one point during Supreme Court Justice Samuel A. Alito Jr.'s Senate confirmation hearings, New York Democrat Charles E. Schumer pressed him on whether he agreed that the sentence was a "fairly clear and straightforward provision of the Constitution."

"All persons means all persons," Schumer said encouragingly. "That's pretty easy."

It was not easy enough for Alito to answer on the spot, however. "It may turn out to be a very simple question; it may turn out to be a complicated question," he said. "I would have to go through the whole judicial decision-making process before reaching a conclusion."

Simple or not, Schumer's question — whether those words would prevent Congress from passing a law denying citizenship to someone born on U.S. soil — lies at the heart of an intensely emotional debate. For now, it is on the periphery of congressional consideration of illegal immigration, but someday relatively soon the question of birthright citizenship may reach the Supreme Court.

That outcome would suit Republican Rep. Nathan Deal of Georgia just fine. Deal, leader of an effort in Congress to bar the children of illegal immigrants from receiving automatic citizenship, says the language in the 14th Amendment is murky and has been misinterpreted over the years. Furthermore, he says, the words of the amendment have been a magnet for immigrants who enter the country illegally, have "anchor babies," then claim that deportation would cruelly separate them from

CQ Weekly Feb. 13, 2006

their family.

The Supreme Court has never directly addressed the ambiguities in the Constitution that are seen by Deal and others who want to limit the 14th Amendment's scope. That creates an opening for Congress to restrict birthright citizenship — and then let the courts decide whether that limit is constitutional. In Deal's view, the phrase "subject to the jurisdiction thereof" is ambiguous enough

> ❝All persons born or naturalized in the United States and subject to the jurisdiction thereof are citizens of the United States.❞
>
> — The 14th Amendment

that it might exclude children of parents who are foreign nationals. Automatic citizenship is now granted to anyone born in the United States, even the children of tourists.

Opponents say Deal and his supporters — his legislation had 83 cosponsors as of early February — are overreaching. All immigrants, legal or not, are subject to the jurisdiction of U.S. laws, says California's Howard L. Berman, the No. 2 Democrat on the House Judiciary Committee. Furthermore, Berman says he is baffled at conservative Republicans, who normally insist on a textual reading of the Constitution, building a case that the court must "interpret" the 14th Amendment. "The fact that the court has not had reason to explore this is because Congress has not had the incli-

nation to adopt something that is so contrary to the plain meaning of those words," he said.

Schumer had used much the same argument in framing his questions to Alito. "President Bush has stated his beliefs that judges should be strict constructionists, rigidly adhering to the letter of the Constitution," he told the judge. But Alito refused to be drawn in. "There are active legal disputes about the meaning of that provision at this time," he said.

For now, the debate is academic. Republican leaders prevented Deal's measure from being considered in December as a proposed amendment to an already contentious border security bill, which went on to be passed by the House. But even if he had been successful, his legislation would have to pass an even more skeptical Senate, where leading Republicans call the effort "futile."

But with public discontent over illegal immigration growing, Deal believes he has a case and a chance. "I think any vehicle that would get the issue before the Supreme Court is the right vehicle," he said.

JURISDICTIONAL DISPUTE

Should that day come, Deal and others would look for guidance to John C. Eastman, a constitutional law professor at Chapman University in Orange, Calif., and director of the Center for Constitutional Jurisprudence at the conservative Claremont Institute.

Eastman testified before a House Judiciary subcommittee in September that the Constitution's citizenship clause has been misinterpreted for more than a century.

Eastman has zeroed in on what the 1866 Civil Rights Act — a statutory forerunner of the 14th Amendment, which was added to the Constitution two years later— said about citizenship. Drafted to guarantee citizenship to recently freed slaves, the law was more direct in who was eligible: "All persons born in the United States, and not subject to any foreign power, excluding Indians not taxed, are hereby declared to be citizens of the United States." The 14th Amendment employed the more ambiguous clause "subject to the jurisdiction thereof," instead of "not subject to any foreign power."

This leaves little doubt in Eastman's mind that Congress understood a clear distinction between "basic territorial jurisdiction" such as traffic laws, and "complete jurisdiction", which encompasses a person's allegiance to a nation.

The Supreme Court confirmed his assessment in *Elk v. Wilkins*, an 1884 ruling that rejected a citizenship claim by John Elk, an American Indian who was born on a reservation but subsequently moved off, and therefore was denied his right to vote.

But Eastman said the court "misread" the citizenship clause 14 years later in *United States v. Wong Kim Ark*. Wong Kim Ark was born in the United States to Chinese parents. After a visit to China, he was denied readmission to the United States. An 1882 law denied birthright citizenship to the decedents of Chinese nationals, and the government claimed that those children would be subject to the rule of its emperor. But the court ruled that common law and the 14th Amendment guaranteed citizenship to all persons born in the United States, regardless of their ethnic heritage.

Jack M. Balkin, a constitutional law professor at Yale University, said that even though the original understanding of the amendment may be ambiguous, the Wong Kim decision offered clarity.

"Now the question is 'what if Congress passes a law that says children of illegal immigrants are not citizens?'" he asked. "Wong Kim Art seems to suggest the statute would be unconstitutional. But you could distinguish that it does not specifically involve illegal aliens."

What the court would do, however, is difficult to predict, Balkin said, particularly since it has two new members and virtually no modern case law about the issue to rely on.

"We should not assume it's an easy case," Balkin said. He suspects the court would "tilt" toward striking down Deal's bill if it became law. However, "it's not a slam-dunk either way."

Building a legal argument might not matter if the supporters cannot muster the political

will for a vote. And while they might ultimately have the numbers, Deal and company currently lack the muscle to bring the debate to the House floor.

On the House Judiciary panel, Chairman F. James Sensenbrenner Jr., a Wisconsin Republican, and Berman rarely find themselves aligned on issues, yet the two have maintained a cordial, working relationship over the years. Sensenbrenner never told Berman why the

An American Policy

Most of the countries that automatically confer citizenship to all native-born people are centered in the Americas. Most other countries have additional requirements.

Antigua and Barbuda	Ireland
Argentina	Jamaica
Barbados	Lesotho
Belize	Mauritius
Bolivia	Mexico
Brazil	Nepal
Canada	New Zealand
Central African	Nicaragua
Republic	Niger
Chile	Pakistan
Costa Rica	Panama
Cuba	Paraguay
Dominican Republic	Peru
Ecuador	St. Lucia
El Salvador	St. Vincent and
Equatorial Guinea	Grenadines
Gambia	Samoa
Grenada	Trinidad and Tobago
Guatemala	Tuvalu
Guinea-Bissau	United States
Guyana	Uruguay
Honduras	Venezuela

SOURCE: Office of Personnel Management

Deal measure had been sidetracked, but he made a point to put Berman at ease about the amendment. "He did tell me it would not be offered," Berman recalled. "He sort of said it with a smile."

The issue appears to have even less support in the Senate. Deal's bill has no companion leg-

islation, and even some of those taking the hardest line on illegal immigration would prefer to steer away from a debate on the meaning of citizenship.

"I believe it would be futile because the United States Supreme Court would strike down any limitations on citizenship rights for individuals born in the United States," said Republican Sen. John Cornyn. He has offered a broad immigration bill that has been well received by interest groups seeking tighter border security and stricter enforcement of immigration laws. But eliminating birthright citizenship is not part of the measure.

Cornyn, a former Texas Supreme Court judge and state attorney general, noted that the Supreme Court offered a hint in 1982, when it wrote in Plyer v. Doe that public schools could not deny the children of illegal immigrants an education. But Cornyn, who is generally a close ally of President Bush, is not simply hedging his bets. He considers the proposal divisive and unnecessary.

"I think it's important that we come out of this immigration reform not appearing to want to punish people gratuitously," Cornyn said. "I think that would be viewed as harsh and punitive, and I don't think it would be a good idea from a policy standpoint or a political standpoint."

Even some of Deal's biggest supporters doubt the proposal can succeed. Florida Republican Mark Foley has signed on, but he is also sponsoring a proposed constitutional amendment that would achieve the same purpose.

For eight years Foley has been championing the amendment route, which requires a two-thirds vote in the House, the Senate and the approval of 38 state legislatures.

"My view is the 14th Amendment was rather certain in its application," said Foley. "Legislatively, I still am not comfortable with Nathan's solution. I think a court could strike it down."

Deal says that's a common reaction from his colleagues, one that tells him he needs to do a better job educating them. But he's confident the court, if presented with an actual controversy based on his legislation, would be intrigued.

"The crux of the matter is getting a case before the court so they could rule," he said. "Normally you would only pass constitutional amendments where you were trying to overrule a court ruling. We haven't had a square ruling on that yet. I think it all really comes down to that." ■

Privacy Er
A 'Net Los

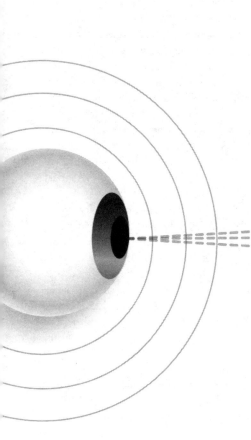

As government snooping on the Web increases, lawmakers are under pressure to find a cyber-age definition of 'unreasonable searches and seizures'

AMERICANS ARE moving much of their lives onto the Internet, along with their love letters, family photo albums, credit card bills and even medical histories. In the process, they risk losing some of the privacy protection the government guaranteed when they kept everything at home.

As the Internet has evolved in the last decade, Congress has taken a hands-off approach, reasoning that regulating a nascent technology would inhibit its development and stifle its growth. But now, with the technology having matured to the point where the Internet is a basic tool of everyday work and home life, it is clear that Washington simply hasn't kept up.

Congress, which has trouble grappling with technology issues in general, has been particularly slow in adapting privacy laws to the runaway evolution of the Internet. The resulting gap between Internet practices and privacy protection has left an increasing amount of personal data on the Internet wide open to government snooping.

"It's the difference between an African cheetah and a Greenland glacier," said Rep. Jay Inslee, a Democrat whose Seattle-area district includes part of Microsoft Corp. "Technology is the cheetah and Congress is the glacier."

Law enforcement investigators once needed

a warrant approved by a judge to gain access to e-mail stored on someone's home computer; now they can obtain much of the same material from the data banks of Internet services such as Yahoo! or America Online with a simple subpoena.

Where laws are out of date and consequently vague about Internet privacy — some don't mention the Internet at all — the Justice Department has stepped in with its own interpretations. It has, for instance, interpreted telephone wiretap laws to give itself authority to track where people go on the Internet and where they send e-mail.

Internet technology, such as the search engine, has run out from under the umbrella of existing privacy laws, leaving the records that companies keep of such searches fair game for any government agency with a subpoena.

"The government is gaining surveillance capabilities without any changes in the law simply because of advances in technology," said James Dempsey, policy director of the Center for Democracy and Technology, a privacy watchdog group. "Technology is outstripping the law."

Two cases this winter have highlighted the Internet's increasing vulnerability to government data collection without court supervision.

In December, the Bush administration acknowledged that the super-secret National Security Agency was eavesdropping on domestic phone calls and e-mail in its hunt for terrorists, without first getting a court's permission.

CQ Weekly Feb. 20, 2006

sion:

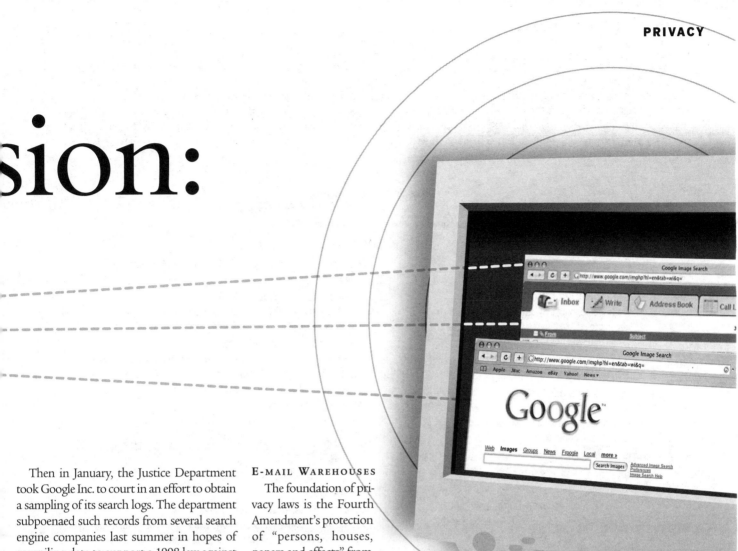

Then in January, the Justice Department took Google Inc. to court in an effort to obtain a sampling of its search logs. The department subpoenaed such records from several search engine companies last summer in hopes of compiling data to support a 1998 law against online child pornography that the Supreme Court has blocked from taking effect. Google is the only one that resisted the subpoenas.

The Bush administration says it is only following the rest of society, and its criminals, onto the Internet. "We would not be meeting our obligations to protect public safety if we let these new technologies pass us by," a Justice Department official said. But privacy groups worry that in the absence of congressional action, the administration is interpreting its power as broadly as possible, in the process shouldering aside personal privacy concerns.

"There is an enormous potential for good in the Internet, but at the same time, there is a potential for Americans to give up all sorts of protections they don't want to give up and shouldn't have to give up," said Sen. Patrick J. Leahy, a Vermont Democrat who has been a leading sponsor of privacy legislation for more than a decade.

Three Internet areas where seams have opened up in privacy protection hold the greatest prospect for friction between the government's quest for information and the public's desire for privacy: e-mail storage, Internet search engine logs and online wiretapping.

E-MAIL WAREHOUSES

The foundation of privacy laws is the Fourth Amendment's protection of "persons, houses, papers and effects" from "unreasonable searches and seizures." The amendment was written at a time when people kept letters and other personal papers locked in desk drawers inside their homes. And it still applies today to files stored on personal computers.

But the Constitution could hardly have envisioned a day when Americans would store much of their most private correspondence — love letters, political musings, financial records — on computer servers owned by search engines, Internet service providers and their own employers.

The Supreme Court has ruled repeatedly that the Fourth Amendment doesn't apply to business records and other information handed over to a third party. That suggests to privacy advocates that the Fourth Amendment may not protect many of the e-mail messages kept in electronic warehouses, even though they think it should.

"Just because the mode of writing is 21st century instead of 18th century, that doesn't mean that the ethos of privacy that the Founding Fathers understood was so vital should be watered down," said Jay Stanley, communications director for the American Civil Liberties Union's "technology and liberty" program. "E-mail has become a dominant means of communication. It serves the same function as the letter writing of old."

Congress recognized this problem years before e-mail became mainstream, back when voice mail, pagers and fax machines were first arriving on the scene. And it tried to legislate a solution with the 1986 Electronic Communications Privacy Act, which set rules for government access to electronic messages.

The law was written at a time when most electronic messages were not held in long-term storage at Internet service providers. Most early e-mail services offered only limited storage space, anyway. So Congress granted strict privacy protection to unopened mail that had been on a server for 180 days or less, roughly anything up to six months. Law enforcement agents must apply to a court for a warrant and show probable cause to believe there is a crime in order to read it.

But Congress provided less protection for unopened mail left on a server for more than

Communication Laws Lag Decades Behind Technology

The privacy of electronic communications is governed by several laws and court decisions, but some laws were written for the telephone age and have not been updated for computers. As Americans store more of their e-mail and other electronic records on the data banks of access providers and Internet catalogs, they also may be losing privacy protection. The Supreme Court has held that documents handed over to a third party are not protected by the Fourth Amendment ban on unreasonable search and seizure.

CONSTITUTION
The Fourth Amendment
Protects against "unreasonable" search and seizure of private property without a warrant demonstrating probable cause.

TELEPHONE

LEGISLATION
Wiretapping Act *(1968)*
Permits wiretapping only as a "last resort" and requires probable cause. Target of surveillance must be notified after the fact.

SUPREME COURT
Smith v. Maryland *(1979)*
Court held that a "pen register," which records the number dialed from a phone, does not violate the Fourth Amendment.

PAPER FILES

SUPREME COURT
Couch v. United States *(1973)*
Court held that the Fourth Amendment does not apply to records handed over to an accountant, as there is no reasonable expectation of privacy.

United States v. Miller *(1976)*
Court held that the Fourth Amendment does not protect bank records, either. Sets precedent that information given to a third party – such as the contents of Web mail and online search information – is not constitutionally protected.

ELECTRONIC COMMUNICATION

LEGISLATION
Anti-Terror Law *(2001)*
The 2001 law known as the Patriot Act expanded the definition of a pen register to include "dialing, routing, addressing or signaling information."

LEGISLATION
Electronic Communications Privacy Act *(1986)*
Extends Wiretapping Act protections to electronic communication in transit, and requires a warrant for probable cause to access the contents of unopened electronic messages in storage for 180 days or less. After that time, messages can be obtained with only a subpoena, but requires eventual notice to the party in question. The Justice Department maintains that all opened e-mail is subject to subpoena.

Local hard drives fall under the same protection as paper files in the home.

six months. To access those messages, the law requires only a subpoena or a court order based on "specific and articulable facts" that the information sought is relevant to an ongoing criminal investigation. And although the target must be notified, notice can be delayed.

Moreover, the law is unclear on how to treat e-mail once it has been opened, no matter how old it is. The 9th Circuit Court of Appeals has ruled that all e-mail, opened or not, can be obtained only with a search warrant if it is less than 180 days old. But the Justice Department maintains that opened e-mails — even those less than 180 days old — have no more protection than e-mail in long-term storage.

All of this means that today, when e-mail is ubiquitous and many people leave years of messages on Web mail servers, much of it is potentially available for government access.

"Many people are completely oblivious to the implications of remote e-mail storage," Dempsey said. "People think of their e-mail as private, as no different than pen and paper files."

Two trends have driven the shift to server-based storage, according to Markham Erickson, general counsel for NetCoalition, a lobbying group that represents Yahoo and Google, among others. The first is the steep drop in storage costs, driven by technology, which allows Internet companies to offer virtually unlimited e-mail warehousing for free. The second is the spread of high-speed, always-on Internet connections. Dial-up users, Erickson explains, tend to download e-mail messages onto their hard drives before reading them. Many broadband users read it where it is.

The Justice Department defends the framework created by the 1986 law. "Congress made this decision that e-mail has less protection if a user makes a deliberate decision to leave a copy of it sitting on a server," said the Justice Department official who spoke on condition of anonymity.

But privacy advocates insist that e-mail users don't make those types of distinctions.

"Most people experience e-mail as a relatively private act," said Deirdre Mulligan, a professor at the University of California at Berkeley School of Law. "It's much like sending a postal letter. People don't distinguish between an opened or an unopened letter, between mail that is less than 180 days old and more than 180 days old."

INTERNET PAPER TRAILS

Most people also don't stop to think about

the Internet search engines, such as Google or Yahoo, that they use every day. But like much of the data on the Internet that might have commercial value, the blizzard of queries on everything from diseases to TV shows is electronically logged and tagged for future reference.

Like e-mail, Internet search logs are sensitive personal records in the hands of online companies, which means they may have little or no protection from government scrutiny. But while e-mail — or at least fairly recent, unopened e-mail — is protected by the 1986 communications law, the status of search logs

> ## "The government is gaining surveillance capabilities without any changes in the law simply because of advances in technology."
>
> — **James Dempsey**, Center for Democracy and Technology

is unclear. Congress has never directly addressed the issue.

Some privacy advocates contend that the 1986 law applies to search logs as well as e-mail, but the Justice Department considers them no different than any other business records that can be obtained by subpoena.

That leaves it to the search engine companies to decide whether and when to hand over user records to law enforcement agents. The only rules that apply, privacy advocates say, are those the companies agree to abide by in their user agreements and privacy policies.

"A search engine is under no obligation to protect search records," said Dempsey of the Center for Democracy and Technology. "We must trust companies to do the right thing."

Internet companies have sophisticated tools to track online behavior. By embedding short strings of software code, or "cookies," inside Web browsers that visit their sites, companies such as Google, Yahoo and Microsoft can identify users and recognize them when they return. Cookies enable search engines to track what visitors search for, what links they click and which pages they view. They use the information to customize online content and advertising and improve the quality of their search services.

Search engines also record the Internet protocol address of any computer that conducts a

Web search. IP addresses, which are typically assigned to users by Internet service providers, identify where on the Internet computers are logged on.

"The search engines are capturing all this data," said Chris Sherman, associate editor of Search Engine Watch, a firm that provides news and analysis about the search engine industry. "For them, it's a gold mine of information."

The existence of such records was not widely known until the Justice Department took Google to court over its search logs.

The department argues that it needs Google's search records to show that Internet filtering doesn't protect children from online pornography and that the Supreme Court should reconsider its decision blocking the 1998 Child Online Protection Act from taking effect. Google's three biggest competitors, Yahoo, Microsoft's MSN and America Online, have complied at least in part with Justice Department subpoenas issued last summer.

The case itself has little to do with privacy, because the government is asking Google to hand over what amounts to a random sampling of search queries that cannot be connected to individual people. But privacy advocates say they worry it will be only a matter of time before the government starts asking search engines to make those connections.

"Search logs are the closest thing to a printout of the goings-on in your brain," said Kevin Bankston, a staff attorney with the Electronic Frontier Foundation, a privacy group based in San Francisco. "They reflect your most private interests, your political and religious beliefs, your medical and financial worries and more. . . . It's incredibly intimate information."

A Justice Department official stressed that it is not always so simple to tie search queries to a particular individual because people often share networks or use multiple computers to conduct Web searches. Still, according to Bankston, the government has several effective ways of making those connections.

For example, he said, under the 1986 communications law, investigators could subpoena an Internet service provider to find out what IP addresses it had assigned to a suspect's account during a given period. Armed with this information, the government could then go back to a search engine and ask it to correlate those IP addresses with search records.

Bankston noted that it is even easier to make such connections if a Web user has registered with a site and conducts searches

Sensitive Election-Year Intel

Why a GOP representative isn't defending NSA taps

THE BUSH ADMINISTRATION'S domestic wiretapping program had a bad week on Capitol Hill, culminating in Pennsylvania Republican **Arlen Specter**, Senate Judiciary Committee Chairman's announcement of legislation to place the plan under judicial review from the Foreign Intelligence Surveillance Court.

But beyond this fairly high-flown constitutional rivalry, there was a more immediate political reversal for the White House: Rep. **Heather A. Wilson** of New Mexico announced she was breaking ranks with her House Republican colleagues to demand a full briefing on the program before the Intelligence Committee.

Wilson chairs the panel's Subcommittee on Technical and Tactical Intelligence. The panel has jurisdiction over the National Security Agency, which administers the controversial warrantless spying efforts. She issued a three-page memorandum citing "serious questions that need answers" about the program's legal status.

Wilson is more than a little motivated

this year to put some distance between herself and the White House, since she's waging one of the House's most competitive re-election bids. So her skepticism could well signal to similarly situated GOP incumbents that the White House program may not be drawing the popular support the president is banking on.

Wilson's Democratic opponent, state Attorney General **Patricia Madrid**, is trying to capitalize on that point, suggesting that the incumbent is publicizing her scruples rather late in the game. "While I've been enforcing the law," Madrid said, "Wilson has been sitting in the House Intelligence Committee apparently ignoring abuses of the law until nine months before an election."

Democrats see Wilson's seat as a linchpin in their

plan for winning House control Nov. 7. It is a classic swing district: **John Kerry** carried it by 3 percentage points in 2004, but it's consistently sent a Republican to Congress since its creation in 1968. The incumbent sees her status as the lone woman veteran in Congress as an asset in a region with strong military ties, while Madrid hopes her Hispanic heritage will prove decisive with the two-fifths of the electorate who are Hispanic.

"We expect it to be an aggressive campaign," says Wilson's campaign spokeswoman **Anne Ekern**. "We expect to again be successful." And clearly, they figure their odds will improve without having to defend the NSA in the bargain.

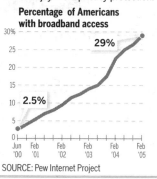

Broadband Boom

Nearly one-third of the U.S. population now has high-speed Internet access. Such connections are a reason many users store their e-mail on remote services such as Yahoo instead of downloading it to home computers, where their messages would enjoy more privacy protection.

Percentage of Americans with broadband access

29%

2.5%

Jun '00, Feb '01, Feb '02, Feb '03, Feb '04, Feb '05

SOURCE: Pew Internet Project

while logged in — to access an e-mail account or a personalized news feed, for instance. In that case, he said, investigators can skip the service provider and go straight to the search engine company.

In their privacy policies, Google, Yahoo and Microsoft all state that they will share personal information about their users with law enforcement when presented with a valid legal request.

Sherman believes consumers are just starting to grasp that the new online services transforming their lives are not totally cost-free. "Privacy and the Web are still new territory for most people," he said. "It's a paradox because we want these tools to be high-quality information tools, but we're not sure we want to make the privacy trade-offs."

For their part, Internet companies stress that they have an incentive to respect user privacy since consumers are more likely to trust them if they do. Still, because of the Google case, privacy advocates hope Congress will step in and provide some protection.

Some lawmakers have already asked why search engines need to maintain such vast databases of user records. In the House, Demo-

crat Edward J. Markey of Massachusetts, who has long been involved in technology and communications issues, is pushing for legislation that would prohibit the long-term storage of personally identifiable search results.

"If you Google something today, someone 20 years from now should not know what you Googled," Markey said. "The warehousing of personal information about people's Internet searches should not be done needlessly."

REAL-TIME WORRIES

At the other end of the surveillance spectrum is the government's quest for access to electronic messages as soon as they are sent. Using technology that even allows investigators to monitor what software a computer is using and what keystrokes an operator types, federal agencies can track where people go on the Internet and whom they correspond with.

The result is a potential bonanza for investigators because the information that Americans reveal about themselves online can be so much lengthier and more detailed than what they say in a phone call.

"Law enforcement, in making the transition to the Internet, has extended its surveil-

lance capabilities," said the ACLU's Stanley.

The key statutes that govern wiretapping on the Internet are the same ones that govern it on phone lines: the 1968 Wiretap Act and the 1986 Electronic Communications Privacy Act, which require law enforcement agents to get a probable-cause warrant to tap phone calls or read e-mail messages in real time.

But the law provides a much lower level of protection for any information that is not the actual content of a conversation.

In the telephone world, this non-content information included phone numbers dialed into a tapped line, which used to be captured with a machine called a "trap and trace" device, and the phone numbers dialed out, which were captured with a "pen register" device. Phone taps are now done digitally, but the terminology remains.

The Supreme Court ruled in 1979 that pen register information has no Fourth Amendment protection. The court concluded that because callers must share the phone numbers they dial with the telephone company to make a call, the information is not private and can be obtained without a warrant.

Using similar logic, Congress decided in

1986 that law enforcement agents should be allowed to obtain the electronic equivalent of pen register information with a simple court order — and no notice to the target of the surveillance — if the government claims the information is likely to be relevant to an ongoing investigation. In practice, privacy advocates say, the courts read this to mean they must give rubber-stamp approval.

Yet the government is still sorting out what qualifies as pen register data on the Internet. The Justice Department says that certain types of information, such as the addresses in the "to" and "from" lines of e-mail messages and Internet Protocol addresses, which identify computers when they are online, clearly fall into the pen register category. Other types of online information, including Web site addresses, might not.

Confusion about what rules apply, privacy watchdogs say, gives the Justice Department leeway to interpret the law as it sees fit. Congress merely compounded the confusion in 2001, when the anti-terrorism law known as the Patriot Act extended the definition of pen register data to include "dialing, routing, addressing or signaling information" without clarifying exactly what that includes.

The trouble, privacy advocates say, is that much of this modern digital information is far more intimate than the phone number data of old. Albert Gidari, a Seattle lawyer who specializes in communications issues, says Internet Protocol addresses are "like DNA on the Internet" since they can be used to track connections between computers and potentially even reveal where people go online.

And Web site addresses offer a window into the documents that people are reading. Although Justice Department officials say they don't think the agency has ever used a pen register to obtain Web site addresses, law enforcement officials can collect this information using a pen register as long as the Justice Department signs off.

"Some could see this as the equivalent of tracking you through a bookstore, tracking you through your daily life," said UC Berkeley's Mulligan. "Web surfing behavior can reveal where you bank, where you get medical information, what your interests and political associations are. It's certainly not contentless information."

So far, there have been few court cases clarifying how the wiretapping laws should apply online. That is in part because many targets of surveillance never discover that they are being tracked. It's also because the 1986 communications law contains no way for those targeted to suppress the evidence collected. Since even information obtained without proper authorization can be used in a trial, few surveillance targets have challenged the statute in court.

Susan Freiwald, a professor at the University of San Francisco School of Law, says this situation leaves Americans with limited protection for some of their most private online behavior.

"The definition of a pen register has evolved from the phone numbers dialed on a paper tape to the electronic records of your entire life," Freiwald said.

The debate over Internet wiretapping has crystallized in recent months over a Federal Communications Commission order requiring companies that provide high-speed Internet access or online phone calls to build wiretapping capabilities into their networks.

A 1994 law required phone companies to provide such law enforcement access, and the FCC has been under pressure from the Justice Department, the Federal Bureau of Investigation and the Drug Enforcement Agency to extend the law's mandate to computer networks.

The FCC ruling has sparked a contentious debate about Internet wiretapping. Universities say surveillance-ready networks could have a chilling impact in academic environments, where students and professors do extensive research online. And libraries warn that there is no way to monitor one patron's online activity without monitoring the activity of everyone who uses a library's computers.

"A core value of the library community is the privacy of our patrons' records, because what you read is only your business," said Prudence Adler, associate executive director federal relations and information policy with the Association of Research Libraries.

A coalition of privacy advocates, library groups and technology companies has challenged the ruling, both at the FCC and in court. They argue that the agency has exceeded its authority and that Congress specifically exempted the Internet from wiretapping obligations when it passed the 1994 law.

But ultimately, privacy groups say, the key to controlling wiretapping on the Internet is adequate legal restraints. And that means updating the law to recognize that much of the information that Americans reveal on the Internet today is just as private, and deserves just as much protection from government surveillance, as the content of their telephone conversations.

"The only way to future-proof the law is to be technology-agnostic," Gidari said. "Whether you are sending information using tom-tom drums or a beam of light, you need the same level of protection for the same type of information."

LACK OF RECOGNITION

It has been six years since Congress last seriously considered revamping laws to regulate government online surveillance. At the time, in the late 1990s, a series of news accounts about how personal information was being mined and sold, and sometimes exploited, on the Internet led to congressional hearings and a number of House and Senate bills. Then in 2000, government surveillance on the Internet became an issue because the FBI was using a computer program called Carnivore to monitor the e-mail and other online activity of criminal suspects.

Congress was moving toward privacy legislation at the time. The House Judiciary Committee even approved a bill that would have addressed many of the issues that still concern privacy advocates. The ACLU's Stanley said lawmakers felt compelled to act because "consumers were scared to do commerce online."

But nothing was done. Instead of restricting Carnivore, Congress asked the FBI for a report on its use, and the bureau soon ditched the program anyway in favor of commercially available software.

The Sept. 11 terrorist attacks swept away much of the remaining concern in the House and Senate about government surveillance. Later that fall, in fact, Congress passed anti-terrorism legislation that gave the government slightly broader authority than it thought it already had to track suspects online.

"Instead of getting extensions of privacy protections, we got the Patriot Act," said Marc Rotenberg, executive director of the Electronic Privacy Information Center.

This year, Congress probably will not get much beyond hearings on Internet privacy.

For one thing, it is hard to get lawmakers to focus on the arcane, technical task of updating electronic surveillance laws, says New Hampshire Republican Sen. John E. Sununu, an authority on Internet privacy issues.

"In Congress, there is a recognition among a small group of lawmakers that this is a problem," Sununu said. "But it doesn't attract a lot of attention or excitement."

Still, he acknowledged, the problem is gaining more visibility because of the domestic spying and Google cases. Leahy, for one, takes that as a sign that the pendulum is shifting toward privacy protection.

"I'm hoping people will now start paying attention," he said. ■

Imbalance Of Power

Lawmakers have offered little resistance to White House claims of authority to write rules in the war on terrorism. Now the NSA surveillance case has many pushing back.

IN SEPTEMBER 2001, as the ruins of the World Trade Center still smoldered and work crews started to repair the charred hole in the side of the Pentagon, a team of Justice Department lawyers quietly began building the Bush administration's legal foundation for the war on terrorism.

In a lengthy memorandum signed by John C. Yoo, the deputy assistant attorney general, administration lawyers methodically laid out a pathbreaking case: that the president had inherent authority as commander in chief of the armed forces not only to do whatever was necessary to retaliate against al Qaeda, but to prevent future attacks from any quarter.

Congress, Yoo wrote, could not "place any limits on the president's determinations as to any terrorist threat, the amount of military force to be used in response, or the method, timing, and nature of the response. These decisions, under our Constitution, are for the president alone to make."

This bold claim of expansive executive authority was only the beginning of what has since escalated into a broader struggle over the balance of powers in wartime. Since Sept. 11, Bush has asserted this claim in several ways: to hold detainees in a prison camp

THE ARCHITECT: John C. Yoo helped lay the foundation for President Bush's broad claim of executive power.

at Guantánamo Bay, Cuba, for example, and to rewrite the ground rules for interrogating them. And Congress has largely gone along, uninterested in impairing the president's ability to protect the nation.

But revelations that the National Security Agency conducted warrantless surveillance of U.S. citizens in its efforts to hunt down suspected terrorists have brought the question of executive power into new territory. Congress is

now at a critical moment in deciding how much to push back against what many legal scholars see as a potential tilt of power to the executive branch in the NSA spying case.

If it accedes to the administration's wishes, as many believe it will, Congress will be giving this and future presidents a ready-made legal rationale for virtually any action they want to take in the name of national security.

That is partly because the conflict from which Bush derives his wartime power — the "war on terror" — is a perpetual battle that, despite the term, combines elements of law enforcement with a military campaign. Unlike most other wars in the past century, it is being waged on U.S. soil as well as abroad. And it will last indefinitely, certainly long after Bush has left office.

"The consequences are monumental, and they're monumental because once one of the branches of government has essentially allowed a different branch to move into its territory and usurp some of its constitutional authority, it's very difficult to get it back," said Mickey Edwards, a Princeton University lecturer and former Republican congressman from Oklahoma.

Edwards and others cast this as a constitutional battle, and in a sense it is, as both sides point to the fundamental powers of the executive and legislative branches in making their case.

But the struggle begins over the 1978 Foreign Intelligence Surveillance Act (FISA), which was passed after congressional hearings revealed widespread abuses by government intelligence agencies. The law established a secret panel of federal judges to process warrants in sensitive foreign intelligence investigations. In the case of the domestic spying program, which the Bush adminis-

tration calls the "terrorist surveillance program," the NSA did not seek FISA warrants. The administration argues that they were not needed.

In wartime, Bush supporters say, the president's power derives directly from the Constitution's designation as commander in chief, and it cannot be altered by an act of the legislative branch.

"Congress cannot use . . . legislative powers to change the Constitution's allocation of powers between the president and Congress in the war power," said Yoo, a professor of law at the University of California at Berkeley, at a Heritage Foundation speech on presidential power.

The duration of the war or the uncertain character of the enemy doesn't change that, the administration argues, and in fact, may heighten the president's need to act without Congress. "Obviously, we would prefer to fight a nation-state, but . . . we may have very limited time to take advantage of information to try to prevent those kinds of attacks," Yoo said. "And imagine the kind of cost that might arise from a delay caused by the need to have to go to Congress for approval for every use of force that would be needed to stop or pre-empt a terrorist attack."

Bush has not been shy about wielding the powers and prerogatives of the presidency. Even before they were elected, he and Vice President Dick Cheney said that one of their objectives was to "restore the power of the presidency," and that message took on new force after Sept. 11.

In most cases, however, Bush has simply exploited less controversial tools that are more clearly at his disposal, such as the right to assert executive privilege over administration documents sought by lawmakers, or to install controversial nominees in executive branch slots and federal judgeships temporarily during Senate recesses. And he has yet to use his veto pen.

But most legal scholars and lawmakers agree that the NSA spying case is different than previous reaches for power by Bush and Cheney. One big difference, according to those critical of the administration, is that this case involves allowing the administration to simply act as if a federal law — in this case FISA — doesn't exist, or that it has no mandatory application in cases such as the NSA spying program. That sets a precedent, Edwards said, that the president "may at his own discretion ignore an act of Congress."

The concern, Edwards and other experts say, is that this and future presidents won't feel obliged to abide by acts of Congress that don't square with their own views of presidential authority. And it could go beyond issues of war.

"The broader claim is that there is an ability of the executive to decide that Congress has invaded the president's prerogatives, and presumably they could claim that outside national security as well," said Duke University law professor Curtis A. Bradley.

So far, senators who have examined the program are splintered over what to do about it, but it appears as if some political solution is likely.

Among those who have misgivings about the legality of the program is Senate Judiciary Chairman Arlen Specter, R-Pa., who is writing legislation that would mandate a judicial review of the surveillance program by the FISA court.

Senate Intelligence Chairman Pat Roberts, R-Kan., one of the administration's staunchest defenders, is also working on legislation in talks with the White House. Although it is not clear what direction they are taking, Roberts has already made it clear, in a 19-page letter to Senate Judiciary leaders, that he thinks what Bush is doing is legal. Several other Republican senators agree.

"These are not Sunday school teachers living in Pakistan that are calling somebody in America to engage them relative to a positive issue," said Georgia Republican Saxby Chambliss.

PUTTING ARTICLE II FIRST

The administration makes a two-pronged defense of the legality of the surveillance program. First, officials point to the use-of-force resolution Congress passed after the 2001 attacks, saying that gives the president a statutory exemption from the FISA law.

But even beyond that, they say, the Constitution in Article II, Section 2 designates the president as commander in chief of the armed forces, and Congress thus cannot constrain the president's constitutional authority to wage a war on terrorism and, in particular, to guard the nation from another terrorist strike.

Bush's lawyers argue that gathering intelligence on the enemy's plans is a fundamental

Nation Evenly Split On Domestic Spying

A pair of CNN/USA Today/Gallup polls found the public split extraordinarily evenly on the propriety of warrantless wiretapping and whether President Bush had the legal standing to authorize it.

Do you think the Bush administration was right or wrong in wiretapping these conversations without obtaining a court order?

Jan. 6-8
(Before Gonzales' Senate Judiciary testimony)

Right 50% | Wrong 46% | No opinion 4%

Feb. 9-12
(After Gonzales' Senate Judiciary testimony)

Right 47% | Wrong 50% | No opinion 3%

Do you think George W. Bush — definitely broke the law, probably broke the law, probably did not break the law or definitely did not break the law?

Feb. 9-12

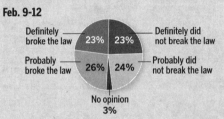

Definitely broke the law 23% | Definitely did not break the law 23%
Probably broke the law 26% | Probably did not break the law 24%
No opinion 3%

NOTE: Telephone surveys of 1,003 adults in January and 1,000 in February both had a margin of sampling error +/− 3 percentage points.

aspect of waging war, akin to spying on the movements of an enemy army — and thus reserved exclusively to the president as commander in chief.

"The history of warfare — including the consistent practice of presidents since the early days of the republic — demonstrates that warrantless intelligence surveillance against the enemy is a fundamental incident of the use of military force," the Justice Department said in a 42-page memorandum sent to Senate leaders in January.

The administration pointed to wartime intelligence-gathering activities ranging from George Washington's interception of British mail pouches during the Revolutionary War, to the wiretapping of telegraphs by both sides in the Civil War, to President Franklin D. Roosevelt's warrantless surveillance of suspected spies during World War II. The Justice Department also cited several Supreme Court cases on the scope of executive power to make its point.

Most of the historical examples the admin-

istration relies on are from before 1978, when the FISA law was enacted. Still, Bush and his supporters say that no law can eliminate a constitutional authority reserved to the executive.

Bush is also relying on a 2003 Supreme Court case, *Hamdi v. Rumsfeld*, in which the justices held that the 2001 force resolution authorized Bush to detain enemy combatants in Afghanistan because "detention to prevent a combatant's return to the battlefield is a fundamental incident of waging war."

If the 2001 resolution authorizes the capture of enemy fighters on fields of battle, the administration argues, it must also authorize the considerably less intrusive power to eavesdrop without a warrant on U.S. citizens in contact with someone overseas suspected of ties to terrorists. "Gathering intelligence on the movements of the enemy and the plans of the enemy is a core part of the ability to wage war," Yoo said.

Presidential supporters also cite a 1952 case, *Youngstown Sheet and Tube Co. v. Sawyer,* in which the court ruled that President Harry S Truman's seizure of U.S. steel mills during the Korean War, after a threatened steelworkers' strike, was unconstitutional. In a concurring opinion, Justice Robert H. Jackson laid out a three-part constitutional test for executive power.

Jackson said that presidents are on the firmest ground when they act pursuant to "an express or implied authorization of Congress." He said that when a president acts without any congressional action, the executive operates in a "zone of twilight."

Jackson concluded that presidential power is "at its lowest ebb" when the chief executive does something "incompatible with the expressed or implied will of Congress." He added that in such circumstances, "presidential claim to a power at once so conclusive and preclusive must be scrutinized with caution, for what is at stake is the equilibrium established by our constitutional system."

Given the 2001 force resolution, the administration argues, the NSA surveillance program falls into Jackson's first category. Critics of the program say that because the force resolution does not apply, Bush is operating within the third category, and is on the shakiest of legal grounds.

Bryan Cunningham, a former CIA officer who specializes in security law, says that even if Bush's surveillance order falls in the third category, it does not mean that it is invalid. "You have to go to what [constitutional authority] the president has left, and my argument is the president has a lot left," he said.

In a Feb. 3 letter to Senate Judiciary leaders, Cunningham wrote that Bush is "constitutionally entitled to decline to adhere to FISA's requirements" if he determines they would "impermissibly impede his ability to carry out his constitutional responsibility to collect foreign intelligence and protect the nation from attack."

"The notion is that you can decline to execute a statute that unconstitutionally impedes your power," Cunningham said.

Indeed, the administration's constitutional argument bypasses Jackson's tripartite test of presidential actions relative to congressional ones altogether.

"If an interpretation of FISA that allows the president to conduct the NSA activities were not 'fairly possible,' FISA would be unconstitutional as applied in the context of this congressionally authorized armed conflict," according to the Justice memo.

Bush employed the same argument at a White House news conference one week later: "Most presidents believe that during a time of war, that we can use our authorities under the Constitution to make decisions necessary to protect us."

WANTING TO BE CLUED IN

The Constitution gives Congress, too, a full array of specific war powers: the power, in Article I, Section 8, to declare war, to raise and support armies, and to regulate the military.

Those war powers, as well as the power to make all laws that are "necessary and proper," are the constitutional ammunition that Congress has to answer Bush's claim that his commander in chief authority gives him the inherent right to conduct warrantless surveillance on U.S. soil, and to insist that he has to follow the FISA law.

"Under our Constitution, Congress is a coequal branch of government, and we make the laws," Democrat Patrick J. Leahy of Vermont told Attorney General Alberto R. Gonzales at a Senate Judiciary Committee hearing Feb. 6. "If you believe you need new laws, then come and tell us. If Congress agrees, we'll amend the law.

"If you do not even attempt to persuade Congress to amend the law," Leahy continued, "then you're required to follow the law as it's written."

The congressional argument in the NSA case is also about how the administration interprets congressional action. Several current and former lawmakers from both parties say they did not contemplate secret, warrantless eavesdropping on U.S. citizens when they voted for the force resolution in 2001 to enable Bush to retaliate against al Qaeda terrorists.

"I don't think that's a fair reading of the force resolution," said Sen. Lindsey Graham, a South Carolina Republican who is a former Air Force prosecutor. Leahy, the ranking Democrat on the Judiciary Committee, has introduced a sense-of-the-Senate resolution to clarify that Congress didn't intend the force resolution to apply to programs such as the NSA surveillance effort.

Bush's opponents paint a frightening picture of the future if the president emerges victorious in this struggle.

Anthony Romero, executive director of the American Civil Liberties Union (ACLU), said that if Congress concedes to Bush on the surveillance program, the president could feel emboldened to take other steps, such as shutting down media outlets or transportation systems if he feels they are necessary to combat terrorism.

"If Congress capitulates in its oversight role and either allows the president to continue with the illegal spying or gives him the power ex post facto, then it will do long-term damage to the system of checks and balances," Romero said.

Graham said he is "urging the administration to reach out to the Congress" to figure out a statutory solution.

"I don't want to, in the name of fighting the enemy, create a constitutional imbalance," Graham said. "That's unhealthy for the future of the country."

Besides Graham and Specter, some key Republicans have indicated that they have strong misgivings about the program's legality.

In a Feb. 17 Senate floor speech, Armed Ser-

The Brains Behind The Executive Power Muscle

Attorney General Alberto R. Gonzales has joined President Bush and Vice President Dick Cheney as the public faces defending the administration's National Security Agency domestic surveillance program since its disclosure in December. But other, lesser-known figures across the government have worked behind the scenes to muster the legal arguments underpinning Bush's broad claim of executive authority in the war on terrorism:

JOHN C. YOO Now a law professor at the University of California at Berkeley, he was a driving intellectual force behind the administration's legal strategy while serving from 2001 to 2003 as deputy assistant attorney general in the Office of Legal Counsel.

WILLIAM HAYNES The Defense Department general counsel. Bush nominated him in 2003 and again in 2005 for a seat on the 4th U.S. Circuit Court of Appeals, in Richmond.

VIET DINH Now a Georgetown University law professor, he helped write the 2001 anti-terrorism law known as the Patriot Act and formulated other aspects of the Justice Department's strategy for the war on terrorism as an assistant attorney general for the Office of Legal Policy from 2001 to 2003.

DAVID H. ADDINGTON While serving as chief counsel to the vice president, he helped draft a memo in early 2002 justifying harsh interrogation techniques, Newsweek has reported. He was promoted to Cheney's chief of staff last summer after the indictment of I. Lewis "Scooter" Libby.

JAY S. BYBEE As an assistant attorney general in the Office of Legal Counsel, he helped write a memorandum in 2002 offering a possible legal justification for aggressive interrogation tactics. He was confirmed as a judge on the 9th U.S. Circuit Court of Appeals, in San Francisco, in 2003, prior to public dissemination of the memo.

DIANE BEAVER An Army lieutenant colonel, she was legal adviser to the commanding general at Guantánamo Bay, Cuba, and wrote a 2002 legal analysis justifying harsh interrogation techniques.

MICHAEL V. HAYDEN As the NSA's director between 1999 and 2005, he was assigned to implement the policy of wiretapping conversations involving parties in the United States. Last year, Bush named him as the principal deputy to Director of National Intelligence John D. Negroponte.

vices Chairman John W. Warner of Virginia said he wants to broaden the charter of the "gang of 14" senators who brokered a deal on judicial nominees last year to include figuring out a legislative response to Bush.

Warner said the group has "given some consideration and may have a position on that" soon. If the group decides to expand its influence into taking the lead on legislation to govern the NSA program, they could make the difference between a tepid congressional response and a robust one.

"I just don't think we can hold tenaciously on this question of the constitutional authorities of the government just being the sole province of the administration for interpretation, having trained in the law myself," Warner said.

On the House side, conservative Arizona Republican Jeff Flake said he is "not comfortable with the response from our party" on the program. He added that the reflexive defense of Bush by many Republican lawmakers "seemed to be a partisan reaction rather than a measured response."

GOP Rep. Heather A. Wilson of New Mexico, who chairs the House Select Intelligence Subcommittee on Technical and Tactical Intelligence, added force to the issue when she raised serious concerns about the spying program. She, too, has signaled skepticism of Bush's argument that his commander in chief authority trumps congressional power.

"The people who wrote our Constitution were very experienced in armed conflict," said Wilson, an Air Force veteran and an employee of the National Security Council during the administration of Bush's father.

Democrats have been blunter. Jerrold Nadler, whose New York City congressional district includes the World Trade Center site, has called the NSA program a "direct challenge" to congressional authority. Nadler said that under Bush's line of reasoning, the president could "authorize murder in the streets of the capital if he thinks doing so would be helpful in defeating terrorism."

Some lawmakers are pushing hard for more congressional oversight and tighter controls, and there has been enough disquiet in both parties to force the administration to engage lawmakers on the issue.

THE JUDICIAL CARD

Many legal experts believe the ultimate solution will lie in a deal between the two branches rather than in the courts. However, two lawsuits have been filed in federal courts, one led by the ACLU and one by the Center for Constitutional Rights, seeking to halt the surveillance on the grounds that it violates not only the FISA law but the First and Fourth Amendments to the Constitution.

The Electronic Frontier Foundation, a privacy and civil rights group, has filed a class action lawsuit against AT&T Corp., accusing that company of unlawfully aiding the NSA program.

On Feb. 16, a federal judge in Washington ordered the Justice Department to comply within 20 days with a Freedom of Information Act request by the Electronic Privacy Information Center, another advocacy group, for doc-

Declaring War: A Look at the Last 65 Years

The Constitution specifically grants the power to declare war to the legislative branch, but Congress has not voted on such an official declaration since World War II. Since then presidents have waged war under the auspices of U.N. resolutions or congressional authorizations of the use of force. In 1973, the enactment of the War Powers Act placed certain restrictions on the president's ability to commit troops without congressional approval, and subsequent authorizations of force from Congress have adhered to the framework of that law.

WORLD WAR II

PL 77-328
Dec. 8, 1941
"Resolved . . . That the state of war between the United States and the Imperial Government of Japan, which has thus been thrust upon the United States, is hereby formally declared."

PL 77-331
Dec. 11, 1941
"Resolved . . . That the state of war between the United States and the Government of Germany, which has thus been thrust upon the United states, is hereby formally declared."

PL 77-332
Dec. 11, 1941
"Resolved . . . That the state of war between the United States and the Government of Italy, which has thus been thrust upon the United States, is hereby formally declared."

KOREA

U.N. Security Council resolution
June 27, 1950
"The Security Council . . . recommends that the Members of the United Nations furnish such assistance to the Republic of Korea as may be necessary to repel the armed attack and to restore international peace and security in the area."

VIETNAM

PL 88-408
"Gulf of Tonkin Resolution"
Aug. 10, 1964
"Congress approves and supports the determination of the President, as Commander in Chief, to take all necessary measures to repel any armed attack against the forces of the United States and to prevent further aggression."
Repealed (PL 91-672) *Jan. 12, 1971*

WAR POWERS ACT

PL 93-148
Nov. 7, 1973
"The president in every possible instance shall consult with Congress before introducing United States armed forces into hostilities . . . and after every such introduction shall consult regularly with the Congress until United States armed forces are no longer engaged in hostilities or have been removed from such situations."

uments related to the surveillance program.

But legal scholars say that because there is much about the surveillance program that remains unknown to the public, plaintiffs mounting legal challenges will have a hard time proving that they have standing to sue. Plaintiffs will have to show that they have actually suffered injury, or are about to suffer injury, because of the surveillance program. Also, parties to lawsuits can assert only their own rights, not the rights of others, with few exceptions.

Because the administration will not divulge substantive details of the program publicly, none of the plaintiffs in the two civil lawsuits know whether they have actually been surveilled. The plaintiffs argue that they have grounds to believe they have; they say that alone is enough for the surveillance to violate their First Amendment free-speech rights.

That is a shaky legal assertion. The Supreme Court ruled in a 1972 case, *Laird v. Tatum*, that this sort of First Amendment claim was not enough for a "justiciable controversy."

Besides the standing issue, courts traditionally are loath to get involved in disputes between the elected branches of government. "I think it's going to be difficult to get a case in front of the courts under the law as it exists now," Cunningham said.

There are a few other legal avenues for critics of the surveillance program to explore besides suing the government. Attorneys for defendants in pending criminal trials are trying to find out whether the government eavesdropped on their clients without a warrant before filing charges against them. But government lawyers could put up procedural roadblocks to such requests.

None of the legal challenges to the NSA surveillance are likely to bear fruit in the near future, however. Government lawyers can spend years fighting all the challenges all the way up to the Supreme Court, if necessary.

"Getting a judicial resolution of this will take a very long time, if at all," said Mark Tushnet, a law professor at Georgetown University. "George W. Bush will not be president at the time there's a definitive judicial resolution of the surveillance issue."

A LEGISLATIVE COMPROMISE

For now, then, Congress has the field to itself when it comes to answering Bush. The administration could decide to broker a deal with GOP leaders before the November midterm elections. That would serve both to defuse the current controversy as a campaign issue and to ensure that a Democratic takeover of either chamber would not weaken the administration's negotiating position.

Bush enjoys strong support from the House GOP rank and file. "We can't believe that we have the ability to constrict a president who is commander in chief in a wartime situation," said Dan Lungren, R-Calif., who serves on the House Judiciary Committee and is a former state attorney general.

The House Judiciary Committee has already moved to squelch two Democratic resolutions of inquiry that would require the administration to turn over records related to the NSA surveillance.

PERSIAN GULF

U.N. Security Council resolution
Nov. 29, 1990
"The Security Council . . . authorizes member States cooperating with the Government of Kuwait . . . to restore international peace and security to the area."
PL 102-1
Jan. 14, 1991
"The president is authorized . . . to use United States armed forces pursuant to United Nations Security Council resolution 678."

KOSOVO

NATO Security Council resolution *June 10, 1999*
"The Security Council . . . decides on the deployment in Kosovo, under United Nations auspices, of international civil and security presences, with appropriate equipment and personnel as required, and welcomes the agreement of the Federal Republic of Yugoslavia to such presences."

AFGHANISTAN

PL 107-40
Sept. 18, 2001
"The president is authorized to use all necessary and appropriate force against those nations, organizations, or persons he determines planned, authorized, committed, or aided the terrorist attacks that occurred on Sept. 11, 2001, or harbored suchorganizations or persons, in order to prevent any future acts of international terrorism against the United States by such nations, organizations or persons."

IRAQ

PL 107-243
Oct. 16, 2002
"The president is authorized to use the armed forces of the United States as he determines to be necessary and appropriate in order to (1) defend the national security of the United States against the continuing threat posed by Iraq; and (2) enforce all relevant United Nations Security Councilresolutions regarding Iraq."

Congress never voted to authorize the U.S. military involvement in NATO operations, under U.N. auspices, in Kosovo in 1999.

But committee Chairman F. James Sensen-brenner Jr., R-Wis., has sent Gonzales a 14-page letter that posed dozens of questions about the program.

Bush, who had kept a select group of House and Senate leaders informed about the program, initially balked at briefing the full chambers' Intelligence panels about the NSA program.

But the president reversed field and agreed to brief the full committees, in part because Wilson demanded it. "They were refusing to brief us on this particular program, and that was unten-able," she said, adding that a closed-door brief-ing of the House Intelligence Committee on Feb. 8 was "the beginning of a process for review."

The administration favors a proposal by Ohio Republican Sen. Mike DeWine that would exempt the NSA surveillance program from the FISA law and provide for regular briefings to a bigger group of lawmakers.

Such legislation would not impose any sub-stantial new curbs on Bush. The administra-tion is likely to oppose any bill with more teeth.

"The president believes that he has the authority necessary [to conduct the surveil-lance], but of course we're willing to work with the Congress if they feel that further codifica-tion of that would be necessary," said White House spokesman Trent Duffy.

After spending a day hearing from Gonza-les, Specter is planning a second Senate Judi-ciary hearing on Feb. 28, with testimony from seven legal experts.

The administration has been resisting Specter's efforts to have former Attorney Gener-al John Ashcroft and former Deputy Attorney General James Comey appear before the Judicia-ry panel. Democrats have urged Specter to keep pushing for Ashcroft and Comey's testimony.

It is not clear how political pressure will come to bear on the issue. Polls show that Americans are supportive of the president in his ability to prosecute the war, but privacy is an increasing-ly important issue to many voters in both par-ties. If more details about the NSA program, or about other secret counterterrorism efforts, leaked out, the public's mood could shift, and more lawmakers from both parties could be moved to pass stringent new laws.

Yoo pointed out that Congress could inves-tigate the program, cut off funding for it, or even move to impeach Bush. But no substan-tive congressional probe into the workings of the program is in the offing, and even Bush's fiercest congressional critics are not calling for the surveillance to be halted.

Conservative Republican congressional leaders are not about to initiate impeachment proceedings against Bush. And even liberals such as Leahy, who have bluntly accused Bush of committing a serious crime, are not sug-gesting that Congress try to punish him.

There are also certain political realities to consider. Bush's critics on Capitol Hill are mindful that in a post- Sept. 11 America, the president can always tap a reservoir of sup-port from the public for any action that he can cast as a defensive measure against terrorist attacks. "When push comes to shove, I don't think anyone will have the stomach for this," said a Senate Republican aide.

Bush might also be helped by the televised riots that have broken out across the Muslim world after a Danish newspaper published car-toon images of the prophet Muhammad. Ross K. Baker, a Rutgers University political science professor, says that episode "convinces Amer-icans that the world is a dangerous place" and reminds them that the nation remains vul-nerable to more terrorist plots.

"Fear favors the White House," Baker said.

Most scholars agree that presidential power ebbs and flows, depending on world affairs and the mood of the electorate.

And nothing in government is permanent. Even if lawmakers give the president a pass on the NSA program, the balance of power between the two branches will continue to be a non-violent front in the four-year-old war on ter-rorism.

"This is not going to be the last instance where the president is going to exert his com-mander in chief authority to do something in the war on terrorism," said Scott L. Silliman, executive director of Duke University School of Law's Center on Law, Ethics and Nation-al Security.

For now, though, even if Congress decides to force Bush to seek judicial approval for the surveillance — which looks to be the strongest congressional response in the offing — Bush will, in a sense, win the argument because he will escape any congressional sanction for going around Congress and ordering the sur-veillance in the first place.

It is imperative that Congress assert itself and its grant of authority in the Constitution to prevent an erosion of power, said David Skaggs, director of the Center for Democracy and Citizenship at the Council for Excellence in Government and a former House Democrat from Colorado.

"If both the Congress and the courts choose not to assert their responsibility and authori-ty," he said, "there will be a de facto accretion of presidential power — not exactly what we think of as the way to operate the republic."

For 200 years, though, such issues have been settled in exactly that way — by debate in the court of public opinion and in contest between the political branches. One side will win more power, and the other side will lose. ■

HELP FOR THE KIDS: Lisa Luceno-Pinski teaches at an Even Start program in Washington that faces closure in light of the 55 percent cut in the program.

The Perils Of a Low Profile

Lacking clout and Hill defenders, smaller social programs are the easiest victims when the GOP decides to curtail spending

ONE DAY AFTER he submitted his annual budget plan to Congress, President Bush flew to Detroit to spell out his plans for ending federal enterprises that don't work. But he cited only one of them as an example of programs he believes have a lackluster track record and little evidence of success. It was a family literacy program called Even Start.

That day, Feb. 8, was the last time during this year's budget debate that anyone would single out Even Start for public attention, good or bad. Bush's speech created a vague impression among some rank-and-file members of Congress that the program was a weak one. But the president didn't make any more speeches about it, and the top Republicans who write the bill that determines the Education Department budget didn't even know about the one speech he did give.

The real danger, in fact, wasn't anything Bush said about Even Start. It was the tight cap on overall spending in the appropriations bill that funds the program — part of a 1 percent reduction in non-security spending set by the budget blueprint Congress approved this spring. Although Even Start was a small enough program to avoid the focused attention that might have killed it outright, it was also too low-profile to be protected from this year's budget squeeze, which may well send the program into a death spiral.

Just before it adjourned for the year, Congress cleared a spending package for the Labor, Health and Human Services, and Education departments that will slash Even Start's federal funding by more than half. It will receive $99 million for the budget year that began in October, down from the $225 million it received in fiscal 2005. Even though the program benefits from state matching funds and some private grants, the officials who run it say the program can't withstand such a substantial loss of federal aid without forcing many of its 1,200 local programs to shut their doors.

It's the kind of cut that is hard, if not impossible, to recover from. If anything, Bush will be under political pressure from his conservative base to make next year's budget even tighter — meaning that the literacy program, which serves approximately 50,000 poor and disadvantaged families, could eventually get squeezed out of the federal budget entirely.

The story of Even Start's decline is a case study in how the budget-cutting atmosphere in Washington — fueled by conservative discontent over rising federal spending — is taking a particular toll on social programs too small to draw much attention from lawmakers.

When budget writers looked for cuts in Medicaid, they had a huge battle on their hands. When appropriators tried to cut rural health programs, House Republicans with rural constituents helped sink the first Labor-HHS bill and forced the appropriators to rewrite it. But when Even Start was tagged to lose 55 percent of its funding, there was virtually no backlash in Congress.

Likewise, there was no price to be paid this year when Congress made a 45 percent cut in aid to help states improve technology in schools. There was little protest over a 30 percent cut to the HOPE VI program to demolish deteriorating housing projects, or a 29 percent cut to rural housing and economic development funds. And few lawmakers had much to

say about cuts to job training, state employment services, and foster care and adoption assistance programs.

It has become such a political chore to trim relatively small slices out of the multi-billion dollar mandatory entitlement programs, such as Medicare and Medicaid health insurance, that lawmakers who want to cut spending are taking a chunk out of discretionary programs that have few political defenders. And by the

> **❝❝I put programs into three categories: 'must dos,' 'need to dos,' and 'nice to dos.' In my mind, this is somewhere between 'need to do' and 'nice to do.'❞❞**
>
> — **Rep. Ralph Regula,** R-Ohio

time the Labor-HHS conference report reached the Senate on its last legislative day of the year, it had become part of a last-minute set of trade-offs to resolve so many major battles before the holidays — involving entitlement program cuts, an extension of the anti-terrorism law known as the Patriot Act and drilling for oil in the Arctic National Wildlife Refuge — that the entire social spending package was cleared almost as an afterthought. Even for Democrats, the Even Start cut was barely a blip.

"A lot of damage can be done to programs that fall below the radar screen because of either size or emotional response," said Richard Kogan, a senior fellow at the Center on Budget and Policy Priorities, a research organization that focuses on programs for low-income people. That's especially true, he said, in a year when dozens of programs are getting cut all at once. "There's only a limited number of things the public can agonize about," Kogan said.

The budget-cutting pressures are forcing moderate Republicans to make agonizing choices. Rep. Michael N. Castle of Delaware, one of the Republicans who voted against the first Labor-HHS conference report because of its tight education funding levels, said his party too often exempts defense and homeland security from the spending cuts it imposes. "What suffers disproportionately are the smaller pro-

grams that don't have a lot of protectors out there," Castle said. "And it's unfortunate."

But he didn't have a lot of options. Had the second version of the conference report been rejected, GOP leaders were threatening to return with a temporary spending package that would have squeezed education funding even more. So when the roll was called, Castle cooled his heels in the back of the House chamber until the second conference report had just enough votes to be adopted — then voted "no" a second time.

LOSS OF INFLUENCE

Just a few years ago, Even Start was considered safe from cuts. That's because it was created by one of the most respected Republicans in the House at the time: Bill Goodling of Pennsylvania, who served 13 terms and was chairman of the Education and the Workforce Committee for six years before his retirement in 2000. A former high school principal and superintendent of schools, he pushed the program into law in 1988 and got it reauthorized — with a big boost in its funding ceiling — just before he retired.

Goodling's bid to save his program played out over many months of telephone calls, letters and meetings with former Capitol Hill colleagues and their aides. He didn't have a huge lobbying army behind him; the program's relatively small size makes its advocacy network pale in comparison to better-funded programs such as Head Start, the early childhood development program. But he knew his former colleagues, particularly in the House, would at least be open to his concerns. "Everyone knows that it's Bill Goodling's project," one Senate Republican appropriations aide said early in the process.

Goodling even had the sympathies of the chairman of the conference committee that wrote the final bill: Ralph Regula of Ohio, the chairman of the House Appropriations Labor-HHS-Education Subcommittee, a former elementary school principal and member of the Ohio Board of Education. "How many years has he spent in schools?" Regula asked, referring to the president. "I've got seven years as a principal. That's probably seven more than he's got."

The program also was viewed favorably by top Republicans on Senate Appropriations, including Chairman Thad Cochran of Mississippi and Pennsylvania's Arlen Specter, chairman of the Labor-HHS Subcommittee, though they were less familiar with it. It had a few other vocal GOP supporters on its side, including Sen. Olympia J. Snowe of Maine and Rep. Todd R. Platts of Pennsylvania, Goodling's successor in the House. It even got a sympathetic plug from Comedy Central's "The Daily Show" in November, which aired a satirical news report that put Even Start in the same category with such "wasteful programs" as school lunches and meat inspections.

But none of that mattered when appropriators confronted a requirement that all discretionary Labor, HHS and Education programs spend $163 million less, in total, than last year. Lawmakers and their aides said the decision to halve Even Start was driven solely by the overall lack of money, not a congressional loss of confidence in the endeavor, and not the fact that the president had publicly taken aim at the program.

In interviews over the course of the year, lawmakers made it clear that they simply had other priorities. Even Regula's enthusiasm for the program went only so far. "I put programs into three categories: 'must-dos,' 'need to dos,' and 'nice to dos,'" he said in a November interview. "In my mind, this is somewhere between 'need to do' and 'nice to do.'"

Goodling was devastated. "It just blows my mind. I don't understand it at all," he said after negotiators signed off on the rewritten package. He had appealed to Regula and Cochran to restore the funds. He even got through by phone to Karl Rove, Bush's deputy chief of staff, who seemed unaware of the controversy.

None of his efforts worked — and Goodling is convinced that state and local governments won't be able to make up for the loss of federal funds, which will cut California's Even Start budget by about $15 million and New York's by $10 million. "They can't come up with that kind of matching money," he said. "So the only literacy program for the poorest of the poor will be gone."

Even Start isn't the kind of program one would expect to have much lobbying clout. It serves some of the most powerless people in society: poor children whose parents can't read to them well because they never graduated from high school, or because English isn't their native language. More than eight out of 10

FINAL CRUSADE: Goodling helped create Even Start while he was a Pennsylvania House member. He says he won't be able to fight for it much longer.

families in the program live below the federal poverty level.

THE FIGHT FOR SURVIVAL

The idea is to teach children to read not only by working with them directly, but also by teaching parents how to read to their kids — the theory being that parents are the most important teachers children have in their early years. The program provides federal funds, matched by state and local dollars and often supplemented by private grants, that link early childhood education, adult literacy and parenting classes together.

In the Adams Morgan neighborhood of Washington, for example, the program serves about 200 low-income families, mostly immigrants from Latin America, Africa and Asia. Parents attend five levels of English instruction and learn computer skills, and their children attend classes that teach basic reading, motor skills and social development. Parents also spend time with their children, learning nursery rhymes and other activities to do together.

"Our families tend to have the lowest literacy and economic levels" of any adult education

and early childhood development programs, said the program's director, Christie McKay, who was featured on "The Daily Show." Many of the parents, she said, had little formal education in their own countries, and some come from cultures that don't stress the importance of interacting with kids to help them learn.

The lobbying effort for Even Start was led by one of Goodling's former aides, Kevin Talley, a former Education and the Workforce chief of staff and now president of the lobbying firm Synergy Partners Inc. He kept less experienced advocates up to date on Congress' actions and counseled them on what tactics would have an impact. When Snowe introduced an amendment in October to restore the program's funding in the Senate Labor-HHS appropriations bill — which did not include anything for the program — its advocates decided not to wage a major fight for it because Talley was convinced it wouldn't pass, an assessment shared by Snowe's staff.

But there was no army of well-paid lobbyists, only an informal campaign of support spearheaded by three organizations: the Goodling Institute for Research in Family Literacy, a research group at Pennsylvania State University established by a $6 million appropriation from Congress right before Goodling retired; the National Even Start Association, based in California; and the Kentucky-based National Center for Family Literacy. It also received some support from Hispanic political groups, such as the National Council of La Raza.

It helped that the program's rationale was embraced by lawmakers such as Platts, who recalls taking his own son to work and reading to him when the boy was an infant. Platts voted against both versions of the Labor-HHS conference report in part because of the Even Start cuts. "I certainly respect the administration's judgment, and we do have to be very careful with our expenditures in this environment," he said. "But I would contend that Even Start is an example of a wise expenditure."

Still, advocates for the program had a number of lobbying missteps, partly because their campaign depended on Even Start staff members and teachers with little experience dealing with Congress.

During the crucial week before negotiators struck their second deal, advocates in town for a conference stopped by the office of one Senate ally without an appointment, virtually guaranteeing that no one would be around to talk to them. They then left a batch of business cards with the phone number of their hotel written on top — not much of an incentive for a busy Senate staff to help them. An aide in the office said that the lobbying effort had been "atrocious."

DOES IT WORK?

The theory behind Even Start was sound, but the program just didn't work, in the Bush administration's view. It cited three evaluations performed over the years by Abt Associates Inc., a research and consulting firm working under contract with the Department of Education, that found little evidence that Even Start families become more literate. The most recent, released in 2003, concluded that Even Start children and parents in 18 local programs "performed as well as, but not better than, control group children and their parents."

This report caught the eye of the Office of Management and Budget, which uses a system called the Program Assessment Rating Tool (PART) to make sure federal programs are doing what they're supposed to do. Based on agencies' answers to 30 survey questions, the programs are rated "effective," "moderately effective," "adequate," "ineffective," and "results not demonstrated." Even Start was rated "ineffective" — and the administration decided to kill it.

And that report, in turn, led Bush to make his speech criticizing the program. "I can't think of anybody in the Congress who is not for helping low-income families become literate," he told the Detroit Economic Club. "The problem is . . . that after three separate evaluations it has become abundantly clear that the program is not succeeding." The bottom line, he said, was that federal officials should "say to the appropriators, 'Show us whether something works.' Even Start is not working, and so I've asked that the program be eliminated and focus resources on things that do work."

The PART evaluations were the centerpiece of OMB's plans to end or reduce funding for federal programs that don't produce results that can be measured by the rating system.

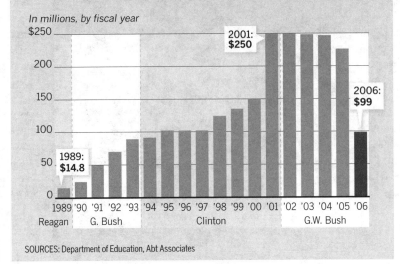

After a Steady Rise, a Sharp Fall

The Even Start adult literacy program began 17 years ago as a tiny project of the Education Department, but annual spending surged 15-fold through the first Bush administration and the Clinton years. Now funding is being cut to its lowest level since fiscal 1995, when the GOP took over Congress.

In millions, by fiscal year

2001: $250

2006: $99

1989: $14.8

1989 '90 '91 '92 '93 '94 '95 '96 '97 '98 '99 '00 '01 '02 '03 '04 '05 '06
Reagan | G. Bush | Clinton | G.W. Bush

SOURCES: Department of Education, Abt Associates

Bush's fiscal 2006 budget called for an end to funding for 99 discretionary programs, a cut for 55 others and the overhaul of 16 to reduce their costs.

Even Start officials insist the program does have benefits that can't always be captured by a measurement tool such as the PART system, because one of its purposes is to prevent bad things from happening. It's supposed to keep adults from lingering in joblessness, they say, or kids from dropping out of school or joining gangs. "It's always hard to prove that prevention programs work, because when they're successful, nobody pays attention," said McKay. Still, McKay's program in Washington has been able to find measurable successes to talk about in reports to private donors, such as increases in test scores on English proficiency exams and improvement in children's reading and math readiness skills.

A bigger issue, Even Start's supporters say, is that the Abt studies were too old to paint an accurate picture of how the program operates now. Abt concedes that all its work precedes the most recent rewrite of the law, in 2000, to include stronger quality standards, including statewide performance measures and a requirement that all programs use scientifically based reading research.

Before those changes, McKay said, students in her program really were "just kind of moved along" once certain topics had been covered. Now, they're expected to prove they've mastered the subjects of their classes, and teachers

are expected to have stronger credentials. "That's the shame of it all," she said. "Now we have it down to a science, and now you're going to cut it?"

ROAD TO A DEEP CUT

In April, as appropriators began the hearings on the year's spending bills, Goodling cited these kinds of complaints in testimony before Regula's panel. "The administration has decided to make something of a poster child of the Even Start program," he testified. "The picture they paint is not the one I, as author of the program, or independent researchers, would recognize."

After that hearing, Regula sent staff members to visit Even Start sites and judge the program for themselves. Their reports were good, he said. And a Specter aide who visited a Pennsylvania program concluded that "it clearly was an example of a program that was doing good work."

In June, the House passed a Labor-HHS bill with $200 million for Even Start — an 11 percent cut, which the program's backers say it would have survived. Republican Rep. Heather A. Wilson wrote an amendment to hold the funding steady at $225 million, but she returned to her Albuquerque, N.M., district for a base-closing hearing, and the amendment was not offered.

The next month, the Senate Appropriations Committee approved its version of the bill, with no money at all for Even Start.

That might have seemed like an ominous sign, but it didn't send Goodling into a panic. The same pattern happened last year, he noted, when the House funded the program, the Senate didn't, and the House got its way. Throughout the fall, there was little indication that this year would be any different.

As long as one chamber funded the program, aides said, it would be an issue in conference. "There are some programs that the House has traditionally supported, and there are some programs that the Senate has traditionally supported," said one Senate Republican appropriations aide. "Because nobody has enough money to pay for everything."

When the bill reached the Senate floor in

Low-Level Targets of Spending Cuts

While most of the budgetary fights in Congress have been about efforts to trim high-profile programs for the poor, such as Medicaid and food stamps, several smaller education and housing programs have been cut or even eliminated with little backlash from lawmakers:

HOPE VI: This program to revitalize public housing was cut 30 percent, to $100 million in fiscal 2006 from $143 million in fiscal 2005. Created in 1992, the program replaces troubled public housing projects with mixed-income housing. The Bush administration wanted to cancel it, saying there are cheaper alternatives.

Rural Housing and Economic Development: Created to help nonprofit organizations pursue innovative rural housing and economic initiatives, it was reduced 29 percent, to $17 million from $24 million.

Safe and Drug-Free Schools: This program to prevent school drug use and violence was reduced 20 percent, to $350 million from $437 million. The administration had tried to eliminate it, saying it had not demonstrated results.

Healthy Communities Access Program: Created in 2002 to coordinate health services for the uninsured and under-insured, it received $82 million last year but will be eliminated once the Labor-HHS-Education package becomes law. The administration recommended ending it, saying it "lacks concrete goals."

Community Development Work Study Program: This $3 million program offered financial aid to help low-income and minority graduate students pursue careers in community development. It was eliminated in this year's Transportation, Treasury, and Housing and Urban Development appropriations law.

October, the program's supporters in Congress, led by Snowe and Platts, circulated letters calling for lawmakers to return the funding to $225 million. Even Start's supporters, however, didn't fight hard for Snowe's amendment to restore the money. Her effort could have backfired, they reasoned, if the amendment failed, because such an overt rejection would have made it harder for negotiators to justify giving it any money at all.

This time, however, the conferees didn't just give the House what it wanted, as they had the year before. Instead, they decided to split the difference between the House and Senate bills. Even Start would receive $100 million — a loss of 55 percent of its federal funds.

OUT OF OPTIONS

The cuts to the program didn't come about because appropriators had something against the program, aides maintain. They say lawmakers had little choice but to cut the program at a time when even high-priority education programs such as special education and Title I funds to poor schools were getting slashed, and when the Labor-HHS appropriators risked the wrath of fellow lawmakers by not including earmarked spending for members' pet projects. "I don't have much to say, because there is not much to say for this conference report," Specter said as its details were unveiled Nov. 14.

"It's that bad."

For a variety of reasons, 22 Republicans and all the Democrats agreed, and they combined to defeat the conference report, the first time the House had rejected a negotiated spending bill in a decade.

Supporters made a last-ditch effort to warn lawmakers what the proposed cuts would mean to the program. Platts, who was concerned about the overall funding levels for education as well as Even Start, told acting House Majority Leader Roy Blunt of Missouri and Chief Deputy Whip Eric Cantor of Virginia: "I'd like to get another chance to vote for this."

Other lawmakers joined in. Rep. Rob Simmons, a Connecticut Republican whose wife works with family literacy programs, wrote to Regula and urged him to reconsider the cuts. Talley circulated a state-by-state estimate by the Congressional Research Service of how much money each state would lose under the proposed cut. Congressional offices noticed an increase in letters and phone calls from grass-roots supporters protesting the cuts.

And Goodling tried to take his appeal to the highest level possible, short of asking for a meeting with the president himself. On Dec. 6, he called Rove, asked why the administration was trying to kill his program, and told the top White House political adviser that he had been the Pennsylvania campaign co-chairman when

Bush's father first ran for president in 1980. Rove told Goodling he was about to talk to Education Secretary Margaret Spellings and would ask her about it.

If he did, it didn't make any difference. The revised conference report didn't add funds for Even Start or any other education program. All the increases were for health care, including rural health programs — a concern of several of the Republicans who voted against the original deal — and new Medicare coverage of Viagra and other erectile dysfunction drugs.

The Labor-HHS conference report barely got through the House, and was so unpopular in the Senate that the only way the GOP leadership could get it through was by cutting a delicate deal with the Democrats to avoid a roll call vote, which almost certainly would have killed the measure. And in one final blow to Even Start, the defense appropriations bill also included a 1 percent across-the-board cut in most federal discretionary spending. That took yet another slice out of the program, reducing its fiscal 2006 funding to $99 million.

Technically, Even Start will continue to receive enough funds to continue some programs through September. But its supporters don't consider that a victory. Some state directors may spread the cuts around and dilute individual programs; others will pour all of the remaining federal funds into a few local programs and shut down the rest.

In Adams Morgan, McKay's program will probably have to close. It takes nearly $400,000 to run, and the District will only have $455,000 for the four programs it currently operates, down from the $1 million it received in fiscal 2005. "What does that tell you?" asked Peggy A. Minnis, the city's Even Start director.

For Goodling, the cuts are a devastating blow to the program that may have been his biggest achievement in Congress. But even before the cuts were announced, he was trying to prepare others to carry on the fight for the program's future. "My time is running out. I'm not a youngster any more," he told his allies at a meeting of the Goodling Institute board in November, a month before his 78th birthday. "So I'm challenging you to get busy and get it done so that by the time I close my eyes for the last time, I can say they've finally gotten the message."

With more rounds of budget-cutting likely next year, though, the reality is that his program — and other social programs that fight the same struggles for visibility — may not even survive long enough for him to pass the torch. ∎

Washington's Rules Put The Squeeze on States

White House liability protections for industry prompts concern among conservatives and local officials

ONE OF PRESIDENT BUSH'S favorite maxims is that the federal government should limit its involvement in local affairs. More than once he has said that his conservative ideology stems from his conviction that "government closest to the people governs best."

But that sentiment increasingly is colliding with the Bush administration's desire to limit the ability of people to sue. In recent months, regulators at the Food and Drug Administration and several other agencies have unveiled regulations that would either limit — or preempt altogether — laws in many states that have been permitting individuals to file civil suits against corporations. Although administration officials say they are not coordinating any effort to block the courthouse door, the proposed new rules have alarmed state officials, consumer advocates and even conservatives in Congress, who worry the White House may be trampling on states' rights and thereby losing some of its conservative bearings.

The concerns reached a crescendo after the FDA included language limiting personal injury lawsuits against pharmaceutical companies in a rule it issued for drug labels. The regulation requires manufacturers to better organize and simplify directions on package inserts, but it also says that companies that comply with the new standards may not be sued in state courts by patients injured by their products.

Similarly, the National Highway Traffic and Safety Administration (NHTSA) is proposing a rule that would shield automobile manufacturers from suits arising from injuries incurred in rollover crashes — as long as the carmakers comply with new federal standards for roof strength. And the Consumer Product Safety Commission approved a look-alike rule limiting suits against makers of mattresses that catch fire, if the companies comply with new standards.

State officials say they were blindsided by some of the efforts and suspect that the administration is using the arcane, often technical federal rulemaking process to avoid drawing attention to itself.

> **"When federal agencies play an arbitrary game of pre-emptive action ... lawsuits are filed and no one gains."**
>
> — Sen. Larry E. Craig, R-Idaho

The National Conference of State Legislatures contends that the FDA went back on earlier assurances that the labeling rule would not pre-empt state or local laws — then refused to provide state legislators with a copy of the revised language or extend the period reserved for the public to comment. (FDA officials say the agency signaled its intent as far back as 2000 and had preempted other state health regulations before that.)

In the case of several of the new rules, including those for drug labels and car construction, regulators placed the language protecting manufacturers in the preamble, or introductory section, which does not customarily deal with changes and is usually treated as accepted fact, not subject to public comment. That has infuriated administration critics, who accuse the White House of planning an elaborate ruse to limit understanding of its anti-litigation efforts.

"Although this policy reversal will substantially undermine the states' ability to protect their citizens, neither affected state and local entities, nor the general public, were given an opportunity to comment," John D. Dingell of Michigan and other senior Democrats on the House Energy and Commerce Committee complained in a Feb. 23 letter to Health and Human Services Secretary Michael O. Leavitt.

Some administration critics view the rules as another chapter in the administration's efforts to shield corporations from litigation, which, among other things, yielded last year's law limiting class action claims.

White House officials say decisions about pre-empting state laws are made agency by agency. In cases like the FDA rule, the pre-emption language reflects views expressed in past court filings.

"In each case, the agency with the appropriate expertise made the determination that a uniform national standard would best protect public health and safety," said Alex Conant, a spokesman for the Office of Information and Regulatory Affairs at the Office of Management and Budget, which oversees regulatory policy.

CONSERVATIVE CRITICISM

Legal scholars question whether rules changes made in preambles, without any corresponding public comment, have the same legal standing as changes subjected to the customary public reviews. However, the administration expects federal judges to give the pre-emptions strong consideration in cases that take up consumers' rights to sue.

CQ Weekly March 6, 2006

Overruling the States

Using its regulatory power, the Bush administration is moving to set federal rules that pre-empt some state laws that permit individuals to sue over environmental and consumer protection concerns, declaring that those state statutes are inconsistent with federal standards. The move has surprised conservatives in Congress, as well as commentators on the political right, who note the administration in the past has promoted states' rights and a more limited role for the federal government. Some examples:

BANKS

The Comptroller of the Currency has proposed a rule that, if adopted and upheld by courts, would exempt nationally chartered banks from state consumer protection laws. States including New York and California currently have laws against predatory lending, guidelines on how and when banks may obtain individual credit reports, restrictions on credit card company activities and particular financial disclosure requirements.

AUTOMOBILES

The National Highway Traffic Safety Administration says that efforts by California and 10 other states to limit automobile emissions that have been linked to global warming amount to an attempt to set fuel economy standards, which it says is exclusively the purview of the federal government. In addition, NHTSA has proposed requiring automakers to construct roofs to better protect drivers and passengers after rollovers. The rule includes language indemnifying the automakers from future rollover-related lawsuits brought under state consumer protection laws.

PHARMACEUTICALS

The Food and Drug Administration is expanding an effort to protect drugmakers against lawsuits brought under state consumer protection laws as long as the manufacturers complied with FDA standards for making and distributing the drugs. The agency in January argued that FDA-approved labels shield companies from many types of litigation that can be brought in state courts.

MATTRESSES

The Consumer Product Safety Commission in February approved a new standard for the flammability of mattresses. But language in the preamble of the rule pre-empts existing state standards and requirements, possibly preventing individuals from seeking court action in states that have higher standards than the federal government.

Some of the most pointed criticism of the rule changes is coming from conservatives in Congress and academics on the political right.

Some conservatives say Bush is flying against the decentralized government spirit espoused by President Ronald Reagan. It was Reagan, they note, who in 1987 imposed an executive order that federal agencies defer to the authority of states whenever possible.

"The prior philosophy was that the federal government . . . should harmonize our enforcement with state enforcement," said Todd Gaziano, director for the Center for Legal and Judicial Studies at the conservative Heritage Foundation. Federal agencies, he said, "ought to be respectful of state decisions and laws, even when I might think that they're foolish."

Michael Greve, a legal scholar at the conservative American Enterprise Institute who supports efforts to limit lawsuits, said the recent rule changes are reminiscent of the regulatory overreaching espoused by some Democratic administrations.

"Am I fond of the trend toward administrative pre-emption? The answer is no. . . . That's a really awful system," Greve said, recalling how the FDA during the Clinton administration redefined the scope of its jurisdiction by declaring it could regulate tobacco.

Some GOP lawmakers worry that pre-emption of state laws could prompt backlash from voters. The FDA rule protecting drug companies against consumer lawsuits is particularly disquieting to them, coming less than a year after a class of popular prescription painkillers was linked to elevated risk of heart attacks and stroke. And conservative lawmakers predict the rules designed to limit lawsuits will themselves trigger expensive legal challenges.

"When federal agencies play an arbitrary game of pre-emptive action, it really costs the taxpayers," said Republican Sen. Larry E. Craig of Idaho, who predicts "a long, drawn-out process because lawsuits are filed and no one gains."

Many conservatives in Congress are not entirely uncomfortable with federal pre-emption, as long as they are consulted. For example, the 2005 class action law requires such cases to be subjected to federal law instead of state procedures, which were deemed friendlier to plaintiffs.

But there is a delicate balance of power inherent in making federal regulations governing commerce. Congress frequently writes laws outlining broad intent, while giving executive branch agencies — which are responsible for policing the activity in question — responsibility for writing the fine print. Tensions rise when agency rules go beyond congressional intent. For example, the proposed rule on car roofs goes beyond what Congress intended when it wrote the Motor Vehicle Safety Act 40 years ago, in the opinion of many. Federal law says that motor vehicle rules do "not exempt a person from liability" in state courts.

"You have to look at it case by case," said Republican Rep. Dan Lungren of California. "Look, there's always been tension between the federal government and its ability to enforce . . . and states' police powers. The question is whether on its face it's clear that pre-emption follows from federal responsibilities."

LAWSUITS COMING

Anticipated court challenges of the Bush rules will take up such questions. The consumer advocacy group Public Citizen plans to sue the government to allege that the roof strength standard is inadequate, because 70 percent of existing vehicles already meet it. The group says the federal pre-emption language removes any incentives to make safer cars and "shuts the courthouse doors" on consumers.

Twenty-six state attorneys general wrote to NHTSA in December arguing that the new rules impedes their state tort system, which serves "as a vital check on government-imposed safety standards."

The specific decision to place the rule change in the preamble of the regulation — which many legal scholars call highly unusual — also is likely come under judicial scrutiny. Thomas W. Merrill of Columbia Law School notes that, when controversial proposals such as pre-emption of state laws are depicted as fact, their legal standing is "more suspect."

Some in Congress appear ready to step in if the actions are found to be overreaching. "Obviously, Congress has the power to pre-empt state law," said Republican Sen. John Cornyn, a former Texas attorney general. "But agencies shouldn't be doing this [without congressional guidance], especially not surreptitiously." ∎

Political Participation

Political participation is the lifeblood of U.S. democracy. This section is devoted to the groups and individuals who help choose the country's leaders and set its course. The articles tackle the outlook for the Republican and Democratic parties as they approach the 2006 midterm elections and the issues of interest groups and their influence on government.

The first article in this section looks closely at the challenges facing Republicans as they strive to maintain their majority in Congress in the 2006 midterm elections. The power of incumbency has only been strengthened due to recent redistricting, and Republicans continue to wield a significant fundraising advantage over Democrats. Nonetheless, a number of nagging issues have beset the GOP lately. Economic concerns and growing discontent over the war in Iraq, as well as mounting scandals and controversies, have engulfed Congress and the White House. As a result, the poll numbers for both the president and the congressional Republicans who rely on his coattails come election time are dismal. All of these developments have put the Republican Party in a defensive posture as the campaign season gets into full swing.

The Jack Abramoff lobbying scandal, with its tales of excessive lobbying fees and ill-gotten political contributions, has brought unwanted attention to Indian casinos and the tribes that run them. The second article focuses on how members of Congress are shying away from contributions from Indians, fearing that any tribal donations will be perceived by voters as tainted. The tribes, for their part, have long been apprehensive of outsiders undermining their sovereignty. The recent fallout over the Abramoff affair has made tribal leaders even more leery of engaging in the political process as they struggle to improve their public image while seeking to advance their interests at the national level.

The third article contemplates Republican prospects not just for a continued majority following the 2006 elections but also into the foreseeable future. Former House majority leader Tom DeLay's exodus from Congress following his indictment by a Texas grand jury on conspiracy charges leaves his party at a crossroads. The "Republican Revolution" that overtook Washington in 1994 appears to have finally exhausted itself, its ideological fervor dampened by the practical necessities of maintaining power. This spirit of revolution, as best personified by DeLay, left a legacy of reshaped government and a bare-knuckled political style that endures to this day. But the party DeLay so ably shepherded for a dozen years has suffered from the scandals and controversies surrounding his departure, making the party's future uncertain.

The impact of grassroots campaigning via the Internet was one of the more intriguing developments in the 2004 elections. The last article in this section details how companies and interest groups are increasingly using the Internet's vast reach to go over the heads of elected officials to bring their message directly to the American people.

The Republicans face newer and thornier obstacles as they strive for a continuing majority in 2006

THERE ARE STILL more than six months to go before Election Day, but the party that has dominated Congress for a dozen years is already locked in a campaign-year vise grip. Weakened by scandal, fractured by ideology and paralyzed by a lack of legislative cohesion, the Republican Party is fighting to control its own political destiny.

The battle is both immediate and long-term. The Republicans, at this still relatively early juncture in the 2006 campaign, remain favored to retain control of both the House and Senate, if only because the party enjoys a set of structural advantages that clearly place Democratic challengers on an uphill slope. Redistricting has locked in scores of safe seats, most of them belonging to the GOP, and the party continues to enjoy a fundraising prowess that will enable its leaders and backbenchers alike to put the best possible face on their legislative records.

In short, Republicans have every political advantage going for them at the moment except one: popularity. Likely voters in the 2006 midterm election are telling pollsters they have little confidence that the party in power is capable of solving any of the problems that matter to them most: the economy, health care, immigration — even homeland security.

A Gallup Poll April 10-13 found Congress with a job approval rating of 23 percent, the same abysmal score that the Democratic-controlled Congress received on the eve of the 1994 midterm election that propelled the Republicans to power. The poll also showed a disapproval score of 70 percent.

The party's standard-bearer, George W. Bush, won't be on any ballots this fall, of course. But the president's own sorry approval ratings could drag down his allies and help determine the outcomes of some of the closest House and Senate races, perhaps with control of the 110th Congress in the balance.

The war in Iraq, the failure to generate any movement on his calls to overhaul Social Security, and now an intraparty debate over border control — which Bush initiated but has yet to step in to resolve — combine with other issues to put Republicans on the defensive on practically every top-tier public policy front.

So whether Republicans will still have their edge after voters go to the polls Nov. 7 depends in large part on what they do, or are unable to do, with their control of Congress during the intervening 28 weeks

Playing

— and especially in the next months. They essentially have between now and the start of the summer recess on July 28 to make progress on a legislative program that convinces the electorate that the GOP should remain in control of the national agenda for another two years. By the time they return after Labor Day, the intensity of the campaign season will be turned up so high that the moment for productive lawmaking will have passed.

The majority party's rather uncharacteristic disarray so far this year suggests that it will have a hard time reversing the downward trend. Before leaving the Capitol for the congressional spring break, both House and Senate leaders were forced to jettison high-priority initiatives more because of Republican divisions than Democratic opposition.

Absent a big (and successful) legislative push, Republicans will go into the fall elections in a defensive crouch — hoping against hope that the bad news from Iraq, the Jack Abramoff and Tom DeLay legal pro-

ON THE SPOT: Whether the majority Senate Republicans, led by Tennessee's Bill Frist, left, or the House GOP majority, under Speaker J. Dennis Hastert of Illinois, get much legislating done in the next three months could have a large impact on this fall's elections.

Defense

SHIFTING SCENARIOS

A thorough, continually revisited analysis of the races in all 435 House seats and 33 Senate seats being contested this year projects that if the election were held today, Republicans would hold at least 54 seats in the Senate — one fewer than today — and 224 seats in the House, seven fewer than now; one contest for the Senate and nine for the House are currently tossups. Majority control is 51 and 218, respectively. (2006 CQ Weekly, pp. 1086-1095)

But this outlook will change, and could change considerably, with each week that passes until Election Day. While the vast majority of Republican seats on the ballot are safe bets for that party to hold — especially in the House — several have characteristics that make them subject to serious competition and thus could swing to the Democrats if the ongoing GOP slump persists.

Democrats have fallen short of their candidate recruitment goals. But it appears they may have found just enough credible challengers to give them long-shot odds at the six-seat net gain they need to win the Senate and the 15-seat net gain they need to win the House.

Two Republican senators seeking re-election are at particular risk. One is Pennsylvania's Rick Santorum, who is defending his conservative record in a state that favored Democrat John Kerry for president in 2004 and who has drawn one of the Democrats' strongest challengers nationally, state Treasurer Bob Casey. The other is Montana's Conrad Burns, who is weakened by reports that he was a leading recipient of campaign donations from Abramoff, who has now pleaded guilty and is cooperating with the Justice Department in a public corruption inquiry that may yet have far-reaching consequences for members of Congress.

Democrats also are staging serious takeover bids in Rhode Island, Ohio, Missouri and Tennessee and underdog bids in Virginia and Arizona. To take over the Senate in January they would have to win most of those while fending off challenges to their incumbents in states such as New Jersey, Maryland and Washington.

On the House side, the Democrats have put more GOP-held seats in play than the other way around — although many of their takeover hopefuls still face long odds.

For Democrats, then, a winning scenario in either chamber depends on events breaking sharply their way between now and November.

And the fact remains that the same polls showing discontent with a Republican-controlled Congress also show that the electorate is not exactly rallying to the Democrats. A Fox News/Opinion Dynamics survey April 4-5 showed that, while 29 percent approved of the job Republicans were doing in Congress and 53 percent disapproved, the ratings for Democrats were almost identical, at 29 percent approval and 51 percent disapproval.

"National Democrats believe that their strongest path to victory is to make the fall elections a referendum on the Republicans," said Dotty Lynch, the longtime political director of CBS News, who's now a fellow at the Institute of Politics at Harvard University. "They want to keep the focus on Republican failures, and they are concerned that if they put forward an agenda they will turn the election [into] a contest of two sets of policies and issues rather than a report card on the status quo."

ceedings, and last year's devastating hurricane season will not be followed by any more such politically debilitating experiences.

If the status quo merely holds, Republicans will almost certainly lose seats even if they manage to maintain their majorities. They would then head into the last two years of the Bush presidency as a greatly diminished political force — far removed from the party that, only 18 months ago, interpreted the last election as evidence that their party had been given a mandate to transform the role of the federal government.

"Republicans will need to demonstrate their common-sense understanding of issues, their compassion for people in need, and their competence as policy makers," said David Rebovich, managing director of the Rider University Institute for New Jersey Politics. "Simply blaming the institution of Congress, a tried and often true campaign tactic of incumbents, or warning voters about the presumably dangerous views of the minority party are not likely to work this fall."

But, Lynch added, "the fact that the Democrats are having such a hard time coming up with a coherent answer to the question 'What would you do differently?' has given the Republicans an opening."

It's not yet clear that the Democrats will be able to rally around a campaign platform similar to the "Contract With America," which the GOP wielded in campaigning before their takeover in 1994. Then again, it's not altogether certain they will need to. Whatever benefit such a manifesto gave the Republicans then was a historic anomaly; most elections with seismic results have been driven by a simple rejection of the party in power. The other side had only to point out what the majority had done wrong and satisfy the public that they wouldn't do any worse.

"If President Bush and the Republican Congress are unable to improve their poll standing in the months ahead, Democrats will probably be able to do quite nicely in November by sticking to a simple, four-word slogan: 'Had Enough? Vote Democratic,' " said Rhodes Cook, who publishes his own political newsletter.

Democrats this year have shown they are increasingly united in their determination to block the Republicans from their legislative goals. But even more worrisome for the GOP was the exposure that recent congressional fights have given to their own internecine rifts — a daunting new development for a party whose leaders harnessed remarkable unity for the first five years of the Bush presidency.

IMMIGRATION IMBROGLIO

Though their party has been politically injured by the public's weariness with the war, the Gulf Coast's rocky recovery from Hurricane Katrina and worries about a growing but uneven economy, Republican leaders decided to press ahead on a Bush priority that has long threatened to divide their ranks in a way not seen for a decade or more: how to deal with an illegal immigrant population estimated at more than 11 million.

One side, which includes Bush and important senators, would tighten border security but also create a guest worker program favored by business interests that have come to depend on immigrants to fill low-wage jobs that they say U.S. citizens don't want. The other side, which includes a majority of the party's House members, would make border security paramount, bar guest workers, and increase criminal penalties on illegal immigrants and those who employ them.

Some in the latter camp warn that the immi-

An iPod Charge to Keep

What goes into a "Special Republican Edition iPod"? Is it something that comes pre-loaded with your own personal **Toby Keith** collection? Maybe a classic or two from the **Charlie Daniels** Band? Does it stream special **Sean Hannity** and **Rush Limbaugh** podcasts? Will it, at the very least, block downloads of **Neil Young's** new single, "Let's Impeach the President"?

None of the above, it turns out. Sure, the Republican National Committee says it's giving customized players as thank-you gifts to the five fundraisers who host the most successful events in a national round of GOP "house parties". But it's only a "Republican iPod" in the sense that it's dressed up on the outside.

It's a standard, 30GB iPod with a video screen and a customized skin, special-ordered from Apple, that features an American flag design. And the back, says RNC deputy press secretary **Josh Holmes**, has a

POTUS-CAST: Bush framed by a special Republican edition iPod.

white patch where President Bush will personally ink his name. "The president's signature is probably the selling point" for the competing fundraiser hosts, says Holmes.

But no pre-loaded Toby Keith. No **Ted Nugent**. Not even **Cream**'s "Sunshine of Your Love" — revealed to be a favorite of Secretary of State Condoleezza Rice, who confessed an unsuspected fondness for "acid rock" in a special **Bono**-edited edition of the UK's Independent. (Ever the politician, Rice also professed a willingness to download "anything" by **U2**.)

Instead, the Republican iPods will let their owners choose which music to download: They'll put the choices in the hands of the people. Still, one suspects if the lucky winners of the party-branded iPods will be swapping MP3s of the **Dixie Chicks'** new release, "Not Ready to Make Nice," they'll be keeping it to themselves.

gration issue could be for the GOP what the North American Free Trade Agreement was for the Democrats. President Bill Clinton hailed the benefits of liberalized trade with Canada and Mexico and pushed the accord through a Democratic Congress. But the effort alienated organized labor and environmental groups, depressing Democratic turnout in November 1994.

Today, some Republicans see a warning sign on the immigration issue in the special election last December in Southern California. John Campbell, a state senator, held what had been a reliably Republican seat for the party — but with a plurality of 44 percent of the vote. While only 28 percent favored a little-known Democrat, 26 percent voted for third-party candidate Jim Gilchrist — a founder of the Minuteman Project, which recruits volunteers to patrol the nation's borders in an effort to limit illegal immigration.

Louis DeSipio, associate professor of politics and Chicano/Latino studies at the University of California at Irvine, said the message of

Gilchrist's campaign "is that there is a core of the Republican Party electorate that holds strong beliefs about illegal immigration, and they are not to be trifled with."

SPENDING SPATS

The other prominent schism in the GOP ranks this spring is on fiscal policy, because many in the party says its leaders have betrayed the "conservative revolution" of 1994 by supporting spending policies that have yielded deepening deficits and rising national debt.

These restive conservatives obtained an agreement from House leaders to enforce procedures aimed at limiting spending, but the deal appears to have collapsed in the face of opposition from Republicans on the House and Senate Appropriations committees — who say it would tie their hands and make it difficult to enact spending bills — and from party moderates who believe that important social programs would be wrongly targeted for cuts. The Demo-

Signposts to Guide the Election Forecasts: An Update

Since last August the CQ political team has been tracking eight indicators, or "signposts," as a means for comparing the Republicans' advantages en route to taking over Congress in 1994 with this campaign's situation for the Democrats. In the eight months since, the GOP's position for 2006 has worsened in at least four categories — and the party isn't even getting acclaim for a statistically strong economy:

Congressional polls

An April 10-13 Gallup Poll of 1,005 adults found only 23 percent approving of the job Congress is doing, while 70 percent disapproved — the exact same assessment that those polled by Gallup gave the Democratic-controlled Congress one month before the Republicans won control of Congress in 1994. The solace for the GOP majority is that other polls show that at the moment, those surveyed dislike congressional Democrats almost as much as they dislike Republicans.

Presidential polls

Already on a down slope last summer, mainly because of Iraq war worries, President Bush's popularity suffered wounds in the wake of Hurricane Katrina that have yet to heal. These days all the widely scrutinized polls show his job approval percentages in the middle-to-high 30s. That support level is slightly below the bottom-scraping scores given to President Bill Clinton just before his party's 1994 election debacle.

President's policies

The issues that were dragging Bush down last summer linger: the Iraq war, his moribund Social Security overhaul plan, the costs of health care and high gasoline prices. Since then, his presidency has been further burdened by Hurricane Katrina, the failed nomination of his friend and lawyer Harriet Miers to the

Supreme Court, revelations about selective White House leaking, the disclosure of Bush's ordering domestic surveillance without judicial oversight and an immigration debate that is dividing the GOP. Bush's situation is at least comparable to that of Clinton, who in 1994 was singed by his failed health care overhaul and backlash against tax increases.

Recruitment

Democrats have found credible contenders for all of their bids to take over Republican Senate seats. They also have expanded their ranks of potentially competitive House challengers. But they haven't matched the GOP's recruiting successes of 1994. Republicans, while mostly playing defense this year, don't need to win many Democratic seats to prevent a takeover of Congress by the other side, and they have solid candidates in a few key races.

Ethics

House Republicans have incurred damage from controversies surrounding power broker Tom DeLay, who is resigning his Texas seat, and Randy "Duke" Cunningham, who resigned his California seat before going to prison for soliciting bribes. The Justice Department inquiry into the relationships of lobbyists and lawmakers could be a ticking time bomb. The Democrats, who were badly damaged by corruption in 1994, now describe the GOP as fostering a "culture of corruption"; to combat that, Republicans point to several ethically challenged Democrats.

Economy

No issue befuddles GOP strategists more than the negative ratings Bush and his party get for their stewardship of the economy. Leading indicators suggest continued growth, but gas prices, high debt, medical costs and foreign competition cause widespread worry. The 1994 Democrats might empathize; voters then held negative views that were also out of sync with statistics.

Retirements

The open-seat outlook provides Republicans with a positive contrast to the Democrats of 1994, who suffered a wave of retirements. There is just one Republican among the four retiring senators. And while outgoing Republicans on the House side outnumber departing Democrats by more than 2-to-1, few of those open GOP seats are vulnerable to partisan takeover.

Pre-election jolt

While two Republican special election takeovers in 1994 were omens for that November's tidal wave, Democrats have only been able to tout near-misses in the two House special contests of the past year. Democrats can crow over their gubernatorial victories last November in New Jersey and Virginia, but those wins only allowed them to maintain their hold on seats they already had.

---

cratic minority, meanwhile, is sure to oppose whatever fiscal priorities the GOP sets.

The result is that the annual budget resolution, which is generally viewed as must-do legislation, is in limbo — again raising the specter of 1994.

That year, it was the leaders of a Democratic majority who faced deep divisions in their ranks and near-united opposition from the GOP minority on nearly every front, and so were stymied in their attempts to push through marquee agenda items — including Clinton's sweeping overhaul of the nation's health care system and an anti-crime bill with new gun controls.

But the echoes of a dozen years ago do not end there. Then, as now, the majority in Con-

gress was watching the approval ratings for a president of the same party sink lower in each new poll. Then, as now, the ethical travails of a relatively small number in the majority's ranks were enough so that the taint of corruption began attaching itself to everyone in the party. The result, now as then, is that the majority had legislative power — but little power to remake its own political fortune.

"The strategy that gets you into office isn't necessarily the one that keeps you there," said Bruce Cain, a political scientist who directs the University of California's Washington Center. "For incumbents generally, what you say you will do if re-elected matters less than what you actually have done to date. And if your

party controls both Congress and the presidency, then you can get blamed for bad conditions or failed administration policies as well."

SHAPING A STRATEGY

Though GOP officials say the party is still guided by the same conservative principles they championed when they took over Congress, they have recognized over the subsequent half-dozen campaigns that enforcing such orthodoxy would prove fatal to its centrist candidates fighting to hang on in politically competitive states and districts — a relatively small group, but one that has been essential to the GOP maintaining its majority by only a dozen or fewer seats.

Under the direction of the current chairman

of the National Republican Congressional Committee, Rep. Thomas M. Reynolds of New York, and his predecessor, Rep. Thomas M. Davis III of Virginia, the GOP has given its candidates free will to shape their own campaigns — even if their emphasis is how independent they are from the party leadership.

Similarly, the National Republican Senatorial Committee this year is fully backing Lincoln Chafee, the Senate's most liberal Republican, in his tough race to retain his seat in Democratic-leaning Rhode Island, even though his challenger in the September primary, Cranston Mayor Stephen Laffey, argues that his conservative views make him a truer Republican.

"While we have a responsibility to govern, all politics is local, and our strategy is to win this majority in the 2006 election. And [those are] the issues that are most important to the districts that these incumbents and candidates are coming from," Reynolds said in briefing reporters on his view of the campaign.

The GOP also clings to the axiom that while voters may hate Congress, they tend to keep loving their own member of Congress. That may be true, but it might be a less reliable buttress than usual. An April 6-9 Washington Post/ABC News poll found that 59 percent approved of their own representatives, down from 65 percent in December.

ENERVATED ETHICS

Aside from Iraq, there appears to be no issue that clouds Republicans' election prospects as much as ethics. Three lobbyists well-connected in the GOP — Abramoff, Tony Rudy and Michael Scanlon — have copped pleas and are telling prosecutors about their dealings with members of Congress; the prospect of one or more incumbents being indicted is taken at the Capitol as almost a given.

Democrats have been trying to convince voters that the Republicans have developed a "culture of corruption" in Congress, and they have a poster boy for this in Republican Randy "Duke" Cunningham, who resigned his California House seat in December after pleading guilty to accepting millions of dollars of bribes from defense contractors.

It is true that Democrats lost their best foil on this issue when Tom DeLay decided to resign his Texas House seat by mid-June. The longtime GOP leader, who denies wrongdoing, is under indictment in Texas on campaign finance charges and is intimately connected to

IN WAITING: Senate Minority Leader Harry Reid of Nevada, at microphone, would be majority leader and House Minority Leader Nancy Pelosi of California, right, would be in line to become Speaker if Democrats took over.

Abramoff, Rudy and Scanlon.

But DeLay also acted as a political lightning rod, and his decision to step aside gave unwanted exposure to other Republicans with past ties to Abramoff — with much of the attention focused on Burns in Montana and Rep. Bob Ney of Ohio. Both deny having done anything wrong and say they will be exonerated, but each faces a serious Democratic challenge in which ethics questions loom large.

In addition, what initially appeared a hellbent rush to tighten rules on lobbying has slowed to a crawl — and Democrats already are using that to bolster their case that Republicans have become weak stewards of congressional integrity.

Still, there is little evidence so far that a critical mass of voters is blaming either Congress as a whole or just the GOP majority for the ethical lapses of individual members.

Republicans argue that this is in part because some Democratic lawmakers also took campaign money from Abramoff and his clients, while others have potential ethical problems of their own. They have newly focused on Alan B. Mollohan of West Virginia, who stepped aside as the top Democrat on the House ethics committee under intense GOP criticism of his personal financial dealings and reports that he steered federal funds to nonprofit groups in his district that were run by some of his contributors.

MARGINS AND MAINTENANCE

In 1994, Republicans fielded enough credible candidates in every region of the country so they could reap maximum benefit from the "tidal wave" that swept the electorate — gaining eight seats in the Senate and an astonishing 52 in the House. Many probably would not have won absent that surge, but they raised enough money and enough support locally and from national interest groups to become viable by the time that wave arrived. Democrats have not been nearly as successful this year at "spreading the playing field" as Republicans were then; the challengers may have been recruited well enough to win narrow majorities if an anti-Republican surge arrives, but they don't have much margin for error.

Along with Pennsylvania's Casey, top-tier Democratic Senate recruits include Rep. Harold E. Ford Jr. in Tennessee, where Majority Leader Bill Frist is retiring; Rep. Sherrod Brown to face two-term GOP incumbent Mike DeWine in Ohio; and state Auditor Claire McCaskill, who only narrowly lost the Missouri governorship in 2004, to challenge Republican Jim Talent's bid for a second term.

Republicans have responded by recruiting former insurance company executive Mike McGavick to challenge Maria Cantwell's campaign for a second term in Washington; state Sen. Tom Kean Jr., the namesake son of a popular former governor, to take on newly appointed Democrat Bob Menendez in New Jersey; and Lt. Gov. Michael Steele to seek the open seat in Maryland.

On the House side, eight of the nine contests that are currently tossups are for Republican-held seats, in part because Democrats have solid recruits in each. They include two candidates in rematches of extremely close 2004 contests: Lawyer Lois Murphy, who again is taking on Rep. Jim Gerlach in the outer suburbs of Philadelphia, and Baron P. Hill, who is seeking to avenge the loss of his southeastern Indiana seat to Mike Sodrel.

The Democrats also have some standouts in contests where Republican incumbents retain only a slight edge. They include Diane Farrell, a former mayor who held Christopher Shays to a career-low 52 percent in southwestern Connecticut last time; state Rep. Ron Klein, who is likely to be by far the best-financed opponent ever for E. Clay Shaw Jr in South Florida; county sheriff Brad Ellsworth, who is seeking to displace John Hostettler in southwestern Indiana; and New Mexico Attorney General Patricia Madrid, regarded as the strongest challenger yet against Heather A. Wilson.

The latest campaign finance reports also suggest that the Democrats have some longshot candidates who could threaten in districts where Republicans are now favored. One of these is lawyer Kirsten Gillibrand, who reported raising $716,000 by the end of March for her challenge to Rep. John E. Sweeney in upstate New York.

But Democrats probably won't be able to win the House unless their own incumbents successfully defend against a handful of serious Republican takeover challenges. Among the GOP's top contenders are David McSweeney, an investment banker ready to spend his money liberally to oust Melissa Bean after one term representing the outer Chicago suburbs; state Sen. Jeff Lamberti, who is taking on Leonard L. Boswell in central Iowa; and state Sen. Craig Romero, who hopes to keep Charlie Melancon's service to one term in southern Louisiana.

Also on this list is a pair of former House members from Georgia: Mac Collins, who is challenging Democratic Rep. Jim Marshall; and Max Burns, who's in a rematch with the Democrat who ousted him in 2004, John Barrow.

VULNERABILITY QUOTIENT

The factor on which 2006 Republicans are clearly in better shape than were the Democrats in 1994 is the number of vulnerable seats left open by departing members.

In 1994, Republicans won in large measure

because of a glut of Democratic departures — many of them in districts, especially in the South, that had mainly conservative constituencies that had been favoring Republicans for many offices for some time. That year, the GOP captured 22 of 31 House seats and all six Senate seats left open by Democrats' retirements.

The Republican majority this year faces no such exposure. With more than half the states already past their filing deadlines, Frist is the

> ## "If your party controls Congress and the presidency, then you can get blamed for bad conditions or failed administration policies."
>
> — **Bruce Cain,** University of California

only Republican senator retiring. While Democrats are contesting his seat, they are also working to hold the other three open Senate seats, now held by retiring Mark Dayton in Minnesota, Paul S. Sarbanes in Maryland and James M. Jeffords of Vermont, an independent who caucuses with the Democrats.

Republicans have done a little less well, but not as badly as the 1994 Democrats, at keeping their incumbents in the running for another term in the House: 20 GOP members so far have announced they are leaving to seek another office or to enjoy retirement, compared with seven Democrats and Vermont's Bernard Sanders, the Democratic-affiliated independent who is favored to take Jeffords' Senate seat.

Most of the outgoing Republicans, though, represent strongly GOP districts that would not go Democratic under any conceivable circumstance. As a result, the competitive impact of House retirements is close to parity: Seven races for open seats currently held by Republicans are highly competitive, compared with four Democratic-held open seats.

MIXED SIGNALS

Lacking any other measuring stick, party strategists and political observers dissect the results of "off-year" and special elections to determine whether a partisan swing might be in the making. Republican takeovers in two House special elections held in 1993 were viewed as omens of their 1994 upsurge.

The verdict so far in this election cycle is

mixed: Democrats can reasonably claim some progress, but the elections since 2004 have not provided evidence of any sea change. Democrats have staged serious efforts in two special House elections for seats that had been held by Republicans, and while the results were close, they came up short in both.

The latest was the April 11 first round of a special election to fill Cunningham's seat. Democrat Francine Busby, a college instructor and school board trustee, took 44 percent of the vote to finish first in a primary in which 18 candidates, regardless of party, appeared on one ballot. That was 8 points better than her showing as Cunningham's 2004 challenger in the normally Republican-voting San Diego-area district. But it was still short of the majority she needed to win the seat outright and avoid a runoff against former Rep. Brian P. Bilbray, who finished first among 14 Republican primary candidates.

Given the area's voting pattern, Busby's hopes for a paradigm-shifting upset may depend on a continued rift within Republican ranks: Businessman Eric Roach, whom Bilbray narrowly edged in the primary, has not ruled out contesting the nomination for the general election; that primary is June 6, the same day as the special-election runoff.

Democrats had to settle for a moral victory in this cycle's other competitive special election for the House. Paul Hackett, an Iraq War veteran turned critic, came within 4 points of winning the reliably Republican seat left open in the Cincinnati suburbs by Rob Portman — who left to be Bush's trade representative and is now his choice for White House budget director.

Democrats won both off-year elections for governor in 2005: Sen. Jon Corzine won in Democratic-leaning New Jersey, and Lt. Gov. Tim Kaine was victorious in Republican-leaning Virginia. The latter victory was accorded added significance because Bush, who had carried the state by 9 points a year earlier, made an election-eve appearance in the state in behalf of the Republican nominee, former state Attorney General Jerry Kilgore.

But both victories were "holds" for the Democrats: Kaine succeed Democrat Mark Warner in Virginia, and Corzine replaced Richard J. Codey in New Jersey. As a result, the Democrats since 2004 have not gained a seat that they did not already hold. ◼

Scrutiny on Tribes Keeps Stakes High

American Indian leaders urged to press on with Hill agenda despite flak from Abramoff lobbying scandal

DISGRACED LOBBYIST Jack Abramoff had dealings with only a handful of American Indian tribes, but the scandal he left behind has touched every tribe everywhere.

In fact, the Abramoff affair, with its tens of millions of dollars in lobbying fees and political contributions from Indian tribes with casinos, has become a political millstone for the Indian gambling business in particular and tribal governments in general. It has drawn more scrutiny to Indian casinos and is driving talk in Congress of new restrictions on tribal gambling, which is the fastest-growing segment of the gaming industry.

The extraordinarily large amounts that some tribes paid Abramoff, in some cases to try to undercut potential Indian competitors, feed a public perception that tribes have become just another wealthy special interest — or worse, have become corrupt themselves. No tribes have been accused of wrongdoing during a Justice Department inquiry that dates to the middle of 2004. But the perception alone will make it harder for all Indians to sell their agenda and defend their interests on Capitol Hill and in statehouses around the country. Conflicts between tribes and surrounding communities already have been increasing with the success of the multibillion-dollar gambling business.

The Abramoff scandal "is going to pollute the waters for everybody, for all tribes," says political scientist David Wilkins, a Lumbee Indian from North Carolina who teaches at the University of Minnesota.

Some in Congress are shying away from contributions from any Indians this election year, for fear the public can't distinguish one tribe from another and will believe that all tribal money is somehow tainted, says Republican Rep. Tom Cole of Oklahoma, a member of the Chickasaw Nation and the only American Indian now serving in Congress.

It is for that reason that poorer tribes badly in need of federal aid might try to distance themselves from those with thriving gambling operations — only about 40 percent of the 567 federally recognized tribes are involved in gambling, according to the National Indian Gaming Commission.

Tribes were already conflicted about getting involved in politics, for fear that would invite meddling outsiders into reservation life and encroach on tribal sovereignty, says Wilkins. "It just exacerbates internal tensions within tribes and among tribes."

As tribal leaders gather in Washington for a series of meetings culminating at the end of February in the winter session of the National Congress of American Indians, the question is how tribes can bolster their public image and defend their interests at the national level.

Many of their Washington allies are urging the tribes to stay engaged in both the political and legislative process, whatever the challenges and despite their disgust at the way Abramoff misused and manipulated his tribal clients. "This is not the time, in my view, for tribes to back out of the process," Cole said. "They have a great story to tell, and for the first time in 500 years, opportunity is moving toward us, not away from us."

And indeed, the stakes for tribal governments in their dealings with Congress and federal agencies have never been higher. The success of Indian gambling has drawn envy and attention. Last fall, for instance, the National Labor Relations Board ruled that federal labor laws apply on Indian land, siding with a union that had been trying to organize workers at a tribal casino in California. It was a major blow to tribal claims of sovereignty, which Indians say puts their land outside the reach of such federal regulations. Tribes now want Congress to try to undo the ruling.

At the same time, Indian communities around the country are still struggling to overcome generations of poverty and privation — and they are looking to the federal government for money to improve education, health care and other services on reservations.

"It's a tough job for us, no question," says Ron Allen, chairman of the Jamestown S'Klallam Tribe in Washington and a member of the executive committee of the National Congress of American Indians. "We're not naive about this. We're very cognizant that it's a very challenging time for us."

DOWN HOME TOUCH

The National Indian Gaming Association is also urging its members to stay involved. But it puts less emphasis on using lobbyists and more on getting members to Washington to meet with lawmakers and staff face to face. "There's no question the role of the hired lobbyist will be receding," said Jason Giles, the association's legal counsel.

Giles explains that part of the concern is that K Street lobbyists have public image problems of their own in the wake of scandal, which could hurt the tribal cause. But more than that, tribal leaders making their case personally have always been the Indians' most effective lobbyists — and for all the complications of traveling to Washington from remote areas, Giles said, "that will probably be the best policy for the foreseeable future."

Giles and others say they are confident that their support on Capitol Hill is strong and deep enough to weather this scandal. Jacqueline Johnson, executive director of the National Congress of American Indians, says her conversations with lawmakers have assured her that those who are "solid on tribal issues are still solid on tribal issues."

Tribes also understand that they need a strong, united voice on issues that cut across Indian Country, particularly the overarching concerns about protecting their sovereignty. They say that history has taught them the importance of unity. "The practice has always been to divide and conquer," Johnson said. "We've resisted it in the past, and I think you'll find that we'll resist that in this case."

Behind efforts to regulate Indian gaming, for example, Indians see jealousy, tinged even with racism, with roots that stretch back generations. "At some level, people like poor Indians," Cole says. Successful Indians, on the other hand, are a threat, he says. "The time of maximum opportunity for Indians is usually the time of maximum danger."

The large sums generated by their casinos is actually one big assurance that American Indian will continue to have access to the political process and that their businesses will continue to grow. Not only are politicians hungry for money to fuel their campaigns, more and more cash-strapped state and local governments have been encouraging the growth of Indian gambling to get a cut of the revenue. The public's appetite for gambling seems nearly bottomless.

Tribes have yet to determine exactly how much they will be giving to political campaigns this year and to whom, but contribute they will, Giles says. And he says he's confident that when it comes down to it, politicians will take the money and will be able to explain to people back home the difference between the legitimate interests of tribes and the questionable behavior of Jack Abramoff. There is also sympathy for people abused and dispossessed for generations.

But Cole is not the only one who has sensed that politicians, at least for a time, will be skittish about being linked with tribes and tribal money. One lobbyist with years of experience representing tribes on a variety of issues in Washington says that while Indians must stay engaged with politics, they will have to be sensitive to those concerns and take care to maintain a lower profile in the capital — contributing to campaigns, for example, but not prominently sponsoring fundraisers.

That lobbyist would not allow himself to be quoted by name out of concern that he stay well away from any discussion of the Abramoff scandal. "Will I continue to advocate for my clients? Yes," he said. "Will I have to work harder to be sure that we're purer than Caesar's wife? Yes."

And despite the imperative to stick together, there are signs of fissures among tribes. While there is plenty of anger at Abramoff, who pleaded guilty to three fraud felonies and promised to tell federal investigators about his efforts to trade favors and contributions for favorable consideration of his clients, the tribes

> ## "[The Abramoff scandal] is going to pollute the waters for everybody, for all tribes."
> — David Wilkins, University of Minnesota

Life in Indian Country

A surge in gambling revenue has done little to reduce the oppressive poverty of many American Indians. Nearly half the available workforce on or near tribal reservations was unemployed in 2001, for example — and the newest Indian Labor Force Report will show that the economic situation had not improved appreciably by 2003.

1.8 million American Indians are enrolled in federally recognized tribes.

1.5 million (84 percent) of them live on or near reservations and are eligible for federal aid services.

49 percent of the workforce, those older than 16, is unemployed.

33 percent of those who are employed earn wages below poverty guidelines.

66 percent of the total workforce is unemployed or living in poverty.

$19.6 billion in revenue was generated from Indian gaming facilities in 2004, with 228 tribes operating 405 venues.

SOURCES: Bureau of Indian Affairs, National Indian Gaming Commission

who hired him have been criticized for using Abramoff to go after fellow Indians who were rivals in the gambling business.

In a recent issue of the newspaper Indian Country Today, columnist Suzan Shown Harjo gave those tribes a "mantle of shame award" for using Abramoff and his colleagues as "attack dogs against other Indian tribes" and for thinking that "paying megabucks to white men gets

the best job done for Native peoples."

TELLING THEIR STORY

What tribes and their national organizations hope to do now is seize control of their public image, and there's talk of national advertising campaigns and documentaries in which tribes would tell their own stories — their history and culture, the benefits they say casino money has brought to many reservations.

They will be looking for ways to communicate to the public and Congress the broad diversity among tribes and remind them that great needs are still facing much of Indian Country. They hope to orchestrate briefings in the House and Senate about their needs, their issues and their business. The National Congress of American Indians will present their legislative priorities to lawmakers at its winter session.

That group's president, Joe Garcia of New Mexico's San Juan Pueblo, plans to deliver a "State of Indian Nations" speech as a counterpoint to President Bush's State of the Union address.

The National Congress has been raising money to purchase a tribal "embassy" in Washington — a longstanding project that would have special significance for Indians now as they seek to improve their image and stress their claim to sovereignty.

Among tribes' top priorities is updating and expanding the law that provides special medical care programs and services to Indians, tribal organizations and urban Indian organizations. They want to strengthen federal programs for suicide prevention and mental illness. They want to finally settle a dispute over the Interior Department's handling of timber, grazing, oil and mineral lease royalties on lands held in trust by the federal government, which has resulted in years of litigation.

Tribes also hope to win a share of authority and federal money to become an active partner in homeland security and efforts to control outbreaks of pandemics such as bird flu. Because they occupy large tracts of land and territory along the nation's borders, Indians are natural allies in such efforts, says Johnson of the National Congress of American Indians.

DEBATE HEATS UP

But the most pressing matter now, which strikes at the livelihood of many tribes, is the congressional debate over Indian gambling.

There is plenty of talk in the House and Senate of revising the 17-year-old law that paved the way for the explosive growth in Indian casinos to strengthening oversight and regulation of the gaming operations or put new restrictions on them. And the number of proposals has been multiplying since the Abramoff story broke. GOP Rep. Mike Rogers of Michigan, for example, wants to give the states veto power over new Indian gambling facilities. Rep. Charlie Dent, a Pennsylvania Republican, would bar tribal casinos that were not on or near existing Indian reservations.

At the same time, anti-gambling activists outside Congress, such as Tony Perkins at the Family Research Council, have been working hard to keep Abramoff's excesses linked to Indian gambling.

Tribal leaders such as Allen, Johnson and others hotly contest that connection. The scandal was a lobbying scandal, not a gambling or Indian scandal, with Abramoff the guilty party, they say. In the end, the tribes who hired him were victims, too, they say. Abramoff insulted them behind their backs, charged exorbitant fees and played one tribe against another.

"Our money is untainted money, it's good money," says Allen, whose tribe operates a casino. "Our cause is just. We think we should walk with our heads high and continue to champion our cause."

Wilkins, of the University of Minnesota, says tribes must strike a difficult political balance, made even more challenging now. Historically, Indians have maintained a "measured distance" from national politics, since any engagement with Washington potentially opens the door to outside meddling.

But because Congress regulates tribal gambling, the first reservation enterprise to really take off in a significant way, the business has drawn them inexorably into the political process — even as it gave them the money to become political players. Tribes justifiably want to protect their interests, Wilkins says.

"This Abramoff situation is just going to intensify the urge of state and federal lawmakers to corral and contain and squeeze tribes," he says.

His advice to tribal leaders is to look to their own resources, their own money and talent, to defend their interests, rather than turning to outsiders like Abramoff. But the way forward for tribes now is far from clear, Wilkins says. And he'll be watching as tribes plot strategy in the coming weeks and months.

"I'm really anxious to see how tribal leaders respond to this," he said. ■

THE HOUSE THAT NEWT BUILT had become the party that Tom DeLay built to last. The "Republican Revolution" of 1994, which overtook Washington with a combination of ideology and high-minded attitude, turned into a tightly controlled machine fueled by high-handed behavior and lots of money — gobs and gobs of money. The power of their ideals — small government and lower taxes, global strength and free markets, citizen lawmakers and states' rights — was ultimately eclipsed by the idea of power. They had to keep it in order to exercise it. And to keep it, they had to behave like political goodfellas, defending their turf, breaking the arms of their underlings, belittling their enemies, and always — always — staying on the lookout for the next big score.

Newt Gingrich, the Visionary, may have created the Republican majority with his mixture of brains, oratory and passion for the cause. But it was Tom DeLay, the Hammer, who constructed an internal operation that employed all the levers of power to keep it humming day and night. He built a whip operation in the House that could deliver the minimum 218 votes at will. He saved the day after Gingrich's fall from grace by plucking J. Dennis Hastert of Illinois from obscurity and

The End of the Republican REVOLUTION

It's still the majority party, but the potent mix of vision and will that won it control of the Capitol has all but evaporated

installing him as Speaker. He engineered the "K Street" project, which not only forced lobby shops to hire Republicans, but gave them specific assignments for writing legislation, raising money and delivering votes.

And he redrew the map of Texas so that more Republicans and fewer Democrats would win election to Congress. Whatever it took, DeLay found a way to preserve and protect the GOP majority in the House and thus enable the Republican Party to remain as Top Cat in the jungle of Washington politics.

Now DeLay is gone, resigned to fight his own lonely cause in court instead of the Capitol. In his wake, he leaves a party weakened by controversy and scandal, fractured at almost every legislative turn, and clearly weary of the constant din of battle. His replacements, immediate and to be determined, together don't measure up to his capacity for winsome optimism and sheer ruthlessness. Without DeLay's will and sense of righteousness, the center does not hold.

And so ends the revolution.

In its place comes — well, no one really knows. DeLay's departure may actually serve to inoculate Republicans in an otherwise dicey election year, leaving them unencumbered by his uncertain fate in the courts. And Democrats have yet to show organizing force of their own, either in new ideas or bridge-building with swing voters.

But even though Republicans hold the still-slim odds to remain in power in both the House and Senate for the next two years, they will be hard-pressed to dominate the agenda like they have for the past six Congresses. In all probability, ad hoc coalitions will emerge on this issue or that to interrupt the operative gridlock.

Republicans will argue, as DeLay himself

continues to insist, that the spirit of the revolution that swept Republicans to power in Congress and helped give them control of the White House lives on, that they and President Bush continue to set a conservative agenda for the government and that new leaders are emerging to guide the movement. "We've never lost our way," DeLay said.

But if the fire still burns, the flame no longer blinds. The unique combination of big ideas about reshaping government and the bare-knuckle politics to make them happen, which was the hallmark of DeLay, Gingrich and Dick Armey, the leaders of the 1994 revolution, no longer rules the day.

Indeed, many conservatives say the revolution had died even before DeLay's ethical, legal and electoral troubles forced him to resign first his post as majority leader, then his seat in the House. The revolution had succumbed, they say, to the exigencies of governing and maintaining political power in a closely divided nation, to the new realities and financial cost of a post-Sept. 11 America, and to a shift in the Republican Party's center of gravity from the congressional wing to the White House.

DeLay's abrupt departure was just the coda to the final movement. "It's spent," said Bill Whalen, a Republican consultant and a research fellow at Stanford University's conservative Hoover Institution.

In its wake have come intraparty factionalism, a rise of political pragmatism over ideological purity, and — as University of Minnesota political scientist Lawrence Jacobs puts it — the sort of party incoherence that Republicans once lambasted Democrats for.

The party that champions smaller government has simultaneously expanded an entitlement program, Medicare, with hopes of winning the votes of senior citizens. The party of fiscal discipline jams a highway bill with billions of dollars in pet projects at a time when the government is burdened with costly natural disasters and wars in the Middle East.

In the House, the party that for years has opposed stricter campaign finance limits as an abridgment of free speech pushed through new fundraising restrictions on political committees called 527s, which are important to their Democratic opponents. That move angered conservative loyalists already frustrated with the direction of the party under its current leaders. "I find this no less shocking than if the Republican leadership decided that to get re-elected this fall they need to raise taxes," said David Keating, executive director of the anti-tax Club for Growth, itself a 527.

Most disconcerting of all to party loyalists is the GOP's loss of direction after more than a decade of knowing exactly where it wanted to take the country and how it wanted to get there. It was a purposefulness epitomized by the 1994 "Contract With America" drafted by former college professors Gingrich, who would become House speaker, and Armey, who would be elected majority leader.

Even Bush, the party's titular leader and embodiment of the Republican agenda, is so beset by problems and controversy that nearly two-thirds of Americans in an AP-Ipsos poll published recently disapprove of the job he is doing. It will be all Bush can do to rescue his legacy, let alone his party.

Building and Holding a GOP Majority

March 1989: Newt Gingrich of Georgia is elected House minority whip to succeed Dick Cheney of Wyoming, who resigned from Congress to become Defense secretary. Gingrich wins by two votes over Edward Madigan of Illinois, the Republican establishment's candidate, whose campaign is managed by Tom DeLay of Texas.

May 1989: Jim Wright becomes the first House Speaker ever to quit in midterm, pushed out after a yearlong inquiry into his financial dealings pressed by Gingrich.

November 1990: The GOP loses eight House seats, but the Republican winners include freshmen who dub themselves the Gang of Seven. This group, which includes John A. Boehner of Ohio, Jim Nussle of Iowa and Rick Santorum of Pennsylvania, leads the charge in 1992 for full disclosure of overdrafts at a House bank run for the benefit of lawmakers.

November 1992: The GOP picks up nine House seats even as President George Bush is defeated for re-election, the first time in 100 years that a party has gained congressional seats in an election when it lost the White House.

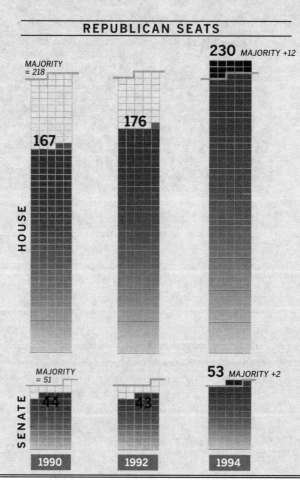

REPUBLICAN SEATS

MAJORITY = 218

230 MAJORITY +12

176

167

HOUSE

MAJORITY = 51

53 MAJORITY +2

44

43

SENATE

1990   1992   1994

November 1994: Republicans win control of Congress for the first time in 40 years, gaining eight Senate seats (for a majority of 53) and 53 seats in the House (for a majority of 230). No GOP incumbent is defeated in either chamber. Republicans win a majority of Southern House seats for the first time since Reconstruction. Democrat Thomas S. Foley of Washington is the first House Speaker defeated for re-election since 1862.

December 1994: Gingrich is the unanimous choice of House Republicans for Speaker, and Dick Armey of Texas is unchallenged for majority leader. DeLay wins a three-way race for majority whip with J. Dennis Hastert of Illinois as his campaign manager — and without Gingrich's backing. Boehner is elected GOP Conference chairman. In the Senate, Bob Dole is unopposed to reclaim the post of majority leader, which he held in 1985-86. But the conservative wing of the caucus engineers the 27-26 election of Trent Lott of Mississippi as whip over Alan K. Simpson of Wyoming.

Congressional Republicans face the most difficult political environment of any election year since they seized control of the House. Problems that are out of their control — the war in Iraq, the aftermath of Hurricane Katrina, rising gas prices — are compounded by an ongoing investigation of an ethics and lobbying scandal that threatens to become the tipping point for the whole mess, possibly turning the public decisively against them.

The party has lost its cohesion, too. With DeLay's strong hand to hold together the coalition of cultural and economic conservatives and moderates, the Republican House had kept the party agenda moving and served as a goad to the balky and slow-moving Senate. Now the House is cracking under pressure, and the Senate as usual is tied in knots on such issues as immigration.

Hastert and the new House majority leader, John A. Boehner of Ohio, pulled the plug on two measures the Republicans consider central to their ability to govern: a budget resolution setting limits on spending for the next fiscal year, and a House-Senate conference agreement to extend $70 billion worth of tax cuts. They didn't have enough votes to move the budget, and they couldn't come to terms with the Senate on the tax cuts.

PRAGMATISM AND LOCAL POLITICS

Thus stymied in the House, Bush and other Republican leaders may suddenly be forced to move their legislative initiatives first through the Senate — a scary proposition to anyone familiar with the glacier-like inertia that prevails in that chamber. *(Senate, p. 50)*

To re-energize the party and help Republicans make the case for a continued majority, conservatives inside the House are agitating for a return to the bedrock principles of 1994, particularly a rededication to cutting spending and limiting the size of government. But many doubt that the congressional wing of the party has the strength or vision to do much at all to change the subject this election year, or to alter the political realities before them.

Among Republicans in Washington, "I don't think there's much agreement anymore about what the revolution means," said David Brady, another conservative fellow at Hoover. "It looks to the country like the president isn't leading and congressional Republicans aren't leading. They're split on spending, they're split on immigration, they're split on the war. They're split on everything."

January 1995: Now in control, the GOP reduces House committees and staff, institutes term limits for chairmen, ends proxy voting and enacts a law ending the congressional exemption from 11 federal workplace laws.

April 1995: The House passes most of the 10 items in the "Contract With America," the campaign manifesto more than 350 House GOP candidates signed by the previous September.
President Bill Clinton reminds the nation that "the Constitution gives me relevance."

January 1996: At least half of the bills promised in the GOP Contract have become law, including limits on unfunded federal mandates and curbs on lawsuits by disgruntled investors. But the party's chief aspiration — that Clinton agree to balance the budget on Republican terms — ends in humiliating defeat as congressional leaders agree to end the second partial government shutdown they had engineered in a bid to force the president's hand.

June 1996: Dole leaves the Senate to focus on his presidential campaign; Lott ascends to

majority leader without challenge.

November 1996: In a bipartisan shift in tactics, both Clinton and the GOP push compromise over confrontation and agree on bills to revamp welfare and to rewrite farm and telecommunications policy. Republicans strengthen their majority in the Senate by two seats but lose nine seats in the House, and Clinton becomes the first Democratic president since FDR to win a second term.

January 1997: Gingrich is only narrowly re-elected Speaker after admitting the previous month that he gave incomplete and inaccurate information to the House ethics committee about the role of a political action committee called

GOPAC in a college course he had taught. The House votes to formally reprimand him and assesses a $300,000 fine.

May 1997: Clinton and GOP leaders agree on a plan to balance the budget within five years by cutting some taxes and restraining the growth in Medicare, Medicaid and other entitlements.

July 1997: A group of mostly junior GOP conservatives, who have come to view Gingrich as too conciliatory and ethically tainted, conspire to oust him and enlist Armey, DeLay and Boehner to their cause in varying degrees. But they cannot agree on who should be Speaker and abort their coup plot.

228 MAJORITY +10

HOUSE

55 MAJORITY +4

SENATE

1996

November 1998: With polls showing the public opposed to the GOP drive to impeach Clinton, Democrats pick up five House seats in the first midterm election since 1934 in which a party in the White House has gained strength in the House of Representatives. Gingrich announces his resignation as Speaker three days later. Republicans pick Robert L. Livingston of Louisiana to succeed him and replace Boehner as conference chairman with J.C. Watts of Oklahoma.

December 1998: The House impeaches Clinton on charges that he lied about and conspired to cover up his sexual relationship with Monica Lewinsky, a White House intern. During the debate, Livingston announces that he is resigning from the House because of his own sexual indiscretions. By nightfall, DeLay has arranged for Hastert, his chief deputy, to be the new GOP nominee for Speaker.

February 1999: After a five-week trial, the Senate rejects both articles of impeachment. The lingering discord leads to a desultory Con-

The internal contest to succeed Bush as the party's presidential nominee in 2008 may well become a battle over what brand of Republicanism, what national vision, ought to replace the Republican Revolution of Delay, Gingrich and Armey. But until then, with the November midterms approaching fast, Republicans are adopting a localized campaign strategy: doing whatever it takes to win, district by district, even if it means bucking Bush or the larger party in certain sections of the country on issues such as the Iraq War.

That's been the pattern for the party for the past few elections, and it's what Brady and other conservatives expect this time. They say the party also will have to hope that efforts by GOP operatives such as DeLay over the past decade to gerrymander safe seats will help the party weather its present troubles.

Such a pragmatic, head-down strategy is a

reversal from the one Gingrich and other Republican leaders employed in 1994, when they worked to nationalize the elections first around their "Contract," then around tax cuts and most recently around the war on terrorism.

"When there is not a coherent ideology, then pragmatism becomes the ideology," said Andrew Rudalevige, a political scientist at Dickinson College in Pennsylvania.

That mode is not unusual in politics, nor is it necessarily catastrophic for Republicans. Truly revolutionary moments in American politics are rare, says University of Georgia political scientist Charles Bullock, a veteran Congress watcher. Much of the arc of American political history has been backing and filling, elaboration on the ideas that periodically burst onto the scene in the way that the GOP Revolution of 1994 did.

And the revolution could well have a lasting impact on U.S. politics. With their emphasis on limiting the reach of government and lowering taxes, Gingrich, Armey, DeLay and other leaders, building on the conservative movement begun by President Ronald Reagan before them, fundamentally changed the terms of debate about the nature of government.

To a great extent, politicians of both parties are still responding to the 1994 calling cards, fighting on the GOP revolutionaries' terms. The intense rivalry between the parties, the sharpened, polarized debate in Congress, are a legacy of the 1994 election and its immediate aftermath as Gingrich and his lieutenants consolidated their power.

The current leaders say the spirit of the revolution still undergirds the Congress. They say it drove the budget process last year, which

gress in which the GOP's principal achievement is raising the spending caps imposed by the 1997 budget-balancing deal.

November 2000: The election yields not only a disputed presidential outcome but also a House with a razor-thin GOP majority of 221 seats (50.8 percent) and a 50-50 Senate, which falls under GOP control only after the Supreme Court effectively awards Florida's electoral votes (and thereby the election) to George W. Bush and Dick Cheney, who, as vice president, gets to break tied Senate votes.

May 2001: Congress clears the deepest tax cut in two decades — reductions in income tax rates, alleviation of the so-called marriage penalty, a phase-out of estate taxes and other breaks worth $1.35 trillion over a decade. But unilateral GOP control of Congress ends the

same week, when James M. Jeffords of Vermont quits the party to become an independent who caucuses with the Democrats, giving that party control of the Senate.

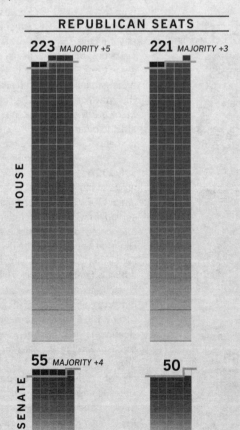

House Republican leaders ceremoniously called President Bush in 2001 after they passed his first tax cut legislation, a key part of the GOP agenda.

September 2001: The attacks on New York and the Pentagon spawn an unusual wave of bipartisan collaboration, which produces laws that authorize military force against al Qaeda, spend $40 billion on recovery, federalize airline security and grant law enforcement sweeping new power to combat terrorists.

November 2002: The GOP picks up two seats to retake the Senate and strengthens its House majority by seven seats. DeLay, unopposed for promotion to majority leader upon Armey's retirement, helps his new protégé Roy Blunt of Missouri become majority whip without opposition.

December 2002: Lott is forced out as Senate GOP leader after he praises the segregationist

promised the first reduction in non-defense discretionary spending since Reagan was president and called for the first cuts in entitlement spending since 1997. They even argue that it shaped the Medicare expansion that has so angered many conservatives: The GOP was able to bring free-market principles to the entitlement program for the first time, delivering prescription drugs and other health care through an expanded system of competing private plans, they say.

"If you look at our agenda, we're on the same path we've been on for 11 years," said Boehner of Ohio, one of the authors of the "Contract With America."

The party as a whole is also more conservative today than it was when Republicans first seized control of the House. The ranks of moderates and those willing to seek a middle ground with Democrats have thinned. One

of the most prominent remaining moderates, New York's Sherwood Boehlert, announced he is retiring.

DEEP FRUSTRATIONS

Today's GOP leaders also face significantly different issues than the revolutionaries were dealing with a decade ago, which has made governing all the more difficult. The war on terror in particular has scrambled priorities and stretched government resources. Immigration, too, which now dominates the Congress and may be a deciding issue in this November's elections, was not on the radar back then. All of those things "present real challenges that as the governing party we have to deal with," Boehner allowed.

But those kinds of trade-offs and tough choices are also what fuels the anger and frustration among many conservatives at what

they view as a betrayal of the Republican Revolution in the years since.

Their list of grievances includes the Medicare drug bill of 2003 and the "No Child Left Behind" education law of 2001, which Boehner helped pass when he was chairman of the committee on Education and the Workforce. The education law, which imposed federal standards and testing requirements on grade schools, was an extension of federal involvement in local education, an idea Bush has since proposed extending to high schools.

Some Republicans had hoped that both the Medicare and education bills would allow the party to seize the initiative on issues where Democrats historically have held the edge with voters. But now many conservatives view them as an abandonment of the party's creed against expanding government.

Conservatives say they trust Boehner and

CQ / SCOTT J. FERRELL

1948 presidential campaign of Strom Thurmond. The White House is complicit in the ouster and helps engineer the election of Tennessee's Bill Frist as the new majority leader.

November 2003: A law creating a prescription drug benefit and otherwise expanding Medicare, a principal target for cuts when the GOP first took control eight years earlier, is enacted only after DeLay holds the House floor vote open for almost three hours in order to

persuade enough reluctant Republicans to vote for it.

October 2004: DeLay is admonished by the House ethics committee for soliciting

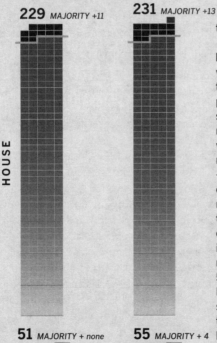

229 MAJORITY +11   **231** MAJORITY +13

HOUSE

51 MAJORITY + none   **55** MAJORITY + 4

SENATE

2002   2004

help from the Federal Aviation Administration in finding Democratic Texas state legislators who had left the state in an unsuccessful attempt to thwart a congressional redistricting that DeLay had orchestrated to benefit his party. DeLay is also admonished by the panel for two other ethical lapses.

November 2004: Bush wins a second term and is the first presidential candidate since 1988 to take a majority of the popular vote. The GOP picks up a net of three House seats — with the effective gain of seven seats under the redrawn Texas map offsetting Republican losses elsewhere. The party also increases its Senate majority by four seats, to 55 — and 25 of those Republican senators had served in the House since the GOP "revolution" began in 1989.

September 2005: DeLay is required by House GOP rules to step aside as majority leader after he is

indicted in Texas on a conspiracy charge related to his fundraising efforts for GOP legislative candidates in Texas in 2002. In October, he is indicted on charges of laundering campaign contributions in that effort.

February 2006: A month after DeLay decides to give up his leadership job for good, House Republicans elect Boehner as majority leader over Blunt and Arizona's John Shadegg.

March 2006: Lobbyist Tony Rudy, once DeLay's deputy chief of staff, is the third person close to DeLay to plead guilty and agree to cooperate in a Justice Department investigation of lobbying fraud and public corruption. Lobbyist Jack Abramoff had done so in January; publicist Michael Scanlon, once DeLay's spokesman, had done so in November.

April 2006: A month after winning the GOP nomination for a 12th term in the House with just 62 percent against three under-funded opponents, DeLay announces that he will resign from Congress by June.

Bush Loyalist for a New Strategy: 'Senate Goes First'

FOR A DECADE, THE SENATE has been the more troublesome member of the ruling Republican majority in Congress, time and again delaying, weakening or just refusing to pass President Bush's priorities and other party initiatives that had been readily embraced by the House. In recent months, though, a loss of Republican cohesion in the House, caused in part by the downfall of Majority Leader and party disciplinarian Tom DeLay of Texas, is putting more pressure on Senate GOP leaders to advance their party's agenda.

The responsibility for making such a "Senate goes first" strategy work will fall increasingly to the soft-spoken but tough-minded Republican whip in the Senate, Mitch McConnell of Kentucky.

Though Bill Frist of Tennessee is the Senate majority leader and the party's public face, he is leaving office at the end of the year by his own choice and already seems focused on a presidential campaign for 2008. McConnell, who was first elected to the Senate in 1984, is the most likely successor to Frist. In fact, the two men have by their own statements been sharing power since Frist was elected to replace Mississippi's Trent Lott three years ago.

"We're a partnership," Frist said in an interview. McConnell says the two men jointly choose which bills McConnell's whip organization will work on. "We make the decision together," McConnell said.

At a political dinner in Kentucky in February, Frist joked that he was "joined at the hip" to the man he calls "the next majority leader."

In recent months, while Frist has received most of the attention, and a good deal of criticism, for what Senate Republicans have and have not accomplished, McConnell's behind-the-scenes diplomacy and gentle but persistent persuasion has been increasingly important to the party on such issues as the budget.

Among GOP insiders, McConnell seems to have just as much clout, if not more at times, than Frist.

With DeLay's imminent departure, House Speaker J. Dennis Hastert of Illinois and new Majority Leader John A. Boehner of Ohio have paid visits to McConnell to get an early view on how major issues are taking shape in the Senate. McConnell has also been a hot ticket on the stump, appearing at a fundraising event for Hastert in Illinois at the end of March.

As the Bush administration's troubles have mounted, McConnell has been if anything more loyal to the White House, arguing that the party can gain ground politically by unifying behind President Bush and some modest, achievable goals he sets.

"The more we're together, the stronger [Bush] will look," McConnell said in an interview in his high-ceilinged office just off the Senate floor. "The stronger he looks, the better it will be for us in the fall."

But political observers warn that getting too close to Bush could hurt McConnell's standing with rank-and-file Republicans, and even with voters back home in his own 2008 re-election campaign, if Bush's public standing continues to slide. A recent poll had Bush's approval rating at 36 percent, matching the lowest point in his presidency.

McConnell's dogged oppositio[n to]
campaign finance law has ove[rshadowed his]
reputation in the GOP as a de[al-maker,]
appropriator's eye for horse-tr[ading.]

Lewis L. Gould, an emeritus history professor at the University of Texas who has written a history of the Senate, "The Most Exclusive Club," says that "in a year, McConnell will look like a genius if Bush's poll ratings go up, and if the GOP does well in the election. But if things go badly, and Bush becomes toxic, his loyalty to the president will become a a liability."

STUBBORNNESS PAYS OFF

Though McConnell's public image is almost as fearsome as DeLay's, thanks mainly to his determined and very public opposition to campaign finance limits over the past decade, he lacks the Texan's hard edges. This is partly due to the nature of the Senate, where individual members have more autonomy than in the House and where party leaders, in McConnell's well-known phrase, have "almost all carrot and no stick."

His aggressive push to overturn parts of the 2002 campaign finance law, in fact, has overshadowed McConnell's reputation among senior members of both parties as a consummate professional, a dealmaker with an appropriator's eye for horse trading.

hanging
owed his
ker with an

McConnell's stubbornness, akin to Bush's, has served him well politically. Democrats, though they decry McConnell as a "Darth Vader," also express grudging admiration for his defense of free speech, including his opposition to a constitutional amendment to ban flag burning, a perennial favorite of many Republicans.

Frist gives McConnell credit for deals that moved two GOP measures through the Senate in the past year: legislation that directs more class-action lawsuits to federal court, where they are less likely to succeed; and changes in bankruptcy law that make it more difficult for debtors to avoid payment. The deals grew in part from McConnell's efforts to improve communications with the House.

A recent compromise on the Senate version of Bush's budget plan demonstrated McConnell's central role in trying to eke out victories for the White House by nudging dissident Republicans and even a few Democrats to join forces. Fearing an embarrassing loss because of defections by Republicans who disagreed with Bush's spending priorities, McConnell began wooing a secret Democratic ally — Mary L. Landrieu of Louisiana — days before a showdown Senate floor vote.

"I thought Landrieu might be the decisive vote," McConnell said, referring to the prospect of a 50-50 tie vote that could have been broken by Vice President Dick Cheney. At the whip's behest, Frist made an opening to Landrieu. McConnell, who also is an Appropriations subcommittee chairman, worked with fellow chairman Judd Gregg of New Hampshire to put together a package of additional hurricane recovery funding for Landrieu's state. Her lone Democratic vote for the budget gave political cover to wavering moderate Republicans, who fell in line behind the plan, providing a narrow but decisive 51-vote majority on the floor.

McConnell tacitly backed efforts to promote Bush's immigration plan, and got close, though Republican leaders were unable to get an agreement on the issue before the spring recess.

LONGTIME LOYALIST

McConnell's political loyalty to Bush grew out of his support for the president's father in the 1988 Republican primaries, when he ran against Senate Minority Leader Bob Dole of Kansas.

It was during that campaign that McConnell met the candidate's eldest son, who was working in the campaign's Washington office. "We had a similar political point of view," McConnell said.

His support for Bush now helps make possible a GOP strategy of previewing legislation and taking difficult votes first in the Senate. Boehner has said that will help build consensus on issues and help protect vulnerable House Republicans this fall.

This year, House leaders are looking to McConnell not for global deals, but to develop Senate touchstones on contentious Bush priorities that demonstrate their viability. McConnell has made clear that he wants action on the president's agenda. And when his two patrons have disagreed, he has leaned toward Bush and against Frist, while doing so quietly.

Frist, for instance, was an early critic of the administration's approval of a corporate merger that allowed a company based in the United Arab Emirates to take over operations in six U.S. seaports. McConnell supported Bush's position that the deal was proper and that any congressional action to block it would send the wrong signal to U.S. allies in the Middle East.

What looked like a collision over the deal between Bush and Hill Republicans was headed off when the Dubai company announced that it was transferring the port operation to a U.S. concern.

McConnell has also backed Bush on the difficult immigration debate. McConnell said in an interview that he agreed with Bush's overall vision for a guest worker plan — something intensely opposed by many Republicans, who call it a form of amnesty for illegal immigrants. McConnell quietly stood his ground, while making sure that his whip team remained neutral.

McConnell kept the heat on by refusing to let party leaders unify behind a bill that defied Bush. "We will be a divided conference on immigration," he said at the start of the debate. "Sen. Frist and I will not be trying to whip that one way or the other. . . . It's unusual where we have a bill on the floor where we don't have a point of view. But this is really one where we don't."

FRONT-RUNNER

The immigration fight provided a showcase for McConnell's bulldog tenacity and his reputation as the consummate inside player, a Republican counterpart to another appropriator who became a party leader, Democrat Robert C. Byrd of West Virginia.

To be sure, McConnell must demonstrate that he can move Bush's priorities over the next year to prove he is worthy of the top Republican's mantle. He is not guaranteed the party leader's job next year, of course. Allies such as Robert F. Bennett of Utah say he already has tacit support from more than 40 of the Senate's 55 Republicans, well more than the simple majority needed to defeat a potential challenger.

Such a challenger could be Trent Lott of Mississippi, who was forced out of the job in late 2002 after he remarked during a 100th birthday party for South Carolina Sen. Strom Thurmond that the country would have had fewer problems if it had elected Thurmond president in 1948 as a segregationist "Dixiecrat."

Lott has raised $1.5 million through his leadership political action committee, twice as much as McConnell, but has not said whether he will try to reclaim his old title. "Every time a story runs about what I might do," he said last week, "Mitch McConnell comes and asks me what I'm up to. I tell him I haven't decided."

respect him for his role in the 1994 revolution, where he emerged as the fourth-ranking member of the leadership.

Leaders from the House Republican Study Committee, who are among the most conservative members of the House, met with Boehner to discuss budget changes to begin restricting spending, with their focus on stopping "earmarks" like the ones that loaded up the highway bill. They believe he wants to rein in spending, but will have to overcome divisions in the House and institutional inertia.

"Whether he can move the beast, I don't know," said Rep. Jeff Flake of Arizona, one of the study committee leaders who met with Boehner.

But others are even more pessimistic. Former Rep. Bob Barr of Georgia, a member of the class of 1994, says there's nothing incoherent about the Republican Party's position in Washington today. "To me, it's painfully coherent: It's about bigger government. There's nothing to even disguise it any more."

When Bush did try to take on one of the pillars of the New Deal last year, with a plan to reshape Social Security and add individual investment accounts to the government pension system, it never got off the ground in Congress. That was as sure as sign as any that the Republican Revolution was over, said Jacobs, the Minnesota political scientist: "The political taste for big, bold conservative ideas has clearly faded."

Franc of the Heritage Foundation points to a budget drafted this year by the Republican Study Committee. In its goals, including cutting taxes and reducing the deficit, it was consciously modeled after the budget of 1995 that got the support of all but one House Republican. Now, Franc says, Republicans, and particularly moderates, view the study committee's plan as draconian.

One of the moderates he was referring to, Michael N. Castle of Delaware, called that argument "empty." Castle is among those pushing now to add $7 billion to the 2007 House budget resolution for domestic spending. The situation today is fundamentally different than in 1995, Castle says. The nation is dealing with new issues, a war and other burdens, he says. He also says he is in favor of many of the proposals from conservatives to overhaul budget rules and rein in spending, but he argues that the current budget would balance the govern-

DIFFICULT JOB: The new House GOP team, led by Hastert and Boehner, left, lacks DeLay's ruthlessness in rounding up support.

ment's books on the backs of important domestic programs.

Protecting those programs, for health, child care, medical research and other programs, is what people want and is the right thing to do, Castle says. It's also good politics for Republicans, he said.

"When you talk to people back home, they talk about day care, about federally supported health program, medical research, education," he said.

WHERE'S THE FIRE?

The difficulty Republican leaders are having on the budget — sorting out the disputes among moderates such as Castle, conservatives such as Flake, and members of the House Appropriations Committee — is emblematic of the muddle of competing demands and viewpoints facing the Republican majority.

A group of academics from conservative think tanks met several months ago in Washington with Bush administration officials to discuss the agenda for the next three years. At

least one of the visitors walked away disappointed. Talking with White House officials was like talking with "a bunch of academics," he said. "It was 'on the one hand, on the other hand.'"

"Where's the fire?" he asked.

In this year's campaigns, Republican leaders say they will make their case for a continued majority by pointing to what they call a record of accomplishments, including the Medicare drug bill, tax cuts, legislation restricting class-action lawsuits, perhaps an immigration bill.

Republicans have an aggressive agenda under way, all of it in keeping with the 1994 revolution, said Ron Bonjean, spokesman for House Speaker J. Dennis Hastert of Illinois.

"The best thing we can do is get things done and produce," Bonjean said. That, he said, and define sharply what Democrats stand for.

But a few days after DeLay announced that he would step down, the House was caught in the deadlock among various factions over spending, forcing leaders to abandon their plans to push through a budget resolution before a two-week spring break. At the same time, efforts to strike a deal between the House and Senate on the $70 billion tax cut package stalled out, and lawmakers left for home without that, too.

The Senate left town tangled up over an immigration overhaul. Even if Republicans could agree to something, they will have to resolve deep differences with the House over the issue.

Perhaps the 2008 presidential campaign will bring clarity and a new sense of direction to the party, as Jacobs at the University of Minnesota and others speculate.

And perhaps the majority coalition built by DeLay and the other revolutionaries will simply continue rolling forward for some time, just as the New Deal coalition hung together and kept Democrats in power for years after the fire had gone out of that movement.

But some conservative lawmakers who want a return to the spirit of 1994, which they say their party has lost, wonder if it won't take harsher medicine to bring the GOP around. The party has gone through several election cycles "relying on redistricting and handing out money to get re-elected," said Flake.

Now, he said, "we may have to spend two years in the political wilderness of the minority before arriving back in the promised land." ■

A New Medium For the Message

Grass-roots advocacy has exploded on the Internet, giving business and interest groups a powerful tool for rallying troops to their cause. But will an e-mail to your congressman be heard above the electronic din?

FROM ITS QUIRKY boarding system, in which passengers line up for seats, to its irreverent in-flight announcements — "There may be 50 ways to leave your lover, but there are only six ways off this aircraft" — Southwest Airlines has built a loyal following among the nation's travelers. Dodging competitors, the company in essence created its own industry by using secondary airports instead of major fields, flying direct from city to city rather than through mega-hubs and selling low-price tickets through its own agents rather than travel services.

So last year, when Southwest launched a lobbying campaign to persuade Congress that it should lift restrictions on long-distance flights from one of those airports — Love Field in Dallas, the airline's birthplace and head-quarters — the company engaged its passengers in that effort, too, and called it "Set Love Free." The airline's pitch to the public is that by helping the airline expand, they would increase competition and lower airfares.

Southwest bought ads, rented billboards, strung banners over boarding gates and even handed out cocktail napkins printed with the campaign slogan — all directing people to a Web site, setlovefree.com. At the site, customers can register, read corporate polemics on the Love Field issue, alert their local newspapers and TV stations to the gravity of the case, and send e-mail to their members of Congress.

In effect, Southwest passengers became

Blogging With A Mute Button

PITY THE CONGRESSIONAL BLOG-GER. Sensing that the freewheeling tenor of debate in the blogosphere might offer some political advantages, a handful of legislators have launched blogs of their own — there is no definitive count, but it seems to be in the high single-digit range. But the very thing that makes blogs entertaining reading — no-holds barred disputation, interactivity, the occasional coarsely worded flame war — can be kryptonite to the image-conscious politician.

So Capitol Hill's blogging pioneers are not exactly pushing the envelope. Much of the activity on congressional blogs tends merely to duplicate the content of press releases that staffers compose and send out in multiple fax- and e-mail-form. Republican **John A. Boehner** of Ohio, the new House majority leader, has a nominal blog called Majority Matters. Here's one of the latest entries: Democrats should "set aside their partisan goals and focus on what's in the best interests of American seniors." Nothing, in other words, that's going to stir up raging online debate — or keep many seniors awake.

Not that things are any more lively on the other side of the cyber-aisle. House Minority Leader **Nancy Pelosi**, a California Democrat, has guest-blogged a few times on Huffingtonpost but mainly just parroted the party's anodyne slogan for the 2006 election: "Together, America can do better."

"Too often, what we see is, 'Oh, I'll just get one of my staffers to write something and send it to Huffingtonpost.' It's not like we can't see through that," says **Jerome Armstrong**, founder of the liberal blog MyDD and co-author of "Crashing the Gate," which lays out a strate-

gy for the Democrats to harness the Web in the service of building greater grass-roots support.

However, interactivity — a key building block of cyber-activism — presents logistical problems of its own. Partisans on both sides are quick to exploit opposition blogs' weaknesses in Web hosting. "What would happen is, Daily Kos will put up something saying, '**Denny Hastert** has a blog. Let's go tell him what we think,'" says **John Hinderaker**, one of the founders of the conservative Powerlineblog.

Senate Majority Leader **Bill Frist** and Speaker Hastert may have struck a happy medium, by offering up blog-style comments hosted at other Web sites. Frist mainly posts his (somewhat) unbuckled political reflections at the site of his political action committee, VolPAC. Hastert doesn't let readers post comments on his Web site, but he cross-posts with some of the established conservative blogs, which do have message boards.

Still, at least one House member is plunging fearlessly into the great bloggy unknown: **Jack Kingston**, the vice chairman of the House Republican Conference from Georgia, just added a comments section to his blog. He's blogging for the same reason he recently let himself in for ridicule on the "Colbert Report" — he's keen to employ any unconventional method to get beyond what he contends is the chronic bias of the liberal mainstream media. "Yeah, we're going to get hammered sometimes, no question about it," says Kingston's communications director, **David All**, who maintains the blog. "But that's the great thing about America, and that's the great thing about the blogosphere."

Southwest lobbyists.

"We really feel like the public is going to push this effort over the top," said Susan Goodman, a Southwest lobbyist who is in charge of grass-roots advocacy. "The more pressure we can get from constituents on legislators, the better chance we've got."

Southwest and other companies, trade associations and interest groups are increasingly using the Internet to reach beyond the Beltway and traditional lobbying techniques to bring more voices to bear on Congress. Technology has made it faster, cheaper and easier for companies and interest groups to enlist employees, customers and sometimes the general public in their causes, creating new, more impressive-looking coalitions that might have taken months or years to assemble in the days of postcards and phone banks.

Ophthalmologists, for instance, used the Internet to help mobilize military veterans for a campaign to stop the Department of Veter-

ans Affairs from allowing optometrists, who are not physicians, to do laser eye surgery in VA facilities.

Dealers in herbal remedies and dietary supplements have been signing up their customers as online activists to defend the controversial products from government regulation.

Major organizations such as the U.S. Chamber of Commerce, the American Medical Association and the Business Roundtable have invested millions developing databases of like-minded people who can be marshaled at a moment's notice to flood Congress with e-mails or phone calls on any issue the groups consider vital.

"I'm just a mouthpiece," said Bruce Josten, executive vice president and chief lobbyist for the Chamber. "It's what's behind me. The real influence game here is if I can get 200 of your constituents to contact you, or 300 or 400. These are people who will pull a lever to decide if you're going to be elected or not. You're not

going to ignore them. You can't afford to ignore them."

Groups that can demonstrate a broad base of support will be more welcome among members of Congress trying to show, in the wake of the Jack Abramoff lobbying scandal, that they are not beholden to corporate or other influence. And that, in turn, makes Internet organizing even more attractive to the lobbying industry.

"This is one of the outcomes of the Abramoff scandal that should be very positive," said Doug Pinkham, president of the Public Affairs Council, an organization for lobbyists and public affairs professionals that has been closely tracking use of technology for grass-roots advocacy. "Input from constituents ought to trump campaign contributions or a personal friendship with a well-connected lobbyist."

Grass-roots organizing has always been "the ultimate advocacy weapon," said Dirk Van

Dongen, president of the National Association of Wholesaler-Distributors. But it has changed since he first came to Washington years ago, when grass-roots meant expensive and time-consuming mailings, long waits for a response and no reliable way of tracking how many people actually wrote or called Congress as a result.

A LOT OF NOISE

Even though Internet organizing has grown rapidly since it was first pioneered by activists a decade ago, it is not magic. Southwest Airlines reports that its Set Love Free campaign and Web site have generated "several hundred thousand" e-mails to Congress.

The campaign has helped feed a debate in Texas and Washington over Love Field and airline competition. Lawmakers have introduced bills to remove the long-distance flight restrictions that Congress imposed on Love Field, and by extension Southwest Airlines, in 1979 as a way to protect the newer Dallas-Fort Worth International. But the restrictions remain in place, and opponents of lifting them them in Texas, including the Dallas-Fort Worth airport, have started their own Internet campaign called "Keep DFW Strong."

The downside of these kinds of efforts, of course, is that the sheer volume can end up seeming like just a lot of noise, and lose meaning in the process. Congress is already being overwhelmed with the electronic data and mail. In 2004, House and Senate offices received nearly 201 million messages, 90 percent of them e-mail, according to a recent study by the nonpartisan Congressional Management Foundation. The volume had increased fourfold since 1995.

That torrent of e-mail puts congressional aides in a tough position, torn between their suspicions that mass e-mails are bogus and their desire to respond to constituents, said Rick Shapiro, executive director of the foundation, which trains congressional staff.

As their in-boxes fill up, members of Congress and their staffs have a hard time figuring out exactly who is sending some of the mail, what groups might be organizing the onslaught and how genuine the grass-roots "movement" really is. They also don't know who is paying for the efforts and how much is being spent on them. Groups engaged in grass-roots organizing and lobbying are not required to disclose such information.

"We just know this has been a huge growth area in recent years," said Fred Wertheimer, president of the political watchdog group

Democracy 21. He thinks that spending on grass-roots lobbying now could well exceed the cost of direct advocacy.

For trade groups and other interests, meanwhile, the challenge becomes how to break through the babble to make their voices heard. For that, say experts in the field, sincerity rules, as it always has.

Without a compelling message, carefully targeted, from credible and compelling messengers, the e-mail will wash over Congress without effect. Technology, lobbying groups say, is no substitute for a message and a smart strategy.

Even in a post-Abramoff Washington, lobbyists still wield great power and influence.

> ## "These are people who will pull a lever to decide if you're going to be elected or not . . . You can't afford to ignore them."
>
> —**Bruce Joston,** executive vice president and chief lobbyist, U.S. Chamber of Commerce

They have information that lawmakers need — legislative and political. They have connections to members and their staffs. And they are an important source of campaign money for both parties. Indeed, interest groups and the consultants working for them say grass-roots lobbying works best in tandem with traditional lobbyists.

TRUE BELIEVERS

Yet Southwest and others who have tried the new strategies are almost evangelical in their faith in the power of Internet grass-roots advocacy to send a strong message.

The technique, which was effectively used in the 2004 presidential primaries when Howard Dean's campaign and the liberal group MoveOn.org used it to sign up volunteers and raise money, has taken hold among business and industry groups in particular. Organizations such as the Chamber believe that mobilizing vote by vote, constituent by constituent, is critical to winning elections and the legislative debates that follow. That realization hit them after Republicans nearly lost the 2000 presidential election. Business groups started to see their member companies — including their employees, shareholders and even cus-

tomers, as in the case of Southwest — as potential credible voices to carry their message to Congress.

The Chamber spent more than $1 million in advance of the 2002 congressional elections to design and launch a Web-based initiative called "Vote for Business" to educate and mobilize its member companies, associations, employees and others who may be sympathetic to its positions. Then the Chamber quickly retooled its system to organize the same constituencies for lobbying, beginning with President Bush's 2003 tax cut package. It has since been replicating the system for state chambers of commerce and members.

The system makes it convenient and simple for people plugged into the network to contact their senators or representatives. It can sort people by region, by issue of interest and by company, association or industry to be sure the Chamber is getting the right voices to speak to Congress on an issue.

The group can use the network to organize phone banks to lobby targeted lawmakers in advance of tough votes. To help defeat amendments to a tax cut package last fall that would have increased taxes on the oil industry, the Chamber fired up its database overnight and directed more than 1,000 phone calls to targeted senators from employers back home.

"We keep getting better and better at this," said Bill Miller, the Chamber's national political director.

Another business group, the Business-Industry Political Action Committee, better known as BIPAC, has developed a Web-based system around what it calls the "Prosperity Project," which enlists the help of workers on lobbying campaigns for business with the argument that their financial well-being is tied to the success of their employer or industry.

BIPAC built the system to mobilize business interests for elections, and it has replicated and tailored those tools for state chambers of commerce, trade associations and individual companies. The organization has spent $500,000 just to protect the data from break-ins, and it raised $6 million in 2004 to develop state-focused grass-roots programs.

More than 900 companies and business associations are now part of the Prosperity Project. One, the Pittsburgh-based glass and paint company PPG Industries, used the electronic tools to mobilize its employees and retirees to lobby for the 2003 Medicare overhaul — making the case to them that the law would ease a financial burden on the company and so

Surrendering to the 'Blogosphere'

WHEN THE NATIONAL ASSOCIATION of Manufacturers hosted a seminar recently on Internet blogs for corporations and associations, interest was so great that organizers had to cut off registration a week early, at 90 people. That's all the reserved room would hold.

Nearly every organization with a cause to promote or an interest to protect seems to be trying to figure out how to fit blogging into their public relations and lobbying strategies — to make the "blogosphere" work for them.

Blogs were invented 12 years ago by a college student in Pennsylvania and have since grown to roughly 30 million, according to Technorati.com, a search engine devoted to tracking them. Readership has leveled off in the past year, and less than 10 percent of those in a recent Gallup poll reported reading blogs frequently.

Yet politicians are paying attention to blogs, as are traditional news organizations. One reason is that blogging appeals to the young. According to Gallup, nearly 20 percent of those between the ages of 18 and 29, or one person in five, reads blogs frequently. Both political parties set aside space for bloggers at their 2004 conventions, and some political leaders invite well-known bloggers in for interviews.

Since politicians are watching blogs and even occasionally starting them, business groups and others looking to influence policy have taken an interest too. Ignoring the phenomenon is not an option, says Mike Krempasky, a conservative blogger from RedState.org and now a consultant with Edelman Public Relations. It's the most fundamental rule of PR: Opting out of the conversation, letting criticisms go unanswered or assertions unchallenged, is foolhardy.

Businesses and big, traditional organizations don't tend to blog well themselves. The qualities that make a blog a hit — irreverence, unpredictability — often don't mesh well with corporate culture.

One exception to that is Shopfloor.org, run by the National Association of Manufacturers (NAM). According to David Sifry, a computer entrepreneur and founder of Technorati, Shopfloor is one of the few association blogs that captures the essentials of the blogging spirit — a personal voice, a loose tone and humor. That is because the person behind the blog, NAM senior vice president Pat Cleary, is funny, affable and at least mildly irreverent. "This is a blog dedicated to manufacturing and related issues, more or less," Cleary explained in a recent posting. Among his features: A weekly visual trip to a factory floor, called Cool Stuff Being Made, and a vintage manufacturing poster displayed every Wednesday.

Cleary has big ambitions for Shopfloor as a mobilizing center. "My goal is for the buzz on Capitol Hill to be, 'Whatever you do, you don't want to get those Shopfloor people stirred up.'"

In fact, the power of blogs to affect policy issues rests on their

BUSINESS BLOGGER: NAM's Pat Cleary uses his site, Shopfloor.org, to promote activism and engagement.

informal interconnections. Bloggers often share, or borrow, information from each other and amplify arguments, so that any story, thought, rumor or criticism can spread fast from blog to blog.

FINDING FRIENDS

What consultants are telling companies and others about blogging is that even if they don't have a Pat Cleary on their staff, they almost certainly have a champion in the blogging world. The key is finding successful and like-minded bloggers and giving them resources — exclusive interviews, facts and talking points, even video or audio — to help make their arguments.

"It doesn't matter what your cause is," Krempasky says, "You can be for more regulation or less, you can find people who are writing passionately about your issue."

Krempasky won't share what specific advice he's giving his clients, but Edelman is doing what he suggests for Wal-Mart Stores Inc., which has been attacked on the Web by organized labor and other activists. Edelman has been reaching out to bloggers sympathetic to the company's position, sending them information and story leads.

The rules for such give and take in the world of blogs are still being worked out. A recent New York Times story raised questions about how bloggers are using information provided by Edelman on behalf of Wal-Mart. The article pointed to postings on some blogs that appeared to come directly, without clear attribution, from e-mails sent by Edelman representative Marshall Manson.

The story put the bloggers on the defensive. It "makes way too much of a very few bloggers who simply cut and pasted from Marshall Manson's e-mails," wrote one of them, Marquette University professor John McAdams. "This is lousy journalism, but it's hardly sinister. How many newspapers have either printed press releases verbatim, or simply rewritten them slightly for publication?"

Meanwhile, anti-Wal-Mart activists are reaching out to bloggers sympathetic to their cause. Wal-Mart Watch, a group affiliated with the Service Employees International Union, circulates information to blogs that bolsters its position.

Krempasky says the best policy for everyone is to be open and honest about whose interests they represent and where information comes from. Attempts to manipulate blogs or plant information on the sly will almost certainly be discovered. Manson urged the bloggers he contacted not to cut and paste text from his e-mails.

For most interest groups, the goal of blogging is not discussion but activism — reaching a policy goal. On Shopfloor, Casey has made a start by organizing e-mail campaigns around such issues as restricting lawsuits. "The payoff is activism and engagement," Cleary says. "All else is chatter."

Using the High-Tech Toolkit

THE U.S. CHAMBER OF COMMERCE BILLS itself as the world's largest nonprofit business federation, representing 2,800 state and local chambers, 830 business associations and 3 million individual businesses. Count the employees of all those companies, and that is the chamber's core constituency for its grass-roots lobbying. But the Chamber wants more. It has been working to engage a broader and broader circle of what Bill Miller, the organization's national political director, calls "business sympathetics" — people who see eye to eye with business on public policy issues and might be willing to help the Chamber with its lobbying.

The tools available for finding those people get more powerful all the time. The Chamber and other business groups have used Internet ads at sites likely to be viewed by people who are interested in business and investing. As part of a campaign to cut taxes on capital gains and dividends, they paid for an ad on the Google search engine that would appear when anyone typed the word "dividend" into the search field.

The Chamber, like other interest groups and political parties, also buys databases and sifts through them for the names of likely "sympathetics."

For competitive reasons, Miller won't disclose the lists and databases the Chamber buys to mine for names. But its efforts might focus on, for example, subscribers to Inc., a business magazine. Chamber staff members also sort by income as they look for small business owners and others with a stake in pro-business lobbying campaigns.

From an advocacy perspective, data-mining is risky. With Americans increasingly concerned about the security of personal information in electronic data banks, some may see a group's outreach as a potential breach of privacy. The buying and selling of personal information from subscriber lists, product warranty cards and a number of other sources is wide open for abuse, says Lillie Coney, associate director of the Electronic Privacy Information Center, a nonprofit research group in Washington.

"There are just no rules in the marketplace now about data use, management and retention," Coney says. "We're at the mercy of whoever."

Consultants, including B.R. McConnon of Democracy Data & Communication, the company that designed the Chamber's grass-roots lobbying initiative, say that any lists used by these groups should be "opt in"— that is, people on them have given their permission to be contacted.

There is a chance, Miller says, that some people contacted might be annoyed or feel that their privacy has been invaded, and a group's success rate falls when it contacts people outside its own member-

> In the end, no technology can replace old-fashioned human connections based on common interests and nurtured over time.

ship. But each additional person willing to contact Congress on behalf of the Chamber has a cumulative effect. The cost-to-reward ratio of data mining, Miller says, "is pretty good."

That's also true for Internet ads, which link viewers to Web sites where they can volunteer for the particular cause, share information about themselves and even contact members of Congress by e-mail.

Another option for advocacy groups is to buy ads on e-mails sent to customers by mail providers or other Internet services. Such companies know a great deal about their clients and their interests, which allows advocates to target their messages to a particular audience.

Internet ads don't work for every issue. Supporters of the Central American Free Trade Agreement last year tried to find grass-roots advocates through Web site ads, but got responses mostly from the East and West coasts, not middle America where the lawmakers they needed to reach were concentrated, says John Castellani, president of the Business Roundtable.

But many thousands of people responded to business groups' ads looking for support for President Bush's 2003 tax cut package, according to Castellani. All told, 200,000 to 300,000 e-mails were sent to Congress on that issue. And of those who responded to the groups' outreach, Castellani says, about 95,000 agreed to be placed on a permanent list of activists to be called on in the future on other issues.

PERSONAL CONNECTIONS

In the end, however, no technology can replace old-fashioned, human connections, based on common interests and nurtured over time.

That's especially true in a high-tech world, says Greg Casey, president of the Business-Industry Political Action Committee. Some groups using the Web-based organizing tools that his group has developed mine databases for names to try to broaden their reach, but the heart and soul of the effort is educating and mobilizing those with a stake in the particular company or organization. He thinks that is the best way to build a powerful grass-roots network for the long haul.

Names mined from consumer databases get stale fast, and in Casey's judgment, such people are far less likely to read and believe the messages that an outside group might send them, as opposed to an e-mail from their employer or an association they have an established relationship with.

The Chamber of Commerce also considers its own membership its greatest strength. For everyone plugged into its advocacy network, the organization spends time providing them with background on issues and keeping them regularly posted on congressional votes and other fruits of their activism. The aim is to build a stable network of activists who will respond when the Chamber needs them to lobby Congress.

If the Chamber can persuade those in its network that everything happening in Washington affects them, that they have a stake in the process, and make it easy for them to engage, Miller says, "they absolutely will participate."

help protect their individual benefits. The company says that more than 6,000 letters supporting the bill were faxed to Congress through its Web site. About 1,000 letters were faxed from PPG facilities around the country.

PPG, a heavy user of natural gas, plans to use the same technique to support efforts to expand domestic energy production.

Also using the Prosperity Project tools, the Financial Services Roundtable mobilized its member companies and their employees early last year to lobby the Senate for limits on class action lawsuits. The Chamber also joined in that effort. The legislation passed.

CAUGHT IN THE SPAM FILTER

But standing out amid the huge quantities of e-mail that have begun flooding Congress, not to mention faxes, telephone calls and letters, is only going to get more difficult. Cut-and-paste e-mails are more likely to get lost in the noise — and congressional aides get those in large quantities.

Congressional offices that receive e-mail through Web-based services, where correspondents must use a lawmaker's own mail form, have installed filters to block messages that don't come from their states or districts. If a group organizing an e-mail campaign is using software that doesn't interact properly with those filters, messages can get dumped and no one ever sees them.

"The sad thing is, people sometimes think they are taking an action, and they're not being heard," said Brad Fitch, co-author of the Congressional Management Foundation's study of citizen advocacy. He has since become CEO of a new company, Knowlegis, that is developing software to help groups better coordinate their traditional lobbying with grass-roots advocacy.

Half of the congressional aides surveyed by the foundation said they believe that identical messages sent as part of grass-roots advocacy campaigns don't have real people behind them. Another 25 percent doubted the legitimacy of such e-mails. Shapiro, the Management Foundation's director, says that virtually every congressional office has a story of a lobbying campaign backed by e-mails or phone calls supposedly from constituents who later say they don't remember contacting Congress at all.

Lawmakers, too, are suspicious. During a discussion of lobbying rules and disclosure in the Senate Homeland Security and Governmental Affairs Committee, Democrat Mark Pryor of Arkansas said groups looking to stir up grass-roots support for their causes at times will misinform and mislead the public. "This is big business," Pryor said. "It's just political reality today, and it's getting more sophisticated all the time."

If the Web makes it easy for people to have their say, it's also easy to manipulate the conversation unseen. As Carol Darr, director of the Institute for Politics, Democracy & the Internet at George Washington University, points out, the virtual, faceless nature of the Internet makes it more difficult to figure out whose interests really are speaking or who is orchestrating a message.

That's true of the most public form of correspondence, called Web logs, or blogs — free-form diaries and commentaries crowding the Web. Both politicians and interest groups have begun cultivating and reaching out to bloggers, since some have extensive followings. There have been unconfirmed reports that public relations executives have paid bloggers for positive posts and that companies try to surreptitiously spin blogs with corporate PR disguised as messages from individual readers.

"You've just got a Wild West out there," Darr said. "A global Wild West."

As part of the debate over lobbying rules in Congress, some members have proposed requiring interest groups, and the consultants working with them, to disclose how much they spend on grass-roots lobbying. But this question quickly gets complicated, especially because influential religious and conservative groups have such extensive grass-roots operations. "If you believe there ought to be disclosure of lobbying expenditures," said Wertheimer, "then you can't leave out what could be the largest part of the lobbying expenditures."

GETTING PERSONAL

Those who use grass-roots lobbying say they are facilitating democracy: finding people who have a stake in the process and giving them an opportunity to participate. "It's an important way to further involve people who ought to be involved," said Miller at the U.S. Chamber.

Businesses say they never tell their employees how to vote or what to think, and they don't require them to take action. PPG, for example, tracks how many e-mails and faxes go out about a particular issue, but according to the company's director of governmental affairs, Judy Maskrey, the system doesn't tie them back to individual employees.

BIPAC has commissioned studies it says show that employees welcome information about issues that affect their company or industry. And while congressional offices report being overwhelmed by the resulting

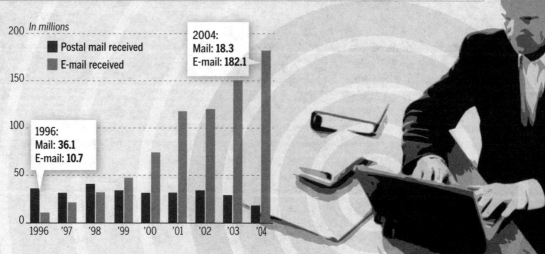

A Hill Covered In E-mail

The volume of electronic mail to Congress has quadrupled over a period of five years, straining the ability of lawmakers to deal with it. Some try to filter out messages that don't originate from their states or districts. Meanwhile, the volume of postal mail has been dropping.

SOURCE: Congressional Management Foundation

In millions

- Postal mail received
- E-mail received

1996:
Mail: 36.1
E-mail: 10.7

2004:
Mail: 18.3
E-mail: 182.1

1996 '97 '98 '99 '00 '01 '02 '03 '04

e-mails, there are also times when they court big shows of support.

When the legislation to send more class action suits to federal courts came to a vote in the Senate a year ago, an aide to the bill's sponsor, Republican Charles E. Grassley of Iowa, contacted the Chamber, the Financial Services Roundtable and others for help. Grassley wanted to demonstrate that there was broad support for the bill, and he also wanted real-life stories from back home to help make the argument for change.

The groups responded, and it was the first time the aide, Rita Lari Jochum, could recall getting so many responses by e-mail. She said that made it easy to review the messages by Blackberry while she went about her business in the Senate. The bill passed, and Jochum said the e-mails helped. "I think it reinforced the grass-roots support that was there," she said.

Aides to members of Congress trying to overturn the VA rule allowing optometrists to perform laser eye surgery say that the veterans mobilized by ophthalmologists played an important role. Convinced that their vision might be at risk, many contacted their lawmakers through a Web site set up by physicians called VetsCoalition.org.

"That's a group that's retired, they're active, and they're finally Internet savvy," said Wendy Taylor, an aide to Republican Rep. John Sullivan of Oklahoma, who led the fight in the House to overturn the rule.

If there's a compelling personal story included in the mail, it also helps lawmakers who are trying to make public policy debates real and immediate. What's more, every lawmaker's career depends upon staying tuned to constituents. As lobbyists work the halls of Congress, approaching members again and again on a particular issue, sooner or later they hear the question, "If it's so important, why don't I hear from people back home about it?"

Indeed, the ability of interest groups to identify people who are motivated enough on a single issue to send an e-mail — or even phone or visit their lawmakers — is one of the big benefits of grass-roots advocacy, said B.R. McConnon, CEO of Democracy Data & Communications, the company that designed the Chamber of Commerce's technology. "The end game is not the millions of e-mails going to the Hill," he said. "The end game is to find people who are genuinely interested and have a personal stake in the issue and are willing to communicate it."

MAIL CALL: Brad Fitch, who studied congressional communications, said some e-mail is lost in the flood and never read.

A Social Revolution

And once those people are identified, they can be more active in the process. Observers of the industry say the new grass-roots technique can open up new conversations between people and their elected representatives and even redistribute power by bringing more people into the system who in the past may not have felt they could participate. It can open new lines of communication, bring fresh ideas, and even give workers in an industry or members of trade associations more say over the industry's agenda.

In the Congressional Management Foundation study, 79 percent of congressional aides surveyed said they believe the Internet has made it easier for people to get involved in public policy, and 55 percent said it has increased public understanding of what goes on in Washington. A plurality of 48 percent said they believe it has made members of Congress more responsive to their constituents.

It can also connect people with common interests who in the past might never have found one another. "Grassroots and the Internet are a revolutionary development in democratic government," said Pinkham of the Public Affairs Council. "It's complicated, it can be messy, it makes it harder to make a decision sometimes. But it also improves the process."

As long as everyone is being honest with one another and is not trying to manipulate constituencies, Pinkham said, it is an exercise in the oldest of political arts: coalition building. "That's finding someone who is likeminded and getting them to join your campaign," he said. "And that's OK."

And for lawmakers, like it or not, their very survival depends on finding a way to sort through the many voices — and respond. More and more, people communicate through the Internet — sometimes even if their desks are six feet apart. Indeed, for many people these days, e-mail is as personal as a written letter or a phone call.

If Congress doesn't learn how to sort through and respond to the growing Internet traffic, and heartfelt messages from constituents go unanswered, it may make lawmakers seem more remote rather than more approachable.

When people speak, whatever channels they use and whoever organizes them, Congress can't afford to simply tune them out, say those who have worked with Internet lobbying.

"If you're turning off your fax or filtering your e-mail," said BIPAC president Greg Casey, "you're doing it at your peril. Because people back home are going to remember that." ∎

Government Institutions

The articles in this section provide insight into the workings of the major institutions of the U.S. government, focusing in turn on Congress, the presidency, and the federal judiciary. The first two articles explore the possibility of a change in leadership in one or both houses of Congress as election-year politics dominate the 2006 political landscape. The first of these articles takes a close look at some of the legislative successes that the Republican Party will be touting as a counter to a somewhat anxious 109th Congress burdened by blossoming scandal and concern about growing voter discontent. Among the accomplishments Republicans will seek to highlight in shoring up their base are the appointments of two conservative justices to the Supreme Court, an economy considered healthy by most indicators, and success in passing a tax cut package. The second article analyzes recent roll call votes to demonstrate how a hopeful Democratic Party—buoyed by the flagging poll numbers of President George W. Bush and the Republican-controlled Congress—is experiencing a season of uncommon unity. This article examines how this trend might affect Democrat's chances in the 2006 election.

The next two articles, on the executive branch, present Bush as a leader more humble in the sixth year of his presidency than in years past. Slam dunked are the ambitious proposals and the sweeping rhetoric that characterized the start of his second term. One article looks at the growing unease of some of the president's most ardent supporters in the Senate over the nation's prolonged military commitment in Iraq. With public support for the war having significantly waned, Bush's pledge to keep troops there "as long as it takes" has been quietly replaced by a subdued rhetoric with less emphasis on Iraq as a model for democracy in the Middle East. The second article spotlights Bush's 2006 State of the Union address, noting its modest agenda and undercurrent of election-year caution, especially in contrast to his far-reaching proposal to transform Social Security featured as the hallmark of his 2005 address.

With the Supreme Court appointments of John G. Roberts as chief justice and Samuel A. Alito as an associate justice, the ideological direction of the new Court became the focus of much attention and speculation. The first article on the judiciary illustrates how in the confirmation process for federal judges, the commonly invoked respect for precedent embodied in the concept of *stare decisis* is now read as more a reflection of a nominee's stance on abortion than an indication of any overarching judicial philosophy. In fact, the overruling of precedents is far more commonplace than is generally believed. The second article on the Court contends that by voting along a party line or on an ideological basis against conservative justices such as Alito, Democrats may be courting disaster in the event of regaining control of the Senate.

Focusing On A Fresh Start

Having seen their legislative blueprint crumpled last year by a mix of hard losses and victories that failed to inspire the party base, Republicans are eager to get 2006 rolling

CONGRESS AS A RULE is always most prolific when it is actually time for members to leave town. The overworked joke in the Capitol is that lawmakers begin to smell the fumes of the jets that will take them home. In reality, the bursts of last-minute legislating are inspired by the prospect of leaving Washington without some "record of accomplishment" to take back to the voters.

So it was the week of July 25, when, in a pre-recess flurry, the Senate cleared two long-stalled items on the GOP agenda: a sweeping energy policy overhaul that had been on the Bush administration's wish list since 2001, and a bill authorizing $286.5 billion for the nation's highway and public transit programs. That week it also cleared legislation to implement the Central American Free Trade Agreement (CAFTA).

Republicans left Washington confident that their productivity would play well with constituents, and ultimately be rewarded by voters in 2006. And at the time, they needed the boost. The war in Iraq was growing ever more violent and its end point more uncertain. Ethics controversies had ensnared and distracted some important legislative players, including then-House Majority Leader Tom DeLay of Texas, who would later be indicted on felony money laundering and conspiracy charges in his home state. And polls showed that Congress' decision earlier in the year to intervene in the case of brain-damaged Terri Schiavo, contrary to public sentiment, had left many voters feeling that the government was out of touch with their interests.

As a result, action on issues of tangible import such as energy, highways and trade, combined with earlier victories including new restrictions on class action lawsuits and legislation to curb bankruptcy filings, was viewed by many lawmakers as essential.

But whatever credit they might have been given did not last long. On Aug. 29, Hurricane Katrina made landfall on the Gulf Coast, and the resulting damage and despair was viewed as a failure of government at all levels. Suddenly the Republican-led Congress was charged with rebuilding not just Baghdad, but New Orleans and much of the Gulf Coast as well — with a combined price tag that was difficult for many fiscal conservatives to stomach.

After that, it became much harder for the GOP Congress to finish its business, and even the end-of-session rush could not loosen the legislative gears completely. A deficit reduction bill, which took the tie-breaking vote of Vice President Dick Cheney to pass the Senate, still needs final action in the House. The two chambers did not agree on a long-term extension of the 2001 anti-terrorism law known as the Patriot Act. And while it was clear earlier in the year that Congress would put the president's proposal to overhaul Social Security and create personal investment accounts on the back burner, more urgent matters such as hurricane relief sealed that initiative's fate for the year.

The majority party's agenda ground to a halt, and Republicans were left scrambling for direction and a unified message. Many analysts say that if 2006 is the year the Republicans lose ground, or even lose control of Congress, the events of 2005 might be the reason.

A CORPORATE FOCUS

But analysts also say that Republicans can be expected in 2006 to attempt to counter the impression of a lack of direction by emphasizing the health of the U.S. economy, which has been humming along with above average growth for two and a half years, and by pointing to the benefits to companies of the legislative actions of the past year. "There are lots of good things happening in the economy that candidates can talk about," says Republican strategist Ed Goeas.

GOP leaders are eager to do so. "We've been one of the most productive Congresses in recent history," said Deborah Pryce of Ohio, who chairs the House Republican Conference. "If you go through the list it's amazing. It's a huge list of significant successes."

Any member of the House or Senate Republican leadership can tick off that list. In addition to the summer's passage of CAFTA and the energy and highway bills, Republicans early in the year pushed through legislation shifting many class action lawsuits to federal courts, where the burden is often greater for plaintiffs. It was the first major plank in the GOP's "tort reform" platform to pass Congress.

In mid-April, Congress cleared legislation long sought by the credit and finance industries that makes it harder for consumers to file for bankruptcy by raising filing fees and requiring more documentation.

In the fall, in the weeks after Katrina caused

FINAL ACTION: Lawmakers led by Sen. Pete V. Domenici, left, enacted an energy bill to enactment last summer after years of trying.

billions in property damage and more than 1,000 fatalities, Congress quickly doled out more than $62 billion in emergency relief, and followed up with legislation designed to address the various social needs of the evacuees, including health care, housing and education.

The big winners of 2005 were the corporate constituencies. The energy bill features $14.6 billion in tax credits and deductions over the next decade to spur increased domestic production of oil and natural gas, develop coal technology, and promote the use of nuclear power and alternative fuels. The highway bill is expected to induce billions of dollars in construction. The credit card and financial industries got their bankruptcy overhaul, and the business world generally cheered the legislation on class action. Passage of CAFTA was a priority of the U.S. Chamber of Commerce, which argued that it will open up vast new markets for American products and services.

BACK TO THE BASE

Tax incentives for energy producers, legal protections for gunmakers and new bankruptcy rules, however, don't make up the kind of portfolio Republicans will need to sell in a midterm election year, which is about catering to base voters. "Nobody cares about the bankruptcy bill," says Republican strategist Glen Bolger. "That's too convoluted for the average Republican to understand. Any Republican who talks about that on the stump ought to be fined."

Party strategists say the GOP can be expected to jump-start its legislative engine in the coming election year with initiatives designed to energize their conservative core, such as tax cuts, immigration overhaul, and possibly even a constitutional ban on gay marriage.

In retrospect, there was very little for social conservatives to point to in 2005, except for the Schiavo legislation, and it is unclear how much that helped the GOP politically.

On the policy side, spending and tax cuts always top the list. The final vote on an almost $40 billion spending cut measure will probably come early this year, but conservatives want more — much more.

"That is not enough," said Grover Norquist, president of Americans for Tax Reform. "That was step one. Now we have to go through the long road to spending sobriety." Norquist wants to see lawmakers take aim at "earmarks" — the items tucked into appropriations bills that serve some parochial purpose for a member.

Republicans are expected to turn their attention to the other side of the ledger as well. The House and Senate each have plans to produce more than $50 billion in tax cuts, but differ significantly on the details. Proposals to extend Bush tax cuts that reduced rates on dividend and capital gains income will be in play immediately, as well as proposals to exempt middle-income Americans from the alternative minimum tax, which threatens to cover a greater segment of the population every year because of inflation.

"As always, taxes and spending are issues that resonate a lot within the Republican party," said Sen. John Cornyn, R-Texas. "People need to be reassured that we've maintained

Highlights: 109th Congress, First Session

CONGRESS DID

- Confirm John G. Roberts Jr. as the first new chief justice of the United States since 1986 and the first new member of the Supreme Court since 1994.
- Complete work on all 11 fiscal 2006 appropriations bills.
- Appropriate $102.7 billion for the military operations in Iraq and Afghanistan but dictated that 2006 be a year of "significant transition" to Iraqi sovereignty and required quarterly reports from President Bush on progress toward that goal.
- Appropriate $62.3 billion, provided about $19 billion in tax relief and altered federal policies on many fronts to assist Gulf Coast states in recovering from Hurricane Katrina, the most economically damaging storm in U.S. history.
- Overhaul federal energy policy, with an emphasis on enhanced production, four years after a similar plan was proposed by the president.
- Authorize $286.5 billion for federal highway, mass transit and road safety programs through 2009.
- Bar cruel, inhuman or degrading treatment of enemy detainees, but limited access to federal courts by prisoners at Guantánamo Bay, Cuba.
- Provide $3.8 billion for preparations against a potential flu pandemic and shield makers of flu vaccine from liability.
- Implement a free-trade agreement between the United States and five Central American countries and the Dominican Republic.
- Require uniform national standards for state-issued drivers' licenses and tighten limits on people seeking asylum.
- Shield gun and ammunition manufacturers, distributors and dealers from civil liability when third parties misuse their products.
- Limit class action litigation by shifting more such cases to federal court.
- Speed the process for reconstituting the House after a catastrophic attack.

CONGRESS DID NOT

- Complete work on a bill to reduce expected entitlement spending over the next five years by $39.7 billion.
- Take any action in response to the president's top second-term domestic initiative, an overhaul of the Social Security program to allow future beneficiaries to divert some of their payroll taxes to investment accounts.
- Extend 16 expiring provisions of a 2001 law, known as the Patriot Act, that had enhanced law enforcement powers to investigate suspected terrorists.
- Enact or extend any tax reductions, the first year since 2000 without a new tax cut.
- Open the Arctic National Wildlife Refuge in Alaska to energy exploration.
- Create a compensation pool for victims of asbestos exposure.
- Expand the federal role in embryonic stem cell research, although it did fund research on umbilical cord blood cells.
- Update federal policy toward immigrant workers and the treatment of businesses that violate immigration law.
- Confirm John R. Bolton as ambassador to the United Nations; Bush instead used his recess appointment power to install that envoy.
- Reauthorize programs run by the Homeland Security and State departments, the Coast Guard and the Army Corps of Engineers.
- Update the Head Start early childhood education program.
- Reauthorize the federal law regulating higher education policy.
- Revamp governance of the U.S. Postal Service.
- Advance a constitutional amendment to ban gay marriage.
- Reach bipartisan agreement to increase the federally guaranteed minimum wage above $5.15, which was set in 1997.
- Rewrite the Clean Air Act to enact the president's "Clear Skies" initiative to curb power plant emissions.

our core principles."

Hearings in early January on Bush's nomination of Samuel A. Alito Jr. to the Supreme Court can be expected to allow conservatives to showcase some of their priorities, and if Alito is confirmed it will allow Republicans to point to both him and Chief Justice John G. Roberts Jr. as successes for the base.

Still, the showdown many conservatives were hoping for — a change in the Senate rules that would outlaw filibusters on judicial nominations — never materialized. A bipartisan group of 14 senators struck an agreement that allowed some controversial appellate nominees through, but allowed filibusters in future "extraordinary" circumstances.

The episode was widely viewed as a proxy fight over abortion, the most controversial issue before the courts and the one most likely to derail the nominees that conservatives want: those who would vote to overturn the landmark Roe v. Wade ruling, which legalized abortion.

One wild-card issue that Republicans could raise to change the political dynamic during election season is gay marriage. It's not clear

how far the White House will push the point, but there are some in Congress who would like to see Round 2 of the same-sex marriage debate in 2006. "I really hope the president gets out and campaigns on it," said Sen. Sam Brownback, R-Kan., who is pushing a measure that would amend the Constitution to define marriage as the union of a man and a woman, exclusively. Brownback moved the legislation last fall through the Senate Judiciary Subcommittee on the Constitution, Civil Rights, and Property Rights.

Here, too, there is a lack of unanimity in the party. "I don't think there's total agreement on whether we should pursue that further than we have," Pryce said.

Immigration, another issue that divides Republicans, is also sure to be teed up in the early months, according to GOP lawmakers and aides. Republicans are under pressure to do something about the continuing flow of illegal immigrants into the United States, and to address the 10 million to 11 million who already live here.

"Immigration reform would be very positive for the country and very positive for the econ-

omy," GOP strategist Goeas says.

But Republicans don't agree on just what kind of "reform" is necessary to fix what all sides say is a broken system. Bush wants to create a guest-worker program that would allow illegal immigrants already in the country to become legal residents — a plan backed by much of corporate America, which relies on those workers to fill low-wage jobs.

But others see such an approach as effectively offering amnesty to people who have broken the law. The House passed legislation late in the session that would beef up border security, criminalize illegal immigration for the first time, and penalize companies that don't monitor whether they have illegal workers on their staffs.

Pryce said it's possible to balance the interests of corporate America with the need to stem the flow of illegal immigrants, but acknowledged the wide divide between the different approaches. "It's going to be difficult," she said, "but people know it needs to get done."

NATIONAL SECURITY FOCUS

The biggest challenge for Republicans,

though, is that regardless of how they sell themselves and their domestic agenda, their fate will be most influenced by matters that are out of their control and thousands of miles away.

"When you ask Americans what's at the top of the list of problems facing the country, Iraq is still the top issue," said Karlyn Bowman, a public opinion expert at the American Enterprise Institute.

Public support for the war slid in 2005. More than half of all Americans now disapprove of the way the Bush administration has handled the situation in Iraq, and a similar percentage think on the whole the invasion was a mistake.

How Democrats handle these national security issues is itself fraught with conflict. The minority party has not been able to fully exploit the issue because members haven't agreed on a unified approach. Rep. John P. Murtha of Pennsylvania, a decorated ex-Marine, called for a quick withdrawal of troops, while others, such as Joseph R. Biden Jr. of Delaware, the ranking member on the Senate Foreign Relations Committee, were unwilling to go that far.

In fact, comparing themselves with the Democrats might be the strategy for Republicans on all manner of issues, party strategists say, from ethics to the war to an array of domestic policy issues. Maybe Republicans have had some bumps in the road, the argu-

ment goes, but what would Democrats have done? Would they do any better?

"The bottom line is at some point the Democrats will have to stand up and say what they've done," Goeas said.

The poll numbers on Iraq have ticked upward in recent weeks, along with Bush's approval ratings, but they still have far to go before Republican strategists and politicians can say Iraq isn't weighing down their campaigns.

In the meantime, lawmakers, especially Democrats, are expected to keep the pressure on Bush on national security matters, particularly on the question of when troops will come home from Iraq. With an eye toward the midterm elections, members of Congress in recent months have identified 2006 as the year in which the president should begin to hand over much of Iraq's security to its new government.

More broadly, the administration's handling of the war on terror has become a debate of greater intensity. Lawmakers have been less willing to sign off automatically on the extraordinary measures Bush has sought to use against suspected members of al Qaeda, and late last year Congress passed legislation to ban abusive interrogations of detainees in U.S. custody and demand more information on the war. The 2006 defense authorization bill requires the White House to submit quarterly

reports on progress in Iraq. Lawmakers also voted in favor of a provision demanding classified reports on any CIA prisons overseas, but that measure was dropped on a technicality. Nevertheless, Congress was on record as wanting a strong oversight role.

While the issue of detainee abuse was settled — after weeks of intense negotiations between Republican Sen. John McCain of Arizona and the White House — others say the legal status of enemy combatants must be revisited. Senate Judiciary Chairman Arlen Specter, R-Pa., objected to a provision included in the defense authorization bill that mostly bars detainees from accessing federal courts and sanctions secret military tribunals.

Another legal question for lawmakers will be the extent to which the president can violate the privacy of U.S. citizens when tracking suspected terrorists. After The New York Times disclosed Dec. 16 that Bush in 2002 authorized the National Security Agency to spy on Americans without court permission, lawmakers refused to agree to a long-term extension of the Patriot Act. After the House refused to extend the provisions for six months, the Senate agreed to a five-week extension. That ensured that the issue will be one of many on Congress' plate this year.

What follows is a bill-by-bill rundown of what happened in Congress in 2005 and what lawmakers have left for the year ahead. ■

Learning To Stick Together

House Democrats reached record unity in 2005, as The Senate GOP's loyalties swayed slightly

FEELING BOLDER: House Democratic Whip Hoyer, center, and other leaders pushed party members to a record degree of unity in 2005.

THERE WAS A TIME when to be a Democrat in Congress was akin to belonging to a luncheon club just so you could eat the food and enjoy the people. Staying for the program wasn't such a priority. No longer. Democrats on Capitol Hill are relying more on what has been the GOP political playbook, staying in step and sometimes getting tough with those who miss a beat.

A decade after Republicans determined there was value in strict adherence to party discipline, the message has sunk in on the other side of the aisle, and 2005 was a breakout year. Over the past half-century, Democrats in the House were never more unified than last year, an analysis of roll call votes by Congressional Quarterly shows. And only twice before, in 1999 and 2001, were Senate Democrats more united than in 2005.

At the same time, House Republicans, who have played at this game much longer, increased their party loyalty a bit last year over 2004, though they didn't quite meet the record they set in 1995 — the year they took command of the chamber for the first time in four decades — and reached twice since in 2001 and 2003. Only Senate Republicans fell off the pace in 2005, dropping well below the level of partisan cohesion they reached in 2003. That year, in fact, still appears to have been the most partisan in Congress since World War II.

One manifestation of the leaders' demand for loyalty is a rising number of roll call votes on which a majority of Republicans line up against a majority of Democrats: These are party unity votes as defined by CQ. Last year, almost half of the 669 recorded votes in the House met this definition, as did almost two-thirds of the 366 Senate roll calls. Overall, party unity scores show Congress is becoming more divided on more issues more often, leaving little room for compromise on major issues.

CQ Weekly Jan. 9, 2006

Partisanship High as Democrats Still Lag Behind GOP

House Democrats were more unified than ever in 2005, voting on average with the party majority 88 percent of the time. House Republicans remained the most united group in Congress, with a 90 percent party unity score, close to an all-time high. In the Senate, Republicans supported the party position slightly less often than a year earlier, while Democrats rallied together more frequently.

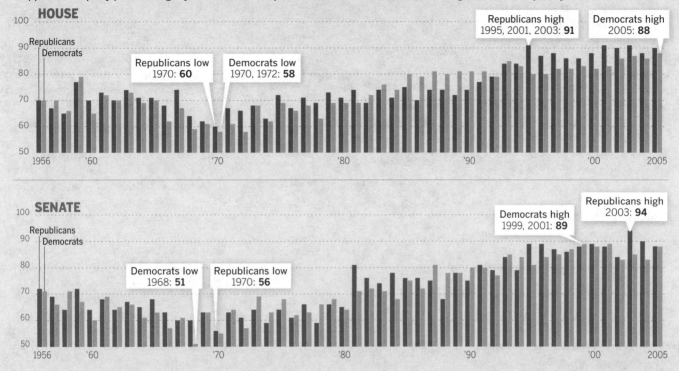

HOUSE

Republicans
Democrats

Republicans low
1970: **60**

Democrats low
1970, 1972: **58**

Republicans high
1995, 2001, 2003: **91**

Democrats high
2005: **88**

1956 '60 '70 '80 '90 '00 2005

SENATE

Republicans
Democrats

Democrats low
1968: **51**

Republicans low
1970: **56**

Democrats high
1999, 2001: **89**

Republicans high
2003: **94**

1956 '60 '70 '80 '90 '00 2005

Moreover, rising Democratic unity has forced the majority Republicans to work harder to win — and resulted in a few high-profile GOP defeats that also jeopardized the legislative agenda of President Bush.

An utter lack of Democratic support, for example, required Republican leaders to twist arms and make promises to preserve very narrow victories in both chambers on a spending cut bill that still must survive one more test in the House early this year. Likewise, most Democrats refused to vote for the Central American Free Trade Agreement — the centerpiece of Bush's trade agenda — leaving Republicans to scramble to win sufficient support from within their own ranks. And when House Democrats held tighter than the Republicans on a bill to permit federally financed medical research using embryonic stem cells, the GOP and the president both suffered a loss.

It's no coincidence that all three of those votes show up in a companion CQ analysis of the president's influence last year and were picked by CQ's editors as among the 28 "key votes" of 2005. *(2006 CQ Weekly, pp. 80 and 108)*

"Democrats are emboldened," said Sarah Binder, a senior fellow at the Brookings Institution in Washington. "Democrats ... are going to be more cohesive when they're in the minority when they think they have an incentive to regain the majority."

House Democratic Leader Nancy Pelosi of California showed last year that she has learned from former House Majority Leader Tom DeLay of Texas and other GOP practitioners of strong-arm tactics to keep her caucus aligned.

So serious have Democrats become about catching up — both at the ballot box and in party discipline — that in mid-December, Pelosi lambasted Edolphus Towns of New York for being absent during a crucial roll call on the spending cut bill that Republicans won by two votes.

Pelosi threatened to yank Towns' seat on the Energy and Commerce Committee, which would ordinarily be a high price to pay for a single missed roll call. But Towns was a repeat offender in Pelosi's book, having helped the opposition by voting in favor of the Central America trade pact in July. Then, as well, the GOP had prevailed by two votes.

"Traditionally we haven't been this unified," said Rep. Jim McDermott, D-Wash., who voted with his party colleagues 99 percent of the time in 2005.

He gave credit to Pelosi, a liberal Californian who critics said early on would be too out of step with the mainstream to be an effective leader. "It's primarily a reflection of Nancy's leadership as a persuasive voice to people all across the board," he said. "You can't dismiss her as some wild-eyed San Francisco liberal."

The evidence of rising unity is in the numbers: House Democrats voted with their party colleagues a record 88 percent of the time in 2005, just below the 90 percent average party support score House Republicans posted. The previous high for House Democrats was 87 percent in 2003; House Republicans reached 91 percent that year, in 2001 and in 1995.

In the Senate, both parties stuck together 88 percent of

2005 DATA
AVERAGE PARTY UNITY SCORE

All Republicans: 90 percent
All Democrats: 88 percent

HOUSE
Republicans   Democrats
90%   88%

SENATE
Republicans   Democrats
88%   88%

VOTES

	SENATE	HOUSE
PARTISAN VOTES	229	328
TOTAL	366	669
	63%	49%

FOR MORE INFORMATION

Top scorers	96
Background	97
History	98
Senators' scores	99
House members' scores	100

the time in 2005. For Democrats, that was a jump from an 83 percent average party support score in 2004, and just a hair below their record of 89 percent set in 1999 and 2001. For Senate Republicans, the drop in support from a record 94 percent in 2003 and a 90 percent score in 2004 helps explain why they lost several critical votes in the days before Congress adjourned for the year.

"In the last six months, it's clearly been a more partisan place," said Todd Akin of Missouri, one of five House Republicans who voted with his party more than 99 percent of the time in 2005. "It's a precursor to a rigorous election season."

Still, GOP leaders scoff at the idea that Democrats are making any headway. And Republicans say they have remained remarkably unified considering the political pressures that accompany public sentiment about the war in Iraq and the task of running Congress in the face of increasingly aggressive tactics by the minority Democrats.

"On the issues that are most important to the American people, the Republicans have been united," said Amy Call, a spokeswoman for Senate Majority Leader Bill Frist of Tennessee, who at times has struggled to control his chamber.

IT'S UNANIMOUS

Rising Democratic unity can also be seen in the frequency with which lawmakers voted unanimously on party unity roll calls. For years, GOP leader have managed often to squelch defections in their ranks — and in the notable partisan year of 2003, Republicans on both sides of the Capitol were unanimous on 239 party unity votes.

Democrats rose to the occasion last year, voting unanimously 82 times in the House and 69 times in the Senate. Those totals essentially matched the 91 times that Republicans voted unanimously in the House and the 59 times they did so in the Senate.

"I can't remember as many votes with 100 percent Democrats as we've had in the past couple of months," said House Minority Whip Steny H. Hoyer of Maryland.

Hoyer attributed the cohesion of his party's caucus to a coming of age of Pelosi's leadership — which has been under fire as Democrats struggled the past few years — and to what he termed "an exclusively partisan agenda" on the part of GOP leaders. "Whether you are conservative, liberal or moderate you find yourself disagreeing with the Republicans," he said.

He may have a point that is borne out in declining individual party unity scores for at least a dozen moderates in the Republican Party who feel alienated, as well as for some fiscal conservatives in the House who voted against Republican spending initiatives they thought were too

Unanimous Votes Are More Common

This graph shows the number of times that members of one party unanimously opposed a majority of the other party on roll call votes. Unanimous votes have become more frequent. That is especially true for Democrats, who recorded a record 151 unanimous roll calls in both chambers in 2005.

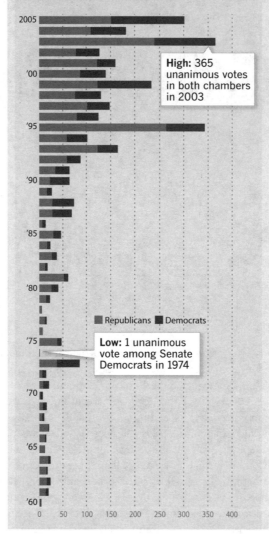

High: 365 unanimous votes in both chambers in 2003

■ Republicans ■ Democrats

Low: 1 unanimous vote among Senate Democrats in 1974

expensive. At the same time, party unity scores for some moderate Democrats also fell in 2005, suggesting that disaffection with the deeper partisan strains of the leadership extends across the aisle.

The shift by moderates was especially evident among blue-state Republican senators, such as Susan Collins and Olympia J. Snowe of Maine, who have found it increasingly difficult to stick with their party on close votes. Collins' support score declined 19 points to 59 percent, and Snowe's score dropped 15 points to 56 percent.

Their defections, like that of Lincoln Chafee of Rhode Island, who backed his party less than half the time in 2005, will undoubtedly make it harder for Frist to accomplish his goals. This is Frist's last year to make his mark as a legislator and a leader in preparation for a possible presidential run in 2008. He will not seek re-election to the Senate when his term ends in 2006.

Chafee, who represents a state that Democratic Sen. John Kerry carried by 20 points in the 2004 presidential election, says he isn't ashamed that he stayed with his party on only 47 percent of last year's party unity votes.

"I strive for consistency," he said with a chuckle when informed that his party support score was dead last among Republicans for the sixth straight year. "I would hope that consistency is there and that's what Rhode Islanders want."

Senate moderates have always been an important bloc in a chamber where the minority can block almost any legislation if they can muster 40 votes to sustain a filibuster. But over the past year, GOP moderates became a more significant voting bloc in the House, too.

Michael N. Castle of Delaware, Christopher Shays of Connecticut, Mark Steven Kirk of Illinois, Sherwood Boehlert of New York and Nancy L. Johnson of Connecticut are among a handful whose party support scores dropped. While moderates have often been ignored by conservative leaders in the House, their power was on display briefly when they blocked passage of the spending cut measure and demanded that a provision be removed that would have allowed oil and natural gas drilling in the Arctic National Wildlife Refuge.

"Moderate Republicans represent that old silent majority," said Wayne T. Gilchrest of Maryland, whose party support score dropped to 80 percent from 85 percent. "This is the dawning of a new day."

Some moderate Senate Democrats also shied from their party last year. Thomas R. Carper of Delaware, Mary L. Landrieu of Louisiana, Ben Nelson of Nebraska and Kent Conrad of North Dakota all voted with Republicans more often in 2005 than in 2004. Nelson was last among Democrats, voting with his party only 46 percent of the time.

ELECTION WORRIES

And while Nelson's supporters in the strongly Republican state of Nebraska may remain comfortable with his record of defections, some GOP senators facing tough re-election fights in 2006 are finding similar reasons to occasionally abandon their party.

Mike DeWine of Ohio, who has trailed in his 2006 re-election campaign in some public opinion polls, saw his party support score drop to 70 percent from 79 percent. Chafee, who already has a primary challenger, dropped to 47 percent from 65 percent. Even the reliably conservative Rick Santorum, who trails in Pennsylvania surveys, dropped to 92 percent in his party support score from 96 percent. That put the chairman of the Republican Conference in the middle of the pack among fellow GOP senators.

Santorum dismissed his decline in party loyalty as having nothing to do with his election. "I'm sure it fluctuates every year," he said. "It just depends on what the votes are on."

And Jim Talent of Missouri, who trails in early public opinion surveys and whose party support score dropped to 84 percent from 96 percent, said he is willing to stand apart from his party on core issues and that his overall loyalty to the GOP is not in question. "I'm not aware of the [party unity] scores, but I am aware when I'm disagreeing with my party or when I criticize the administration" on an issue, Talent said.

The impact of election-year politics wasn't limited to GOP senators. Democratic Rep. Harold E. Ford Jr. of Tennessee, who is running for Frist's Senate seat in a firmly Republican state, came across as more moderate in 2005, as his party support score dropped 7 points to 83 percent.

OPTIMISTIC DEMOCRATS

Rising Democratic unity is boosting the confidence of the party's leaders. In the Senate, by banding together and winning a few GOP allies, Democrats derailed renewal of the 2001 anti-terrorism law known as the Patriot Act. In fact, they closed the year by winning seven of the last eight party unity votes.

In the House, Democrats rarely win major votes because they are badly outnumbered and the Republicans closely control the debate. But Pelosi has made her GOP counterparts work harder to win. "When I became leader, the Democrats were sort of a co-op. It was an amalgamation of ideas," Pelosi said. "We've decided to define ourselves and our priorities."

On the CAFTA vote, for example, House Republican leaders had to hold the roll call open after midnight July 27 while cajoling some of their more hesitant rank-and-file members to vote for the trade agreement. And on Nov. 17, the first time House leaders brought the conference agreement on the fiscal 2006 Labor/Health and Human Services spending bill up for a vote, all 201 Democrats voted against it, joined by 22 Republicans. Together, they temporarily killed the measure until it could be retooled and brought back to the House floor.

Republicans, meanwhile, have been working to instill party discipline in the next generation of House leaders — freshmen such as Patrick T. McHenry of North Carolina and Bobby Jindal of Louisiana. McHenry backed his party 99 percent of the time on party unity votes. Jindal voted with Republicans 97 percent of the time, and emphasized the few occasions he did not go along with party marching orders. "More important than the number is looking at the particular issue," Jindal said. "There have been times where I voted against the party, like CAFTA."

THE MORE THINGS CHANGE . . .

Despite a handful of significant partisan departures, several reliable trends continued in 2005.

For instance, Southern Democrats representing Republican states were the least loyal to their party, while Northern Republicans parted ways with the GOP more often than colleagues from other regions. And strong delegation-wide support for their parties was logged by Texas Republicans, California Democrats and Massachusetts Democrats.

There is no reason to expect the divisive atmosphere in either chamber will change in the current year, with an election 10 months away and Capitol Hill captivated by the latest installment in the saga of super-lobbyist-turned-confessed-criminal Jack Abramoff, whose Jan. 3 guilty plea rattled the ranks of lawmakers and lobbyists alike.

"Parties aren't letting up," said Binder, the Brookings scholar. "They may look even more partisan in an election year. The minority won't have much incentive to hand victories to the majority."

The GOP majority, in turn, is likely to be highly motivated to stay unified as it strives to give its members opportunities to show a record of accomplishment to the voters who will decide how many Republicans return to Congress next year.

As 2005 wound down, Blunt reflected on the first session of the 109th Congress and public opinion polls showing a negative opinion of the legislative branch, and he professed to see a silver lining in those clouds: the expectation of a positive reaction to the session-closing votes to trim government spending, provide funding for military operations, and provide help for the states devastated by hurricanes Katrina and Rita.

"People's dissatisfaction with gas prices and the war has had an effect," he said. "What we've done over the last three weeks will have a positive impact on people's view of Congress." ■

Taking 'As Long As It Takes' No Longer

Congress is saying 'enough' to the president it has always backed on Iraq, demanding realistic goals and a timely drawdown of U.S. troops

IN A SINGLE VOTE last week, Senate Republicans, President Bush's most loyal supporters since the United States first sent troops to Iraq in April, 2003, sent him a clear message. They essentially gave him one year to turn over the conflict to Iraqis and to begin to bring U.S. troops home.

While their resolution did not lay out a timetable — it calls for 2006 to be "a period of significant transition to full Iraqi sovereignty" — these politicians reminded Bush that their party's political fortunes, indeed, their own more than his, rest on the administration's ability to make significant progress in Iraq in the coming 12 months.

In effect, Bush has been put on notice that even his own party's patience is wearing thin. Republicans who have to face the voters next year are finding that Bush's favorite refrain,

CQ Weekly Nov. 21, 2005

that the U.S. will remain in Iraq "as long as it takes," is no longer an acceptable answer. "We worry about our troops," said Republican Sen. Mike DeWine of Ohio, who faces a tough re-election race.

But what is possible in a year? Washington these days is a town of diminished expectations when it comes to what the United States realistically can accomplish in Iraq.

The most that can be hoped for, foreign policy experts say, is an Iraq with a degree of stability, but certainly not the flowering of Middle East democracy that Bush talked about in his inaugural address in January. The worst, they say, is civil war, chaos and a war that draws in Iraq's neighbors and destabilizes the Middle East even more.

Most likely, though, 2006 will be a year in which the U.S. administration simply "muddles through," registering enough progress in training Iraqi forces and in helping the new Iraqi gov-

ernment stand on its own two feet to mollify its critics enough to stay on the president's course.

Bush, for his part, has gone on the offensive, repeatedly pointing to the October vote on Iraq's constitution and December's parliamentary elections as proof that the country is on the way to the democratic future he had always envisioned. During a recent trip to Asia, he pledged that as Iraqi forces become capable of assuming responsibility for their country's security, U.S. troops will stand down. He also kept up his attacks on Democrats who have criticized his handling of the war. "I expect there to be criticism," Bush said, "but when Democrats say that I deliberately misled the Congress and

STEPPING UP: Iraqi Army soldiers stand at attention during a ceremony to restore Iraqi border security in the restive city of Kusaiba, near the Syrian Iraq border. Iraqi troops are expected to take over more security duties from U.S. forces and will be crucial to the country's stability.

the people, that's irresponsible."

The administration might be able to rescue the situation in Iraq, and its party's chances at home next year, if it can train enough Iraqi troops and police to ensure stability in the country and therefore significantly reduce the U.S. military presence by next fall.

But Middle East experts caution against forming any great expectations for progress in 2006. The most likely prognosis for next year is that the conflict will grind on for the foreseeable future.

As Anthony H. Cordesman, an expert on the Middle East at the Center for Strategic and International Studies, put it: "The most we can real-

ly hope for at the end of 2006 is enough progress to give us very good reasons to go on into 2007."

HOPING FOR THE BEST

Bush's goal in Iraq two and a half years ago was the establishment of a full-blown democracy in the heart of the Middle East. Today, most analysts believe that is no longer attainable. The best Bush can hope for is a scaled-back version of Iraqi statehood in which the government remains viable and pro-Western and does not reconstitute its programs on weapons of mass destruction.

Making do with less in Iraq will not be easy for an administration that went in with such

high expectations. Former ambassador David Mack, a retired Arabist at the State Department, said a successful U.S. exit strategy from Iraq depends on the administration's willingness to shed its "illusions" about establishing a modern, Western-style democracy there.

That goal, he said, is no longer realistic, given the mistakes the administration has made in Iraq and the time, money and political capital it would require to correct them.

Detainee Rights Remain at Issue

NO MATTER HOW HARD President Bush tries, the images from Abu Ghraib prison won't fade away.

Nearly two years after U.S. troops were found to have abused some Iraqi captives at the prison outside Baghdad, and despite repeated assurances from Bush and his administration that they do not countenance torture, the treatment of detainees is more of an issue than ever. Embarrassing revelations, ranging from the Abu Ghraib abuse to a recent report of secret overseas prisons for al Qaeda captives, continue to complicate the administration's prosecution of the war in Iraq and the broader war against terrorism.

The Senate stepped in with two amendments to an annual defense authorization bill that sponsors say would clarify the treatment and rights of detainees and put the issue to rest. The Senate, like the rest of the country, is of two minds on detainees: Suspected terrorists and those with connections to terrorists should not have the same rights to the court system as U.S. citizens, but neither should they be abused or mistreated. The amendments the Senate overwhelmingly adopted reflect this dichotomy. The provision sponsored by Arizona Sen. John McCain, a POW in the Vietnam War, would prohibit torture. Another, proposed by South Carolina Sen. Lindsey Graham, would mostly bar detainees from the courts, allowing one review of serious sentences.

"I think that it's been long overdue," Graham said. Congress has not acted sooner, he said, because "I think we've been afraid that we'll be seen as meddlers" or "friendly to the terrorists."

Though McCain and Graham say their separate proposals would resolve the continuing controversy over detainees, some legal experts contend that they would not, and that the issue will continue to plague the administration. Human rights experts say the bill would give detainees no legal recourse if interrogators used abusive tactics. Nor would the Graham proposal address the rights of suspected terrorists held anywhere other than Guantánamo Bay in Cuba. Legal experts say the provisions are so broad that they will lead to more court battles.

"We're actually going to the fundamental question of war powers" and what the president, or Congress, is entitled to decide, said Scott L. Silliman, executive director of Duke University School of Law's Center on Law, Ethics and National Security. "There's a lot at stake in this."

McCain's amendment, which the Senate added to the Defense appropriations bill by a 90-9 vote in October and on Nov. 4 agreed to include in the authorization legislation, would ban cruel and inhumane treatment of suspects — bolstering existing anti-torture laws — and require interrogators to rely on an Army field manual that complies with standards set by the Geneva Conventions.

McCain said the legislation would make U.S. policy on detainees clear and give military commanders firm guidance on how to treat prisoners.

The administration does not think such legislation is either necessary or advisable. The "United States doesn't do torture," Bush has declared, but the White House has threatened to veto the legislation and proposed that Congress exempt CIA operatives from McCain's abuse ban. Graham's provision also did not fall in line with what the White House wanted, which was essentially no involvement from Congress whatsoever.

DAY IN COURT

The second and more controversial amendment by Graham would essentially remove the rights of detainees being held at Guantánamo Bay to protest their detention in federal courts. It would allow detainees to appeal their status if a military tribunal determined they were "enemy combatants," and those sentenced by a tribunal to death or more than 10 years in prison would have their sentences automatically reviewed by a federal appeals court in Washington. But that would be the only recourse.

Graham said the legislation would go above and beyond standards set by the Geneva Conventions and assure every detainee a "day in court" while reducing the number of habeas corpus petitions.

The administration has held most terrorism suspects outside the country and denied them access to U.S. courts. But the Supreme Court ruled in 2004 that foreigners being held at Guantánamo Bay have a right to protest their detentions. That resulted in more than 160 habeas corpus petitions contesting more than 300 detentions.

But according to Silliman, the proposal is probably far too broad to keep enemy combatants out of the U.S. court system entirely. And he did not think the bill explicitly endorses the existence of military tribunals Bush created after the Sept. 11 terrorist attacks. Accordingly, detainees could argue that the secret trials are unconstitutional and that they should not be subjected to the tribunals, he said.

"If I were to push that language as far as I could, that's what I would say" to defend a detainee, Silliman said.

And explicit congressional authority might be what Bush needs to fend off challenges to the constitutionality of the tribunals.

Supreme Court Justice Robert H. Jackson spelled out such a requirement in a 1952 ruling that President Harry S Truman had unconstitutionally seized control of the nation's steel mills to manage production of critical munitions.

From now on, Mack said, Bush must strive to create a non-threatening Iraq that will not turn against the United States or its allies in the region. Such a state would require a prolonged, if smaller, U.S. military presence to provide backup for Iraqi troops, who will take the lead on security operations. "That is the best they can hope for," he said.

Sen. Joseph R. Biden Jr. of Delaware, the top-ranking Democrat on the Senate Foreign Relations Committee and one of the most knowledgeable lawmakers on the Iraq situation, said an optimistic goal would be "a country that is not a haven for foreign terrorists, that is not a threat to its neighbors and that has a shot over time of developing into a democracy."

That shot at democracy, Biden and other experts warn, also depends upon a number of political and economic developments that must convince Iraq's Sunnis, Shiites and Kurds that they have a common stake in the country holding together as a nation-state.

For example, following the Dec. 15 parliamentary elections, Iraq's new leaders will have to show that they can peacefully amend the country's constitution, which left unresolved important issues such as the relationship between mosque and state and the powers of the central government under Iraq's loose fed-

Different Circumstances, Different Rights

The legal status and treatment of suspected terrorists has been hotly debated since November 2001, when President Bush authorized their detention and trial by military tribunals. The administration decided that since terrorist organizations, such as al Qaeda, are not states, and since Afghanistan at the time of the U.S. invasion was a "failed state," those detained were "illegal enemy combatants" not protected by the Geneva Conventions for the treatment of prisoners of war, though they should be treated humanely. Since almost all of the detainees were captured and held outside the United States, the administration has argued that they are not entitled to protest their detention in the federal courts, although a number have tried. Subsequent legal battles have developed around the three main categories of detainees described here, including an example of each.

Foreigners captured outside the United States and held at Guantánamo Bay, Cuba

SHAFIQ RASUL was a British citizen working for al Qaeda when he was captured and sent to Guantánamo Bay in 2002. The Bush administration has deemed all of the detainees to be unlawful combatants who may be held indefinitely without trial. The Supreme Court ruled last year in *Rasul v. Bush* that such detainees must have access to federal courts to appeal their detentions through habeas corpus petitions, which are used to challenge the legality of a person's confinement. An amendment the Senate adopted to the annual defense authorization bill would greatly limit that access. The Pentagon has established military commissions to try the detainees for violations of the laws of war, but the legality of these commissions is under review by the Supreme Court.

American Citizens captured *outside* the United States

YASER HAMDI was an American citizen when he was captured in Afghanistan in 2001 after allegedly participating in hostile action against U.S. military forces. He was then held by the military for two years without charge and access to legal counsel. In response to a petition by Hamdi's father, the Supreme Court ruled in his case that the president had the authority to detain him under the law, enacted just after the Sept. 11 terrorist attacks, that authorized the use of military force in Afghanistan, but that he was entitled to challenge the basis of his detention before "a neutral decision-maker." Hamdi was deported to Saudi Arabia last year after he agreed to renounce his U.S. citizenship and never return.

American citizens captured *within* the United States

JOSÉ PADILLA was arrested in Chicago three years ago and accused of being a terrorist by the government, which declared him an unlawful enemy combatant and put him under the military's control. Lawyers acting on his behalf argued that he should be charged in federal court and given the same rights as any criminal defendant. Earlier this year, a federal judge in South Carolina ordered the government to charge Padilla or release him, arguing that his case differed from that of Hamdi because Padilla was arrested on U.S. soil. The government argued that Padilla had previously fought in Afghanistan against U.S. forces, and the 4th Circuit Court of Appeals subsequently reversed the trial judge's decision and ruled that Bush does have the authority to detain Padilla without charges.

"When the president acts in absence of either a congressional grant or denial of authority, he can only rely upon his own independent powers," Jackson wrote. "But there is a zone of twilight in which he and Congress may have concurrent authority, or in which its distribution is uncertain."

Legal experts also agreed that Graham's amendment probably makes it impossible for a detainee to alert a civilian judge to abuse, potentially raising more legal concerns and challenges.

In a letter to senators, the American Civil Liberties Union said Graham's proposal would gravely undercut the power of McCain's anti-torture amendment because it would "unconstitutionally remove the system of checks and balances for anyone claiming the federal government engaged in torture or abuse."

"Congress is still cutting short constitutional protections," said Christopher E. Anders, legislative counsel at the American Civil Liberties Union.

Debate is also expected on the legal rights of those held in secret CIA prisons. Graham's amendment is restricted to those at Guantánamo Bay, the military's sole detention center for suspected terrorists.

The result of all this is continued and perhaps even accelerated litigation on detainees.

"I have never seen so much movement in the area of national security law," said Silliman, who spent 25 years as a military attorney in the Air Force. "It's exciting, but it's a little frightening too."

---

eral system. The constitution has already codified the autonomy that the Kurdish areas in the north have enjoyed since 1991. But it also holds out the possibility of a similar autonomous arrangement for the southern Shiite-dominated provinces.

In 2006, Iraq's Sunnis, disenfranchised after the fall of Saddam Hussein in 2003, will be negotiating to strengthen the central government's powers over these regions, especially their oil resources. Their success or failure will play a major role in the reconstruction of Iraq's economy and the reliable delivery of basic services such as electricity and clean water.

Other issues that will have to be resolved are the future of the northern city of Kirkuk, which the Kurds claim as part of their autonomous region but which Saddam had populated with Sunnis, and the weakness and corruption of the Iraqi government.

It is hoped that such questions will be resolved through negotiation and compromise. If the past is any indication, however, they will more likely be marked by bombings, shootings and assassinations.

"The fantasy is that everything is perfect by the end of the year, and we all live happily ever after," Cordesman said. "But I don't know why the hell we should regard it as a meaningful scenario."

Still, many of those who study the region, including foreign policy realists such as Mack and Cordesman, believe 2006 will see the beginning of a drawdown of U.S. forces in Iraq, if only to help beleaguered Republicans on Capitol Hill. It is too early to know how many troops might be leaving, but these experts all agree that many American soldiers will remain there to help keep together the war-battered country.

According to several military analysts, U.S. troops will be pulled back from the front lines and garrisoned in bases as Iraqi forces take over responsibility for most counterinsurgency operations. The Americans will be called up for special missions and border security.

Right now about 150,000 U.S. and coalition troops are in Iraq, with perhaps 50,000 well-trained Iraqis. Biden expects that "if all goes well, at this time next year we will have 50,000 to 80,000 troops in Iraq, and in two years 15,000 to 50,000, and in three years, zero to 15,000."

WORST-CASE SCENARIOS

In Iraq, however, things have seldom gone as planned, and conditions have generally grown worse. The outcome over the next year will depend partly on how U.S. forces are managed and the mission they receive. Kenneth M. Pollack, a former Middle East specialist at the CIA and the National Security Council, said forecasts such as Biden's are wishful thinking. If anything, he said, troop levels should be increased to as many 400,000 to cover the new government's back as it struggles to hold the country together.

Moreover, he said, the troops in Iraq are being misused. Instead of giving priority to counterinsurgency operations — a tactic that proved unsuccessful in Vietnam — Pollack said commanders should be using soldiers first to protect Iraqi civilians and enable the reconstruction of their cities and towns. Under the current strategy, which leaves the population centers unprotected, the United States cannot count on the loyalty of the Iraqi forces, no matter how well they are trained, he said.

"I have a lot of reservations about Iraqi forces," said Pollack, who is now a scholar at the Saban center for Middle East Policy at the Brookings Institution. He notes that most of the Iraqi forces are made up of men from the Kurdish Pesh Merga and Shiite Badr militias. "As long as Iraq moves in a good direction, Kurdish leaders will be glad to be in the Iraqi army. But they will pull back if they don't like it." The same goes for the Shiites, he said. "They are as effective as their masters want them to be."

"I expect there to be criticism, but when Democrats say that I deliberately misled the Congress and the people, that's irresponsible."

— President **Bush**

Thus the biggest danger facing Iraq's new government after the elections is the growing sectarian violence between Sunnis and Shiites. Pollack notes that the inability of Iraqi and American forces to halt this violence has created a downward spiral toward sectarianism. "The more people worry about their own security, the more they are drawn to the militias" to protect them, he said.

Moreover, they say, increasing communal violence between Sunnis and Shiites — including wholesale massacres of men by one religious group or the other — is outpacing the political milestones that Iraqis have achieved and straining the country to the breaking point.

At some point, say Middle East experts and lawmakers, the sectarian violence could simply push Iraq into full-blown civil war — the worst of all possibilities for Bush.

"I don't think civil war is a distant possibility," said Pollack, who recently returned from a visit to Iraq. "When I was there in 2003, it was a distant possibility. During this trip, people were talking about civil war as if it could happen this year. It is a much more present concern now."

Such a war would probably see the Shiite and Kurdish militias join forces to retaliate massively against the Sunnis, a development that could draw in Jordan, Saudi Arabia and other Sunni neighbors. Their intervention would probably prompt Iran to get involved on

the side of its Iraqi Shiite co-religionists. Meanwhile, any move by the Kurds toward greater autonomy would draw in the Turks, who worry that their own Kurdish population will want autonomy. As the conflict escalates, "the United States is perceived as not only having failed in Iraq, but having failed in the region," Cordesman said.

"If that's the case, all the king's men couldn't put Iraq together again," Biden said. "It may happen in eight months or in 18 months. But if the status quo continues and we don't get lucky, I don't know. . . ." His voice trailed off.

MUDDLING THROUGH

Between the administration's shimmering vision of a stable, fully democratic Iraq and the nightmare scenario of civil war, Middle East experts agree that the administration still has an opportunity to salvage the situation by speeding up the training of Iraqi troops and giving the country's new leaders the breathing room they need to peacefully resolve their sectarian differences.

Middle East expert Cordesman sees the United States "muddling through" in Iraq over the next year. "We won't have as successful an effort politically as we would like, but it won't be something that denies us hope or shows no progress," he said. "And the same will be true for the development of Iraqi forces, Iraqi secu-

themselves into the Iraq debate.

Increasingly, that scrutiny is coming from Republicans, who will be extra sensitive to the public mood on the war as the November 2006 elections draw closer. Inevitably, political experts say, such pressure will begin to erode Bush's position as commander in chief, forcing him to make critical choices on Iraq that could prove fateful. Lawmakers will test and debate each of those choices — a stark contrast to the wide latitude Congress has so far given Bush on the war.

"If he resists congressional and public pressure, maintains our forces, and the insurgency continues to fester, public support for the war will continue to go south," said Thomas E. Mann, a scholar of American presidents and politics at the Brookings Institution. "But if he pulls out the troops, the risk is that Iraq really will become a breeding ground for terrorists."

Mann and other experts believe that political imperatives will dictate a decision by Bush to begin withdrawing U.S. troops from Iraq before the midterm elections.

"He simply must to be able to show — or claim — that the Iraqis are standing up militarily, allowing us to begin to withdraw," Mann said. "Then he has to hope that the negative consequences from that don't manifest themselves before the midterms."

Calls for a quicker withdrawal only underscore how limited Bush's options are in Iraq. When Democratic Rep. John P. Murtha of Pennsylvania proposed an immediate withdrawal, it was widely regarded by both Republicans and Democrats as a path to disaster. But it nevertheless struck a chord that the president's current policy is not working and that the United States may need to lower its expectations.

Former ambassador Mack told the story of how, after a speech he gave on Iraq, a woman in the audience stood up and demanded to know how her son, a Marine officer serving in Iraq, could be expected to fight for such a diminished version of Iraq statehood — one, she pointed out, where women might not have the kinds of rights that U.S. officials had promised to ensure. He gave a frank answer.

"There are things that are absolutely necessary from a strategic point of view; there are things that are nice but would take a lot more resources that we can put in; and there are things that are totally unobtainable," said Mack.

"And I think we are at the point where we have to settle for what is absolutely necessary." ∎

rity and Iraqi governance. If you ask my opinion as to whether that will actually happen, I think the odds are at least even."

Right now, Cordesman said, citing Pentagon figures, 88 battalions of Iraqi army soldiers are deployed alongside U.S. troops, as well as another 26 battalions of Iraqi police. The Pentagon, however, will not specify to what level they have been trained. Cordesman assumes that their capabilities will improve over the next year, allowing some U.S. force reductions by mid-2006.

One of the reasons the U.S. military mission is having such difficulty standing up a new Iraqi army is that it has had to begin from scratch.

Because the original Iraqi army was disbanded, many of the soldiers found their way into the insurgency, said retired Lt. Col. Rick Francona, a former Air Force intelligence officer with extensive experience in Iraq. He said the U.S. decision to disband the Iraqi army after the invasion was disastrous. "Not only did we lose all that military expertise, we're fighting it," he said.

He also said the effort to build up Iraq's army is hobbled by the U.S. army's lack of interest in training Iraqi soldiers. The attitude in the U.S. military is that "the best and the brightest don't train," he said.

Muddling through in 2006 will also require administration initiatives on the diplomatic front. Biden and other lawmakers say the odds for success next year can be improved if the administration makes a greater effort to get other countries involved. Biden notes that European nations offered to "adopt" Iraqi ministries to help them get on their feet, but the Bush administration refused because the Europeans proposed carrying out their duties from their home countries.

"The administration should have accepted," Biden said. "It would have sucked them in" and given the Europeans a stake in Iraq's reconstruction.

Biden has also proposed a high-level regional security conference including all of Iraq's neighbors and Egypt, plus the United Nations, the European Union, NATO and the World Bank. Sen. Chuck Hagel of Nebraska, the second-ranking Republican on the Foreign Relations Committee, embraced the idea in a Nov. 15 speech to the Council on Foreign Relations in Washington, saying such cooperation "lessens the possibilities that further instability and violence in Iraq will spread like a raging inferno throughout the region."

The administration has not responded to the proposal, but it is indicative of the ways in which lawmakers are increasingly inserting

Bold, Sweeping Agenda: Not This Time
Bush defends war, wiretapping but ratchets down big plans

IN LAYING OUT THE AGENDA for the sixth year of his presidency, President Bush delivered a State of the Union address that lacked the bold proposals and soaring rhetorical vision that have marked his previous addresses to Congress, reflecting the reality of a humbled White House intent on finishing the job in Iraq while pursuing modest domestic plans.

Playing to his strengths, Bush was adamant about not retreating in the war against Iraq, gave a stern warning to Iran regarding its nuclear weapons programs, and offered a firm defense of his controversial wiretapping program. He was quick to assert his view of presidential power over foreign policy, spying and troop levels overseas. And he took on his Democratic critics of the war.

"Hindsight alone is not wisdom," the president said. "And second-guessing is not a strategy." *(2006 CQ Weekly, p. 352)*

But, after using the first half of his speech to reiterate familiar refrains about freedom, democracy and vigilance in the war on terrorism, Bush left Congress with a rather modest to-do list.

Notably chastened by last year's failure to get any movement on an overhaul of Social Security, the president simply called for a commission to study changes in entitlement programs. Realizing that Democrats and some Republicans have repeatedly blocked proposals to drill in the Arctic National Wildlife Refuge, Bush did not mention this proposal once. He gave only a mild swipe at the problem of corruption — even as debate over Jack Abramoff, lobbying and ethics rages in Washington — calling for leaders to be more honest. And he offered few new ideas for the struggling Gulf Coast as it rebuilds after Hurricane Katrina.

Bush did lay out a few initiatives for Republican congressional leaders to carry out, some of which will run into significant opposition from Democrats filled with ambition for the midterm elections and some of which have bipartisan support.

The boldest proposals were in the area of energy consumption, where he admitted the country was "addicted to oil." Bush pitched a slew of goals such as dramatically reducing

MODEST TO-DO LIST: Bush gives his fifth State of the Union address to a joint session of Congress on Jan. 31.

dependence on foreign oil while increasing funding for research into alternative fuels.

He also tried to lay the foundation for changing, but not overhauling, the U.S. health care system, proposing health savings accounts and medical liability legislation.

And he acknowledged the nation's declining competitiveness in the area of math and science, noting that economic giants China and India are catching up if not surpassing the American economy in some areas.

ELECTION YEAR CAUTION

The president called for the 2003 tax cuts to be made permanent, and warned that the 2001 anti-terrorism law known as the Patriot Act (PL 107-56) should not be allowed to expire. One of Bush's proud moments of the night was seeing Samuel A. Alito Jr., who had been confirmed by the Senate just hours earlier, sitting in his new black Supreme Court justice robe in the front row of the House chamber. *(2006 CQ Weekly, pp. 340 and 349)*

While giving Congress a modest wish list, Bush also chided lawmakers on spending, called for a crackdown on earmarks and asked for the line-item veto, a perennial proposal that was enacted during the administration of Bill Clin-

ton in 1996 but later struck down by the Supreme Court. *(1998 Almanac, p. 6-17)*

Republican lawmakers praised the address, but their enthusiasm was tempered by the realism that Congress could easily become gridlocked in an election year shadowed by scandals that have touched the White House and the former majority leader of the House, Tom DeLay of Texas.

"Partisan Democrats might try to criticize the president for not having a long list of new agenda items in his speech," Senate Finance Chairman Charles E. Grassley, R-Iowa, said in a statement. "Well, I'd rather see him focus on the most important issues over the course of his presidency than offer a laundry list of new initiatives."

Democrats bought very little of the speech, and their optimism heading toward November was summed up by their choice to give their formal response: Virginia Gov. Timothy Kaine, a Democrat who won the statehouse in a firmly "red" Republican state last fall.

"If we want to replace the division that's been gripping our nation's capital, we need a change," Kaine said in a televised address from the governor's mansion in Richmond. "Democrats are leading that reform effort,

Handicapping State of the Union Goals

President Bush devoted much of his State of the Union address Jan. 31 to foreign policy issues, defending the war in Iraq and the administration's handling of the war on terrorism. But he also gave Congress a list of election year legislative goals. Here are some of the things Bush requested and the outlook for them on Capitol Hill:

TOPIC	BUSH PROPOSAL	CONGRESSIONAL OUTLOOK
Health care	Bush called for an expansion of health savings accounts — created in 2003's Medicare drug law (PL 108-173) — by allowing premiums to be paid from the tax-free account by patients in high-deductible health plans. The aim is to reduce costs by encouraging patients to negotiate prices and comparison shop for medical services, eventually driving down prices throughout the system. He called for helping small businesses afford insurance through legislation that would make it easier for them to join together to increase bulk purchasing power by bypassing state coverage mandates. He also renewed his perennial call for an overhaul of the medical malpractice system.	Senate Majority Leader Bill Frist, R-Tenn., wants his chamber to consider Bush's health care proposals by April, but he faces significant obstacles. The House has passed a small business health insurance bill, but it has little support in the Senate. Democrats argue that tax incentives do little to help low-income Americans who either pay only a small amount of taxes or do not have the extra money to lock up in a health savings account. It is unlikely that stand-alone bills on some of the tax breaks could muster enough support in the Senate this year, so the most likely scenario would be to go through a budget reconciliation bill.
Energy	Bush proposed increasing alternative fuel research funding by 22 percent and increasing support for new fuel-efficient automobile technology. He said his initiative would address electricity demand through "zero emission" coal technology, wind and solar power and "clean" nuclear power. Automobile research would focus on batteries for hybrid and electric vehicles, hydrogen fuel cells and new methods of producing ethanol using wood chips and other plant materials rather than just corn.	Lawmakers expressed disappointment in Bush's proposals, saying they had already been addressed in the energy law (PL 109-58) enacted last year. Some said the president missed an opportunity to have a more immediate effect on oil and gas consumption by endorsing steps to reduce demand. But several Republicans said the president's initiative would lead Congress to appropriate more money for alternative energy.
Education/ Competitiveness	Bush wants to double funding for basic research in the physical sciences, train 70,000 teachers for advanced placement math and science high school courses and bring 30,000 private mathematicians and scientists to teach part-time.	Several bills, including one (S 2197) by Sen. Pete V. Domenici, R-N.M., already have been introduced that would address these proposals. But any such programs are likely to come with a fight over cost, and Democrats may oppose efforts to cut spending on other education programs as a way to fund these proposals.
Immigration	Bush said the country needs to have a "rational, humane guest-worker program that rejects amnesty, allows temporary jobs for people who seek them legally and reduces smuggling and crime at the border."	The House last year, ignoring the guest-worker issue, passed a bill (HR 4437) aimed at strengthening border security and interior enforcement, with new penalties for illegal immigrants and mandates for businesses to verify legal status of workers against federal databases. But the bill must pass the Senate, where several lawmakers advocate a more comprehensive fix that balances border security with a guest-worker program and policies that allow illegal immigrants to earn legal status.
Entitlements	Acknowledging that his Social Security proposal of 2005 was effectively dead on Capitol Hill, Bush proposed a joint bipartisan executive-congressional commission to study the sustainability of the three big entitlement programs — Social Security, Medicare and Medicaid.	Even if leaders do appoint members to such a commission, it's not likely that any significant changes would be decided during an election year.
Tax cuts	Bush again called on Congress to indefinitely extend his signature tax cuts enacted in 2001 and 2003.	While making those tax breaks permanent is not in the cards for Congress anytime soon, GOP leaders are trying to win final passage of a package of tax cut extenders this winter, and may force a vote this year on making permanent the scheduled estate tax repeal.

working to restore honesty and openness to our government, working to replace a culture of partisanship and cronyism with an ethic of service and results." *(2006 CQ Weekly, p. 357)*

ENERGY INITIATIVES

When Bush turned his attention to energy consumption, his comments seemed a long way from his early presidential image as a Texas oilman who believed drilling for more oil was a critical part of the solution.

Bush said that "the best way to break this addiction is through technology." He called for a 22 percent increase in clean-energy research at the Department of Energy, and investments in more low-emission plants, solar and wind technologies and safe nuclear energy. He promoted hybrid vehicles, proposed reducing dependence on Middle East oil by 75 percent by 2025 and called for research funding to produce ethanol from grass and other vegetation.

These are all initiatives that could be funded by Congress through the appropriations process, and have widespread support. Some of the proposals, however, are really just extensions of last year's energy law (PL 109-58) *(2006 CQ Weekly, p. 37; provisions, 2005 CQ Weekly, p. 2337)*

Pete V. Domenici, R-N.M., chairman of the Senate Energy and Natural Resources Committee, said the speech marked a "sharp departure" from previous addresses.

"Traditionalists may be disappointed that oil and gas weren't the centerpieces of his energy remarks, but the president is absolutely right to map out an expanded strategy in alternative energy," Domenici said in a statement. However, Domenici added that Bush's goal of reducing imports will also necessitate development of "our own abundant resources such as oil shale."

Moreover, early details of the president's fiscal 2007 budget request, to be released Feb. 6, showed that recommended spending on major parts of the plan is less than what was authorized in the energy law.

For example, the White House said it will recommend spending $150 million in fiscal 2007 on research aimed at making biofuels more competitive with oil — $59 million more than the current appropriation but about $50 million less than the energy bill authorizes.

Bush's proposals to spend $148 million next year on solar power research and $44 million on wind also represent increases over current spending but are less than the totals authorized in the energy bill, which called for $2.2 billion in total funding for clean-energy research

and development in fiscal years 2007-2009.

The administration also said it would propose $281 million in fiscal 2007 for low-emissions "clean coal" research and development and $54 million to build a prototype zero-emission coal-powered generating plant.

Bush will request $30 million to develop new batteries for hybrid vehicles and $289 million to make hydrogen-powered vehicles commercially viable by 2020, a goal set in his 2003 State of the Union speech.

HEALTH CARE

While the energy proposals may have some legs in Congress, Bush's health care ideas could face stiff opposition from Democrats and perhaps moderate Republicans.

He called for an expansion of Health Savings Accounts — created in the 2003 Medicare drug law (PL 108-173) — by allowing premiums to be paid from the tax-free account by patients in high-deductible health plans. The aim is to lower costs by encouraging patients to negotiate prices and comparison shop for medical services, eventually driving down prices throughout the system. *(Medicare law, 2003 Almanac, p. 11-3)*

Democrats are dead set against such an idea, arguing that tax incentives do little to help low-income Americans who either pay only a small amount of taxes in the first place or do not have the extra money to lock up in a health savings account. "A health savings account is great for someone who can save . . . but for 46 million Americans who are uninsured, this does nothing at all," said Senate Minority Leader Harry Reid of Nevada.

Bush also called for limiting medical liability, echoing a priority of Senate Majority Leader Bill Frist, R-Tenn., who plans to bring a malpractice overhaul to the floor this year. However, Frist's efforts to crack down on malpractice suits have fallen short in recent years, and Democrats in the Senate are unlikely to give the majority leader an easy victory on one of his top priorities. *(2004 Almanac, p. 12-12)*

ADDRESSING COMPETITIVENESS

Bush gave a nod to the power of the global economy and acknowledged the need for the United States to catch up in certain areas.

"In a dynamic world economy, we are seeing new competitors like China and India," Bush said. "And this creates uncertainty, which makes it easier to feed people's fears."

Bush proposed a new "American Competitiveness Initiative" and called on Congress to fund training for 70,000 high school teachers to lead instruction in advanced placement for

math and science. He also called for 30,000 math and science professionals to be brought into classrooms to teach.

"Preparing our nation to compete in the world is a goal that all of us can share," Bush said.

The education initiatives were among the few in the State of the Union Address that received significant bipartisan applause, suggesting that these proposals may make it out of Congress this year.

"I thought his education initiative putting more math and science teachers in the classroom was exactly the right thing to do," said Senate Minority Whip Richard J. Durbin, D-Ill.

In his fiscal 2007 budget request, Bush will seek $380 million to train teachers, research effective math curricula and lure people who work in math and science fields to schools to teach as an "adjunct teacher corps," according to a White House summary of the program.

And while Democrats may like the focus on education funding, they will probably fight the president's continued push to make a slew of tax cuts permanent. Republicans and Democrats in Congress remain divided over whether to extend tax cuts, but Bush insisted that "America needs more than a temporary expansion, we need more than temporary tax relief." *(Background, 2005 CQ Weekly, p. 788)*

Republicans are also likely to struggle with the other piece of Bush's "competitive" agenda — immigration. Bush again called for a "rational, human guest-worker program," but also called for stronger enforcement at the borders. Republicans, especially in the House, have been divided over the best way to approach an immigration overhaul. *(2006 CQ Weekly, p. 44)*

ON THE CUTTING ROOM FLOOR

The 2006 State of the Union address in some ways may also be remembered for what the president did not say.

Bush spent just two paragraphs on ethics, even though much of Washington is consumed by the Abramoff scandal, DeLay awaits a trial on money laundering charges and former Rep. Randy "Duke" Cunningham, R-Calif., is possibly headed to federal prison after pleading guilty to bribery charges late last year. *(2006 CQ Weekly, p. 174)*

"Honorable people in both parties are working on reforms to strengthen the ethical standards of Washington," Bush said. "I support your efforts."

That gave Democrats an opening to criticize what they persistently call a "culture of corruption" among Republicans.

Bush "spoke for 46 minutes before he finally dedicated less than 60 words to ethics reform," said Sen. Barack Obama of Illinois. "This isn't acceptable. We need a serious commitment to reform."

On a priority for social conservatives, especially in an election year, Bush avoided endorsing a constitutional amendment to ban gay marriage — something Frist and Rick Santorum, R-Pa., plan to bring to the Senate floor this year. Bush made only a passing mention of the topic, criticizing "activist courts that try to redefine marriage."

HURRICANE RELIEF

Democrats and Republicans from the Gulf Coast were also disappointed with the short shrift they believe Bush gave to one of the biggest disasters in American history: Hurricane Katrina. Bush proposed no new money or new programs, but highlighted ongoing efforts.

"I was very disappointed in how small a part it was of his speech," said Sen. David Vitter, R-La.

Rep. William J. Jefferson, D-La., who represents a large portion of New Orleans, believed Bush devoted "the most cursory treatment you could imagine" to his destroyed city. "I think some of our people are more bewildered after the speech than before it," Jefferson said.

Bush's administration was highly criticized last year for its initial response to the storm that devastated New Orleans and the Louisiana and Mississippi coastlines.

On Feb. 1, the Government Accountability Office (GAO) issued a preliminary report finding that a confused chain of command and a failure of leadership hindered the federal response to Hurricane Katrina. The findings were released at the behest of the House select panel investigating the Katrina response.

Neither Homeland Security Secretary Michael Chertoff nor any of his deputies served as a "focal point" of the response effort, said Comptroller General David M. Walker, head of the GAO, which conducted its study at the request of the select committee.

House Government Reform Chairman Thomas M. Davis III, R-Va., who also heads the select panel, said the findings were nothing that his investigators had not examined.

But Davis said the GAO review would help "amplify" the report due from his select panel Feb. 15 and tracks closely with what the committee has learned. ■

Precedent Heeded, But Not Revered

While respect for settled law is Topic A in nomination hearings, the high court has a history of reversing itself

AFTER A RECENT VISIT from Supreme Court nominee Samuel A. Alito Jr., Republican Sen. Susan Collins, a moderate from Maine, went before a battery of cameras and pronounced herself satisfied that he had "tremendous respect for precedent."

The subtext, of course, was the *Roe v. Wade* decision that guaranteed a woman's right to abortion 32 years ago. Since the first opening on the court last summer, the notion of "respect for precedent" has almost become code for whether a nominee would consider overturning the 1973 decision.

But this new insistence by lawmakers on a devotion to precedent and respect for the "settled law" established by court decisions — at least the ones they agree with — has also become something larger. Because Alito was chosen to replace centrist Justice Sandra Day O'Connor, he could help form a new conservative majority that also strikes down, or steers away from, precedents on affirmative action, separation of church and state and many other issues.

So now the phrase *stare decisis* — Latin for "to stand by that which is decided" — has entered the political lexicon of the day. Pennsylvania Republican Arlen Specter, chairman of the Senate Judiciary Committee, in hearings on the nomination of John G. Roberts Jr. for chief justice, talked about the importance of "super precedents," and then elevated the concept

even more by referring to something called "super duper precedents."

And the interest in stare decisis will almost certainly continue to be a central theme when the debate over Alito heats up again this January.

But for all the discussion of settled law, the justices overturn, narrow and ignore their own precedents more often than the public debate suggests, particularly after significant changes in the court's lineup.

"In spite of what Judge Alito says, the fact that he's joining the court along with Chief Justice Roberts means we're likely to see reconsideration of precedents across the board," said David M. O'Brien, a University of Virginia government professor.

HOW SETTLED IS SETTLED?

This undoing of precedent generally happens either directly or through steady erosion. The court may expressly overturn one or more of its own decisions in the course of deciding a case. Or it may technically leave a precedent standing, but chip away at or even destroy it in subsequent decisions.

Justices do not void precedents on a whim. They subscribe to the doctrine of stare decisis to promote continuity and stability in federal law and to give state judges and lower federal court judges guideposts for deciding subsequent cases.

"In most matters it is more important that the applicable rule of law be settled than it be

settled right," Justice Louis D. Brandeis wrote in a 1932 dissent that has been quoted in subsequent decisions.

The justices have always been willing to strike down precedents, though, when a new majority feels that a case was either improperly decided or overtaken by societal changes.

In a 1991 case, *Payne v. Tennessee*, Chief Justice William H. Rehnquist wrote an opinion that struck down two precedents from 1987 and 1989 on the admissibility of "victim impact statements" at sentencing hearings for capital crimes, and of prosecutors' statements about a crime victim's personal qualities.

Rehnquist had dissented from both of the earlier cases, which had held that such evidence and statements were not admissible. He was finally able to assemble a majority for his reasoning after two justices retired.

"We are now of the view" that states can allow juries to consider such evidence, Rehnquist wrote. As far as the two precedents were concerned, Rehnquist wrote, "they were wrongly decided and should be, and now are, overruled."

Rehnquist said that while precedents should be closely followed in property and contract rights cases in the interest of stability in those areas of the law, prior decisions did not deserve the same deference in cases that decided what sort of evidence is admissible at trial. "Stare decisis is not an inexorable command," Rehnquist wrote.

Justice Thurgood Marshall wrote a dissent in the case that castigated the abrupt shift. "Neither the law nor the facts supporting [the two precedents] underwent any change in the last four years," Marshall wrote. "Only the personnel of this court did."

HOLLOWING OUT

Besides overturning precedents outright, the Supreme Court can eviscerate them with subsequent rulings that hollow out their legal underpinnings without expressly overturning the old cases.

In 1896, the court famously ruled in *Plessy v. Ferguson* that separate but equal accommodations on railway cars were constitutional. That rationale was later applied by segregationist governments in defense of separate school systems for blacks and whites.

Several education discrimination cases in the first half of the 20th century rejected the constitutionality of segregated law schools and graduate schools without striking down *Plessy*.

Finally, the court ruled 9-0 in *Brown v. Board of Education* in 1954 that the separate but equal doctrine "has no place" in public education.

Writing for a unanimous court, Chief Justice Earl Warren said the *Plessy* doctrine had to be considered in light of the fact that public education had since become pervasive and compulsory in American society.

"We cannot turn the clock back . . . to 1896, when *Plessy v. Ferguson* was written," wrote Warren for a unanimous court. Although *Brown* did not overturn *Plessy* outright, it effectively voided the 19th-century segregation precedent. In a later case, the court cited *Brown* in rejecting segregation in public transit.

"*Brown* did not explicitly overrule *Plessy* . . . but *Brown* nonetheless clearly left *Plessy* for dead," said David J. Garrow, a Supreme Court historian at Cambridge University.

CHIPPING AWAY

For all of the debate about overturning the court's 1973 decision in *Roe*, it appears more likely to fall victim to attrition than to an out-

Perishable Precedent

Just as the Supreme Court can reverse itself, Congress can use legislation to attempt to overturn court decisions it disagrees with. On occasion, it takes more than one attempt. The Supreme Court and Congress engaged in a 15-year tug-of-war, for example, over the extent to which states could infringe on religious practices.

1990: The Supreme Court ruled in *Employment Division, Department of Human Resources of Oregon v. Smith* that Oregon could ban peyote, a hallucinogenic drug made from a cactus, even though it was used by some American Indians in religious ceremonies. A 6-3 majority, in upholding an Oregon law, agreed that religion could not be used as an excuse for violating an otherwise valid law.

1993: Partly in response to lobbying efforts by religious groups that criticized the court for harming the free exercise of religion, Congress passed the Religious Freedom Restoration Act (PL 103-141), which had the effect of reversing the 1990 decision. The law restored an earlier standard that said state laws restricting religion had to serve a "compelling" government interest that posed the least possible burden on religious freedom. Congress claimed authority to act under the 14th Amendment, which granted it broad power to enforce civil rights through legislation.

1997: The Supreme Court, in *City of Boerne v. Flores*, invalidated the 1993 law. The ruling held that Congress exceeded its constitutional authority to regulate state activity and that the broad authority granted to Congress by the 14th Amendment applied only to civil rights, which are distinct from the right to free exercise set out in the First Amendment.

2000: In response to the *Flores* case, Congress passed narrower legislation (PL 106-274) that made it harder for local governments to enforce zoning or other land-use regulations against religious groups and required governments to allow those institutionalized in state facilities to practice their faith according to the "compelling" government interest standard. Drafters of the law aimed to get around the Supreme Court's ruling by applying it only to organizations that received federal money or when a conflict over religious practices was linked to interstate commerce.

2005: The Supreme Court unanimously upheld the 2000 law in *Cutter v. Wilkinson*. Ohio had challenged the law's constitutionality, saying it promoted an establishment of religion because it encouraged prison inmates to become religious to secure certain benefits.

right overruling. For much of the past decade, abortion rights activists have said abortion opponents have used the "chipping away" strategy to undermine the precedent.

O'Connor and Justices Anthony M. Kennedy and David H. Souter co-wrote the court's opinion in a 1992 case, *Planned Parenthood of Southeastern Pa. v. Casey*, that reaffirmed the "essential holding" of *Roe* against the wishes of Rehnquist and Justices Byron R. White, Antonin Scalia and Clarence Thomas, who wanted to overturn what was then a 19-year-old ruling. "Liberty finds no refuge in a jurisprudence of doubt," O'Connor and her allies wrote.

But the trio abandoned the graduated

trimester-based system of permissible government regulation established in *Roe*. Instead, states could regulate abortions performed before fetal viability as long as they did not create an "undue burden" on the woman. Justice Harry Blackmun, the author of *Roe*, wrote a lengthy dissent in *Casey*, clearly worried that *Casey* was a step toward overturning *Roe*.

"I am 83 years old," Blackmun wrote. "I cannot remain on this court forever, and when I do step down, the confirmation process for my successor well may focus on the issue before us today."

Blackmun proved prescient. Abortion has been one of the main issues in every Supreme Court nomination of the past 20 years. Senators who favor abortion rights are watching for any sign that Alito would vote with Scalia, Thomas and perhaps Roberts to overturn *Roe*.

But even if he doesn't go that far, Alito could help weaken *Roe* further in future cases. On Nov. 30, the justices will hear arguments in *Ayotte v. Planned Parenthood of Northern New England* to test the constitutionality of New Hampshire's parental notification law.

The current court could easily split down the middle, as the Rehnquist court often did, with O'Connor the fifth and deciding vote for a 5-4 majority. If it did, the justices could decide to postpone a final decision in the case until after O'Connor's replacement arrived.

As early as next year, the high court could hear a challenge to a 2003 federal law banning the late-term procedure that opponents call "partial birth" abortion.

Given what is at stake, Alito's devotion to stare decisis will probably play a starring role in his January hearing. But his answers about whether he would try to overturn or weaken past opinions are not likely to shed much light on what kind of justice he would be, experts say.

Said Erwin Chemerinsky, a Duke University law professor: "I think it's very difficult to get a sense of a nominee's views about precedent in a way that tells anything useful." ■

A Risky Strategy For Judging Judges

Democrats, by sowing the wind with ideological opposition to Alito, risk reaping the whirlwind

As THIS MONTH'S Supreme Court confirmation hearings wound down, Harvard Law professor and liberal gray eminence Laurence H. Tribe was once again at the Senate Judiciary Committee witness table to criticize the nominee's judicial philosophy.

Tribe hewed to the argument, which he first laid out in 1985, that senators should evaluate potential justices on their judicial philosophies and political views — not mainly on their qualifications and temperament, as was customary at the time. The Senate Democratic leadership soon embraced the concept and has applied it in opposing five of the subsequent seven nominees put forward by Republican presidents — including the current one, Samuel A. Alito Jr.

"There is every reason to expect that he would live up to the expectations that the president and the president's ideological base have for him," Tribe said of Alito, whose views have been articulated during 15 years as a federal appeals court judge.

And all of the panel's Democrats, followed by a solid majority of Democrats on the Senate floor, are expected to take Tribe's advice and vote against Alito on the basis of his conservatism. He seems certain to be confirmed anyway, because almost all of the majority Republicans have concluded Alito's conservatism suits them fine.

Unfortunately for Tribe and his liberal allies, their tactical victory a generation ago in changing the shape of the judicial war's battlefield is now shaping up as a long-term strategic blunder. By citing their ideological differences in voting in large numbers against both Alito and Chief Justice John G. Roberts Jr., Democrats have opened the door to Republicans some day opposing a Democratic president's nominees for no other reason than their perceived liberalism.

The debates on all three of President Bush's nominees — Alito, Roberts and White House counsel Harriet Miers, who foundered because she lacked sufficient conservative bona fides for many Republicans — have made clear that judicial philosophy is now the most important factor for most senators in evaluating aspirants.

MAJORITY RULES

But the Republicans who sank Miers last fall, like the Democrats who engineered the rejection of Robert H. Bork in 1987, had an overriding advantage: They were in the majority. So Democrats who want to block GOP nominees on ideological grounds — or get their sort on the court — are beginning to face the reality that they'd do better spending less time berating nominees and more time figuring out how to win more Senate seats and recapturing the White House.

"Democrats will have to face the fact that at some point in the future the tables will be turned and some of the tactics may actually come back to haunt them," said Richard Davis, a Brigham Young University political science professor and author of "Electing Justice."

The new focus on ideology means that judicial confirmations are increasingly becoming a numbers game, no different than any piece of legislation.

The majority has the power to kill a bill by never putting it on a committee's agenda and the ability to scuttle a judicial nominee the same way. The Senate GOP exercised that prerogative to stop about two dozen of President Bill Clinton's picks for the circuit courts of appeal. That is a less public method of combating a president's efforts to shape the judiciary than a vote on the Senate floor, and it can be justified with the argument that the nominee lacked majority support.

Beyond that, most senators in the majority stand willing to use procedural maneuvers to overcome a judicial filibuster by the minority. Such a move by the Democrats against Alito, now all-but-officially abandoned, would have put last spring's carefully negotiated agreement about the use of the filibuster to a hard test and increased the partisan tone of the process.

Finally, the party in control of the Senate can force its own president to withdraw a nominee, as happened with Miers last fall. While that option might be used sparingly, it is a high hole card for the most ideologically committed senators to hold.

"We're in a stage now where we're going to get party-line votes," predicted Davis. "The minority party will vote against the president's choice merely because he or she represents the president's choice." He predicted an end to the days of lopsided votes for Supreme Court nominees as presidents focus on building the minimum coalition necessary to win confirmation by asking, "How many votes do I need, and how close to my views will this person be to get that."

The process may well reach the point where senators such as Nebraska's Ben Nelson — who said the intelligence and résumés of both Alito and Roberts were sufficient to win his party-line-crossing endorsement — become relics. Nelson was among 13 Democrats representing states that Bush carried in 2004 who voted for Roberts. Just three in that group opposed him.

SIGN OF THE TIMES

That is a marked change from the 1980s, and 1990s, when nominees as conservative as Antonin Scalia and as liberal as Ruth Bader Ginsburg won confirmation almost unanimously.

Democrats say the comparison is inexact, arguing that Clinton sought advice from Senate Republicans before nominating Ginsburg, former counsel to the American Civil Liberties Union, and that she is closer to the political center than either Alito or Roberts. But the contrast is nonetheless stark.

Roberts, whose professional qualifications were unquestioned and performance before the Judiciary Committee flawless, was supported by precisely half of the Senate's 44 Democrats. Far fewer are likely to vote for Alito, as signaled by three Roberts supporters who announced their opposition: Max Baucus of Montana, Ken Salazar of Colorado and Patrick J. Leahy of Vermont, the top Democrat on Judiciary.

The implications for a future Democratic president facing a GOP Senate are clear. "The Republicans will say that Democrats did this to a highly qualified conservative; we'll do this to a highly qualified extreme liberal," said Jeffrey A. Segal, a political science professor at Stony Brook University in New York and co-author of "Advice and Consent: The Politics of Judicial Appointments."

Republican senators have noted the contrast and already issued what amounts to thinly veiled threats.

Lindsey Graham of South Carolina told Alito during his hearing that if Ginsburg "were here today and a Democratic president had nominated her and we take on the role that our colleagues are playing against you, not only would she not have gotten 96 votes, I think she would have been in for a very rough experience."

The current emphasis on judicial philosophy is not altogether without precedent.

As Tribe pointed out in the 1985 book, "God Save this Honorable Court," that helped spur the Democrats' tactical shift, the views held by Supreme Court nominees or the presidents who tapped them have influenced the Senate for as long as the republic has existed.

George Washington's nomination of John Rutledge for chief justice in 1795 foundered in part because of Rutledge's opposition to the Jay Treaty with Great Britain. More recently, the likely impact of adding Lyndon B. Johnson's nominees Thurgood Marshall and Abe Fortas to the liberal Warren Court left conservatives unsettled, though they couched their opposition in terms of cronyism and inexperience.

But concerns about nominees' judicial phi-

Confirmation and Partisanship

For two decades, both parties have moved to block appellate court nominees based on their ideology. Democrats have gone a step further, voting in sizable numbers against three GOP Supreme Court nominees on largely philosophical grounds, while Republicans overwhelmingly supported President Bill Clinton's two high court selections.

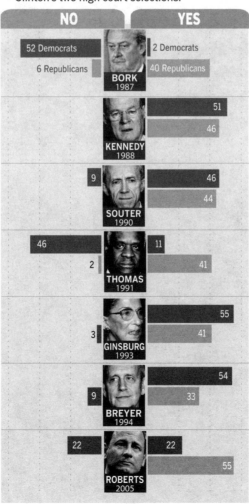

NO	YES
52 Democrats	2 Democrats
6 Republicans	40 Republicans
BORK 1987	
	51
	46
KENNEDY 1988	
9	46
	44
SOUTER 1990	
46	11
2	41
THOMAS 1991	
	55
3	41
GINSBURG 1993	
	54
9	33
BREYER 1994	
22	22
	55
ROBERTS 2005	

losophy have grown in both parties in recent decades as the courts have become the forum for deciding contentious social issues ranging from segregation to abortion and gay marriage.

And, despite the customary disclaimer from nominees that they will always have open minds, empirical research suggests that a candidate's judicial philosophy is a good predictor of how he will vote in any given case. As the latest evidence, liberal activists pointed to the 6-3 Supreme Court decision that Attorney General John Ashcroft did not have authority under a federal drug law in 2001 to thwart Oregon's legalization of physician-assisted suicide. Dissenting were Roberts and conservative bulwarks Scalia and Clarence Thomas.

So interest groups of all persuasion have come to see a seat on the court as an enormous prize and put pressure on their Senate allies to toe their party line. But not until Bork's nomination did judicial philosophy become the central focus of the battle. Democrats spent lavishly and mounted an election campaign-style crusade against Bork, a former Yale Law School professor with six years as a federal appellate judge. They spotlighted his originalist judicial philosophy, citing a long record filled with controversial academic and judicial writings that they worked hard to market to the public as out of the mainstream. Opponents also benefited from the nominee's arrogant manner and, perhaps most important, their party's Senate majority at the time.

That proved to be the high-water mark for the Democratic efforts to derail conservative nominees. But the right learned its lesson. As this year's trio of nominations showed, both sides now stand ready with equally large war chests for commercials and grass-roots organizing, as well as armies of legal experts and bloggers ready to offer their views of a nominee's record.

The fates of Bush's picks signal that partisan control of the Senate remains the biggest factor in determining whether a focus on judicial philosophy succeeds. Conservatives — concerned about Miers' views and her lack of standing in the conservative legal community that has blossomed since the 1980s — successfully pressured the president to withdraw her nomination before hearings began. By contrast, Democrats consigned to the minority had no such luck defeating Roberts and are on their way to losing on Alito, despite their misgivings.

"This is not a strategy that's ever worked from a minority position," said Segal, who argues Democrats are actually worse off for their opposition to Alito and Roberts on philosophical grounds. "It's failing miserably. You put up a fight and lose, you're worse off than if you never put up a fight. Republicans didn't look bad for agreeing with Ginsburg. They were able to take the high ground."

Democrats and their liberal allies are unapologetic. "The Senate is not fulfilling its constitutional obligations if it does not take judicial philosophy into account, most especially at a time when the president has elevated judicial philosophy as one of the most important criteria for the selection of a nominee," said Marcia Greenberger, co-president of the National Women's Law Center, a liberal legal advocacy group.

Democrat Charles E. Schumer of New York, the most vocal Senate advocate for focusing on judicial philosophy, said that he still believes "ideology is the best criteria" for judging justices. "That's the reason you want people on the court," said Schumer, who added that the Alito and Roberts nominations "vindicated" his focus on judicial philosophy.

Yet Schumer may have less impact on the composition of the court as a member of the Judiciary panel than in his capacity as chairman of the Democratic Senatorial Campaign Committee, which is charged with winning the six seats needed for Democrats to retake the majority. That explains why Schumer spent more time chiding Republicans about the growing lobbying corruption scandal than on the Alito nomination.

'CRYING WOLF EFFECT'

If they don't take over the Senate, Democrats and their liberal allies intent on attacking a nominee's judicial philosophy appear to need some new arguments. After a quarter-century warning that every Republican nominee — from Sandra Day O'Connor and David H. Souter to Alito — would spell the fall of the court's 1973 *Roe v. Wade* ruling that established a right to abortion, the American public may be tuning out the alarm.

"You get a 'crying wolf' effect that people aren't going to believe you when you say that Roe is under serious threat and say it over and over again," said Keith Whittington, a visiting professor of law at the University of Texas.

But the dilemma is that few other issues resonate as widely with the public, as Democrats found this year. Their attempts to talk about Roberts' potential threat to the regulatory state under the Constitution's Commerce Clause fell flat, as did their run at Alito's record in favor of a strong executive — even at a time when the president's unilateral authorization of domestic spying was in the headlines.

The left's best hope of winning the judicial war and jarring an indifferent public might be what they fear the most: the success of a more conservative court.

Alito and Roberts could steer the court in a more conservative direction and scale back affirmative action or abortion rights more than the public favors. Democrats could then use those votes to argue the court has skewed just as far out of the mainstream as conservatives complain the Warren Court did in the 1960s. And those Supreme Court rulings might then become useful ammunition in presidential and congressional elections.

"The bottom line is they need to win more elections," said Stefanie Lindquist, a Vanderbilt University law professor. "They are in a position where their failure to win elections has resulted in the loss of important Supreme Court seats. This is a consequence of that." ■

Politics and Public Policy

This section focuses on political issues that directly affect the everyday lives of the American people. The articles examine the potential for obesity litigation in the "food court," the port security controversy, and the arguments for and against medical savings accounts, as well as immigration and tax code reform.

Medical studies have revealed an alarming increase in obesity among Americans in the last quarter century, and the health care costs associated with this dramatic national weight gain are rising rapidly. Some nutrition experts and consumer advocates point to deceptive marketing practices in the food, beverage, and restaurant industry and plan to file consumer protection lawsuits similar to those that led to blockbuster settlements between big tobacco companies and a number of states. The first article in this section looks at how the food industry is gearing up for a possible protracted legal battle by framing the fundamental issue as a matter of personal choice.

The recent debate over foreign ownership of U.S. port facilities served as a reminder that security fears are an ever-present feature of post-9/11 America. Opposition to the Dubai Ports World deal was cast as legitimate concern over security or as racism. The second article argues that the controversy over foreign investment just scratches the surface of a complex set of issues in an interconnected global economy.

On the domestic front, President Bush, congressional Republicans, and big business are seeking to gain control over spiraling health care costs by encouraging private, market-based approaches. The third article explores the possibility of allowing consumers to comparison shop for medical services as they do for goods and services. Some health care experts worry that such programs will primarily benefit those who are well off, leaving those most in need with inadequate coverage. Others argue that escalating costs will force companies to drop many workers' and retirees' coverage, leaving even more people uninsured and saddling the government with the bill, thus making a "consumer-driven" plan a potential solution to making health care more affordable.

The debate over immigration reform has caused a growing rift in the Republican Party and inspired thousands of Hispanic Americans as well as illegal immigrants to march in protest over attempts to make illegal entry into the United States a felony. Although the American public generally supports legislation to curb illegal immigration, it is uncomfortable with the idea of building a wall between the United States and Mexico. The fourth article examines the positions of the key political players in this debate.

The last article in this section explores how attempts to overhaul the tax code are politically dangerous for elected officials—every loophole in the code seems to have its entrenched defenders. Although it is notoriously complicated, the tax code provides numerous deductions, the loss of which could cause the kind of fallout that politicians caught up in reelection campaigns can scarcely afford.

Obesity on the Docket

Industry is bracing for a tough battle in the 'food court' as the rising cost of obesity has states looking for relief in litigation

FOOD FIGHTER: Schwartz, who recently testified before the Senate Judiciary Committee, is at the forefront of the industry's legal defense.

WHEN THE influential Washington lawyer Victor Schwartz invites business associates to lunch, he occasionally steers them to a Subway sandwich shop near his 14th Street office, where the ascetically thin 65-year-old can select from the chain's menu of low-fat items. Schwartz always makes sure to tell his dining partners that he doesn't expect them to mimic his healthful habits. "They have a meatball sub with cheese on the menu. People have a right to eat it," he explains.

It's an observation Schwartz is likely to repeat again and again in the coming months. As one of the nation's leading experts on product liability law and an adviser to the National Restaurant Association, Schwartz is helping choreograph the defense in a coming legal showdown over how fast food, snacks and sodas are sold to the public — a high-stakes fight that bears a resemblance to the battle over tobacco in the 1990s.

Consumer advocates and nutrition experts have sent notices to several of the nation's largest food companies that they intend to file consumer protection lawsuits charging the companies with deceiving the public by selling nutritionally worthless products and making consumers vulnerable to obesity-related illnesses. The groups, led by the Washington-based Center for Science in the Public Interest (CSPI), are getting help from trial lawyers who were involved in the 1998 legal settlement between states and tobacco companies, and who think they can employ some of the same strategies against the food, beverage and restaurant industry, whose annual sales approach $900 billion.

The companies are taking the threat seriously enough to have engaged in preliminary talks about curbing some of their marketing practices. But industry executives suspect that plaintiffs' attorneys will press forward with the suits, intent on using the ensuing publicity to spur copycat actions in other states and, possibly, inspire attorneys general to sue to recover the costs of treating diabetes, high blood pres-

sure and other conditions linked to being overweight. For that reason the industry is depending on strategists such as Schwartz to fight the litigation — they call it the "food court" — with a legal, legislative and public relations campaign built around the notion that eating is one way people exercise their free will.

Foremost among the executives' fears is that a judge will allow one of the cases to go forward and give attorneys access to documents revealing marketing strategies and other internal deliberations. Company officials worry about the damage that could be done by the disclosure of a seemingly routine memo on how to depict the nutritional content of a fast-food product or, say, an e-mail assessing how many more families would visit a fast-food establishment with an adjoining playground. They expect that such a revelation would touch off a tempest in which the information would be used to portray companies as manipulative profit seekers.

The cases have an added emotional component because they concern the marketing of food and beverages to children. And they play into mounting public awareness about the health concerns linked to obesity, which Surgeon General Richard H. Carmona, in making the case for changed eating habits, equated recently with the threat of terrorism.

In one case, CSPI is threatening to sue Kellogg Co. and Viacom Inc. (owner of the popular Nickelodeon cable channel for children) to halt the marketing of high-calorie or high-sugar food to children under the age of 8, seeking damages that plaintiffs estimate could exceed $1 billion. A second expected suit brought by a group of public interest lawyers against Coca-Cola Co.,

PepsiCo Inc. and their bottlers would seek to halt sales of sugar-laden sodas in schools. Lawyers expect to file both cases in Massachusetts, where there are fewer legal hurdles to bringing mass tort cases and where the law does not require that a plaintiff be harmed by the alleged deceptive conduct.

It was almost inevitable that the fight over fat would be decided in court. Congress and presidential administrations have been reluctant to wade very deeply into what constitutes healthful eating or set guidelines for selling food, caught between competing impulses to protect commercial speech and care for the welfare of children. But the prevalence of obesity is beginning to factor into other policy debates. The cost of treating obese and overweight individuals is increasingly cited in discussions on how to control health spending and insure the population. A number of states, confronted with soaring Medicaid costs, have set nutritional guidelines and passed laws governing the sale of food in schools, citing a compelling public interest in promoting good health. (*Gov. Mike Huckabee, p. 90*)

A TASTE FOR TORT

With his legal chops and Beltway connections, the garrulous Schwartz is ideally positioned to influence the debate. A former law school dean and veteran of the Ford and Carter administrations, he led efforts in the late 1970s to establish federal standards for product liability suits and is co-author of a widely used law school textbook on tort law. He's also a fixture on Capitol Hill, where he testifies on behalf of such groups as the U.S. Chamber of Commerce and American Tort Reform Association and can swap stories with senators about their law school professors. Despite railing against media-savvy plaintiffs' lawyers, Schwartz also knows how to play to the crowd, frequently breaking into unsolicited and devastatingly accurate impersonations of Senate Judiciary Chairman Arlen Specter and former President Bill Clinton.

Though Schwartz specifically speaks for chain restaurants and smaller, independent establishments, he serves as the public face for a loose-knit coalition of grocers, beverage companies, food processors, agricultural interests

LUNCH FROM A MACHINE: As part of their campaign, nutrition advocates have convinced some states to prohibit snack and soda vending machines in schools.

and libertarian academics that is coalescing in response to the suits.

"The vast majority of American people think this stuff is ridiculous and that it doesn't belong in court," he said. "Lawsuits send the absolute wrong signal to people who are obese. But the lawyers behind this are like Alexander the Great: they need new worlds to conquer."

The timing of the threatened suits is no accident. Academic and government studies have documented America's weight gain in increasing detail. The Centers for Disease Control and Prevention (CDC) says the incidence of obesity among Americans has doubled in the last quarter century and tripled among teens. (Obesity is defined as having a body mass index over 30; the measurement is derived by dividing one's weight in kilograms by height in meters.) A government study found that immigrants tend to arrive in the country in a better state of health than their American counterparts, only to grow fatter and less fit the longer they stay.

The focus on how food is marketed was sharpened in December, when the Institute of Medicine, a division of the National Academy of Sciences, issued a report finding that 80 percent to 97 percent of the food products targeted at children and teens are of "poor nutri-

tional quality." It added that food advertising aimed at children changes their dietary preferences. The institute urged companies to promote products that are lower in salt, fat and sugar and higher in nutrients.

Yet despite a growing body of evidence that Americans are packing on pounds and growing unhealthy, many legal experts predict that it will be difficult to demonize Big Macs, corn chips and chocolate bars. None of the items pose the kind of deadly health risks that tobacco does. Americans, moreover, like to eat, regard many food products in a positive light, and tend to display more brand loyalty to them than to other consumer products.

Perhaps more important, the majority of the public views eating as a personal choice, and Americans, polls show, are not sympathetic to the individuals who overindulge nor to the "fat suits" lawyers bring on their behalf. Food companies additionally argue that obesity is a complicated condition, influenced not just by diet but by how physically active a person is, as well as genetics and environment. For that reason, it is difficult to link being fat to a single cause, such as eating at a particular restaurant.

One of Schwartz's goals is to reinforce in the public's mind that obesity is a preventable condition, not a disease. Categorizing obesity as a

clinical malady would, in many people's view, remove the element of personal responsibility from the debate and automatically confer the status of medical victim, increasing the chances the person could recover damages.

"Look, if I choose to skydive or drink too much, that's a choice," he said. "I really think some plaintiffs' lawyers are embarrassed by this because they see the day when they'll sue restaurants just because their clients got fat."

A factor that could influence this argument is whether food is somehow addictive, as tobacco was found to be. No evidence is known to exist, but a recent report in the Chicago Tribune that Kraft Foods Inc. and its then-parent, Philip Morris USA, collaborated from the 1980s to 2001 on making more alluring foods and cigarettes have plaintiffs' attorneys suspicious. They want to know the extent to which the taste or content of snacks or beverages was manipulated in company labs to influence consumers' sense of satisfaction. Kraft, which along with Philip Morris is now part of Altria Group Inc., says it doesn't conduct or fund research aimed at creating dependency on any of its products or limiting consumers' ability to control their eating habits. The exchange of information is routine among corporate affiliates, it says.

Schwartz is also portraying his antagonists as

meddlesome opportunists who are trying to impose their tastes on the rest of the country — and get huge monetary settlements in the process. He and other industry defenders contend that the suits abuse the legal system by trying to force judges to set broad public policies.

"When lawsuits against tobacco companies were getting started, we viewed it as just the tip of the iceberg. We knew trial lawyers would keep going from industry to industry until they get more traction," said Matthew Webb, vice president of legal reform policy at the U.S. Chamber of Commerce.

As Schwartz and groups such as the Chamber lay out their case, other industry defenders are firing broadsides at their attackers. One visible player is the Center for Consumer Freedom, a nonprofit Washington think tank established in 1995 with funding from Philip Morris and still supported by food and beverage companies. The center takes on groups such as the CSPI and other populist crusaders such as People for the Ethical Treatment of Animals, and calls into question health studies on obesity, including one the CDC issued in 2004 that found that obesity is associated with 400,000 premature deaths annually in the United States. The agency later significantly revised its estimates downward, to about 26,000 deaths.

BIG GUNS FROM TOBACCO WAR

Food companies have come under legal attack in the past. However, most successful cases involved instances of negligence or deliberate misrepresentation. For example, McDonald's Corp. in 2002 paid $10 million to settle a suit brought by vegetarian groups after it was disclosed that the company enhanced the flavor of its french fries by cooking them with beef tallow, despite representations that it was using pure vegetable oil. In another more notorious case, the Jack in the Box chain was found liable in 1993 for undercooking hamburgers containing a strain of *E. coli* that killed four children and sickened another 700 people.

Overweight individuals on several occasions have sued fast-food chains, claiming that the companies did not alert them of the risks of eating fast food. The best-known case was filed in 2002 by a group of obese New York City teenagers and their parents, alleging that fast food consumed at McDonald's made them vulnerable to diabetes, cardiovascular disease and other health problems. The complaint was dismissed by a federal court judge in 2003 but part of the case was reinstated in January 2005 when the 2nd Circuit Court of Appeals ruled that the presiding judge misinterpreted the

state's consumer protection law. The ruling leaves open the possibility that lawsuits alleging misrepresentation can go forward, even if plaintiffs do not prove a direct connection between the misrepresentation and the alleged harm.

The suits threatened in Massachusetts go in a similar direction by focusing on the way food is sold. Echoing arguments used in the tobacco litigation and in suits involving lead-based paint and asbestos, attorneys contend that the food and beverages in question are a "public nuisance" — essentially a harmful substance that endangers public welfare — and that buying the products automatically subjects the purchaser to inherent health risks.

The focus on marketing to children under the age of 8 adds an extra twist to the arguments. The CSPI contends that young children who watch advertising on television don't recognize the messages as ads and are being manipulated into consuming unhealthful products. The products' appeal is enhanced by companies' widespread licensing of popular cartoon characters, as is the case with Kraft Macaroni and Cheese in SpongeBob Square Pants, Rugrats or Scooby Doo varieties, or Nabisco Dora the Explorer cookies and snacks.

Similarly, lawyers behind the suit against the beverage companies and their bottlers are expected to make the case that students in schools are captive consumers, and that the bright signage on soda machines is an inescapable lure.

Companies could face staggering penalties if plaintiffs prevail. Violations of the Massachusetts consumer protection act brings penalties of $25 per incident, meaning a fine every time a child under 8 is exposed to advertising for a product the suit contends is unhealthful. What is more, the Massachusetts Supreme Judicial Court has ruled that cases can proceed even when plaintiffs can't demonstrate that they were actually harmed by a deceptive practice.

John F. Banzhaf III, a George Washington University law professor involved with the suit and veteran legal activist who in the 1960s began the crusade to end tobacco advertising on television, says the case illustrates a fundamental truth about the marketing of food: consumers can't make informed choices if they don't know what is healthful and unhealthful.

"The food industry says it's about personal responsibility, but it's also about corporate responsibility," Banzhaf said. "A lot of people think Chicken McNuggets are healthier than

Companies' Big Helping for Advertising

With great profit comes great amounts of marketing. Many food companies spend in excess of 15 percent of total sales on advertising, much of it targeted at children.

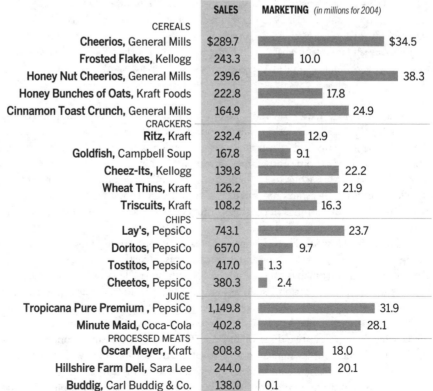

	SALES	MARKETING *(in millions for 2004)*
CEREALS		
Cheerios, General Mills	$289.7	$34.5
Frosted Flakes, Kellogg	243.3	10.0
Honey Nut Cheerios, General Mills	239.6	38.3
Honey Bunches of Oats, Kraft Foods	222.8	17.8
Cinnamon Toast Crunch, General Mills	164.9	24.9
CRACKERS		
Ritz, Kraft	232.4	12.9
Goldfish, Campbell Soup	167.8	9.1
Cheez-Its, Kellogg	139.8	22.2
Wheat Thins, Kraft	126.2	21.9
Triscuits, Kraft	108.2	16.3
CHIPS		
Lay's, PepsiCo	743.1	23.7
Doritos, PepsiCo	657.0	9.7
Tostitos, PepsiCo	417.0	1.3
Cheetos, PepsiCo	380.3	2.4
JUICE		
Tropicana Pure Premium, PepsiCo	1,149.8	31.9
Minute Maid, Coca-Cola	402.8	28.1
PROCESSED MEATS		
Oscar Meyer, Kraft	808.8	18.0
Hillshire Farm Deli, Sara Lee	244.0	20.1
Buddig, Carl Buddig & Co.	138.0	0.1

SOURCE: National Academy of Sciences

Huckabee Sells What He's Lost

IT WASN'T SO LONG AGO that Gov. Mike Huckabee of Arkansas was afraid to show his face, along with his substantial girth, at health policy events. "Heck, I didn't want to be up on the stage," he said. "I was afraid they'd point at me and say, 'If you don't do these things you could end up like him.'"

That was before a doctor's diagnosis of diabetes — along with the warning that Huckabee would die soon if he didn't lose weight — changed all that. He took up a vigorous diet and exercise regimen, shed more than 100 pounds in the process and earned the nickname of "Skinny" from President Bush.

LOSS CRUSADE: In November 2002, Huckabee weighed more than 280 pounds. He weighed about 170 when he ran his third marathon, in March 2005.

As a result, Huckabee, 50, no longer shies away from health forums. On the contrary. In addition to sharing his story in countless media appearances, Huckabee, a Republican, has pursued as ambitious an anti-obesity agenda as any governor and keeps a spotlight on health issues as chairman of the National Governors Association (NGA).

Policy makers frequently get their religion on an issue from personal experience. The sweeping 1990 Americans with Disabilities Act, to cite one of the most prominent examples, was the bipartisan project of Democratic Sen. Tom Harkin of Iowa, who has a deaf brother, and former Sen. Bob Dole, R-Kan., who lost the use of his right hand in World War II.

Health advocates are particularly delighted that the turnaround by Huckabee — who is exploring a run for president in two years — has led him to spread their message. "It's a 'pinch me' that Gov. Huckabee has taken this on," said Julie L. Gerberding, director of the Centers for Disease Control and Prevention.

Huckabee isn't even sure what weight he topped out at — because it exceeded the 280-pound limit on the scale at the governor's mansion — but he jokes that, at 5-feet 11-inches, he was "approaching the weight of a cement truck." Taking a 12-minute walk was once a strain, but he now runs regularly and has completed his third marathon in Little Rock.

---

cheeseburgers when, in fact, they have more fat and calories. If people are consciously aware of a risk and frequently reminded, they'll make reasonable choices at least some of the time."

Banzhaf hopes the Massachusetts lawsuits will spur look-alikes in other states and lead to the placement of health warnings labels, similar to those on cigarettes and liquor bottles, on snack food packages. He would like to see signs above counters in McDonald's warning about the dangers of eating too much fast food. And he foresees other spin-off actions, such as patient lawsuits against doctors who don't tell them about the dangers of obesity.

Michael Jacobson, executive director of CSPI, says the threatening lawsuits amount to a last resort because Congress and federal regulators have been unwilling to police nutrition in a serious way, by, for example, imple-

menting policies to cut consumption of sodium and hydrogenated oils known as trans fats.

"There's a range of public health problems related to what we eat, and the government does precious little due to pressure from the food industry, though it has to shovel more money to the National Institutes of Health to come up with treatments [for obesity-related disease]," Jacobson said. "Litigation is the right tool in cases like this."

A number of legal and food marketing experts believe Banzhaf and Jacobson are overreaching, ignoring the fact that the law doesn't protect consumers from making bad decisions.

"The people who are most concerned about their health probably don't walk in the door of a McDonald's or Burger King in the first place," said John Stanton, a professor of food marketing at St. Joseph's University. "Even if

you put up a sign, what people think and do is two different things. McDonald's sold the McLean burger in the 1990s, and it was a failure. This is about a small group of people saying the world doesn't want something."

Banzhaf is but one of the tobacco-suit veterans seeking to press a case against food companies. Another is Richard A. Daynard, an associate dean at Northeastern University School of Law, who says state courts are a venue of last resort because Congress is unwilling to enact marketing restrictions.

Schwartz, who went to Columbia Law School with Banzhaf, says his adversaries nonetheless are trying to use the cost of litigation to levy a tax on unhealthful food. In doing so, he asserts, they are disregarding the traditional separation of government powers and bypassing state and federal legislators.

An ordained Baptist minister who will celebrate his 10th anniversary as governor in July, Huckabee continually preaches the benefits of healthy habits. He has published his own weight loss book and made health the main theme of NGA's winter meeting — persuading one of his gubernatorial predecessors, former President Bill Clinton, to offer a testimonial about his own lifelong struggle with his weight and his newfound crusading for healthier eating habits.

Better health is not only a good idea for individuals, Huckabee says, but something that governors should promote as a public policy issue to rein in rapidly escalating costs in Medicaid and other medical care programs. Huckabee estimates that his state could save 15 percent of its annual $161 million bill for the health insurance of its workforce if it could convince state workers to quit smoking, lose some weight and exercise more. However, Huckabee does not endorse suing food companies to recover Medicaid costs of treating obesity-related illnesses, as the nutrition advocates and trial lawyers now threatening suits against food companies are hoping.

FROM PHILOSOPHY TO POLICY

But Arkansas now rewards employees who adopt healthier habits. For instance, workers who clock enough steps on their personal pedometers gain credits toward days off. In addition, the state has banned soda vending machines from elementary schools, reinstated physical education requirements and now runs the most ambitious childhood obesity screening program in the country.

So far, the results of these efforts have been modest. State rates of childhood obesity haven't gone down yet — although even halting the rapid growth of the problem is a major accomplishment — and Arkansas still has the 11th highest rate of adult obesity among the states, at 25 percent, according to the Trust for America's Health, an advocacy group.

Huckabee is unperturbed, saying that obesity is a generational challenge that will take years to combat. He compares it with other issues such as smoking, seat belt usage and drunk driving, in which shifts in cultural attitudes took years in coming.

The underlying idea that government has a role to play in the personal health choices of millions of individuals — as well as the limits

on its role — reflects Huckabee's broader political philosophy. As much as any contemporary politician, Huckabee has governed as a compassionate conservative. He has cut taxes deeper than any other politician in his state's history and supports a ban on abortion, but at the same time he has regularly pulled on the levers of government to offer direct help to Arkansas citizens.

Huckabee has brought down the number of uninsured Arkansas children through his ARKids First program and has greatly increased education spending. A lifelong guitar player who fronts a rock band called Capitol Offense, Huckabee has put a special emphasis on the importance of arts education.

But for all the attention and emphasis he has put on greater health, his policy efforts have been relatively modest. Most states have pursued some sort of anti-obesity campaign in recent years, but they have been largely small-bore efforts requiring minimal expenditures. "Our strategy in Arkansas is one that really had to require no additional funding," said Joe Thompson, the state's chief health officer.

Some health advocates wish that states would push back harder against a culture larded with fat-saturated snacks, gigantic restaurant portions and sedentary jobs and lifestyles. Some argue that states should pursue a legal strategy akin to their 1990s lawsuits against cigarette manufacturers. "If we want to get serious about obesity, we've got to use governmental action with regard to this problem," said John F. Banzhaf III, a George Washington University law professor and strategist in both tobacco and obesity cases.

But Huckabee derides the concept of suing foodmakers and fast-food restaurants as "absurd" and "ridiculous," saying there is a fundamental difference between tobacco, which has no healthful purpose, and food, which everyone must eat to survive. He doesn't want government to become what he calls the "grease police," for both philosophical and pragmatic reasons.

If government starts trying to dictate what people eat and how much of it, he warns, the argument will turn to questions of personal liberty, not health. "We don't want to lose the argument by fighting it on an unfriendly battlefield. The key is creating incentives so people are driven to make the right choices because it's good for them, not because somebody's told them they have to."

In discussions with lawmakers and in law journal articles, Schwartz has outlined a multi-layered defense for the food industry. He begins by arguing that past cases have already held food companies liable for making defective products, or because they didn't warn consumers about inherent risks — for example putting peanuts, a well-known allergen, in candy bars. According to his reasoning, if traditional rules are followed, plaintiffs in the food suits can prevail only if they demonstrate that their condition was caused exclusively by food — and that a particular company's food caused the harm. For plaintiffs to win, judges also would have to substantially change their interpretation of what constituted a "product defect."

Schwartz goes on to argue that litigation based on weight gain will discourage consumer choice by making gun-shy restaurants withdraw

some fattening products. He notes that restaurants chains such as McDonald's and Wendy's have struck a happy balance by varying their menu offerings and selling salads, wraps and bottled water side-by-side with cheeseburgers and fries. Schwartz adds that lawyers who invite state attorneys general to file obesity lawsuits might violate a central principle of law — that an injured person's claim is greater or at least equal to those who allege indirect harm — because the government in question might be given greater legal rights than the injured person.

However legally sound those arguments might be, Schwartz acknowledges that they will fail if a single judge decides to change requirements in existing law.

"Common law is amoebic, alive, organic," he said in a rising voice. "If the public starts to think these guys are like tobacco companies or

begin seeing themselves as David and food chains and marketers as Goliath, and a very pro-plaintiff judge feels the public mood has shifted, things will change."

A NATIONAL SOLUTION?

Precisely because a single court is capable of setting legal precedent for the entire country, the food industry, as part of its multipronged campaign, is arguing that Congress needs to step in and cut off obesity lawsuits. It is pressing for liability legislation that Schwartz helped write and that is commonly referred to as the "cheeseburger bill." The measure would block civil suits against food manufacturers, sellers or trade associations in federal or state courts when a claim was based on an individual's weight gain, obesity or any weight-related health condition. Plaintiffs still could sue when a food manufacturer or seller "knowingly" violated a federal or state law regarding the manufacture or marketing of a product.

The bill has passed the House twice, most recently last October, only to die in the Senate, which is less friendly to "tort reform" measures. The National Restaurant Association has aggressively lobbied for similar measures at the state level, persuading legislatures in 21 states to approve the curbs.

Schwartz argues a that federal "cheeseburger bill" remains essential because the food service industry is the largest private-sector employer in the nation, with 11.7 million workers, and is engaged in interstate commerce. "Congress has a history of acting in the area of tort law when a national solution is appropriate and necessary," he said.

The food industry additionally backs a bill that would impose stronger penalties on lawyers who file lawsuits that are deemed to be "meritless" by eliminating a rule in civil procedures that allows lawyers to avoid sanctions by quickly withdrawing such claims. That measure also passed the House in October but is unlikely to be taken up in the Senate.

The food companies' lobbying clout was evident when the House passed legislation aimed at establishing national food safety standards. The measure, which has not yet been taken up by the Senate, would prevent states from setting or enforcing different standards, such as those in several states that require mercury warnings for fish. The food industry had complained about the difficulty of meeting an array of different state standards, drawing criticism from consumer groups and 39 attorneys general.

Nutrition advocates and others pressing forward with the obesity suits say such liability protections are a smoke screen that relieves food companies of any obligation to act responsibly and could, in fact, encourage reckless behavior.

The nutrition advocates have been scoring some victories of their own at the state level, persuading legislatures to restrict vending of food and beverages in schools. California lawmakers last year passed the nation's toughest school nutrition guidelines, extending to high schools a ban on the sale of sodas during school hours that already was in effect for elementary and middle schools and setting new standards for food sold in schools. That law was supported by Republican Gov. Arnold Schwarzenegger, who complained that obesity-related illness was costing his state $28 billion a year for health care.

The food industry says such efforts are off the

Child Obesity Rising

Over 40 years, the percentage of obese Americans under the age of 20 has quadrupled, to 16 percent.

Percent of age group that is obese

12-19 year olds
6-11 year olds

1963-70	1971-74	1976-80	1988-94	1999-02
4% / 5%	4 / 6	7 / 5	11 / 11	16 / 16

SOURCE: Centers for Disease Control and Prevention

mark. Groups including the American Beverage Association and the Grocery Manufacturers Association argue that the measures seek to impose a one-size-fits-all approach without addressing the root causes of obesity through education programs. The groups also note the bans could hurt schools that have licensing agreements with soft drink companies and bottlers, which support athletic programs.

DOWNSIZING THE SUPERSIZE

Food and beverage companies say they can confront the obesity problem by tweaking their product lines and developing voluntary guidelines. The American Beverage Association, which represents the $90 billion non-alcoholic drink market, last year announced a voluntary program to sell only water and 100 percent juice in elementary schools. The policy would be extended to provide sports drinks, no-calorie soft drinks and low-calorie juices in middle schools and soft drinks in high schools. The association denied that the move was influenced by state laws such as California's and said it was instead aimed at promoting common-sense solutions.

Food companies increasingly are aiming products at older, health-conscious consumers, hoping the availability of more nutritional offerings can snare a potentially lucrative market niche. Candymaker Mars Inc. is marketing a line of heart-healthful chocolates called CocoaVia that are rich in flavanols, a class of compound extracted from the cocoa plant that is thought to have antioxidant properties.

PepsiCo has added a "Smart Spot" symbol on more than 100 products — including Baked Lay's Potato Crisps, Quaker Instant Oatmeal and Quaker 100 percent Natural Granola — to highlight their nutritional value. PepsiCo and other snack makers have stripped most saturated fats and trans fats from products in response

to evidence that those fats raise cholesterol and put people at greater risk of heart disease.

But looming over the healthful marketing efforts are experiences such as McDonald's with its low-fat McLean burger. The burger, introduced in 1991, had just 12 grams of fat, compared with 28 grams for a Big Mac. The difference was noticeable. Sales flopped, and the item was quickly pulled from the menu.

"Consumers still prefer the taste of a product with a lot of fat, texture and other sensory attributes," said Gale Strasburg, chairman of Michigan State University's department of food science and human nutrition. "There's a potential market if you can convince the public something tastes good and it's good for you."

Such a phenomenon is taking effect in the beverage world. The popularity of bottled water, sports and energy drinks, coupled with warnings from nutritionists about sugary sodas, prompted soda sales to decline in 2005 for the first time in 20 years.

Yet many companies are reluctant to entirely break with traditional tastes. A middle ground some are staking out, according to St. Joseph's University's Stanton, is limiting the portion size of popular products, thereby saving consumers from overindulging while acknowledging that people seek out the taste they're accustomed to. Kraft Foods has embraced the strategy by introducing 100-calorie packages of Oreo and Chips Ahoy! thin crisps and miniature Wheat Thins. McDonald's similarly stopped "supersizing" fries and drinks at its more than 13,000 restaurants nationwide.

"You know what my ideal serving size is for potato chips? Whatever the size of the bag I'm eating," Stanton said. "But the fact is you can be satisfied with fewer calories. There's nothing that says you can't reduce the size of a ready-to-heat meatloaf portion you pick up at the supermarket. One of the reasons Subway is healthy is they actually give you less food [in the 6-inch subs that have become popular with dieters]."

Schwartz, the Subway patron, agrees, but says enterprising lawyers would devise a case that makes the sandwich chain look bad, given the chance. For that reason, he views the threatened suits as a watershed moment in tort law and is urging the food industry to dig in or risk a continuing cycle of litigation.

"When you start paying people to go away, more checkbooks start coming out," he said. "The cases won't go away. The prospect of a settlement makes people hang in there even longer." ■

Defining 'Ours' In a New World

Foreign investment in U.S. industry and infrastructure worries many, but proponents say capital without borders is key to the global economy — and America's prosperity

IT'S BEEN A GENERATION since foreign ownership of America's prized assets generated such consternation about U.S. sovereignty and competitiveness.

Then, it was the rise of Japan Inc. that alarmed voters and set lawmakers to hand-wringing. The result was a series of new laws intended to protect the most crucial parts of the nation's security infrastructure from foreign control.

The perceived threat was first raised when Fujitsu Ltd., a large Japanese computer manufacturer, attempted in 1987 to buy a controlling stake in Fairchild Semiconductor Corp., a California company and one of the early pioneers of U.S. high-technology manufacturing. Fujitsu ultimately retreated under pressure from federal government officials.

Two years later, however, the high-profile acquisition of the iconic Rockefeller Center complex on New York's Fifth Avenue suddenly raised the issue of foreign ownership to a fever pitch in newspaper headlines, best-selling books and political debates. That purchase, by a subsidiary of Japan's Mitsubishi Group, was as much about the loss of U.S. pride and prestige as it was about the risk that critical U.S. production facilities might somehow be compromised by foreign takeovers.

Today, China's economy has supplanted

Japan's as the biggest perceived global economic threat; Mitsubishi unloaded Rockefeller Center years ago. China's wide-reaching economic clout, and its commensurate political influence around the world, have only fueled other American fears emanating from the Sept. 11 terrorist attacks, pushing the issue of who owns America beyond economic nationalism to concerns about the very safety and security of the nation.

It is that attitude that has inflamed public debate about a Middle Eastern government-owned company managing facilities at six of the largest U.S. ports — including two within sight of Ground Zero in Manhattan.

"Foreign control of our ports, which are vital to homeland security, is a risky proposition, riskier yet is that we are turning it over to a country that has been linked to terrorism previously," said New York Democratic Sen. Charles E. Schumer, one of the most outspoken critics of the port acquisition. "This deal seems to have been unnecessarily fast-tracked, and the American people are entitled to greater and more open scrutiny."

But national and economic security concerns — some would call it xenophobia or even a latent form of racism — are in many respects just the surface issues in the debate over foreign ownership of prime American assets. Lawmakers, pundits and bloggers have pounced on genuine fears among Americans that U.S. ports are vulnerable to terrorist attack and that com-

petition for oil and natural gas could weaken our standing in the world.

The more fundamental question revolves around the global economy and the fact that investment capital in today's world has very little regard for national boundaries. If lawmakers decide to place new limits on foreign ownership as a way to stanch those rising fears, they might bring lasting harm to an economy that thrives on the desirability of American assets to non-U.S. investors.

Foreign owners controlled almost 16 percent of non-financial U.S. corporations in 2003, up from about 11 percent a decade earlier. And almost 5 percent of the U.S. workforce toils for foreign bosses.

Those are "striking" numbers, according to Edward M. Graham, a senior fellow at the Institute for International Economics. Graham and David Marchick, a Washington lawyer who specializes in foreign investment, are co-authors of a soon-to-be-released book, "U.S. National Security and Foreign Direct Investment," that addresses the widening role of foreign investment in the United States and the need for limits.

The United States has amassed a trade deficit that exceeded $725 billion last year alone and totaled an almost incomprehensible $3.6 trillion over the past decade. Americans have given that much money to the rest of the world to buy oil, clothing, electronics, toys and myriad other goods. Those dollars are coming

RALLYING CRY: Schumer is among those lawmakers who seized on the Dubai port deal as a post-Sept. 11 threat to New York's security.

money brought the Industrial Revolution to U.S. shores, with Europeans leading the charge. At the same time, international investment in the United States isn't easily categorized by nationality or scope of control, beyond noting its concentration in manufacturing.

Statisticians at the Commerce Department's Bureau of Economic Analysis have calculated that foreign-owned companies produced 5.8 percent of private industry output in 2003, up from 3.8 percent in 1988. Much of this is in automobiles, chemicals and heavy manufacturing, although there are also large holdings in financial services. Because of the 2001 recession, which hit manufacturing particularly hard, the 2003 contribution from foreign-owned companies was actually a bit below the previous peak of 5.9 percent of non-government output.

Annually, foreign investors have been adding to their stock of U.S. investments at the rate of just under $100 billion a year since the recession, down from $200 billion or more a year at the end of the last decade and $336 billion in the year 2000 alone.

At the end of 2004, Commerce figures show that the purchase price of foreign-owned assets in the United States was about $1.7 trillion, or $2.7 trillion when a rough gauge of current market value is used. Graham calculates that foreign-owned assets amount to about a fifth of all U.S. corporate net worth.

Europe and Canada account for about 75 percent of all foreign companies operating here, but while investors based in the United Kingdom form by far the biggest bloc, the Japanese are second, ahead of corporate owners from Germany, the Netherlands, France, Canada and Switzerland.

The foreign face of Corporate America is also not always well known. Many, if not most, Americans may know that Shell Oil, which has operated in the United States for a century, is a foreign-owned company, a Dutch-British consortium. And it's obvious to all that the tens of thousands of autoworkers who assemble cars in Alabama, Indiana, Ohio, South Carolina, Texas and elsewhere for Honda, Toyota and BMW report to parent companies

back to buy U.S. factories and other businesses, which Graham, Marchick and most economists contend is a good thing because such investments produce jobs for Americans and add to U.S. economic growth.

These proponents of investment worry that if the United States raises new barriers to foreign ownership — or if overseas investors perceive that their overtures are more likely to be rejected — those dollars will go elsewhere.

"There is an unfortunate and almost a neg-ative taint about foreign investment in Washington," said Marchick, a partner in the firm of Covington & Burling. "We depend on foreign investment not only to bridge the gap between what we save and what we consume, but our manufacturing base is heavily supported by foreign investment."

STEEL AND SCHOOL LUNCHES

Foreign ownership of U.S. business is nothing new. As far back as the 1870s, foreign

Overseas Owners: Who, What, Where

A majority of the direct ownership of U.S. companies by international investors comes from Europe, with the largest share — one-fifth — from the United Kingdom. Almost half of foreign-owned U.S. companies are involved in manufacturing, followed by wholesale and retail trade. Foreign-owned companies are in all regions of the country, though they are somewhat more heavily concentrated in the South. Figures are based on 2003 statistics:

Top industries of foreign-owned companies in the U.S.

Manufacturing	46.8%
Wholesale trade	17.2%
Retail trade	5.7%
Information	5.5%
Finance/Insurance	5.3%
Professional/Technical	3.7%
Real estate	2.1%
Other	13.7%

Total: $486.3 billion
Contribution to private GDP

Countries with the largest share of all foreign-owned U.S. companies

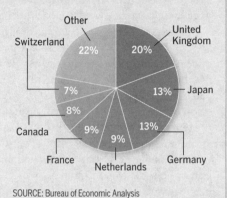

Other 22%
Switzerland 7%
Canada 8%
France 9%
Netherlands 9%
Germany 13%
Japan 13%
United Kingdom 20%

SOURCE: Bureau of Economic Analysis

Regional distribution of U.S. workers employed by foreign-owned companies

West 19%
Northeast 27%
Midwest 23%
South 32%

NO SPARKS HERE: British-owned National Grid has offered to buy New York-based electric utility KeySpan Corp.

---

overseas, not to mention that DaimlerChrysler is no longer headquartered in Detroit.

But other, less obvious foreign companies are ingrained in the U.S. economy.

The largest food service company in the country is Sodexho USA, formerly part of the Marriott hotel empire. Now owned by France-based Sodexho Alliance, the company employs 120,000 people in the United States — earning $6.3 billion in 2005 and supplying almost half of the parent company's revenue. It serves millions of meals a day in school and college cafeterias, on Marine Corps bases and in corporate and government offices.

And while the security of U.S. ports is a leading topic of discussion, the country's largest protective service — guarding banks, corporate offices and some port facilities — is Securitas Security Services USA Inc. This Sweden-based company made its first inroads in the United States in 1999, when it bought Pinkerton's Inc. Later, Securitas acquired Burns International, the Wells Fargo security company and other prominent names that date to the mid-1800s. The U.S. division supplies about half of the parent company's revenue, according to company official James McNulty. And while port security "is not a huge amount of business" for Securitas, the company is watching the Dubai company issue closely, he said.

National Grid, Britain's largest utility, recently announced that it would buy KeySpan Corp., which supplies electricity and natural gas to New York and parts of New England, for $7.3 billion. That will make National Grid, which first entered the U.S. market in 2000, the third-largest utility delivery company in the country, serving almost 8 million customers across the Northeast.

While Congress is focused on foreign ownership in America, U.S. companies continue to expand overseas. And the value of U.S.-owned companies abroad remains far greater that foreign assets here: $2.4 trillion when measured at cost and $3.3 trillion at market value.

Broadly, U.S. companies add between 1.5 percent and 5 percent to economic output in other industrialized countries, including 5.3 percent of Australia's gross domestic product (GDP) and 1.9 percent of Italy's. In both cases, the U.S. contribution is almost half of the amount added by all foreign-owned companies.

THE ROOTS OF CFIUS

Still, the reciprocal nature of increasingly global capital flows is frequently overshad-owed by domestic security concerns, and many lawmakers raise outright objections to foreign ownership of any business deemed essential to the U.S. economy.

That was the issue behind recently expressed apprehensions about the Chinese buying a U.S. oil company, and it is playing out again in the current uproar over who runs America's ports.

Last summer, the $18.5 billion bid by China National Offshore Oil Corp., the country's third-largest petroleum producer, for California-based Unocal Corp. sparked a firestorm on Capitol Hill. The opposition led the Chinese government-backed company to quickly withdraw its offer, although many close observers say there never was a security threat raised by the acquisition.

The even louder outcry that began recently against the involvement of Dubai's DP World in operations at the Port of New York and New Jersey, plus ports from Philadelphia to New Orleans, has pitted outraged lawmakers from both parties against President Bush, who hastened to defend the deal and has threatened to veto any legislation that would block it.

On its face, this conflict between Congress and the White House is reminiscent of the late 1980s, when some lawmakers pressed to tighten the screws on foreign investment, reversing course after decades of welcoming other countries' money with open arms.

Mostly, those efforts weren't successful, although the procedure for executive branch review of potential national security risks in a foreign takeover was written into law in 1988 and broadened in 1992 — both times in response to specific acquisitions that worried lawmakers. During that same period, Congress also required the government to collect a limited amount of data on foreign ownership of U.S. assets, resisting demands for greater disclosure of private company information that might have discouraged investment.

But the current debate hits hot-button issues that go beyond both national security and globalization, touching upon the exercise of presidential power and even influence peddling. Among the Dubai company's advisers was the firm run by former Secretary of State Madeleine Albright.

"The politics have certainly changed in the last year," Marchick said.

That's evident in the continued drumbeat of opposition on Capitol Hill to the port transaction. The Dubai company's offer to submit to a new 45-day investigation by the federal government's Committee on Foreign Investments in the United States (CFIUS), which already cleared the deal once, hasn't calmed the waters on Capitol Hill. The rhetoric has in fact been ratcheted up.

"Don't let them tell you that it's just a transfer of title," said New Jersey Democratic Sen. Frank R. Lautenberg on Feb. 27. "Baloney. We wouldn't transfer the title to the Devil; we're not going to transfer it to Dubai."

The politically charged fight may very well force the Dubai company to abandon its U.S. holdings in the end, observers say. And lawmakers may try to impose stiffer controls on international ownership of U.S. assets, particularly when a foreign government is involved.

"Everything in this country can't be for sale," said Richard C. Shelby, an Alabama Republican and chairman of the Senate Banking Committee. "While I strongly support our open investment policy and recognize that it is vital to our national economic interests, I do not believe it should stand at any cost," he said at a March 2 committee hearing.

Most opponents of the port deal insist that their concern is a narrow one, focused on the threat of so-called critical infrastructure falling into the hands of a foreign government that hasn't always been the most responsive to U.S. demands.

This worry that a Middle Eastern company operating "within our defense perimeter," as New York Republican Rep. Peter T. King put it, might harbor terrorists comes at a time when industrial countries around the world are asking tougher questions about foreign ownership. In France — long a bastion of economic nationalism — and in other European countries, there are signs of growing resistance to the flood of overseas investment, particularly from China and the Middle East, but even from within Europe and from the United States.

"Everything in this country can't be for sale."

— Sen. Richard C. Shelby, R-Ala.

REMEMBERING THE BRIEFCASE

For a country that thinks of itself as homegrown, the United States has since the 19th century been dependent on foreign investment. And for almost as long, that arrangement has been reciprocal, with U.S. investment serving as a dominant force overseas. Possibly no country other than Britain has been more willing to accept international ownership of central pieces of its economy, said Graham.

From the beginnings of the Industrial Revolution, imported from Europe, foreign investors built chemical plants, radio broadcasting facilities, telecommunications companies and automobile factories. In some cases, Graham said, those investments lost their foreign status when the owners were naturalized as U.S. citizens. Andrew Carnegie's U.S. Steel was the largest industrial corporation in the country and was a Scottish company until Carnegie became a citizen.

By 1914, foreign direct investment in the United States, defined as an ownership interest of 10 percent or more in factories, real estate or other tangible assets, totaled $1.3 billion. In dollar terms, that may seem quite small, but when combined with non-ownership holdings of stocks, it amounted to about 20 percent of GDP, a measure of the total size of the economy. Today, foreign direct investment is equal to about 16 percent of GDP, according to Commerce Department figures.

The amount of foreign ownership raised few red flags until World War I, when Americans began to fret about German involvement in the U.S. economy. Those fears intensified in

1915 when a German diplomat accidentally left his briefcase on the platform of a New York train station. Materials found in the briefcase indicated that some German investments in the United States were aimed at building up Germany's war capability.

The briefcase incident confirmed for some lawmakers that German commercial interests weren't to be trusted.

So when the United States formally entered the war in the spring of 1917, Congress passed the Trading with the Enemy Act. President Woodrow Wilson used it to seize assets held by many German companies. Under U.S. law those companies should have been turned back to the Germans after the war, but instead many assets were transferred to U.S. ownership.

That explains why the New York company Sterling Drug Inc. for decades sold aspirin under the trademark previously held by Bayer AG, the German chemical giant that once had large U.S. operations. Through U.S. acquisitions over the past two decades, including the purchase of Sterling Drug in 1988, Bayer again owns the U.S. trademark. DuPont Co. was also a huge beneficiary of this nationalization episode, winning hundreds of German patents.

A decade after the war, Congress passed the Radio Act of 1927, which, in the name of national security, severely restricted foreign ownership in radio broadcasting and telecommunications. Ownership limits in other industries followed.

As a result, foreign investment in the United States dried up for a time, but it began to increase in the early 1940s, largely as a result of Allied help during World War II. Investment picked up slowly in the 1950s and more robustly during the 1960s and 1970s. Still, relative to the size of the economy, foreign investment was small compared with what it had been early in the century.

That began to change in the 1980s, and by the end of that decade, with Japan's economic surge and the corresponding rise in the U.S. trade deficit, foreign ownership was again surging and becoming a source of political concern.

Thanks in part to the decade-long U.S. economic boom of the 1990s, and Japan's stagnation during that same time, these fears disappeared even as the flow of international investment continued.

Until now, that is.

CRITICAL OR NOT?

Sept. 11 changed the debate. Before, when national security was raised in the context of foreign investment, two issues were paramount: Would sensitive military technology be put at risk, and might foreign producers of needed defense-related goods be able to thwart U.S. national interests if they had a stranglehold on the supply. It's not insignificant that the primary law governing foreign ownership in the United States is a provision of the 1950 Defense Production Act, which gives the president authority to command factories to produce essential materials in times of strife.

"One could make the case that we do not want international investors to take a controlling share in Lockheed-Martin, but this would surely be the extreme example," said William Keller, director of the Matthew B. Ridgway Center for International Security Studies at the University of Pittsburgh, in an e-mail.

"If we want to maintain our military advantage, then it makes sense to keep the military technology and industry at home and generally to keep foreign firms out," Keller said.

But he and others warn against taking that level of concern too far. "We certainly do not want to encourage U.S.-based companies to become lax and uncompetitive by offering them protection from foreign investment," Keller said. Since Sept. 11, however, the focus in parts of the executive branch and on Capitol Hill has shifted toward protection of critical infrastructure.

That shift actually began almost a decade earlier with the 1993 bomb blast in the World Trade Center garage and the deadly 1995 truck bombing in Oklahoma City. President Bill Clinton created a commission in 1996 to evaluate how to protect critical infrastructure, almost all of which is privately owned. Two years later, he issued the first presidential directive on critical infrastructure policy, which emphasized information-sharing between government and industry in eight broad areas, ranging from banking to the water supply.

After the attacks on New York's World Trade Center and the Pentagon, Congress defined critical infrastructure in the 2001 anti-terror law, commonly called the Patriot Act, as "systems and assets, whether physical or virtual, so vital to the United States that the incapacity or destruction of such systems and assets would have a debilitating impact on security, national economic security, national public health or safety, or any combination of those matters."

The Bush administration followed with a national strategy in 2003, expanding the Clinton-era list of eight critical areas to 11, and adding five more "key assets" that could, if attacked, result in major loss of life or damage national morale.

U.S. Companies Invest Heavily Abroad

Purchases of foreign companies by U.S. investors have been twice as large in recent years as overseas purchases of ownership interests in U.S. companies.

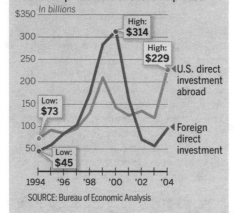

SOURCE: Bureau of Economic Analysis

A new presidential directive that year elaborated on which agencies are responsible for which parts of the critical national infrastructure, and the newly created Department of Homeland Security was given the task of coordinating this strategy and building an inventory. The department was also included as a regular participant in national security reviews of foreign investment by CFIUS.

The inventory of critical infrastructure as first compiled by the department has drawn criticism for both its omissions — nuclear power plants weren't always included — and for being short on rationale.

"They might have a clear definition, but it doesn't make sense," said James Lewis, a senior fellow at the Center for Strategic and International Studies, a Washington-based think tank. "It's far too broad."

At the same time, efforts by Homeland Security to persuade fellow participants in CFIUS to pay closer attention to critical infrastructure concerns haven't always been successful. "In this department, protecting critical infrastructure influences our view of national security and particular transactions," said Stewart Baker, assistant secretary of Homeland Security, in an interview. "Other agencies are certainly free to criticize us and say we don't think that's national security."

A September 2005 report by the Government Accountability Office found that CFIUS tends to view the nation's open investment policy as its top priority, and that Homeland Security, along with representatives of the Pentagon and Justice Department, have argued that the committee's definition of national security "is not sufficiently flexible to provide

for safeguards in areas such as protection of critical infrastructure."

The lack of emphasis on infrastructure by CFIUS bothers some lawmakers. "I'm not sure it's been considered much at all," said Indiana Democratic Sen. Evan Bayh, who has proposed legislation to expand the committee's definition of national security. "Last year, involving the acquisition of a major energy company . . . that was given no weight whatsoever. . . . In the case of Magnequench, the majority production of a sensitive weapons component here — no weight whatsoever," Bayh said.

Yet some lawmakers, in the wake of the Dubai ports fight, have gone far beyond what Bayh has proposed.

Democratic Sens. Hillary Rodham Clinton of New York and Robert Menendez of New Jersey want to prohibit companies controlled by foreign governments from conducting operations at U.S. seaports. And Dubai's DP World is far from alone in that field. The other leading bidder for the port operations acquired by the Dubai company is owned by the government of Singapore, which already has extensive operations in the United States.

Minnesota Republican Sen. Norm Coleman would take that a step further and bar foreign government-controlled companies from managing a national security-related "facility or investment," such as a seaport, unless its day-to-day operating structure was formally insulated from the foreign government.

And Duncan Hunter, a California Republican who chairs the House Armed Services Committee, would bar all current and future foreign investment in critical infrastructure.

"Dubai can't be trusted," said Hunter. "United Arab Emirates officials have been instrumental in the transshipment of nuclear materials and weapons of mass destruction components."

STRINGS ATTACHED

There is a feeling among those who deal on a regular basis with CFIUS national security reviews and who understand the ways in which the interagency group acts that the ports fight is more a public relations disaster than a potential breach of security.

"The irony is that the perception from the DP World transaction is that CFIUS has a light touch," said attorney Marchick. "In fact, it has been much tougher and much more rigorous, imposing more Draconian conditions on companies."

But because the agency conducts its work in secret, both to protect the national security

Foreign Investors Often Meet Resistance in U.S.

International acquisitions of U.S. companies isn't a new topic of concern. Since 1988, the president has had the authority to block any takeover that he judges might compromise national security, following an investigation by the interagency Committee on Foreign Investment in the United States. On several occasions, foreign bidders have withdrawn after meeting stiff opposition from U.S. lawmakers.

ROCKEFELLER CENTER

In November 1989, the Japanese company **Mitsubishi Estate Co.** paid $846 million for a 51 percent interest in the **Rockefeller Group,** whose properties included the iconic Rockefeller Center in Manhattan, later increasing the holding to 80 percent. The 1988 Exon-Florio amendment to the Defense Production Act allows the president to prevent any acquisition judged to pose a threat to national security, but President George Bush didn't interfere with this highly publicized deal.

LTV MISSILE

After **LTV Corp.** filed for bankruptcy reorganization in 1992, France-owned **Thomson CSF** made a successful bid for the steel company's missile division, alongside a coordinated bid by the Washington-based **Carlyle Group** for the company's aircraft division. **Lockheed Corp.** and **Martin Marietta Corp.** complained after losing the bidding war, prompting an investigation by the Committee on Foreign Investment in the United States (CFIUS), which reviews such transactions under the Exon-Florio provision. But Thompson withdrew its bid when it became clear that the committee would recommend a presidential veto. Shortly thereafter, Congress passed the Byrd amendment to Exon-Florio requiring a formal investigation in any case where a bidding company is owned by a foreign government or acting on its behalf.

LENOVO GROUP LTD.

At the end of 2004, **IBM Corp.** completed the $1.75 billion sale of its personal computer division to **Lenovo Group Ltd.,** a giant Chinese computer maker partially owned by the government. Several lawmakers raised concern that the transaction might give the Chinese government access to sensitive and complex technology, while the deal's backers argued that the personal computers contain only very common equipment. CFIUS ultimately approved the deal after assurances were made that Lenovo would not have access to sensitive IBM technology.

CNOOC

In June 2005, the **China National Offshore Oil Corp.**, which is majority-owned by the Chinese government, outbid **Chevron Corp.** by $2 billion to take over of California-based **Unocal Corp.,** which had significant oil and natural gas properties around Asia. The proposed sale raised immediate concerns on Capitol Hill, and the House voted twice to show its displeasure with the deal, though neither vote was likely to stop it from closing. Shortly after the House action, and in the face of rising opposition, CNOOC withdrew its bid, and Chevron made the acquisition.

---

matters at hand and the proprietary information of the companies involved, those conditions are rarely publicized.

Marchick, who worked on the sale of IBM's personal computer division to China's Lenovo Group last year, won't discuss the details of that transaction or any agreement regarding sensitive national security matters.

But in congressional testimony, William Reinsch, president of the National Foreign Trade Council, described agreements that were intended to protect sensitive technology that Lenovo wasn't acquiring from IBM, but that was located in the same buildings where Lenovo would be operating.

"Often, the applicant is willing to make commitments that address any concerns the government has raised," said Reinsch, a long-time congressional aide and former Commerce Department official in charge of controls on sensitive exports.

And it may just be that the parties to the Lenovo case did a better job of convincing skittish politicians that the deal wasn't a security threat. "The Lenovo deal didn't quite trigger a firestorm, but it was headed in that direction," Graham said.

From time to time, deals fall through when such conditions are imposed. The Hong Kong conglomerate Hutchison Whampoa Ltd. backed out of the purchase of bankrupt Global Crossing Ltd. in 2003 because of conditions requiring the company to allow the CIA and FBI to conduct surveillance through its fiber optic networks.

Similar conditions may have been part of the DP World transaction. Stewart Baker, assistant secretary of Homeland Security, testified that the Dubai company agreed to an "open book" policy that permits government officials access to its records at any time without a subpoena. Graham added that it would not be unusual to require U.S. citizenship and screening of workers in certain cases, although he said he had no knowledge that such conditions were imposed in this case.

Still, it would be in DP World's interest and in the interest of the emir of Dubai — the company's owner — to spell out the details, Graham said. "I were his close adviser, I'd say open up on this."

CHILLING THE WATERS

It isn't clear yet how the Dubai port case will play out, how quickly it might be resolved, and whether there will be significant political and economic casualties — either at home or abroad. Revelations of a second Dubai-based company's acquisition of a British company with U.S. defense plants has raised new concerns among lawmakers.

Marchick and other observers predict that the continuing congressional outcry will chill investments and make CFIUS more cautious. But Marchick says there are ways to give lawmakers a fuller picture of foreign investment national security reviews without giving them a veto, and without risking a public firestorm.

One option, he said, would be regular — annual or quarterly — reports by CFIUS to Congress, roughly parallel to those required under the 1976 Hart-Scott-Rodino antitrust law. Those reports would cover the number of filings, with details by economic sector, and take particular note of government-owned acquisitions. "None of this data is out there," he said.

And he endorsed classified briefings for relevant committee chairman and ranking minority members on the details of reviews. "Congress wants to know about it, and if there is more transparency there would be a greater comfort level," he said.

But even if the current controversy dies down and Congress accepts some form of enhanced reporting without imposing statutory limits on investment, irreparable damage may have been done to overseas perceptions of

Americans and to the ability of the United States to gain cooperation in the Middle East.

Lawmakers angrily reject any notion that xenophobia or bigotry has played a role in their outrage in the port case. But even Bush has leveled the accusation that critics of the Dubai deal are applying a different standard because it involves a Middle Eastern country.

And at the same time, many — though not all — knowledgeable observers say they see no real threat in this case. "My friends in the intelligence community tell me that there is no reason to think that security at our ports would be altered if the ports were managed by DP World as opposed to the British firm that does it now," said Keller from the University of Pittsburgh. "If this is true, then blocking the DP World investment relies on the same fallacy as thinking that every Muslim is an al Qaeda sympathizer, which is untrue on its face."

"This is a terribly negative message we are sending to the Arab nations in the Middle East" about free trade and geopolitical cooperation, said Reinsch in testimony to the House Financial Services Committee.

And the outcry may have damaged public perceptions both in the United States and abroad, said Steve Canner, a longtime Treasury official who handled CFIUS matters in the first few years after 1988 and who is now at the U.S. Council for International Business.

"It's hard for the man in the street to get into the facts and go beyond the sound bite," Canner said. "The foreign press and others have seen the politicization of the process." ∎

A Nation Of Health Shoppers

Bush sketches a 'consumer driven' plan to fight rising health care costs, but critics question the savings and say key problems are unaddressed

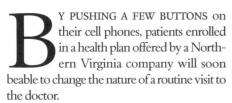

BY PUSHING A FEW BUTTONS on their cell phones, patients enrolled in a health plan offered by a Northern Virginia company will soon be able to change the nature of a routine visit to the doctor.

The company will offer a service that allows patients who receive a diagnosis to type drug names into their cell phones and instantly get a list of cheaper name-brand and generic drugs. The insurer, Lumenos Inc., expects its clients to use the information to negotiate with doctors for low-cost alternatives for treating their back pain, high cholesterol or hypertension. Because of the way the company structures its coverage, the savings will hold down the consumer's overall costs.

The service is part of a larger vision of the future of health care that President Bush, congressional Republicans and big business believe will begin to rein in the nation's soaring health care costs. It is built around the notion that consumers can be persuaded to comparison

CQ Weekly Feb. 13, 2006

shop for the best bargains in health care, just as they do for other goods and services, if they are given enough financial incentives and transparent pricing information.

In this world of "consumer-driven health care," patients will use Internet-based services to comparison shop for lower-priced drugs and visit walk-in clinics instead of doctors for ear aches and other minor maladies. Doctors and hospitals will be paid for performance and receive bonuses if patients don't experience complications. There will be minimal government control over the market.

The administration is staking a lot on the concept. With national health spending now exceeding $1.9 trillion — and with tens of millions of aging baby boomers certain to drive up costs in the coming decade — public officials worry that medical inflation will prompt many employers to gradually drop workers' and retirees' coverage, leaving more people without insurance and the government on the hook for more charity care.

This vision is rooted in the belief that private market competition can be harnessed to stop

the upward spiral and, in the process, silence calls from Democrats for increased government regulation of health care.

"To make our economy stronger and more productive, we must make health care more affordable, and give families greater access to good coverage and more control over their health decisions," Bush said in his State of the Union address Jan. 31.

Will it work? Experts of all political stripes agree that something needs to be done to slow health care inflation, and in some respects they say, it makes sense to give consumers more control of the process. On a broader level, though, many are skeptical about whether the plan will result in any real savings in the U.S. health care system. Health economists note that most consumer-driven plans primarily will control the cost of outpatient visits to doctors and prescriptions, not hospital stays and care for individuals with chronic conditions, such as diabetes and heart disease, which are both among the prime drivers of medical inflation.

What's more, experts say it will take a major transformation to clear up what many charac-

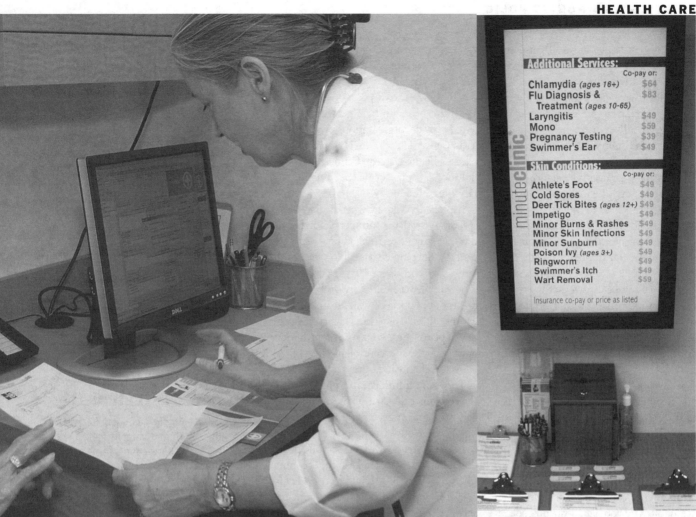

Additional Services:

	Co-pay or:
Chlamydia *(ages 16+)*	$64
Flu Diagnosis & Treatment *(ages 10-65)*	$83
Laryngitis	$49
Mono	$59
Pregnancy Testing	$39
Swimmer's Ear	$49

Skin Conditions:

	Co-pay or:
Athlete's Foot	$49
Cold Sores	$49
Deer Tick Bites *(ages 12+)*	$49
Impetigo	$49
Minor Burns & Rashes	$49
Minor Skin Infections	$49
Minor Sunburn	$49
Poison Ivy *(ages 3+)*	$49
Ringworm	$49
Swimmer's Itch	$49
Wart Removal	$59

Insurance co-pay or price as listed

NEW OPTIONS: The shift to consumer-driven health care includes walk-in clinics, such as this MinuteClinic, located in a CVS Pharmacy in Bethesda, Md., where Loretta Kingdon, left, consulted with nurse Trish Hudgespat. Prices for procedures are posted, fast-food menu style.

terize as the opaque, arbitrary way that many providers set prices. Asking patients to navigate the current system, with its complex diagnostic codes and techno-speak, is, in the view of one leading economist, akin to blindfolding consumers, setting them loose in a department store, then only paying for certain items.

"Here I am, I have chest pain. What am I going to do? I call up a group of doctors and say, 'What is your price for treating chest pain?' I just don't see how that would work," said Princeton University economist Uwe E. Reinhardt, who devised the department store analogy.

Despite such misgivings, the private market approaches will continue to gain prominence. Bush and his Republican allies have long resisted government intervention, such as mandating universal health coverage through government-regulated networks of providers, as President Bill Clinton proposed in 1993. Instead, they place their faith in the idea that patients can be empowered to ration their own

"We must make health care more affordable, and give families ... more control over their health decisions."

— President Bush, Jan. 31 State of the Union speech

care without imperiling their well-being.

Insurers, who long bore the burden of having to limit medical services and were the object of considerable public enmity during the advent of "managed care" in the 1990s, are welcoming the chance to transfer the responsibility of rationing care to consumers. Businesses similarly see the shift as a way of transferring more of the financial risk of getting sick to their workers while saving money on health coverage.

"We're at the tipping point of this movement," said Chip Tooke, a founder of Lumenos in 1999 with an eye toward promoting consumer-driven care. He sold the division in 2003

to health insurance giant WellPoint/Anthem. "Six years ago, people thought I was nuts. Now, Fortune 500 companies are interested in this."

The shift will put the onus on consumers to save money in specially designated accounts, sort out their personal health needs and find objective sources to evaluate the merits of one treatment over another. More fundamentally, they will have to abandon the notion perpetuated by the current system of employer-sponsored coverage that they are entitled to the best care available, without regard to cost.

The transformation to a more market-based system comes at a particularly critical time for America's health system. Health care spending now accounts for about 16 percent of the economy, compared with about 13 percent in 2000. The government is certain to bear a greater burden of those costs as more employers decide they can no longer afford to offer coverage to workers and retirees. The premiums companies pay to provide health insurance for workers rose a cumulative 60 percent over the past five years.

To slow the trend, Bush is heavily promoting new employer-sponsored health care packages built around health savings accounts, or HSAs, which were created by the 2003 Medicare prescription drug law. Workers are given health insurance policies with comparatively high annual deductibles ranging from $2,100 to more than $10,000 for a family. To offset the added cost, they typically pay lower monthly premiums and can squirrel money for future medical expenses tax-free in the HSAs. Any unspent money in a given year can be carried over to the next year, and workers may take the HSA accounts with them when they change jobs. After age 65, account holders can spend the balance on anything but must pay taxes on non-health-related items.

Conservative politicians consider HSAs — and a similar savings vehicle known as a health reimbursement account, or HRA, which allows employers to keep the funds if a worker leaves a job —as a panacea. The plans are becoming increasingly popular with employers, who see them as more affordable alternatives to comprehensive health coverage. About 3 million high-deductible policies are being used today, a figure that is expected to rise to 14 million by 2010.

Advocates say plans with HSAs will lower medical spending because of the way they force workers to pay a bigger share of up-front costs through the higher deductibles. The theory is that patients will have an incentive to look for cheaper care when appropriate, decline unnecessary tests and, as in the case of Lumenos' clients, seek out cheaper medicine. It's a departure from conventional employer-sponsored health care, in which patients enrolled in managed care make a co-payment for an office visit but typically are unaware and unconcerned about the costs of the services, drugs or tests their doctors order.

"As people take on more responsibility, either freely or because they are pushed, they will look more at value [they receive] for the money," said Stuart M. Butler, a health care expert at the conservative Heritage Foundation. "As we move away from a strictly employment-based system, people will take more control of their spending."

Early evidence suggests that the plans are delivering some of their intended effect. The premiums businesses paid for plans featuring HSAs or HRAs rose an average of 2.8 percent from 2004 to 2005, compared with an 8 percent increase for traditional health maintenance organizations, 8.5 percent for less-restrictive point-of-service managed care plans and 7.2 percent for preferred-provider organizations, according to a survey of 152 major U.S. employers released by the Deloitte Center for Health Solutions, a project of the consultancy Deloitte & Touche.

Experts don't know whether the slower spending growth in consumer-directed plans was the result of patients doing more comparison shopping or bargaining for health services, or whether it reflected a decision to simply use fewer health services because of higher out-of-pocket costs. Also unknown is whether individuals received higher quality of care in plans whose costs rose more quickly, or whether the cost-controlling effect of the HSAs will endure in future years.

The Bush administration argues that the consumer-directed plans are working, and is intent on expanding use of HSAs. The White House has proposed spending $52 billion over five years to, among other things, allow workers to keep the accounts when they change jobs and to provide tax breaks for individuals who purchase insurance packages featuring HSAs on their own, as opposed to receiving them at work. Administration officials say that if Congress adopts the proposals, HSA enrollment will total about 21 million Americans by 2010.

"We think HSAs are the prudent way for people to insure themselves in America," said Al Hubbard, chairman of Bush's National Economic Council.

ANY REAL IMPACT?

But will HSAs have any significant effect on national health spending? Many health care economists believe the accounts primarily appeal to healthier, wealthier individuals, who can use them to stash money tax-free for future medical expenses. Even if this relatively healthy population limited its spending significantly, medical inflation would continue to surge.

Experts note that the routine visits to doctors that HSAs address do not constitute the biggest source of health care spending. Instead, it is the huge medical bills incurred by the sickest patients.

Studies show that about 20 percent of patients, including those with chronic diseases or within six months of death, account

Consumer-Driven Plans May Slow Spending . . .

The management consultant Deloitte Touche Tohmatsu says consumer-driven health plans (CDHPs) appear to be delivering on their early promises to lower medical inflation. The firm found that such plans' cost to employers rose at about one-third the rate of some traditional managed care plans last year.

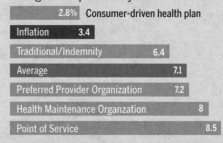

2.8%	Consumer-driven health plan
Inflation	3.4
Traditional/Indemnity	6.4
Average	7.1
Preferred Provider Organization	7.2
Health Maintenance Organzation	8
Point of Service	8.5

SOURCE: Deloitte Center for Health Solutions 2006 annual survey of 152 large employers.

. . . But They're Leaving Patients Dissatisfied

Last fall, the Employee Benefit Research Institute and Commonwealth Fund found that workers in CDHPs are more likely to forgo medical care because of the cost and are generally less satisfied with their plans than with traditional comprehensive health coverage. The study differentiated between workers in CDHPs with and without health savings accounts (HSAs).

Are you satisfied with the quality of your health care?

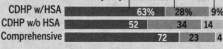

	Extremely/Very	Somewhat	Not
CDHP w/HSA	63%	28%	9%
CDHP w/o HSA	52	34	14
Comprehensive	72	23	4

Have you ever delayed or avoided health care due to cost?

	Yes	No
CDHP w/HSA	35%	65%
CDHP w/o HSA	31	69
Comprehensive	17	83

Have you ever not filled a prescription due to cost?

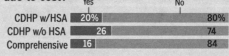

	Yes	No
CDHP w/HSA	20%	80%
CDHP w/o HSA	26	74
Comprehensive	16	84

Would you be likely to stay with your current health plan given the opportunity to change?

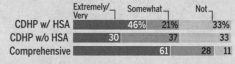

	Extremely/Very	Somewhat	Not
CDHP w/ HSA	46%	21%	33%
CDHP w/o HSA	30	37	33
Comprehensive	61	28	11

SOURCE: Survey of 1,204 adults Sept. 28- Oct. 19. Margin of sampling error +/− 3 percentage points

for 80 percent of the U.S. health care tab at any given time. HSAs would probably do little for these individuals, who spend thousands of dollars a year on medical costs and have little incentive to reduce spending because they need constant care.

Indeed, those with chronic illnesses requiring several types of drugs might incur even higher out-of-pocket costs with the high-deductible plans than they would in more traditional managed care arrangements.

Even experts who back the concept of HSAs acknowledge that their effect could be marginal, at least initially. "There are huge challenges [to overcome] before consumer-driven heath care can affect things in any significant way," said Joseph Antos, a health care economist at the conservative American Enterprise Institute and a supporter of HSAs.

Adds Harvard Business School professor Regina E. Herzlinger, another HSA advocate, "There is no magic. Are HSAs good? Yes. But are they for everyone? No. There must be more than one solution."

Some of the skepticism stems from the fact that patients with HSAs lose the incentive to save money after they pay the deductible in the accompanying insurance plan. Once a ceiling on out-of-pocket costs is reached, patients get coverage similar to what is offered in traditional employer-sponsored plans.

Patients also need pricing information and other tools to find less expensive health providers, assuming their conditions are not life-threatening. Virtually all health care economists note that there is a severe lack of user-friendly information for people to consult before selecting health services. Hospitals currently use a "chargemaster," or lengthy list of prices for procedures, to establish the cost of care rendered. The lists may include tens of thousands of items, and prices are changed in an ad hoc fashion. That leads to variations in the cost of basic services, such as a chest x-ray, even among hospitals in the same county. Patients now see the charges only when they or their insurers are billed after a procedure.

Beyond the questions about how economically effective HSAs will be, there is evidence to suggest that patients do not like the new insurance arrangements. A recent survey of 1,204 workers ages 21-64 by the Employee Benefit Research Institute, a nonpartisan think tank funded by major employers, and the Commonwealth Fund, a health research organization, found that individuals with traditional health insurance were more satisfied with their coverage than their counterparts in consumer-directed plans. Patients in consumer-driven plans with health problems or annual incomes under $50,000 were more likely to avoid, delay or skip necessary medical procedures. The study found that few health plans of any variety provided cost and quality information to help individuals make informed decisions about their care.

The findings parallel earlier surveys, such as a 2005 survey of 2,500 adults by the consulting firm McKinsey and Co., that found workers in consumer-driven plans were less satisfied with the arrangements than with their previous insurance. Lack of information about options was a primary reason for the discontent.

Supporters of HSAs in the business community maintain that they will have a positive effect, even if they fail to suppress medical inflation. By lowering costs for individual businesses, the accounts will allow workers to continue to be covered by some form of health insurance and take a much more hands-on role in deciding what level of care they receive.

"We've moved on from managed care to the idea of trying choice," said Maria Ghazal, director of public policy for the Business Roundtable. "Employers have been interested in HSAs because the control of the dollars shifts to employees. It's the biggest thing to hit."

Hospital Pricing: Complex, and Seemingly Arbitrary

Experts say that patients in consumer-driven medical insurance plans will not be able to adequately comparison shop for services unless they can obtain easily understood menus of prices. That is particularly difficult in hospitals, which generally offer thousands of distinct products and services — with the charges for consumers (and, most often, their insurers) set in a seemingly ad hoc fashion.

The hospital's comprehensive price list is known in the industry as the "chargemaster," but California is the only state that requires the lists be made public. Comparing 2005 prices at a sampling of five of the 35 hospitals in Orange County, a large urban and suburban jurisdiction with a socio-economically and racially diverse population, illustrates the wide disparities for common services.

	Brain CT Scan	ER Visit (moderate injury)	Mammogram	Echocardiogram	Aspirin (325 milligrams)
CHAPMAN MEDICAL CENTER (114 beds in the outer suburbs of Anaheim, recently sold by Tenet Healthcare Corp. to Integrated Healthcare Holdings)	$2,392	**$694**	$348	$936	$2.50
COASTAL COMMUNITIES (178 beds in densely populated Santa Ana, also IHH-owned)	1,790	381	323	876	6.25
FOUNTAIN VALLEY REGIONAL (400 beds in small, well-educated suburb of Fountain Valley, owned by the Tenet Healthcare Corp.)	**3,284** (most expensive)	477	**626**	**1,228**	**6.25**
HOAG MEMORIAL (419 beds, not-for-profit Presbyterian hospital on the waterfront in Newport Beach, rated best in the county)	**1,050** (least expensive)	375	218	955	free
ANAHEIM MEMORIAL (217 beds in northwest Anaheim, part of the Memorial Care health system, which owns five hospitals in California)	1,854	446	**185**	859	.05

A Revolution In Health Care

STEVE CASE FOUNDED America Online on the bet that consumers would want a convenient, user-friendly way to connect to the Internet. Now, he is moving into health care, and his bet this time is that patients can and want to navigate the health care system on their own.

Case, 47, is spending upward of $500 million on a venture called Revolution LLC that consists, so far, of eight separate health care ventures. The companies include two that help employers manage health savings accounts, a chain of walk-in clinics in stores and Internet sites that may one day include consumer-friendly content such as patient reviews of doctors modeled on the customer reviews found on the online bookseller Amazon.com.

The popularity of these ventures will provide an early assessment of how Americans are responding to new consumer-driven health care plans that give patients responsibility to shop for health care. Case believes aging baby boomers will naturally gravitate to the services, drawn both by the desire to take more direct control over their well-being and balance their families' health needs with busy schedules.

"I'll probably spend the next 20 years trying to fix the health care system," he said. "Many people think the health care system is broken and getting worse. I'd want them to know there is a better way. It's not going to happen overnight, but we're on the cusp of a wave of change that'll ultimately give consumers more choice and control and convenience."

Case founded Revolution in 2003 after a controversial two-year stint as chairman of AOL-Time Warner Inc. The Hawaii native engineered the controversial merger that created the media conglomerate but left under pressure after AOL's market value plummeted. Case still exhibits the nuanced language and quick delivery that made him a star in the go-go 1990s. And he is big on specifics, pausing during an interview to muse on whether the health care market is undergoing "fragmentation" or "segmentation."

Case has attracted several high-profile Washington collaborators. Revolution's general counsel is Ron Klain, former chief of staff to Attorney General Janet Reno and Vice President Al Gore in the Clinton administration. Ex-Bush administration Secretary of State Colin L. Powell sits on Revolution's board of directors, as does former Fannie Mae Chairman and Clinton budget director Franklin Raines.

Case says he became more aware of patients' needs while watching his brother, Dan, an investment banker, battle and ultimately succumb to brain cancer in 2003. Case says he bristled at the long hours Dan Case spent waiting to see specialists during the final months of his life.

The father of five also says he understands how hard it is to find time during the workweek for medical appointments.

The underlying concept behind all of Case's ventures is that consumers will willingly seek out alternatives for some types of medical care and shop for services if they have enough choices and easy-to-understand information about prices. Case puts faith in market competition, saying the health care system can be fixed without passing major new laws.

The most visible part of Revolution's effort is Redi Clinic, a growing chain of walk-in clinics found in Wal-Marts, HEB groceries and Duane Reade pharmacies that are staffed mainly by nurse-practitioners. The clinics offer an array of basic health services for prices below what doctors charge in offices. Clinic staff doesn't accept insurance but give customers receipts that they can submit to their carriers.

Redi Clinic is not alone. A rival, MinuteClinic, has 71 has locations

> **"I'll probably spend the next 20 years trying to fix the health care system."**
> — Steve Case

MEASURING PERFORMANCE

The push for HSAs isn't the only market-driven effort to control health care spending. Insurers and businesses increasingly are linking payments to doctors and hospitals to the quality of care patients receive. The trend is fueled by the perception that some providers are being overpaid for substandard care, and that patients who have to make multiple visits to resolve a medical problem are a prime reason for increased health care spending.

"You want to reward ... providers who do it well the first time," said Gail R. Wilensky, senior fellow at the health research organization Project HOPE and a former Medicare administrator in the administration of President George Bush. "That is a fundamentally different dynamic than what we have now. If you screw it up, you get paid twice. It's a terribly perverse system."

The "pay-for-performance" movement originated in the late 1990s, fueled by business and insurer concerns about patient safety. Public and private corporations that provide health benefits formed a coalition known as The Leapfrog Group in 1998 to advocate for higher quality care. The group, which now consists of more than 170 Fortune 500 companies, encourages large employers to identify health plans and hospitals that provide exemplary service, then prod workers to use their services. The Commonwealth Fund, which helped establish the group, counts close to 100 pay-for-performance programs nationwide.

The movement has prompted some unusual alliances. The American Board of Internal Medicine has signed on with one program called "Bridges to Excellence" that is administered by large employers including General Electric Co., Procter & Gamble, and Verizon Corp. Internists who agree to monitor their performance might qualify for bonus payments if they meet certain benchmarks.

In California, a state on the vanguard of the movement, half of all physicians will be graded by pay-for-performance programs within five years.

The efforts are providing an important benefit to patients by generating report cards they can use to shop for medical services. Pay-for-performance programs for hospital care, for example, measure such quality-of-care criteria as the prevalence of post-surgery infections or how often heart-bypass patients have to return to surgery within 24 hours because of complications. They also often gauge how long patients wait in emergency rooms before getting treatment or how quickly someone reporting chest pain gets an electrocardiogram. The programs sometimes measure such patient

in retail stores and in corporate buildings across the country. MinuteClinic's chairman is Glen Nelson, a surgeon and former chairman of Medtronic Inc., a Fortune 500 medical equipment developer.

The menu of services at a MinuteClinic in Bethesda, Md. — posted fast-food style — recently listed pregnancy testing for $39, treatment of minor burns and rashes for $49, wart removal for $59, and flu diagnosis and treatment for $83.

Some health experts believe the clinics will persuade many patients to avoid seeking out a doctor whenever they are ill.

"If they're successful, it means the American public will be satisfied with going to a nurse and not requiring a doctor to be there for these well-defined services," said Jack Rowe, chairman and chief executive officer of the insurance giant Aetna, which covers treatments at MinuteClinics in Maryland and Pennsylvania. "That's always been the question. Many nurses are fully capable of taking care of these problems, but there's been a resistance to that on the part of society."

The viability of clinics is enhanced by consumer-driven health care featuring HSAs and high-deductible insurance plans. These people may be more selective consumers because they face potentially higher out-of-pocket costs for medical services than if they were in traditional employer-sponsored health plans. Case thinks these patients will gravitate to conveniently located, low-cost providers, only visiting a doctor or hospital for more serious ailments.

Some health care analysts worry that the use of clinics and other providers could weaken the doctor-patient relationship. A survey of 43,600 MinuteClinic customers over the past half-year found 64 percent of respondents would have otherwise sought care for their medical problem from their primary-care physician. Another 23 percent would have gone to an emergency room or urgent care center while 8.5 percent would have not sought any care at all.

Experts note increased reliance on the clinics could create problems in the larger system. Some analysts worry that the already-splintered health care system could suffer from even less coordination.

"You have trade-offs with this," said Stuart Butler, vice president of domestic and economic policy at the Heritage Foundation, a conservative think tank. "The upside is more convenience, and it's less expensive. The downside is that it's bad enough in the health care system anyway to get communication between the people serving you. If you don't see good transfers of information, yes, you are going to see fragmentation, a lack of follow up and miscommunication in the system."

PLAYING BOTH ENDS

Case not only is running clinics but also is actively selling consumer-driven health plans to businesses, as well as helping administer the benefit packages for smaller companies. A Revolution division called Extend Benefits LLC began offering consumer-driven and other health plans to members of Sam's Club, the warehouse shopping chain that is part of Wal-Mart Stores Inc. Sam's Club is waiving fees for members who sign up for themselves, or their businesses. Yet another Revolution division, ConnectYourCare Inc., helps employers who already offer workers consumer-driven plans to administer the accounts.

Case is using his expertise with Internet businesses to cater to the needs of patients with HSAs. A Revolution company called SimoHealth offers patients spreadsheets to track visits to clinics, out-of-pocket expenses and prescriptions. It even provides sample letters that people can use to lodge appeals when an insurer denies coverage for a service. The market leader for such software is Intuit Inc.'s Quicken Medical Expense Manager.

The former Internet executive also is assembling a network of health care Web sites to help patients in consumer-driven plans navigate the health care system. A venture called 1-800-Schedule that Case bought is pitched as health care "yellow pages," allowing patients to access lists of providers by specialty and make appointments online. Revolution eventually may expand this into a virtual shopper's guide to health care, including patient comments about providers. Later this year, Revolution also will launch a Web service providing consumer-oriented health news, entering a field dominated by such medical Web sites as WebMD.

---

safety criteria as whether a hospital has a computerized system to enter drug prescriptions.

The pay-for-performance concept has caught the attention of federal and state officials, who are adapting it for Medicare and for Medicaid, the federal-state program for the poor. The budget reconciliation package that became law Feb. 1 requires the secretary of Health and Human Services to develop a plan to implement pay-for-performance programs for hospitals beginning in fiscal 2009.

Despite the programs' widespread appeal, some health care experts warn that the pay-for-performance concept should not be viewed as a panacea.

A Harvard School of Public Health study of the initiative of the big insurer PacifiCare Health System, published in October in the Journal of the American Medical Association, concluded that paying health care providers to reach a fixed performance goal might not yield significant gains in quality for the money spent. The researchers said doctors with historically high standards of care collected the most bonuses, even though they only had to maintain the status quo. Physicians who previously provided lower-quality care but significantly improved their standards were not comparably rewarded.

The market-based approaches to controlling health spending go beyond grading doctors and hospitals. Insurers are promoting more frequent screening for serious diseases as well as wellness programs that advocate healthier lifestyles.

Lumenos, for example, offers health incentive accounts that award individuals credits for using preventive care services that they can later apply to out-of-pocket medical expenses.

In Florida, Republican Gov. Jeb Bush is taking a similar tack by experimenting with a Medicaid pilot project that includes giving beneficiaries cash for participating in preventive care such as weight loss classes or smoking cessation programs.

Health insurers increasingly are agreeing to cover the cost of screening for a variety of types of cancers and are using diagnostic tools such as magnetic resonance imaging (MRI) and CT scans — not to mention genetic screening — to identify early signs of disease or prevent things from going wrong. They reason that spending more when a patient appears healthy is preferable to waiting until he shows signs of a debilitating, hard-to-treat condition.

But the testing must be done judiciously to make a dent in health spending. More frequent use of diagnostic tests has been one of the leading sources of medical inflation. And with the cost of an MRI scan of the breast or spine often exceeding $1,000, health plans could drive up spending on each patient by encouraging more screening if it wasn't necessary.

REINVENTING THE SYSTEM

Doubts about whether any of the market-based initiatives will actually save the health system are certain to be cited by proponents of more sweeping changes, who believe the government must take a more active role setting standards of care and controlling costs.

A series of government-sponsored health care forums under way in 30 cities is already revealing signs of discontent. The forums, mandated by the 2003 Medicare drug law, will prove fodder for a report to Congress due later this year suggesting ways to change the health system.

When 150 Florida residents met at one such gathering in Orlando in late January, 96 percent of the attendees said America's health system was in a "crisis" or faced "major problems." National polls reveal similar alarm. A CBS News-New York Times poll in late January found that nine out of ten Americans think the system needs fundamental change. Such sentiments have not been as prevalent since the Clinton administration advocated a sweeping overhaul of the national health system, including mandatory national health coverage, in 1993 and 1994.

The Clinton plan died in the face of overwhelming opposition from congressional Republicans and health insurers. Since then, GOP leaders have advocated incremental steps toward fixing the health system, convinced that heavy-handed government intervention will crush innovation in the market.

It is unclear whether their vision will prevail. Health care is one of the most unpredictable components of domestic policy, endlessly whipsawed by demographic shifts, market innovations and political pressure. Numerous obstacles could halt the consumer-driven movement early in its existence. Patients and the medical establishment might resent businesses' and insurers' overriding focus on cost control, just as they bitterly fought managed care companies' efforts to ration care in the 1990s. Congress, faced with deepening budget deficits, might decide to scale back the tax advantages behind HSAs, especially if the GOP loses control of one or more chambers.

If the consumer-driven plans do not deliver measurable results within a few years, members of both parties might shift their focus from costs to expanding access to health care, and to the nation's 45 million uninsured individuals.

Advocates of the new movement understand the vicissitudes behind promoting change. Many conservatives threw their hopes behind managed care in the 1980s and 1990s, convinced that HMOs could control runaway medical inflation. The plans did, to some degree. But they were applied with such a heavy hand that consumer backlash forced the insurers to stop rationing care. A similar result this time will probably spur calls for more sweeping change, including a revival of those for universal coverage of all Americans.

"We have to hope all these dominoes will fall into place," said American Enterprise Institute's Antos, an HSA advocate. "Otherwise this will be the latest experiment that didn't get off the launching pad." ■

A Parting of Ways at the Border

The rift in the GOP over Bush's immigration policy reflects the nation's mixed signals on an issue roiled by security fears, regional biases and hard economic realities

PRESIDENT BUSH relied on a coalition of cultural and economic conservatives to win the White House and stay in power. In recent months, though, the alliance that has survived by avoiding internal disputes over questions such as abortion and tax cuts has begun to fracture over the highly charged issue of immigration.

By forcing the Senate to debate immigration, Republican leaders have highlighted rather than hidden the stark differences between them. On one side are pro-business Republicans, who say the nation's economy depends on immigrant labor. On the other stand the cultural or social conservatives, who say illegal immigrants steal American jobs, threaten security and erode the nation's predominant culture.

President Bush, whose public support has been dragged down by the war in Iraq and his administration's mishandling of a succession of issues — the most recent being seaport security — is being forced to defend his own proposal for a guest worker program that critics say would allow those already in the country to gain citizenship.

The backlash against Bush's plan from within his own party was only to be expected, experts on the issue say. Many conservatives consider it little more than amnesty for the 12 million illegal immigrants already in the country, the kind of policy over which they had spent years criticizing President Bill Clinton and other Democrats.

With an eye on public discontent over immigration policy, Senate Majority Leader Bill Frist, a Tennessee Republican with presidential aspirations, has demanded that the Senate debate the issue. If the Judiciary Committee cannot first come up with a bill after five unsuccessful markups, Frist will bring his own proposal to the floor, and it looks nothing like Bush's.

The Senate debate, in fact, will revolve largely around the views and political ambitions of a handful of senators who are looking at a broader context: either their party's prospects or their own; the future of the nation's economy or its cultural identity; the costs of illegal immigration or the costs to immigrants themselves.

Sen. John McCain of Arizona is the front-running candidate for the 2008 Republican nomination and so has the most to lose in the immigration debate. He has sided with Bush on the need for a guest worker program, though his state is the home of the Minutemen — the civilian posse trying to monitor and halt illegal immigration.

Frist is the contender trying to find his feet in the presidential nomination race. As he did last year with the Terri Schiavo debate, Frist is siding with the party's staunchest cultural conservatives, who have also been Bush's most loyal supporters. He wants the Senate to act on border security before it even debates guest workers.

The most urgent voice in the debate, however, is that of Colorado Republican Rep. Tom Tancredo, a self-styled populist from a suburban Denver district who is traveling the country — and presidential primary states — to demand not only control of the borders but enforcement of immigration laws at the workplace. He is joined by Rep. J.D. Hayworth, an Arizona Republican who has called the current flow of illegal immigration an "invasion."

Among Democrats, who are generally keeping a low-profile on the issue while Republicans squabble, Sen. Edward M. Kennedy of Massachusetts has become a potential dealmaker on immigration, in fact going into partnership with McCain on a version of Bush's guest worker plan.

Opinion polls give these central players little advice on how to handle the issue beyond a general public unease about the level of illegal immigration and a general uncertainty about what to do. For instance, 62 percent of voters say undocumented workers should not be allowed to progress toward citizenship, but an even higher percentage does not want to build a wall between the United States and Mexico.

The cross-cutting permutations of the immigration debate, along with the risks and rewards, seem almost endless for both parties. Among Republicans, the fractures extend beyond the main divisions between cultural and economic conservatives. Some evangelical Christian groups are torn between their desire for law and order and a perceived moral duty to help keep immigrant families together.

Faithful Divided On 'Thou Shalt'

AS IF THE BROAD DIVIDE over immigration weren't complicated enough for the different factions of Republicans, the internecine politics gets even more baroque: A core constituency of the party — religious voters — is itself fractured over the moral questions of how the United States ought to respond to the wave of illegal immigrants.

U.S. Catholic bishops, leaders of an important religious group that the GOP has been working hard to win over, call for compassion and understanding for illegal immigrants — and denounce as uncharitable and short-sighted a House-passed bill that focuses solely on border enforcement. So, too, are leaders of World Relief, an aid organization founded by the conservative National Association of Evangelicals, advocating a more Samaritan-like approach.

To make its case, World Relief quotes the Book of Leviticus: "The alien living with you must be treated as one of your native-born. Love him as yourself. . . ."

Then again, other evangelicals, Catholics and religious people just as passionately argue the other side. Their priority is strengthening the borders and cracking down on illegal immigration, which they say threatens the welfare of families here who have followed the rules, including the working-poor.

Conservative commentator Phyllis Schlafly, a Catholic, has written that any "amnesty" for illegal immigrants, including a guest worker program, such as the one proposed by President Bush, is "immoral."

Immigration, unlike abortion, is not a top-tier concern for this constituency. Some of the biggest names on the religious right, such as James Dobson of Focus on the Family, have stayed on the sidelines, saying they need to stick with the moral family issues closest to their mission. But there are strong feelings among other conservative religious leaders on both sides of the debate.

And that further complicates the calculus for congressional Republicans, who need every last vote they can get in this November's midterm elections. Stand one way, and they anger religious conservatives who see things the way Schlafly does. Choose the other side, and they turn off other evangelicals and, perhaps most important, Catholics, with whom they have begun to make successful inroads.

Catholics are still sharply divided politically, "so even secondary issues could make a difference" in the GOP's efforts to make them a part of their coalition, says political scientist John Green of the University of Akron.

The divisions among Christian conservative leaders reflect the conflicted feelings of religion-minded voters. In January, the Pew Research Center for the People & the Press reported that 64 percent of white evangelicals surveyed said that making it tougher for illegal immigrants to enter the United States should be a top priority.

And yet, another Pew survey last year also found members of large religious communities, including evangelicals, "all over the block" in their views toward immigrants, as Green puts it. World Relief is not a left-wing group, outside the mainstream of the evangelical world. Its founder, the National Association of Evangelicals, is the umbrella group for traditionally conservative churches that together claim 30 million congregants.

If the issue is politically complicated, there's also nothing easy about it morally, says conservative Christian leader Gary L. Bauer. The poor families now here legally, who have to compete with illegal immigrants for low-skilled jobs, also have a claim on the conscience of the public, he says. "The justice argument is very muddled at that point."

Some conservative Christians argue that illegal immigration hurts all families by straining the health care system, schools and law enforcement. Assisting illegal immigrants or allowing them to become legal once they have slipped in illegally also encourages law-breaking, something that's counter to Christian morality, they say.

God "would never condone law-breaking," says Sadie Fields, state chair of the Christian Coalition of Georgia.

WHAT SHOULD A CHRISTIAN DO?

Jenny Hwang of World Relief's refugee and immigration program says no one supports illegal immigration, and everyone wants the borders secured. But policy makers should recognize the human toll of an immigration system that has long been broken, she says.

Last fall, that group, the Catholic bishops and others signed a statement calling for a legal, orderly way for migrants to enter and find work. They also want measures allowing "hard-working immigrants who are already contributing to this country to come out of the shadows" and work toward becoming legal residents. They are not talking about amnesty, Hwang says: Immigrants should have to go to the back of the line, pay heavy fines and otherwise earn legal status over time.

Richard Land, a leader of the conservative Southern Baptists, says his denomination might be open to such measures, as long as the border is secure and illegal immigrants aren't getting a free pass.

Some big names on the religious right have stayed on the sidelines of the immigration debate, preferring to stick with moral issues closer to their core mission.

Land, the bishops and others also criticize the House border security bill for, among other things, making it a crime to assist people known to be illegal, something they say would make criminals of Christians trying to do their religious duty to the needy.

For the bishops, there's an added, institutional imperative to this fight: Many Hispanic immigrants are Catholics themselves.

Many are also conservatives, argues Samuel Rodriguez Jr., a conservative evangelical minister and head of the National Hispanic Christian Leadership Conference. That means it's in the interests of both religious conservatives and the GOP to get behind initiatives to put them on the path to becoming citizens, he says.

Polls show that Hispanic immigrants support the social conservative line on abortion and same-sex relationship, among other hot-button social issues. If the GOP turns its back on them, the party risks "alienating, not just for a generation, but forever, the fastest-growing face of the traditionalist conservative voting bloc," says Rodriguez.

Republican leaders want to unite the two wings of their party, but they don't want to lose support among Hispanic voters who might be turned off by a heated debate in the Senate. Tens of thousands of people recently marched in Phoenix, Milwaukee and other cities to protest the House-passed legislation that would make it a felony to be in the country illegally.

"This is a tricky moment for us, and I think it is an important moment for us," said Republican Sen. Mel Martinez of Florida. "The voice that is heard from our party over the next couple weeks will have an awful lot to do with how we are viewed with Hispanic America."

Perhaps the biggest obstacle to a deal on immigration is that there is so little room for compromise between the main factions. Emotions seem to trump almost every effort to find middle ground.

Alan K. Simpson, the former Republican Senator from Wyoming, was at the center of an equally emotional debate on the issue in the mid-1980s and knows how difficult it can be to get to yes.

"You talk about an honest approach of limiting immigration, and you will be called a bigot, a racist or a xenophobe," Simpson recalled. However, if you favor more immigration and caring about immigrants, "people yell, 'Button your shirt, your heart fell out.'"

BILL FRIST
THE CONTENDER

A HELICOPTER TOUR over the Rio Grande was enough to convince the Senate Majority Leader last October that Congress had to do something to control illegal immigration.

Ten days later and back in Washington, Frist joined McCain and Texas Republican Sen. John Cornyn, who have been considered leaders on the immigration issue, for a news conference, announcing that immigration would be a priority for the Senate in 2006.

Cornyn and McCain said the issue required a comprehensive look, with some kind of guest worker program vital to any legislation. But Frist surprised his colleagues by coming out stridently for better border security and enforcement of immigration laws in the rest of the country.

"It is clear that a country that cannot control its own border is going to have a hard time controlling its destiny, and therefore it's time to act," Frist said, echoing a complaint many conservatives have made for decades.

What's driving Frist to follow the House and lean away from the tougher questions may be the simple fact that it is easier that way. As majority leader, he has his caucus to consider. Many members are facing tough re-election bids at a time when Republicans are sagging in the polls. Policies that speak to the public's frustration with porous borders might help overcome growing discontent with the war in Iraq and other unpopular policies.

Frist introduced legislation March 16 similar to what the House passed Dec. 16. Frist's measure would authorize extensive fencing along the Southern border and criminalize those found in the country illegally. That is now a civil violation, and most are simply deported. The bill also would set up a mandatory electronic employment verification process that would be phased in for all businesses within five years. In the past, Frist has been reluctant to burden business with immigration enforcement.

Not only did Frist introduce legislation, he is forcing it to the floor by sticking to a deadline for debate. The Judiciary Committee, which has jurisdiction over immigration, had struggled through markups in March without dealing with the most pressing question: what to do about the illegal immigrants already in the country. Before the Senate left for a weeklong recess, Frist made good on his threat by making his own border security bill the first order of business when the chamber reconvenes March 27.

His impatience might have as much to do with the presidential calendar as the upcoming congressional elections.

"It is not a secret that Sen. Frist is running for president, and he recognizes the need to do something about this," said Tancredo. "That's great. I do think it would be better for him to say, 'I have a good idea and I influenced the passage of legislation we can all be proud of.' He can point that difference out."

Frist also could make a good case with social conservatives and others frustrated by illegal immigration by clearly distinguishing himself on the issue from the president and McCain. "This allows him to draw a sharp contrast," said James Gimpel, a University of Maryland professor and co-author of the 1999 book 'Congressional Politics of Immigration Reform.' "By introducing this legislation, this comparison is being written about all over the country, and Frist looks like an alternative to McCain."

Frist finished ahead of McCain and other Republican candidates during a recent straw poll on his home turf in Tennessee. Though he may be unknown nationally, he retains a solid base in the Southeast, so a strong showing among conservatives in the West could make him a formidable contender.

All of that may be responsible for Frist figuratively holding a stopwatch to the Judiciary panel and forcing the debate before any real consensus can be achieved.

His commitment will be truly tested if the Senate succeeds in passing a bill. Then Frist will be in position to appoint conferees to deal with the House. In those closed-door sessions, the most difficult negotiating is expected. Conferees must find some middle ground between the House bill, which is favored by some of the loudest critics of illegal immigration, and whatever the Senate decides, which is expected

FENCE BUILDER: Frist, who visited a Los Angeles detention center Feb. 21, wants tighter border controls.

to be more moderate.

"This is where we will be able to tell how serious Frist is," Tancredo said. "And if we can keep the president out of it. If the president weighs in, boy, I don't know what will happen."

It is difficult to imagine Bush directly challenging Frist on the immigration issue, since they have been such close allies. But given Bush's public support, it might not matter anyway. "There is obviously the power of persuasion," said Jack Pitney, a professor of government at Claremont McKenna College. "The difficulty is a president is less persuasive when his poll numbers are down."

JOHN McCAIN THE CANDIDATE

WHEREVER HE GOES, McCain can't help but draw a crowd. That happens when you have a rock star quality reserved for only a handful of candidates who reach the upper echelon of presidential politics. He has a story that can play anywhere: a decorated Vietnam veteran and P.O.W. who became a blunt-spoken conservative politician with a maverick streak. His quick wit, affability and popularity among independent voters — the sort who flocked to Ross Perot a decade ago — make him today's most formidable politician next to the president himself.

Yet with all that in his favor, McCain has struggled with the group he needs in order to win the GOP nomination: social conservatives in his own party. And by siding with Bush for a pro-business policy on immigration, he has made himself a target for the very people he needs as voters in the Republican primaries.

McCain has not helped his effort by pairing up with Kennedy, who is arguably the most liberal member of the Senate, on legislation that would allow the nearly 12 million illegal immigrants now in the country to remain and even to earn citizenship.

McCain is under enormous pressure in his home state, where vivid images of Mexicans crossing the Southwest border dominate the nightly news. Arizona spawned the Minuteman Project, the infamous grass-roots organization that volunteers to patrol the border for illegal immigrants, and that group has little love for McCain. In March, the group boasted of having 7,000 volunteers descending on the Southwest border.

Yet McCain remains committed to his effort. He is Bush's biggest ally. They are bank-

SIDING WITH BUSH: McCain, seen here speaking at a rally in New York, favors a guest worker plan.

ing on the economic forces that illustrate the U.S. dependency on immigrant labor. A recent study by the Pew Hispanic Center determined that 7.3 million of the 140 million workers in the U.S. labor force are illegal immigrants — or one in 20. Supporters of the McCain-Kennedy proposal say those are jobs that Americans don't want and that immigrants are more than happy to take: insulation workers (36 percent are illegal immigrants), roofers (29 percent), butchers (27 percent) and dishwashers (23 percent), to name a few.

Some of Bush's allies on Capitol Hill say the problem with the guest worker program he proposed two years ago is one of political strategy and not substance. Many GOP members might embrace some kind of guest worker program, but they wonder why the president pushed the guest worker plan ahead of border security.

Bush "led with his political chin when he decided to talk exclusively in the beginning in terms of a guest worker program," said California Republican Rep. Dan Lungren, who

helped draft sections of the House border security and enforcement bill. "It's an essential part of the solution. But if you start with that, you are losing a lot of people in the beginning."

Bush has recently tried to right the balance by talking about border security at the same time he discusses guest workers.

Some leading conservatives say Bush understands that the issue is more about economics than anything else. Grover Norquist, president of Americans for Tax Reform, says that many of the problems associated with immigration are a function of state welfare policies, and not the nation's borders. That, he says, is why immigration is less of a burden in Texas than California.

"We need more people in the United States to remain a world power and simply to function as an economy," Norquist said. "Our immigration rates are below what our job requirements are. We need 500,000 people more than we allow people in [annually]."

For McCain, speaking to large immigrant groups helps him move toward the political center and reach voters that other members of his party might overlook.

Martinez, who is leaning toward supporting the McCain-Kennedy legislation with some modifications, said McCain is a smart politician who has his eye on a powerful constituency.

"I think he is looking at the glass half-full," Martinez said. "He is generating a lot of enthusiasm for the largest growing minority in American. . . . I'm guessing he sees a huge opportunity with Hispanic Americans."

Simpson does not think McCain's support for a guest worker program will affect his presidential chances. "It won't hurt him at all," Simpson said. Only by seeking bipartisan support can Congress resolve the difficult immigration issues, he says, and McCain is taking the right approach reaching to his left rather than his right.

Congress, Simpson said, needs "a guy with guts. Step up to the plate! Stop trying to please everybody. I can't tell you how to succeed, but I can tell you how to fail: trying to please everybody."

McCain has taken his proposal on the road to Miami and New York, among other places.

And thousands of immigrants have come to see him in Washington, most recently a crowd of Irish-Americans from Boston and New York who arrived March 8 to show support for McCain's legislation. The rally also featured Kennedy and New York Sen. Hillary Rodham Clinton, the Democratic front-runner who has since criticized the border security bill that the House passed as "mean-spirited."

With the three of them, the room had the feel of a campaign stop, prompting McCain to joke that the warm reception was "enough to make a guy want to run for president." And he used the opportunity to remind the crowd of the broad reach of his proposal.

"Your cause today is not just for Irish," McCain told the crowd. "Your cause is for that Hispanic woman who is working, washing dishes in some restaurant in Phoenix who can't come here to join you. Your cause is for the woman from Sudan, who came here with nothing but the clothes on her back. Many of you from New York know there is a lady who stands besides the golden door with her lamp lit for people from Ireland and from all over the world. That's the great tradition of this great nation of ours."

The crowd responded by standing on their chairs and applauding and whistling for several minutes, then swarming around him on his way out.

TOM TANCREDO
THE POPULIST

IN ANOTHER LIFE, Rep. Tom Tancredo would be an anonymous back-bencher in the House or even still teaching social studies to junior high school students in the Denver suburbs. Instead, the Colorado Republican has 12 million illegal immigrants to thank for a mercurial rise in 21st century politics.

Catapulting onto the national scene as a single-issue populist, Tancredo is a hawk in the war on immigration. He has become the face, voice and frustration of ordinary Americans fed up with the growing number of illegal immigrants who are taking U.S. jobs, speaking Spanish, ignoring U.S. culture — even to the point for some of refusing to salute the U.S. flag.

Tancredo offers a simple solution: Congress needs to adopt the most severe policies at its disposal to make life utterly unbearable for illegal immigrants — most of them Mexican.

The Minutemen embrace him as their hero, welcoming him to a rally in front of the Capitol on Feb. 8 with the kind of applause reserved for heads of state. He received a standing ovation Feb. 9 from this year's Conservative Political Action Committee conference, where he told the crowd, "It is the president who is out of step with his party, not Tom Tancredo."

"Tancredo is already a political winner on the issue," Pitney said. "Whatever happens, he has planted the flag for the social conservatives on immigration issues."

Hearing that some view him as a success

despite the outcome of the immigration debate only seems to sadden Tancredo.

"If that is true, that is in a way unfortunate," Tancredo said. "I don't have the power or influence of so many of my colleagues. I'm just a guy who has certainly burned a lot of bridges with the party. My ability to affect change is always going to come from the outside. I have to work harder to get the Congress to respond. If I were in a position of leadership, I'm sure it would be a lot easier."

Some people have accused him of being a racist and a xenophobe. He has endured intense criticism from within his own party; Tancredo said presidential adviser Karl Rove once warned him, "Do not darken the doorstep of the White House."

He views himself as a realist in a post-Sept. 11 culture, simply looking out for America's best interests. For Bush, the world is made up of "trading blocks and not nations," Tancredo says. That is where they fundamentally disagree.

"If you are committed to that kind of world view, then it is easy to understand why you would [ask], 'What, you want to build a fence and make it very difficult to get into this country?' " Tancredo said in describing what he sees as a disconnect between Bush and social or cultural conservatives. "That has something to do with it. What extent, I have no idea. Pure speculation."

Tancredo has been relentless in promoting his vision for controlling immigration. He's kept a busy travel schedule in between sessions, flying off on the weekends to Iowa, New Hampshire, South Carolina and other hot campaign spots to push the immigration debate into the 2008 election. He's a regular on talk radio and cable television — in both English and Spanish.

Perhaps most importantly, he has nurtured the House Immigration Reform Caucus, helping it grow from a handful of members to nearly 100. That ability to attract members to the caucus allowed him to become a player in December when the House debated border security legislation. Tancredo, who once spent lonely nights on the floor of the House denouncing U.S. immigration policy, suddenly had both an audience and influence. The House answered by drafting a bill that would require the government to build nearly 700 miles of fence along the U.S.-Mexican border, make it a felony to be illegally present in the United States and severely punish humanitarian workers — including priests and doctors — caught aiding illegal immigrants.

Norquist of Americans for Tax Reform says

ANGRY POPULIST: Tancredo opposes guest worker programs, which he says would lead to amnesty.

Tancredo's approach works against the party's and the nation's interests because it ignores the economy and the demands for hundreds of thousands of workers that cannot get visas — issues that are paramount to Republicans.

Isolationist conservatives have never been successful in national GOP circles because they cannot rally business conservatives to their side, Norquist said, citing the failed presidential campaigns in the 1990s of Patrick Buchanan and the Virginia governor's race of 2005.

"If this was such a wonderful issue, you would be talking to President [Pat] Buchanan, Gov. Kilgore and Sen. Tancredo," Norquist said. "Ask Tancredo when they were running around looking for someone to run for the Senate, why no one talked to him. He was not electable statewide."

TED KENNEDY
THE DEALMAKER

THE IMMIGRATION DEBATE in Congress presented Democrats with the political choice of keeping quiet and hoping that Republicans would shred each other on the issue, or speaking up and risking the same sort of divisions in their own party.

Most have kept quiet. But Kennedy, who played a big role the last time Congress did an overhaul of immigration policy, in the 1980s, has not been so reticent. He has positioned himself as a middleman on an issue where Bush and McCain need Democratic votes to push the Senate in their direction.

Two decades ago, Democrats controlled the House and had influence at the conference table. But even now, with Republicans holding a majority in both chambers, the elder statesman of Northeastern liberals has emerged as a powerful force and partner for Bush. They teamed up on education during Bush's first term. And now Bush, struggling to strike the right balance within his party on the explosive topic of immigration, is dependent on Kennedy in a fight that some insist cannot be won without bipartisan support.

"The reason [immigration] doesn't go anywhere is because of emotion, fear, guilt and racism," said Simpson, who teamed up with Kennedy in 1986 on legislation that gave amnesty to millions of illegal immigrants. "Those words you use to either beat up on the bill, or pass it. It's sad to watch. There is no such thing as a partisan immigration [policy]. It has to be a bipartisan bill that embraces the

national interest."

This time, Kennedy has used his voice to push for a guest worker program that would allow those in the United States illegally to earn a path to citizenship. And Kennedy has found a new Republican partner in McCain.

The McCain-Kennedy bill has drawn bipartisan support from a wide group of senators, including Republicans Sam Brownback of Kansas and Lindsey Graham of South Carolina, as well as Democrats Barack Obama of Illinois and Joseph I. Lieberman of Connecticut.

Kennedy's role as a dealmaker and partner to McCain even earned grudging respect from Norquist. "Apart from Jane Fonda, nobody is wrong on everything in this world," Norquist said. "Ted Kennedy is an American and shares a lot of American values. He has respect for immigrants. He takes that to a principled standpoint."

Working at the Margins

Most illegal immigrants fill low-skill, low-wage jobs in the agriculture, construction and service industries and have become an important labor source for many businesses. Nationwide, there are an estimated 7.3 million undocumented workers, about 5 percent of the total civilian workforce of 140 million. Figures are from March 2005.

	Percent undocumented	Industry total
 **CONSTRUCTION**		
Construction laborers	25	1,614,000
Painters, construction and maintenance	22	768,000
Carpet, floor, and tile installers and finishers	20	330,000
Roofers	29	325,000
Drywall installers, ceiling tile installers, and tapers	28	285,000
Brick masons, block masons, and stonemasons	25	198,000
Helpers, construction trades	28	145,000
Cement masons, concrete finishers, and terrazzo workers	21	141,000
Insulation workers	36	56,000
DOMESTIC		
Maids and housekeepers	22	1,531,000
Laundry and dry-cleaning workers	15	206,000
Pressers and textile workers	25	83,000
Upholsterers	18	72,000
FOOD SERVICE		
Cooks	20	2,218,000
Food preparation workers	17	758,000
Dishwashers	23	367,000
Butchers and other meat, poultry, and fish processing workers	27	322,000
AGRICULTURE		
Miscellaneous agricultural workers	29*	839,000
Graders and sorters of agricultural products	22	74,000
 **OTHER**		
Grounds maintenance workers	25	1,204,000
Packers and packagers	20	548,000
Cleaners of vehicles and equipment	20	427,000
Packaging and filling machine operators and tenders	20	367,000
Sewing machine operators	18	292,000
Helpers, production workers	23	64,000
Parking lot attendants	19	64,000
Computer hardware engineers	20	54,000

*A separate Labor Department study of agricultural workers put this figure at 53 percent.

SOURCE: Bureau of Labor Statistics.

Only a handful of other Senate Democrats publicly addressed the immigration issue as the floor debate approached.

Senate Minority Leader Harry Reid of Nevada recently visited the border with Mexico and criticized Frist for threatening to circumvent the Judiciary Committee's work by bringing his own legislation to the floor. Reid said he would use "every procedural means" to stop Frist.

The McCain-Kennedy bill, Reid said, was a "good place to start." Any immigration policy must include a guest worker program and offer a "path to citizenship" for those here illegally, he said.

The range of differences that Democrats harbor on immigration was becoming apparent, though. California Sen. Dianne Feinstein has repeatedly said she has not seen a guest worker plan she would support. She thinks additional visas should be issued for agricultural workers, and those in the country illegally should be allowed to stay and transition into those jobs. Over time, by meeting several requirements, the workers could adjust their status and ultimately earn a "green card," a non-restrictive visa that allows non-citizens to accept any job they are offered.

Nebraska Democrat Ben Nelson, however, has joined Republicans Jeff Sessions of Alabama and Tom Coburn of Oklahoma in proposing one of the Senate's toughest border security bills, which includes a proposal for a fence along the entire Southern border with Mexico.

If the Bush administration and congressional Republicans hope to pass any immigration legislation this year, some bipartisan arrangement and at least some compromise will be necessary. That will be difficult on an issue with little emotional leeway for compromise and in an election year when Democrats think they can pick up House and Senate seats.

One person who might help Bush is Cornyn, a loyal supporter of his policies on the Hill and a cultural conservative.

Cornyn, along with Arizona Republican

Where They End Up

Illegal immigrants are spread throughout the country, but the largest populations are still in border states and those with major cities. The states with more than 300,000 undocumented immigrants in 2004:

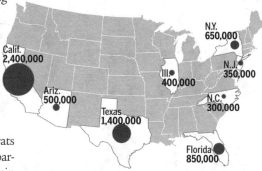

SOURCE: Pew Hispanic Center

WARM WELCOME: Kennedy, here at an April 10 immigration rally, says illegals should have a way to become citizens.

Jon Kyl, has proposed legislation that would allow temporary workers into the country but would force all illegal immigrants to leave before being eligible for guest worker status.

That distinction may be enough to win over some of the cultural conservatives critical of the Bush proposal.

And Cornyn has shown that he's ready to deal across the aisle. When the Judiciary Committee was pressed to act by Frist, Cornyn reached out to Kennedy, making an effort to find common ground on a guest worker plan. The two worked out a last-minute compromise that avoided the issue of what to do about the current population of illegal immigrants.

Whether they can get beyond that is still in doubt. The problem, Cornyn says, is that some people cannot accept any proposal that might be seen as rewarding people for breaking the law.

"No one wants to be punitive or unnecessarily harsh," Cornyn said. "But we have to find a way to build a political consensus to transition those people who have come here illegally, either back to their country of origin or [allow them to] come back after they have left."

But Cornyn is encouraged by the unusual partnerships that have developed between people in both parties. "This is one where the U.S. Chamber of Commerce and La Raza Unida [a Hispanic rights group] are pretty much in lock step," he said. "And you see people like Sen. McCain and Sen. Kennedy with a bill. And you see all sorts of variety. That's one of the things that makes it the hardest, but also one of the most interesting and challenging, to come up with a solution."

Sensing the growing rift in his own party, Bush met March 23 with leaders on this issue, with hopes of building some consensus days before what could be a very public fight among Republicans on the Senate Floor. After the meeting, he cautioned all to watch their tone.

"It's important that we have a serious debate, one that discusses the issues," Bush said. "But I urge members of Congress, and I urge people who like to comment on this issue to make sure the rhetoric is in accord with our traditions. . . . We all may have different family histories, but we all sit around this table as Americans." ■

The Power Of Status Quo

■ The tax gap. If the IRS could collect every penny the law requires, the budget deficit would all but disappear. But despite years of studying the problem, the IRS hasn't begun to close the gap or even devise a comprehensive strategy to do so.

■ Capital vs. labor. The ideological war between those who favor limiting the tax on capital (corporate earnings, personal investments) and those who prefer giving wage-earners a break is largely settled. Through incremental changes in the law, Congress has reduced the tax on capital to the lowest since World War II.

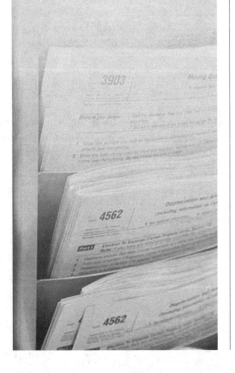

Overhauling the tax code has been a popular idea for years. But fundamental reform will involve disrupting some deeply rooted social and corporate policies.

Just over a year ago, a president flush with re-election victory and "political capital" to spend launched his second term with an ambitious vision to overhaul the U.S. tax system. He created a blue-ribbon commission to evaluate a tableful of restructuring proposals, from modest revisions to the income tax code to more far-reaching ideas, such as a flat tax, a national sales tax and value-added taxes.

"I believe this is an essential task for our country," President Bush said when he created the panel right after the November 2004 elections. "I am firm in my desire to get something done."

In his second State of the Union address since winning re-election, Bush made no mention of the Advisory Panel on Federal Tax Reform or its 272-page report, which was issued last Nov. 1 by its chairman and vice chairman, former Sens. Connie Mack, a Florida Republican, and John B. Breaux, a Louisiana Democrat.

Nor did Bush even utter the words "tax code overhaul." And the White House has signaled that no legislative proposals will be forthcoming in the weeks and months to come. Any initiative to debate the issue in this elec-

CQ Weekly Feb. 6, 2006

tion year will have to come from Congress, where there also seems to be little taste for action in either Republican or Democratic leadership camps.

It's no wonder. Taxes may be Topic A for reform-minded critics on both the right and left, but it's also a potential career killer for any politician who dares to get behind a specific proposal for change. Though everyone complains about the current tax code — it's too complicated, it's inequitable, it's riddled with loopholes — every provision in the law also has its passionate defenders.

Exhibit No. 1 is the leading recommendation of the president's hand-picked tax commission: to scale back the tax break that allows homeowners to deduct the interest paid on their home mortgages.

The reaction to this proposal was swift and brutal. Real estate brokers and home builders squealed that it would pull the rug out from recent buyers who had factored the deduction into their long-term financial plans. Mortgage bankers chimed in against the idea, reflecting the reach and clout of the housing industry that has been the biggest engine of growth in the U.S. economy the past four years.

The fact that brokers, builders and bankers are ubiquitous in nearly every congressional district in the nation wasn't lost on lawmakers,

State of Contention

What do the Teamsters, the National Governors Association and Coca Cola Enterprises have in common? An acute desire to keep state-approved corporate tax breaks coming — a passion they also share with both major parties in every state.

But this featherbedding consensus faces a major challenge in March, when the Supreme Court is expected to rule on a challenge to such tax breaks, which top $50 billion a year.

The case concerns a 2004 ruling on a tax break that Ohio granted to DaimlerChrysler for a $1.2 billion expansion of a Jeep plant in Toledo. The 6th U.S. Circuit Court of Appeals found that the deal violated the Constitution's Commerce Clause by unfairly discriminating against companies that want to develop outside of Ohio. That came as a shot across the bow for the political leaders, corporate lobbies and labor unions with major stakes in such decisions. The Ohio ruling has also galvanized anti-corporate activists, who have filed copycat lawsuits against the state of Minnesota and against Dell Computer in North Carolina.

Kevin Thompson, a lobbyist at the Council on State Taxation, says he's never seen "all three folks" — government, business and labor — unified on the same side. "We have 200 businesses, the big seven state and local government groups, and the Teamsters. It's very rare. But it's refreshing," he says.

Many legal observers are expecting the Supreme Court to send the Ohio case back to the 6th Circuit court on the grounds that the at-the-moment successful plaintiff lacks standing to sue. She is Charlotte Cuno, a Toledo taxpayer who argues that her family is harmed by the DaimlerChrysler tax perk because her public school doesn't have enough money for computers.

Once the case is kicked back, the lobbying strategists will start working in earnest, on behalf of congressional legislation that would make such state breaks unambiguously legal. "We're going to hit the ground running as soon as the Supreme Court decision comes out," says Thompson, who has been keeping lawmakers briefed on the matter.

Ralph Nader, the veteran consumer advocate and perennial presidential candidate, helped put together the Ohio suit and is preparing to fight against the expected legislative campaign. He argues that state-specific business tax breaks erode the tax bases of local communities — and that dozens of economic studies have shown that such localized tax incentives don't boost economic activity but instead shift the tax burden to small businesses and individuals who cannot get the subsidies.

But Nader has also been in Washington long enough to know that winning an argument on points is not enough. "If they lose in the Supreme Court, they get it through Congress instantly. It'll be like walking through the corridors passing out money, getting votes," he laments. And they won't even be seen as looting the federal treasury, since states will ultimately be footing the bill.

who scrambled to the microphones with vows to protect the tax break — and its primary beneficiaries in the middle class.

The commission's proposal was quickly dropped from all discussion in Washington. The silence from the Bush administration, in particular, was deafening.

CONFLUENCE OF COMPLEXITIES

The fact is, the mortgage interest deduction, which has existed since 1913, the year Congress created the personal income tax, is as close as the tax system gets to motherhood and apple pie. It has become embedded in the tax code as the government's way of promoting home ownership — 69 percent of all U.S. households own their homes — even though it costs the U.S. Treasury $70 billion or more a year in forgone revenue.

"Congress has made a longstanding commitment to housing as a preferential element of our society," said Jerry Howard, executive vice president of the National Association of Home Builders. Scaling back the mortgage interest deduction, he said, "would be tantamount to abrogating over 100 years of a federal commitment to housing."

This is the kind of automatic resistance that rises up every time any lawmaker or administration seeks to overhaul the tax system. Rewriting the tax code upends longstanding business practices and disrupts social policies that are rooted in the law. The individuals and businesses that do not want to face the risk and uncertainty — and increased burden — that come with these changes begin to push back, invoking the longstanding benefits of the status quo. And the result is inertia.

The complexities of the tax code may drive people crazy when it's time to figure out their personal or business tax obligations, but the prospect of brand new rules and regulations can be even more fearsome. For companies, changes to the tax code can take months or years to decipher. The Internal Revenue Service, for instance, is still issuing regulations stemming from the 2004 corporate tax law, more than a year after enactment.

Howard, from the home builders' group, allows as much. "Because virtually every element of society . . . is impacted by the tax code, whenever you propose changes, those changes are going to have a ripple effect," he said.

"People will jump to the defense of the status quo. . . . Part of that is fear of change."

To a far greater extent than other tax policy decisions, plans to fundamentally overhaul the tax code almost by definition produce economic winners and losers. Eliminating some of the specialized tax breaks that crowd the law immediately threatens the beneficiaries of those breaks.

"Every person who's going to lose a deduction regards their deduction as having come with the Bill of Rights, or even Moses," said Bob Packwood, the former Oregon Republican senator who is now a lobbyist for Sunrise Research Corp.

Packwood should know. He chaired the Senate Finance Committee and helped pick winners and losers as Congress went through the last overhaul of the tax code, in 1986. "Generally, losers are willing to fight harder than winners," he said.

The mortgage interest deduction happens to be the second-most popular tax "expenditure" in the law. But it is just one of hundreds of existing benefits designed by lawmakers to encourage or reward certain economic and social activities — from having children to corporations' conducting research and development — that have survived attempts to streamline the complicated tax law over the years.

These tax breaks, which are likely to be

Largest Tax Breaks and What They Cost

The U.S. tax code is riddled with hundreds of provisions that reduce the amount of income subject to tax, including the deduction for mortgage interest payments that will save Americans almost $450 billion over the next five years. Together, these so-called tax expenditures are worth in excess of $800 billion in forgone revenue for fiscal 2006. The following list shows the largest of these tax breaks and their projected cost through 2010. Not shown is an economists' convention that credits homeowners with the value of the rent they would receive on owner-occupied houses, which amounts to $185 billion from 2006 to 2010.

In billions of dollars

TAX EXPENDITURES	2004	2005	2006	2007	2008	2009	2010	Total: 2006-2010
Exclusion of employer-paid insurance premiums and medical care	$102.3	$112.2	$125.7	$139.1	$152.6	$166.2	$176.7	$760.2
Deduction for mortgage interest	61.5	68.9	76.0	82.0	89.0	95.8	102.8	445.5
Exclusion for 401(k) plan income	47.7	45.9	48.1	51.8	56.1	60.9	66.4	283.4
Exclusion of capital gains on home sales	29.7	32.9	36.3	40.1	44.2	54.7	72.0	247.2
Exclusion for employer-paid pensions	47.0	50.3	51.1	52.6	47.5	45.3	44.6	241.0
Deductions for charitable contributions	27.4	29.7	32.6	34.5	36.8	39.4	42.2	185.5
Stepped-up capital gains basis at death	24.2	26.1	28.8	31.6	34.8	35.6	33.7	164.4
Child tax credit	22.4	32.7	32.8	32.9	32.9	32.8	32.7	164.0
Deduction for state and local taxes	45.3	39.1	34.6	32.9	31.9	31.8	32.1	163.2
Reduced rate for capital gains (except agriculture, timber, iron ore and coal)	25.2	27.2	28.4	30.5	36.9	26.9	21.6	144.2
Exclusion for life insurance earnings	20.8	22.8	24.1	26.2	28.8	31.0	33.6	143.6

SOURCE: Office of Management and Budget

worth more than $800 billion combined this year — almost as much as the total of discretionary appropriations for fiscal 2006 — span far and wide. The earned income tax credit (EITC), which will cost more than $5 billion in lost revenue this year, according to the Office of Management and Budget, is protected fiercely by advocates for the poor. Veterans guard their tax exclusion for death and disability benefits, which is projected to cost almost $4 billion in 2006. And oil companies seek to maintain about $2 billion in expense allowances and credits for their operations.

As a result, the tax code is riddled with deductions and credits, deeply embedded in the system and hard to dig out. The tax break that costs the Treasury the most annually is the exclusion that benefits workers whose employers provide health insurance and medical care. That benefit was expected to cost about $126 billion in 2006, according to the White House budget office.

The research and development tax credit, ostensibly a way to encourage investment by corporations, often ends up rewarding research that would have been done anyway. Repealing it would generate $6 billion a year in revenue. But lawmakers are loath to discontinue a popular business tax break that is guarded jealously by defense and pharmaceutical companies. Moreover, the issue is never far from the surface. Lawmakers generally extend the tax break for a year or so at a time — meaning that industry supporters are constantly talking with lawmakers about their needs, and also constantly making campaign contributions to influential tax writers.

Moreover, fundamental changes to the tax code inevitably affect corporations and individuals in different ways.

For individuals, a change in the tax code inevitably means a change in tax liability. For corporations, a change in the tax code could mean basic change in the way business is done.

Tweaks to the child credit and other family-targeted tax provisions, for example, would not have the same effect as changes to business tax law, says Tom Ochsenschlager, vice president of taxation for the American Institute of Certified Public Accountants.

"Unlike a business, someone is not going to sit down and say we're going to have more kids" because of the tax advantages, Ochsenschlager said. A business, on the other hand, could well decide to add or drop a product — or lay off employees — depending on its future tax liability.

The institutional resistance to tax changes is not confined to K Street lobbying firms or interest groups, argues Eugene Steuerle, who coordinated the Reagan Treasury Department's tax overhaul effort between 1984 and 1986 and is now a senior fellow at the liberal-leaning Urban Institute.

It includes federal agencies that view various constituencies as their "clientele" — whether it is the Housing and Urban Development Department seeking to maintain a housing tax break, or the Commerce Department defending a business tax deduction. "A lot of interest groups are represented not just by lobbyists on K Street," Steuerle said.

HIDE AND SEEK

Even when a tax deduction disappears, it may not be gone for long.

In 1986, Packwood helped repeal the federal income tax deduction for state and local sales taxes, while retaining the deduction for state and local income taxes. The move drew fierce objections from lawmakers including Sen. Phil Gramm, R-Texas, whose state has no income tax and relies on sales taxes to finance government activities. Lawmakers from Texas, South Dakota and other states without income taxes spent the next two decades fighting to restore the tax break, a battle they won in 2004 when a version of the deduction was included in a corporate tax overhaul law.

Moreover, potential losers tend to be best equipped to wage the fight. Some in the corporate sector are particularly wary of another tax overhaul debate along the lines of 1986, which ended up increasing the tax burden on large corporations. Big manufacturers and retailers are closely watching proposals to institute a value-added tax (VAT) or other consumption-based taxes that might affect different companies in different ways.

"Big business has been reluctant for a number of years because they got burned in 1986," said Chris Edwards, a tax expert at the libertarian Cato Institute who helped corporations assess the potential effect of tax overhaul proposals as an analyst for Price Waterhouse during the 1990s. "Since then, businesses are rightfully leery about tax reform."

All of these factors place obstacles in the way of wholesale "reform" and favor changes in tax law at the margins, if at all.

The complexity of the tax code feeds this inertia. In recent decades, lawmakers have used tax benefits as a way to encourage certain economic activity, such as home buying and research and development. Just last summer, Congress devised a new tax credit designed to get Americans to buy more cars powered by gas-electric "hybrid" technology.

This dynamic is part of what makes equitableness so difficult to achieve. Making the system more equitable requires taking away the targeted tax deductions enjoyed by some specific individuals and businesses, but which don't benefit the public at large.

"These things all have the common feature that they benefit one kind of economic activity at the expense of all others," argued William G. Gale, an economist at the Brookings Institution. "The way reform is supposed to work is to take away those subsidies and take the revenue gained and use it for the general benefit."

Indeed, the political dynamics surrounding most overhaul proposals are quite different from those surrounding more popular tax cut ideas. When lawmakers talk about cutting taxes, they often ignore the less pleasant work of paying for those tax cuts. As a result, everybody appears to win. But when lawmakers talk about overhauling the tax code without changing the revenue the government takes in, that automatically means there will be economic winners and losers.

"The difference is that in tax reform, the losers are visible. In tax cuts, nobody quite knows how we're going to pay for it," Gale said.

Packwood points to the 1986 debate over limiting "passive losses" as a particularly instructive example of the institutional bias against tax overhaul. When the Senate Finance Committee produced its tax overhaul bill in 1986, it included a provision designed to make it more difficult for wealthy individuals to avoid paying taxes by sheltering their income with the aid of "paper losses." Under pre-1986 law, investors in limited partnerships who were not actively involved in the management of a property development project could still take a deduction for losses incurred in the venture. Because those losses would often exceed the limited partner's investment, the resulting tax shelter could be lucrative.

The real estate industry, which benefited greatly from the status quo, had helped halt earlier attempts to roll back the tax break, and erupted against the proposed changes. Real estate developers argued that changing the rules regarding partnerships would jeopardize the financial stability of large development projects, and said the proposed changes were discriminatory because they targeted the real estate industry — despite lawmakers' insistence that the tax overhaul effort was about making the law more fair.

But in the end, the industry lost as congressional leaders and the administration agreed to phase out the "passive loss" rules, raising several billion dollars in revenue, which was then was used to offset losses that resulted from other changes in the act. Yet even here, the inertia facing "reform" was evident. Tax writers exempted some oil and gas companies — represented by a separate powerful lobby — from the new rules.

Achieving even this limited kind of tax overhaul victory in the face of industry resistance resulted from a rare confluence of factors in 1986. It was supported by President Ronald Reagan, who was committed to changing the tax code and to cutting the top tax rate for individuals to 28 percent from 50 percent while removing millions of lower-income taxpayers from the tax rolls. The attempt to lower rates and broaden the tax drew support from both Republicans and Democrats. And at the time there was public outrage over how little major corporations were paying in taxes.

Since then, the lack of such momentum has meant several broad tax overhaul proposals have been confined to the dustbin with little public debate.

For instance, while some leading GOP tax experts advocate a shift to a consumption-based tax, such as a national sales tax or a VAT, the threat of opposition from groups that might be adversely affected, such as retailers and low-income individuals, have helped to keep the ideas far from the center of public debate.

"Analysts of public policy have always indicated that there's a strong bias toward the status quo, especially when you're identifying winners and losers," said the Urban Institute's Steuerle.

CORPORATE WINNERS AND LOSERS

The end result of tax overhaul efforts on businesses can be unpredictable.

At the end of the 1986 debate, large corporations found themselves with an increased share of the burden. Although the new law reduced tax rates for corporations as well as individuals, it made a host of other changes to the corporate tax system that increased corporate tax receipts to pay for the reductions in individual tax rates.

As written, the law was designed to reduce individuals' taxes by $121.7 billion over six years, while increasing taxes on corporations by $120.4 billion. For instance, lawmakers raised the top marginal tax rate on long-term capital gains from 20 percent to 28 percent.

Indeed, top Beltway lobbyists such as Kenneth Kies, a former chief of staff of the Joint Tax Committee and a player in the 1986 debate, have warned companies that they should be concerned that Congress will again shift more of the tax burden onto corporations to pay for "reforms" for individual taxpayers if the president and Congress pursue a debate on fundamental tax overhaul.

"The corporate sector paid more tax to make the individual stuff work.... They're naturally afraid of that re-occurring," said one senior Republican tax aide on the Finance Committee staff.

The Bush White House has gotten the message from all quarters, and is essentially conceding that any debate or action on an overhaul of the tax code will have to wait until 2007 or 2008. Republicans running for re-election won't have to defend something that could be cast as a death knell to popular tax deductions. Instead, candidates can campaign on the general idea of overhauling a tax system that is too complex, inherently unfair and, of course, takes too much money out of voters' pocketbooks.

While taking a second look at the tax code could bring huge benefits to individuals and business owners, at the end of the day, its negative impact is hard to avoid.

As even CPA Ochsenschlager concedes, "Change is very disruptive." ■

Appendix

The Legislative Process in Brief   120

The Budget Process in Brief   124

Glossary of Congressional Terms   125

Congressional Information on the Internet   148

The Legislative Process in Brief

Note: Parliamentary terms used below are defined in the glossary.

INTRODUCTION OF BILLS

A House member (including the resident commissioner of Puerto Rico and nonvoting delegates of the District of Columbia, Guam, the Virgin Islands and American Samoa) may introduce any one of several types of bills and resolutions by handing it to the clerk of the House or placing it in a box called the hopper. A senator first gains recognition of the presiding officer to announce the introduction of a bill.

As the usual next step in either the House or Senate, the bill is numbered, referred to the appropriate committee, labeled with the sponsor's name and sent to the Government Printing Office so that copies can be made for subsequent study and action. House and Senate bills may be jointly sponsored and carry several senators' names. A bill written in the executive branch and proposed as an administration measure usually is introduced by the chairman of the congressional committee that has jurisdiction, as a courtesy to the White House.

Bills—Prefixed with HR in the House, S in the Senate, followed by a number. Used as the form for most legislation, whether general or special, public or private.

Joint Resolutions—Designated H J Res or S J Res. Subject to the same procedure as bills, with the exception of a joint resolution proposing an amendment to the Constitution. The latter must be approved by two-thirds of both houses and is then sent directly to the administrator of general services for submission to the states for ratification instead of being presented to the president for his approval.

Concurrent Resolutions—Designated H Con Res or S Con Res. Used for matters affecting the operations of both houses. These resolutions do not become law.

Resolutions—Designated H Res or S Res. Used for a matter concerning the operation of either house alone and adopted only by the chamber in which it originates.

COMMITTEE ACTION

With few exceptions, bills are referred to the appropriate standing committees. The job of referral formally is the responsibility of the Speaker of the House and the presiding officer of the Senate, but this task usually is carried out on their behalf by the parliamentarians of the House and Senate. Precedent, statute and the jurisdictional mandates of the committees as set forth in the rules of the House and Senate determine which committees receive what kinds of bills. Bills are technically considered "read for the first time" when referred to House committees.

When a bill reaches a committee it is placed on the committee's calendar. Failure of a committee to act on a bill is equivalent to killing it and most fall by the legislative roadside. The measure can be withdrawn from the committee's purview only by a discharge petition signed by a majority of the House membership on House bills, or by adoption of a special resolution in the Senate. Discharge attempts rarely succeed and the Senate procedure has not been used for decades.

The first committee action taken on a bill usually is a request for comment on it by interested agencies of the government. The committee chairman may assign the bill to a subcommittee for study and hearings, or it may be considered by the full committee. Hearings may be public, closed (executive session) or both. A subcommittee, after considering a bill, reports to the full committee its recommendations for action and any proposed amendments.

The full committee then votes on its recommendation to the House or Senate. This procedure is called "ordering a bill reported." Occasionally a committee may order a bill reported unfavorably; most of the time a report, submitted by the chairman of the committee to the House or Senate, calls for favorable action on the measure since the committee can effectively "kill" a bill by simply failing to take any action.

After the bill is reported, the committee chairman instructs the staff to prepare a written report. The report describes the purposes and scope of the bill, explains the committee revisions, notes proposed changes in existing law and, usually, includes the views of the executive branch agencies consulted. Often committee members opposing a measure issue dissenting minority statements that are included in the report.

Usually, the committee "marks up" or proposes amendments to the bill. If the amendments are substantial and the measure is complicated, the committee may order a "clean bill" introduced, which will embody the proposed amendments. The original bill then is put aside and the clean bill, with a new number, is reported to the floor.

The chamber must approve, alter or reject the committee amendments before the bill itself can be put to a vote.

FLOOR ACTION

After a bill is reported back to the house where it originated, it is placed on the calendar.

There are five legislative calendars in the House, issued in one cumulative calendar titled *Calendars of the United States House of Representatives and History of Legislation*. The House calendars are:

The Union Calendar to which are referred bills raising revenues, general appropriations bills and any measures directly or indirectly appropriating money or property. It is the Calendar of the Committee of the Whole House on the State of the Union.

The House Calendar to which are referred bills of public character not raising revenue or appropriating money.

The Corrections Calendar to which are referred bills to repeal rules and regulations deemed excessive or unnecessary when the Corrections Calendar is called the second and fourth Tuesday of each month. (Instituted in the 104th Congress to replace the seldom-used Consent Calendar.) A three-fifths majority is required for passage.

The Private Calendar to which are referred bills for relief in the nature of claims against the United States or private immigration bills that are passed without debate when the Private Calendar is called the first and third Tuesdays of each month.

The Discharge Calendar to which are referred motions to discharge committees when the necessary signatures are signed to a discharge petition.

There is only one legislative calendar in the Senate and one "executive calendar" for treaties and nominations submitted to the Senate.

Debate. A bill is brought to debate by varying procedures. In the Senate the majority leader, in consultation with the minority leader and others, schedules the bills that will be taken up for debate. If it is urgent or important it can be taken up in the Senate either by unanimous consent or by a majority vote.

In the House, precedence is granted if a special rule is obtained from the Rules Committee. A request for a special rule usually is made by the chairman of the committee that favorably reported the bill. The request is considered by the Rules Committee in the same fashion that other committees consider legislative measures. The committee proposes a resolution providing for immediate consideration of the bill. The Rules Committee reports the resolution to the House where it is debated and voted on in the same fashion as regular bills.

This graphic shows the most typical way in which proposed legislation is enacted into law. There are more complicated, as well as simpler, routes, and most bills never become law. The process is illustrated with two hypothetical bills, House bill No. 1 (HR 1) and

Senate bill No. 2 (S 2). Bills must be passed by both houses in identical form before they can be sent to the president. The path of HR 1 is traced by a gray line, that of S 2 by a black line. In practice, most bills begin as similar proposals in both houses.

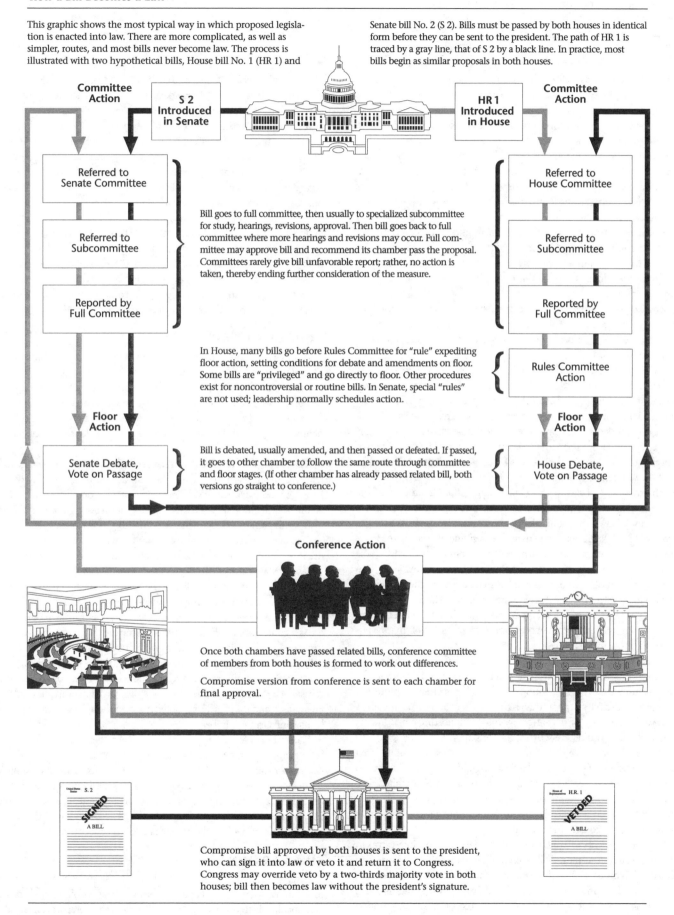

Committee Action

S 2 Introduced in Senate

HR 1 Introduced in House

Committee Action

Referred to Senate Committee

Referred to Subcommittee

Reported by Full Committee

Bill goes to full committee, then usually to specialized subcommittee for study, hearings, revisions, approval. Then bill goes back to full committee where more hearings and revisions may occur. Full committee may approve bill and recommend its chamber pass the proposal. Committees rarely give bill unfavorable report; rather, no action is taken, thereby ending further consideration of the measure.

Referred to House Committee

Referred to Subcommittee

Reported by Full Committee

In House, many bills go before Rules Committee for "rule" expediting floor action, setting conditions for debate and amendments on floor. Some bills are "privileged" and go directly to floor. Other procedures exist for noncontroversial or routine bills. In Senate, special "rules" are not used; leadership normally schedules action.

Rules Committee Action

Floor Action

Floor Action

Senate Debate, Vote on Passage

Bill is debated, usually amended, and then passed or defeated. If passed, it goes to other chamber to follow the same route through committee and floor stages. (If other chamber has already passed related bill, both versions go straight to conference.)

House Debate, Vote on Passage

Conference Action

Once both chambers have passed related bills, conference committee of members from both houses is formed to work out differences.

Compromise version from conference is sent to each chamber for final approval.

S. 2 — SIGNED — A BILL

H.R. 1 — VETOED — A BILL

Compromise bill approved by both houses is sent to the president, who can sign it into law or veto it and return it to Congress. Congress may override veto by a two-thirds majority vote in both houses; bill then becomes law without the president's signature.

The resolutions providing special rules are important because they specify how long the bill may be debated and whether it may be amended from the floor. If floor amendments are banned, the bill is considered under a "closed rule."

When a bill is debated under an "open rule," amendments may be offered from the floor. Committee amendments always are taken up first but may be changed, as may all amendments up to the second degree; that is, an amendment to an amendment to an amendment is not in order.

Duration of debate in the House depends on whether the bill is under discussion by the House proper or before the House when it is sitting as the Committee of the Whole House on the State of the Union. In the former, the amount of time for debate is allocated with an hour for each member if the measure is under consideration without a rule. In the Committee of the Whole the amount of time agreed on for general debate is equally divided between proponents and opponents. At the end of general discussion, the bill is often read section by section for amendment. Debate on an amendment is limited to five minutes for each side; this is called the "five-minute rule." In practice, amendments regularly are debated more than ten minutes, with members gaining the floor by offering pro forma amendments or obtaining unanimous consent to speak longer than five minutes.

Senate debate usually is unlimited. It can be halted only by unanimous consent or by "cloture," which requires a three-fifths majority of the entire Senate except for proposed changes in the Senate rules. The latter requires a two-thirds vote.

The House considers almost all important bills within a parliamentary framework known as the Committee of the Whole. It is not a committee as the word usually is understood; it is the full House meeting under another name for the purpose of speeding action on legislation. Technically, the House sits as the Committee of the Whole when it considers any tax measure or bill dealing with public appropriations. Upon adoption of a special rule, the Speaker declares the House resolved into the Committee of the Whole and appoints a member of the majority party to serve as the chairman. The rules of the House permit the Committee of the Whole to meet when a quorum of 100 members is present on the floor and to amend and act on bills. When the Committee of the Whole has acted, it "rises," the Speaker returns as the presiding officer of the House and the member appointed chairman of the Committee of the Whole reports the action of the committee and its recommendations. The Committee of the Whole cannot pass a bill; instead it reports the measure to the full House with whatever changes it has approved. The full House then may pass or reject the bill — or, on occasion, recommit the bill to committee. Amendments adopted in the Committee of the Whole may be put to a second vote in the full House.

Votes. Voting on bills may occur repeatedly before they are finally approved or rejected. The House votes on the rule for the bill and on various amendments to the bill. Voting on amendments often is a more illuminating test of a bill's support than is the final tally. Sometimes members approve final passage of bills after vigorously supporting amendments that, if adopted, would have scuttled the legislation.

The Senate has three different methods of voting: an untabulated voice vote, a standing vote (called a division) and a recorded roll call to which members answer "yea" or "nay" when their names are called. The House also employs voice and standing votes, but since January 1973 yeas and nays have been recorded by an electronic voting device, eliminating the need for time-consuming roll calls.

After amendments to a bill have been voted upon, a vote may be taken on a motion to recommit the bill to committee. If carried, this vote is usually a death blow to the bill. If the motion is unsuccessful, the bill then is "read for the third time." After the third reading a vote on passage is taken. The final vote may be followed by a motion to reconsider, and this motion may be followed by a move to lay the motion on the table. Usually, those voting for the bill's passage vote for the tabling motion, thus safeguarding the final passage action. With that, the bill has been formally passed by the chamber.

ACTION IN SECOND CHAMBER

After a bill is passed it is sent to the other chamber. This body may then take one of several steps. It may pass the bill as is — accepting the other chamber's language. It may send the bill to committee for scrutiny or alteration, or reject the entire bill, advising the other chamber of its actions. Or it simply may ignore the bill submitted while it continues work on its own version of the proposed legislation. Frequently, one chamber may approve a version of a bill that is greatly at variance with the version already passed by the other chamber, and then substitute its contents for the language of the other, retaining only the latter's bill number.

Often the second chamber makes only minor changes. If these are readily agreed to by the other chamber, the bill then is routed to the president. However, if the opposite chamber significantly alters the bill submitted to it, the measure usually is "sent to conference." The chamber that has possession of the "papers" (engrossed bill, engrossed amendments, messages of transmittal) requests a conference and the other chamber may agree to it. If the second chamber does not agree, the bill dies.

CONFERENCE ACTION

A conference works out conflicting House and Senate versions of a legislative bill. The conferees usually are senior members from the committees that managed the legislation who are appointed by the presiding officers of the two houses. Under this arrangement the conferees of one house have the duty of trying to maintain their chamber's position in the face of amending actions by the conferees (also referred to as "managers") of the other house.

The number of conferees from each chamber may vary, the range usually being from seven to nine members in each group, depending on the length or complexity of the bill involved. But a majority vote controls the action of each group so that a large representation does not give one chamber a voting advantage over the other chamber's conferees.

Theoretically, conferees are not allowed to write new legislation in reconciling the two versions before them, but this curb sometimes is bypassed. Many bills have been put into acceptable compromise form only after new language was provided by the conferees. Frequently the ironing out of difficulties takes days or even weeks. Conferences on involved, complex and controversial bills sometimes are particularly drawn out.

As a conference proceeds, conferees reconcile differences between the versions, but generally they grant concessions only insofar as they remain sure that the chamber they represent will accept the compromises. Occasionally, uncertainty over how either house will react, or the positive refusal of a chamber to back down on a disputed amendment, results in an impasse, and the bills die in conference even though each was approved by its sponsoring chamber.

When the conferees have reached agreement, they prepare a conference report embodying their recommendations (compromises) and a joint explanatory statement. The report, in document form, must be submitted to each house. The conference report must be approved by each house. Consequently, approval of the report is approval of the compromise bill. In the order of voting on conference reports, the chamber that asked for a conference yields to the other chamber the opportunity to vote first.

FINAL ACTION

After a bill has been passed by both the House and Senate in identical form, all of the original papers are sent to the enrolling clerk of the chamber in which the bill originated. The clerk then prepares an enrolled bill, which is printed on parchment paper.

When this bill has been certified as correct by the secretary of the Senate or the clerk of the House, depending on which chamber originated the bill, it is signed first (no matter whether it originated in the Senate or House) by the Speaker of the House and then by the president of the Senate. It is next sent to the White House to await action.

If the president approves the bill, he signs it, dates it and usually writes the word "approved" on the document. If the president does not sign it within 10 days (Sundays excepted) and Congress is in session, the bill becomes law without his signature.

If Congress adjourns *sine die* at the end of the second session the president can pocket veto a bill and it dies without Congress having the opportunity to override.

A president vetoes a bill by refusing to sign it and, before the ten-day period expires, returning it to Congress with a message stating his reasons.

The message is sent to the chamber that originated the bill. If no action is taken on the message, the bill dies. Congress, however, can attempt to override the president's veto and enact the bill, "the objections of the president to the contrary notwithstanding." Overriding a veto requires a two-thirds vote of those present in each chamber, who must number a quorum and vote by roll call.

If the president's veto is overridden by a two-thirds vote in both houses, the bill becomes law. Otherwise it is dead.

When bills are passed finally and signed, or passed over a veto, they are given law numbers in numerical order as they become law. There are two series of numbers, one for public and one for private laws, starting at the number "1" for each two-year term of Congress. They are then identified by law number and by Congress — for example, Private Law 10, 105th Congress; Public Law 33, 106th Congress (or PL 106-33).

The Budget Process in Brief

Through the budget process, the president and Congress decide how much to spend and tax during the upcoming fiscal year. More specifically, they decide how much to spend on each activity, ensure that the government spends no more than that and spends it only for that activity and report on that spending at the end of each budget cycle.

THE PRESIDENT'S BUDGET

The law requires that, by the first Monday in February, the president submit to Congress his proposed federal budget for the next fiscal year, which begins on October 1. To accomplish this the president establishes general budget and fiscal policy guidelines. Based on these guidelines, executive branch agencies make requests for funds and submit them to the White House's Office of Management and Budget (OMB) nearly a year before the start of a new fiscal year. The OMB, receiving direction from the president and administration officials, reviews the agencies' requests and develops a detailed budget by December. From December to January the OMB prepares the budget documents, so that the president can deliver it to Congress in February.

The president's budget is the executive branch's plan for the next year — but it is just a proposal. After receiving it, Congress has its own budget process to follow from February to October. Only after Congress passes the required spending bills — and the president signs them — has the government created its actual budget.

ACTION IN CONGRESS

Congress first must pass a "budget resolution" — a framework within which the members of Congress will make their decisions about spending and taxes. It includes targets for total spending, total revenues and the deficit, and allocations within the spending target for the two types of spending — discretionary and mandatory.

Discretionary spending, which currently accounts for about 33 percent of all federal spending, is what the president and Congress must decide to spend for the next year through the thirteen annual appropriations bills. It includes money for such activities as the FBI and the Coast Guard, for housing and education, for NASA and highway and bridge construction and for defense and foreign aid.

Mandatory spending, which currently accounts for 67 percent of all spending, is authorized by laws that have already been passed. It includes entitlement spending — such as for Social Security, Medicare, veterans' benefits and food stamps — through which individuals receive benefits because they are eligible based on their age, income or other criteria. It also includes interest on the national debt, which the government pays to individuals and institutions that hold Treasury bonds and other government securities. The only way the president and Congress can change the spending on entitlement and other mandatory programs is if they change the laws that authorized the programs.

Currently, the law requires that legislation that would raise mandatory spending or lower revenues — compared to existing law — be offset by spending cuts or revenue increases. This requirement, called "pay-as-you-go" is designed to prevent new legislation from increasing the deficit.

Once Congress passes the budget resolution, legislators turn their attention to passing the 13 annual appropriations bills and, if they choose, "authorizing" bills to change the laws governing mandatory spending and revenues.

Congress begins by examining the president's budget in detail. Scores of committees and subcommittees hold hearings on proposals under their jurisdiction. The House and Senate Armed Services Authorizing Committees, and the Defense and Military Construction Subcommittees of the Appropriations Committees, for instance, hold hearings on the president's defense budget. The White House budget director, cabinet officers and other administration officials work with Congress as it accepts some of the president's proposals, rejects others and changes still others. Congress can change funding levels, eliminate programs or add programs not requested by the president. It can add or eliminate taxes and other sources of revenue, or make other changes that affect the amount of revenue collected. Congressional rules require that these committees and subcommittees take actions that reflect the congressional budget resolution.

The president's budget, the budget resolution and the appropriations or authorizing bills measure spending in two ways — "budget authority" and "outlays." Budget authority is what the law authorizes the federal government to spend for certain programs, projects or activities. What the government actually spends in a particular year, however, is an outlay. For example, when the government decides to build a space exploration system, the president and Congress may agree to appropriate $1 billion in budget authority. But the space system may take ten years to build. Thus, the government may spend $100 million in outlays in the first year to begin construction and the remaining $900 million during the next nine years as the construction continues.

Congress must provide budget authority before the federal agencies can obligate the government to make outlays. When Congress fails to complete action on one or more of the regular annual appropriations bills before the fiscal year begins on October 1, budget authority may be made on a temporary basis through continuing resolutions. Continuing resolutions make budget authority available for limited periods of time, generally at rates related through some formula to the rate provided in the previous year's appropriation.

MONITORING THE BUDGET

Once Congress passes and the president signs the federal appropriations bills or authorizing laws for the fiscal year, the government monitors the budget through (1) agency program managers and budget officials, including the Inspectors General, who report only to the agency head; (2) the Office of Management and Budget; (3) congressional committees; and (4) the General Accounting Office, an auditing arm of Congress.

This oversight is designed to (1) ensure that agencies comply with legal limits on spending and that agencies use budget authority only for the purposes intended; (2) see that programs are operating consistently with legal requirements and existing policy; and (3) ensure that programs are well managed and achieving the intended results.

The president may withhold appropriated amounts from obligation only under certain limited circumstances — to provide for contingencies, to achieve savings made possible through changes in requirements or greater efficiency of operations or as otherwise provided by law. The Impoundment Control Act of 1974 specifies the procedures that must be followed if funds are withheld. Congress can also cancel previous authorized budget authority by passing a rescissions bill — but it also must be signed by the president.

Glossary of Congressional Terms

AA—(See Administrative Assistant.)

Absence of a Quorum—Absence of the required number of members to conduct business in a house or a committee. When a quorum call or roll-call vote in a house establishes that a quorum is not present, no debate or other business is permitted except a motion to adjourn or motions to request or compel the attendance of absent members, if necessary by arresting them.

Absolute Majority—A vote requiring approval by a majority of all members of a house rather than a majority of members present and voting. Also referred to as constitutional majority.

Account—Organizational units used in the federal budget primarily for recording spending and revenue transactions.

Act—(1) A bill passed in identical form by both houses of Congress and signed into law by the president or enacted over the president's veto. A bill also becomes an act without the president's signature if he does not return it to Congress within ten days (Sundays excepted) and if Congress has not adjourned within that period. (2) Also, the technical term for a bill passed by at least one house and engrossed.

Ad Hoc Select Committee—A temporary committee formed for a special purpose or to deal with a specific subject. Conference committees are ad hoc joint committees. A House rule adopted in 1975 authorizes the Speaker to refer measures to special ad hoc committees, appointed by the Speaker with the approval of the House.

Adjourn—A motion to adjourn is a formal motion to end a day's session or meeting of a house or a committee. A motion to adjourn usually has no conditions attached to it, but it sometimes may specify the day or time for reconvening or make reconvening subject to the call of the chamber's presiding officer or the committee's chairman. In both houses, a motion to adjourn is of the highest privilege, takes precedence over all other motions, is not debatable and must be put to an immediate vote. Adjournment of a house ends its legislative day. For this reason, the House or Senate sometimes adjourns for only one minute, or some other very brief period of time, during the course of a day's session. The House does not permit a motion to adjourn after it has resolved into Committee of the Whole or when the previous question has been ordered on a measure to final passage without an intervening motion.

Adjourn for More Than Three Days—Under Article I, Section 5 of the Constitution, neither house may adjourn for more than three days without the approval of the other. The necessary approval is given in a concurrent resolution to which both houses have agreed.

Adjournment *Sine Die*—Final adjournment of an annual or two-year session of Congress; literally, adjournment without a day. The two houses must agree to a privileged concurrent resolution for such an adjournment. A sine die adjournment precludes Congress from meeting again until the next constitutionally fixed date of a session (Jan. 3 of the following year) unless Congress determines otherwise by law or the president calls it into special session. Article II, Section 3 of the Constitution authorizes the president to adjourn both houses until such time as the president thinks proper when the two houses cannot agree to a time of adjournment. No president, however, has ever exercised this authority.

Adjournment to a Day (and Time) Certain—An adjournment that fixes the next date and time of meeting for one or both houses. It does not end an annual session of Congress.

Administration Bill—A bill drafted in the executive office of the president or in an executive department or agency to implement part of the president's program. An administration bill is introduced in Congress by a member who supports it or as a courtesy to the administration.

Administrative Assistant (AA)—The title usually given to a member's chief aide, political advisor and head of office staff. The administrative assistant often represents the member at meetings with visitors or officials when the member is unable (or unwilling) to attend.

Adoption—The usual parliamentary term for approval of a conference report. It is also commonly applied to amendments.

Advance Appropriation—In an appropriation act for a particular fiscal year, an appropriation that does not become available for spending or obligation until a subsequent fiscal year. The amount of the advance appropriation is counted as part of the budget for the fiscal year in which it becomes available for obligation.

Advance Funding—A mechanism whereby statutory language may allow budget authority for a fiscal year to be increased, and obligations to be incurred, with an offsetting decrease in the budget authority available in the succeeding fiscal year. If not used, the budget authority remains available for obligation in the succeeding fiscal year. Advance funding is sometimes used to provide contingency funding of a few benefit programs.

Adverse Report—A committee report recommending against approval of a measure or some other matter. Committees usually pigeonhole measures they oppose instead of reporting them adversely, but they may be required to report them by a statutory rule or an instruction from their parent body.

Advice and Consent—The Senate's constitutional role in consenting to or rejecting the president's nominations to executive branch and judicial offices and treaties with other nations. Confirmation of nominees requires a simple majority vote of senators present and voting. Treaties must be approved by a two-thirds majority of those present and voting.

Aisle—The center aisle of each chamber. When facing the presiding officer, Republicans usually sit to the right of the aisle, Democrats to the left. When members speak of "my side of the aisle" or "this side," they are referring to their party.

Amendment—A formal proposal to alter the text of a bill, resolution, amendment, motion, treaty or some other text. Technically, it is a motion. An amendment may strike out (eliminate) part of a text, insert new text or strike out and insert — that is, replace all or part of the text with new text. The texts of amendments considered on the floor are printed in full in the Congressional Record.

Amendment in the Nature of a Substitute—Usually, an amendment to replace the entire text of a measure. It strikes out everything after the enacting clause and inserts a version that may be somewhat, substantially or entirely different. When a committee adopts extensive amendments to a measure, it often incorporates them into such an amendment. Occasionally, the term is applied to an amendment that replaces a major portion of a measure's text.

Amendment Tree—A diagram showing the number and types of amendments that the rules and practices of a house permit to be offered to a measure before any of the amendments is voted on. It shows the relationship of one amendment to the others, and it may also indicate the degree of each amendment, whether it is a perfecting or substitute amendment, the order in which amendments may be offered and the order in which they are put to a vote. The same type of diagram can be used to display an actual amendment situation.

Annual Authorization—Legislation that authorizes appropriations for a single fiscal year and usually for a specific amount. Under the rules of the authorization-appropriation process, an annually authorized agency or program must be reauthorized each year if it is to receive appropriations for that year. Sometimes Congress fails to enact the reauthorization but nevertheless provides appropriations to continue the program, circumventing the rules by one means or another.

Appeal—A member's formal challenge of a ruling or decision by the presiding officer. On appeal, a house or a committee may overturn the ruling by majority vote. The right of appeal ensures the body against arbitrary control by the chair. Appeals are rarely made in the House and are even more rarely successful. Rulings are more frequently appealed in the Senate and occasionally overturned, in part because its presiding officer is not the majority party's leader, as in the House.

Apportionment—The action, after each decennial census, of allocating the number of members in the House of Representatives to each state. By law, the total number of House members (not counting delegates and a resident commissioner) is fixed at 435. The number allotted to each state is based approximately on its proportion of the nation's total population. Because the Constitution guarantees each state one representative no matter how small its population, exact proportional distribution is virtually impossible. The mathematical formula currently used to determine the apportionment is called the Method of Equal Proportions. (See Method of Equal Proportions.)

Appropriated Entitlement—An entitlement program, such as veterans' pensions, that is funded through annual appropriations rather than by a permanent appropriation. Because such an entitlement law requires the government to provide eligible recipients the benefits to which they are entitled, whatever the cost, Congress must appropriate the necessary funds.

Appropriation—(1) Legislative language that permits a federal agency to incur obligations and make payments from the Treasury for specified purposes, usually during a specified period of time. (2) The specific amount of money made available by such language. The Constitution prohibits payments from the Treasury except "in Consequence of Appropriations made by Law." With some exceptions, the rules of both houses forbid consideration of appropriations for purposes that are unauthorized in law or of appropriation amounts larger than those authorized in law. The House of Representatives claims the exclusive right to originate appropriation bills — a claim the Senate denies in theory but accepts in practice.

At-Large—Elected by and representing an entire state instead of a district within a state. The term usually refers to a representative rather than to a senator. (See Apportionment; Congressional District; Redistricting.)

August Adjournment—A congressional adjournment during the month of August in odd-numbered years, required by the Legislative Reorganization Act of 1970. The law instructs the two houses to adjourn for a period of at least thirty days before the second day after Labor Day, unless Congress provides otherwise or if, on July 31, a state of war exists by congressional declaration.

Authorization—(1) A statutory provision that establishes or continues a federal agency, activity or program for a fixed or indefinite period of time. It may also establish policies and restrictions and deal with organizational and administrative matters. (2) A statutory provision, as described in (1), may also, explicitly or implicitly, authorize congressional action to provide appropriations for an agency, activity or program. The

appropriations may be authorized for one year, several years or an indefinite period of time, and the authorization may be for a specific amount of money or an indefinite amount ("such sums as may be necessary"). Authorizations of specific amounts are construed as ceilings on the amounts that subsequently may be appropriated in an appropriation bill, but not as minimums; either house may appropriate lesser amounts or nothing at all.

Authorization-Appropriation Process—The two-stage procedural system that the rules of each house require for establishing and funding federal agencies and programs: first, enactment of authorizing legislation that creates or continues an agency or program; second, enactment of appropriations legislation that provides funds for the authorized agency or program.

Automatic Roll Call—Under a House rule, the automatic ordering of the yeas and nays when a quorum is not present on a voice or division vote and a member objects to the vote on that ground. It is not permitted in the Committee of the Whole.

Backdoor Spending Authority—Authority to incur obligations that evades the normal congressional appropriations process because it is provided in legislation other than appropriation acts. The most common forms are borrowing authority, contract authority and entitlement authority.

Baseline—A projection of the levels of federal spending, revenues and the resulting budgetary surpluses or deficits for the upcoming and subsequent fiscal years, taking into account laws enacted to date and assuming no new policy decisions. It provides a benchmark for measuring the budgetary effects of proposed changes in federal revenues or spending, assuming certain economic conditions.

Bells—A system of electric signals and lights that informs members of activities in each chamber. The type of activity taking place is indicated by the number of signals and the interval between them. When the signals are sounded, a corresponding number of lights are lit around the perimeter of many clocks in House or Senate offices.

Bicameral—Consisting of two houses or chambers. Congress is a bicameral legislature whose two houses have an equal role in enacting legislation. In most other national bicameral legislatures, one house is significantly more powerful than the other.

Bigger Bite Amendment—An amendment that substantively changes a portion of a text including language that had previously been amended. Normally, language that has been amended may not be amended again. However, a part of a sentence that has been changed by amendment, for example, may be changed again by an amendment that amends a "bigger bite" of the text — that is, by an amendment that also substantively changes the unamended parts of the sentence or the entire section or title in which the previously amended language appears. The biggest possible bite is an amendment in the nature of a substitute that amends the entire text of a measure. Once adopted, therefore, such an amendment ends the amending process.

Bill—The term for the chief vehicle Congress uses for enacting laws. Bills that originate in the House of Representatives are designated as HR, those in the Senate as S, followed by a number assigned in the order in which they are introduced during a two-year Congress. A bill becomes a law if passed in identical language by both houses and signed by the president, or passed over the president's veto, or if the president fails to sign it within ten days after receiving it while Congress is in session.

Bill of Attainder—An act of a legislature finding a person guilty of treason or a felony. The Constitution prohibits the passage of such a bill by the U.S. Congress or any state legislature.

Bills and Resolutions Introduced—Members formally present measures to their respective houses by delivering them to a clerk in the chamber when their house is in session. Both houses permit any number of members to join in introducing a bill or resolution. The first member listed on the measure is the sponsor; the other members listed are its cosponsors.

Bills and Resolutions Referred—After a bill or resolution is introduced, it is normally sent to one or more committees that have jurisdiction over its subject, as defined by House and Senate rules and precedents. A Senate measure is usually referred to the committee with jurisdiction over the predominant subject of its text, but it may be sent to two or more committees by unanimous consent or on a motion offered jointly by the majority and minority leaders. In the House, a rule requires the Speaker to refer a measure to the committee that has primary jurisdiction. The Speaker is also authorized to refer measures sequentially to additional committees and to impose time limits on such referrals.

Bipartisan Committee—A committee with an equal number of members from each political party. The House Committee on Standards of Official Conduct and the Senate Select Committee on Ethics are the only bipartisan, permanent full committees.

Borrowing Authority—Statutory authority permitting a federal agency, such as the Export-Import Bank, to borrow money from the public or the Treasury to finance its operations. It is a form of backdoor spending. To bring such spending under the control of the congressional appropriation process, the Congressional Budget Act requires that new borrowing authority shall be effective only to the extent and in such amounts as are provided in appropriations acts.

Budget—A detailed statement of actual or anticipated revenues and expenditures during an accounting period. For the national government, the period is the federal fiscal year (Oct. 1 to Sept. 30). The budget usually refers to the president's budget submission to Congress early each calendar year. The president's budget estimates federal government income and spending for the upcoming fiscal year and contains detailed recommendations for appropriation, revenue and other legislation. Congress is not required to accept or even vote directly on the president's proposals, and it often revises the president's budget extensively. (See Fiscal Year.)

Budget Act—Common name for the Congressional Budget and Impoundment Control Act of 1974, which established the basic procedures of the current congressional budget process; created the House and Senate Budget Committees; and enacted procedures for reconciliation, deferrals and rescissions. (See Budget Process; Deferral; Impoundment; Reconciliation; Rescission. See also Gramm-Rudman-Hollings Act of 1985.)

Budget and Accounting Act of 1921—The law that, for the first time, authorized the president to submit to Congress an annual budget for the entire federal government. Before passage of the act, most federal agencies sent their budget requests to the appropriate congressional committees without review by the president.

Budget Authority—Generally, the amount of money that may be spent or obligated by a government agency or for a government program or activity. Technically, it is statutory authority to enter into obligations that normally result in outlays. The main forms of budget authority are appropriations, borrowing authority and contract authority. It also includes authority to obligate and expend the proceeds of offsetting receipts and collections. Congress may make budget authority available for only one year, several years or an indefinite period, and it may specify definite or indefinite amounts.

Budget Enforcement Act of 1990—An act that revised the sequestration process established by the Gramm-Rudman-Hollings Act of 1985, replaced the earlier act's fixed deficit targets with adjustable ones, established discretionary spending limits for fiscal years 1991 through 1995, instituted pay-as-you-go rules to enforce deficit neutrality on revenue and mandatory spending legislation and reformed the budget and accounting rules for federal credit activities. Unlike the Gramm-Rudman-Hollings Act, the 1990 act emphasized restraints on legislated changes in taxes and spending instead of fixed deficit limits.

Budget Enforcement Act of 1997—An act that revised and updated the provisions of the Budget Enforcement Act of 1990, including by extending the discretionary spending caps and pay-as-you-go rules through 2002.

Budget Process—(1) In Congress, the procedural system it uses (a) to approve an annual concurrent resolution on the budget that sets goals for aggregate and functional categories of federal expenditures, revenues and the surplus or deficit for an upcoming fiscal year; and (b) to implement those goals in spending, revenue and, if necessary, reconciliation and debt-limit legislation. (2) In the executive branch, the process of formulating the president's annual budget, submitting it to Congress, defending it before congressional committees, implementing subsequent budget-related legislation, impounding or sequestering expenditures as permitted by law, auditing and evaluating programs and compiling final budget data. The Budget and Accounting Act of 1921 and the Congressional Budget and Impoundment Control Act of 1974 established the basic elements of the current budget process. Major revisions were enacted in the Gramm-Rudman-Hollings Act of 1985 and the Budget Enforcement Act of 1990.

Budget Resolution—A concurrent resolution in which Congress establishes or revises its version of the federal budget's broad financial features for the upcoming fiscal year and several additional fiscal years. Like other concurrent resolutions, it does not have the force of law, but it provides the framework within which Congress subsequently considers revenue, spending and other budget-implementing legislation. The framework consists of two basic elements: (1) aggregate budget amounts (total revenues, new budget authority, outlays, loan obligations and loan guarantee commitments, deficit or surplus and debt limit); and (2) subdivisions of the relevant aggregate amounts among the functional categories of the budget. Although it does not allocate funds to specific programs or accounts, the budget committees' reports accompanying the resolution often discuss the major program assumptions underlying its functional amounts. Unlike those amounts, however, the assumptions are not binding on Congress.

By Request—A designation indicating that a member has introduced a measure on behalf of the president, an executive agency or a private individual or organization. Members often introduce such measures as a courtesy because neither the president nor any person other than a member of Congress can do so. The term, which appears next to the sponsor's name, implies that the member who introduced the measure does not necessarily endorse it. A House rule dealing with by-request introductions dates from 1888, but the practice goes back to the earliest history of Congress.

Byrd Rule—The popular name of an amendment to the Congressional Budget Act that bars the inclusion of extraneous matter in any reconciliation legislation considered in the Senate. The ban is enforced by points of order that the presiding officer sustains. The provision defines different categories of extraneous matter, but it also permits certain exceptions. Its chief sponsor was Sen. Robert C. Byrd, D-W.Va.

Calendar—A list of measures or other matters (most of them favorably reported by committees) that are eligible for floor consideration. The House has five calendars; the Senate has two. A place on a calendar does not guarantee consideration. Each house decides which measures and matters it will take up, when and in what order, in accordance with its rules and practices.

Calendar Wednesday—A House procedure that on Wednesdays permits its committees to bring up for floor consideration nonprivileged measures they have reported. The procedure is so cumbersome and susceptible to dilatory tactics, however, that it is rarely used.

Call Up—To bring a measure or report to the floor for immediate consideration.

Casework—Assistance to constituents who seek assistance in dealing with federal and local government agencies. Constituent service is a high priority in most members' offices.

Caucus—(1) A common term for the official organization of each party in each house. (2) The official title of the organization of House Democrats. House and Senate Republicans and Senate Democrats call their organizations "conferences." (3) A term for an informal group of members who share legislative interests, such as the Black Caucus, Hispanic Caucus and Children's Caucus.

Censure—The strongest formal condemnation of a member for misconduct short of expulsion. A house usually adopts a resolution of censure to express its condemnation, after which the presiding officer reads its rebuke aloud to the member in the presence of his or her colleagues.

Chairman—The presiding officer of a committee, a subcommittee or a task force. At meetings, the chairman preserves order, enforces the rules, recognizes members to speak or offer motions and puts questions to a vote. The chairman of a committee or subcommittee usually appoints its staff and sets its agenda, subject to the panel's veto.

Chamber—The Capitol room in which a house of Congress normally holds its sessions. The chamber of the House of Representatives, officially called the Hall of the House, is considerably larger than that of the Senate because it must accommodate 435 representatives, four delegates and one resident commissioner. Unlike the Senate chamber, members have no desks or assigned seats. In both chambers, the floor slopes downward to the well in front of the presiding officer's raised desk. A chamber is often referred to as "the floor," as when members are said to be on or going to the floor. Those expressions usually imply that the member's house is in session.

Christmas Tree Bill—Jargon for a bill adorned with amendments, many of them unrelated to the bill's subject, that provide benefits for interest groups, specific states, congressional districts, companies and individuals.

Classes of Senators—A class consists of the thirty-three or thirty-four senators elected to a six-year term in the same general election. Because the terms of approximately one-third of the senators expire every two years, there are three classes.

Clean Bill—After a House committee extensively amends a bill, it often assembles its amendments and what is left of the bill into a new measure that one or more of its members introduces as a "clean bill." The revised measure is assigned a new number.

Clerk of the House—An officer of the House of Representatives responsible principally for administrative support of the legislative process in the House. The clerk is invariably the candidate of the majority party.

Cloakrooms—Two rooms with access to the rear of each chamber's floor, one for each party's members, where members may confer privately, sit quietly or have a snack. The presiding officer sometimes urges members who are conversing too loudly on the floor to retire to their cloakrooms.

Closed Hearing—A hearing closed to the public and the media. A House committee may close a hearing only if it determines that disclosure of the testimony to be taken would endanger national security, violate any law or tend to defame, degrade or incriminate any person. The Senate has a similar rule. Both houses require roll-call votes in open session to close a hearing.

Closed Rule—A special rule reported from the House Rules Committee that prohibits amendments to a measure or that only permits amendments offered by the reporting committee.

Cloture—A Senate procedure that limits further consideration of a pending proposal to thirty hours in order to end a filibuster. Sixteen senators must first sign and submit a cloture motion to the presiding officer. One hour after the Senate meets on the second calendar day thereafter, the chair puts the motion to a yea-and-nay vote following a live quorum call. If three-fifths of all senators (sixty if there are no vacancies) vote for the motion, the Senate must take final action on the cloture proposal by the end of the thirty hours of consideration and may consider no other business until it takes that action. Cloture on a proposal to amend the Senate's standing rules requires approval by two-thirds of the senators present and voting.

Code of Official Conduct—A House rule that bans certain actions by House members, officers and employees; requires them to conduct themselves in ways that "reflect creditably" on the House; and orders them to adhere to the spirit and the letter of House rules and those of its committees. The code's provisions govern the receipt of outside compensation, gifts and honoraria and the use of campaign funds; prohibit members from using their clerk-hire allowance to pay anyone who does not perform duties commensurate with that pay; forbids discrimination in members' hiring or treatment of employees on the grounds of race, color, religion, sex, handicap, age or national origin; orders members convicted of a crime who might be punished by imprisonment of two or more years not to participate in committee business or vote on the floor until exonerated or reelected; and restricts employees' contact with federal agencies on matters in which they have a significant financial interest. The Senate's rules contain some similar prohibitions.

College of Cardinals—A popular term for the subcommittee chairmen of the appropriations committees, reflecting their influence over appropriation measures. The chairmen of the full appropriations committees are sometimes referred to as popes.

Comity—The practice of maintaining mutual courtesy and civility between the two houses in their dealings with each other and in members' speeches on the floor. Although the practice is largely governed by long-established customs, a House rule explicitly cautions its members not to characterize any Senate action or inaction, refer to individual senators except under certain circumstances, or quote from Senate proceedings except to make legislative history on a measure. The Senate has no rule on the subject but references to the House have been held out of order on several occasions. Generally the houses do not interfere with each other's appropriations although minor conflicts sometimes occur. A refusal to receive a message from the other house has also been held to violate the practice of comity.

Committee—A panel of members elected or appointed to perform some service or function for its parent body. Congress has four types of committees: standing, special or select, joint, and, in the House, a Committee of the Whole. Committees conduct investigations, make studies, issue reports and recommendations and, in the case of standing committees, review and prepare measures on their assigned subjects for action by their respective houses. Most committees divide their work among several subcommittees. With rare exceptions, the majority party in a house holds a majority of the seats on its committees, and their chairmen are also from that party.

Committee Jurisdiction—The legislative subjects and other functions assigned to a committee by rule, precedent, resolution or statute. A committee's title usually indicates the general scope of its jurisdiction but often fails to mention other significant subjects assigned to it.

Committee of the Whole—Common name of the Committee of the Whole House on the State of the Union, a committee consisting of all members of the House of Representatives. Measures from the union calendar must be considered in the Committee of the Whole before the House officially completes action on them; the committee often considers other major bills as well. A quorum of the committee is 100, and it meets in the House chamber under a chairman appointed by the Speaker. Procedures in the Committee of the Whole expedite consideration of legislation because of its smaller quorum requirement, its ban on certain motions and its five-minute rule for debate on amendments. Those procedures usually permit more members to offer amendments and participate in the debate on a measure than is normally possible. The Senate no longer uses a Committee of the Whole.

Committee Ratios—The ratios of majority to minority party members on committees. By custom, the ratios of most committees reflect party strength in their respective houses as closely as possible.

Committee Report on a Measure—A document submitted by a committee to report a measure to its parent chamber. Customarily, the report explains the measure's purpose, describes provisions and any amendments recommended by the committee and presents arguments for its approval.

Committee Veto—A procedure that requires an executive department or agency to submit certain proposed policies, programs or action to designated committees for review before implementing them. Before 1983, when the Supreme Court declared that a legislative veto was unconstitutional, these provisions permitted committees to veto the proposals. Committees no longer conduct this type of policy review, and the term is now something of a misnomer. Nevertheless, agencies usually take the pragmatic approach of trying to reach a consensus with the committees before carrying out their proposals, especially when an appropriations committee is involved.

Concur—To agree to an amendment of the other house, either by adopting a motion to concur in that amendment or a motion to concur with an amendment to that amendment. After both houses have agreed to the same version of an amendment, neither house may amend it further, nor may any subsequent conference change it or delete it from the measure. Concurrence by one house in all amendments of the other house completes action on the measure; no vote is then necessary on the measure as a whole because both houses previously passed it.

Concurrent Resolution—A resolution that requires approval by both houses but does not need the president's signature and therefore cannot have the force of law. Concurrent resolutions deal with the prerogatives or internal affairs of Congress as a whole. Designated H. Con. Res. in the House and S. Con. Res. in the Senate, they are numbered consecutively in each house in their order of introduction during a two-year Congress.

Conferees—A common title for managers, the members from each house appointed to a conference committee. The Senate usually authorizes its presiding officer to appoint its conferees. The Speaker appoints House conferees, and under a rule adopted in 1993, can remove conferees "at any time after an original appointment" and also appoint additional conferees at any time. Conferees are expected to support the positions of their houses despite their personal views, but in practice this is not always the case. The party ratios of conferees generally reflect the ratios in their houses. Each house may appoint as many conferees as it pleases.

House conferees often outnumber their Senate colleagues; however, each house has only one vote in a conference, so the size of its delegation is immaterial.

Conference—(1) A formal meeting or series of meetings between members representing each house to reconcile House and Senate differences on a measure (occasionally several measures). Because one house cannot require the other to agree to its proposals, the conference usually reaches agreement by compromise. When a conference completes action on a measure, or as much action as appears possible, it sends its recommendations to both houses in the form of a conference report, accompanied by an explanatory statement. (2) The official title of the organization of all Democrats or Republicans in the Senate and of all Republicans in the House of Representatives. (See Party Caucus.)

Conference Committee—A temporary joint committee formed for the purpose of resolving differences between the houses on a measure. Major and controversial legislation usually requires conference committee action. Voting in a conference committee is not by individuals but within the House and Senate delegations. Consequently, a conference committee report requires the support of a majority of the conferees from each house. Both houses require that conference committees open their meetings to the public. The Senate's rule permits the committee to close its meetings if a majority of conferees in each delegation agree by a roll-call vote. The House rule permits closed meetings only if the House authorizes them to do so on a roll-call vote. Otherwise, there are no congressional rules governing the organization of, or procedure in, a conference committee. The committee chooses its chairman, but on measures that go to conference annually, such as general appropriation bills, the chairmanship traditionally rotates between the houses.

Conference Report—A document submitted to both houses that contains a conference committee's agreements for resolving their differences on a measure. It must be signed by a majority of the conferees from each house separately and must be accompanied by an explanatory statement. Both houses prohibit amendments to a conference report and require it to be accepted or rejected in its entirety.

Congress—(1) The national legislature of the United States, consisting of the House of Representatives and the Senate. (2) The national legislature in office during a two-year period. Congresses are numbered sequentially; thus, the 1st Congress of 1789-1791 and the 106th Congress of 1999-2001. Before 1935, the two-year period began on the first Monday in December of odd-numbered years. Since then it has extended from January of an odd-numbered year through noon on Jan. 3 of the next odd-numbered year. A Congress usually holds two annual sessions, but some have had three sessions and the 67th Congress had four. When a Congress expires, measures die if they have not yet been enacted.

Congressional Accountability Act of 1995 (CAA)—An act applying eleven labor, workplace and civil rights laws to the legislative branch and establishing procedures and remedies for legislative branch employees with grievances in violation of these laws. The following laws are covered by the CAA: the Fair Labor Standards Act of 1938; Title VII of the Civil Rights Act of 1964; Americans with Disabilities Act of 1990; Age Discrimination in Employment Act of 1967; Family and Medical Leave Act of 1993; Occupational Safety and Health Act of 1970; Chapter 71 of Title 5, U.S. Code (relating to federal service labor-management relations); Employee Polygraph Protection Act of 1988; Worker Adjustment and Retraining Notification Act; Rehabilitation Act of 1973; and Chapter 43 of Title 38, U.S. Code (relating to veterans' employment and reemployment).

Congressional Budget and Impoundment Control Act of 1974—The law that established the basic elements of the congressional budget process, the House and Senate Budget Committees, the Congressional

Budget Office and the procedures for congressional review of impoundments in the form of rescissions and deferrals proposed by the president. The budget process consists of procedures for coordinating congressional revenue and spending decisions made in separate tax, appropriations and legislative measures. The impoundment provisions were intended to give Congress greater control over executive branch actions that delay or prevent the spending of funds provided by Congress.

Congressional Budget Office (CBO)—A congressional support agency created by the Congressional Budget and Impoundment Control Act of 1974 to provide nonpartisan budgetary information and analysis to Congress and its committees. CBO acts as a scorekeeper when Congress is voting on the federal budget, tracking bills to ensure they comply with overall budget goals. The agency also estimates what proposed legislation would cost over a five-year period. CBO works most closely with the House and Senate Budget Committees.

Congressional Directory—The official who's who of Congress, usually published during the first session of a two-year Congress.

Congressional District—The geographical area represented by a single member of the House of Representatives. For states with only one representative, the entire state is a congressional district. As of 2001 seven states had only one representative each: Alaska, Delaware, Montana, North Dakota, South Dakota, Vermont and Wyoming.

Congressional Record—The daily, printed and substantially verbatim account of proceedings in both the House and Senate chambers. Extraneous materials submitted by members appear in a section titled "Extensions of Remarks." A "Daily Digest" appendix contains highlights of the day's floor and committee action plus a list of committee meetings and floor agendas for the next day's session.

Although the official reporters of each house take down every word spoken during the proceedings, members are permitted to edit and "revise and extend" their remarks before they are printed. In the Senate section, all speeches, articles and other material submitted by senators but not actually spoken or read on the floor are set off by large black dots, called bullets. However, bullets do not appear when a senator reads part of a speech and inserts the rest. In the House section, undelivered speeches and materials are printed in a distinctive typeface. The term "permanent Record" refers to the bound volumes of the daily Records of an entire session of Congress.

Congressional Research Service (CRS)—Established in 1917, a department of the Library of Congress whose staff provide nonpartisan, objective analysis and information on virtually any subject to committees, members and staff of Congress. Originally the Legislative Reference Service, it is the oldest congressional support agency.

Congressional Support Agencies—A term often applied to three agencies in the legislative branch that provide nonpartisan information and analysis to committees and members of Congress: the Congressional Budget Office, the Congressional Research Service of the Library of Congress and the General Accounting Office. A fourth support agency, the Office of Technology Assessment, formerly provided such support but was abolished in the 104th Congress.

Congressional Terms of Office—A term normally begins on Jan. 3 of the year following a general election and runs two years for representatives and six years for senators. A representative chosen in a special election to fill a vacancy is sworn in for the remainder of the predecessor's term. An individual appointed to fill a Senate vacancy usually serves until the next general election or until the end of the predecessor's term, whichever comes first. Some states, however, require their governors to call a special election to fill a Senate vacancy shortly after an appointment has been made.

Constitutional Rules—Constitutional provisions that prescribe procedures for Congress. In addition to certain types of votes required in particular situations, these provisions include the following: (1) the House chooses its Speaker, the Senate its president pro tempore and both houses their officers; (2) each house requires a majority quorum to conduct business; (3) less than a majority may adjourn from day to day and compel the attendance of absent members; (4) neither house may adjourn for more than three days without the consent of the other; (5) each house must keep a journal; (6) the yeas and nays are ordered when supported by one-fifth of the members present; (7) all revenue-raising bills must originate in the House, but the Senate may propose amendments to them. The Constitution also sets out the procedure in the House for electing a president, the procedure in the Senate for electing a vice president, the procedure for filling a vacancy in the office of vice president and the procedure for overriding a presidential veto.

Constitutional Votes—Constitutional provisions that require certain votes or voting methods in specific situations. They include (1) the yeas and nays at the desire of one-fifth of the members present; (2) a two-thirds vote by the yeas and nays to override a veto; (3) a two-thirds vote by one house to expel one of its members and by both houses to propose a constitutional amendment; (4) a two-thirds vote of senators present to convict someone whom the House has impeached and to consent to ratification of treaties; (5) a two-thirds vote in each house to remove political disabilities from persons who have engaged in insurrection or rebellion or given aid or comfort to the enemies of the United States; (6) a majority vote in each house to fill a vacancy in the office of vice president; (7) a majority vote of all states to elect a president in the House of Representatives when no candidate receives a majority of the electoral votes; (8) a majority vote of all senators when the Senate elects a vice president under the same circumstances; and (9) the casting vote of the vice president in case of tie votes in the Senate.

Contempt of Congress—Willful obstruction of the proper functions of Congress. Most frequently, it is a refusal to obey a subpoena to appear and testify before a committee or to produce documents demanded by it. Such obstruction is a misdemeanor and persons cited for contempt are subject to prosecution in federal courts. A house cites an individual for contempt by agreeing to a privileged resolution to that effect reported by a committee. The presiding officer then refers the matter to a U.S. attorney for prosecution.

Continuing Body—A characterization of the Senate on the theory that it continues from Congress to Congress and has existed continuously since it first convened in 1789. The rationale for the theory is that under the system of staggered six-year terms for senators, the terms of only about one-third of them expire after each Congress and, therefore, a quorum of the Senate is always in office. Consequently, under this theory, the Senate, unlike the House, does not have to adopt its rules at the beginning of each Congress because those rules continue from one Congress to the next. This makes it extremely difficult for the Senate to change its rules against the opposition of a determined minority because those rules require a two-thirds vote of the senators present and voting to invoke cloture on a proposed rules change.

Continuing Resolution (CR)—A joint resolution that provides funds to continue the operation of federal agencies and programs at the beginning of a new fiscal year if their annual appropriation bills have not yet been enacted; also called continuing appropriations. Continuing resolutions are enacted shortly before or after the new fiscal year begins and usually make funds available for a specified period. Additional resolutions are often needed after the first expires. Some continuing resolutions have provided appropriations for an entire fiscal year. Continuing resolutions for specific periods customarily fix a rate at which agencies may incur obligations based either on the previous year's appropriations, the president's budget request, or the amount as specified in the agency's regular annual appropriation bill if that bill has already been passed by one or both houses. In the House, continuing resolutions are privileged after Sept. 15.

Contract Authority—Statutory authority permitting an agency to enter into contracts or incur other obligations even though it has not received an appropriation to pay for them. Congress must eventually fund them because the government is legally liable for such payments. The Congressional Budget Act of 1974 requires that new contract authority may not be used unless provided for in advance by an appropriation act, but it permits a few exceptions.

Correcting Recorded Votes—The rules of both houses prohibit members from changing their votes after a vote result has been announced. Nevertheless, the Senate permits its members to withdraw or change their votes, by unanimous consent, immediately after the announcement. In rare instances, senators have been granted unanimous consent to change their votes several days or weeks after the announcement. Votes tallied by the electronic voting system in the House may not be changed. But when a vote actually given is not recorded during an oral call of the roll, a member may demand a correction as a matter of right. On all other alleged errors in a recorded vote, the Speaker determines whether the circumstances justify a change. Occasionally, members merely announce that they were incorrectly recorded; announcements can occur hours, days or even months after the vote and appear in the Congressional Record.

Cosponsor—A member who has joined one or more other members to sponsor a measure.

Credit Authority—Authority granted to an agency to incur direct loan obligations or to make loan guarantee commitments. The Congressional Budget Act of 1974 bans congressional consideration of credit authority legislation unless the extent of that authority is made subject to provisions in appropriation acts.

C-SPAN—Cable-Satellite Public Affairs Network, which provides live, gavel-to-gavel coverage of Senate floor proceedings on one cable television channel and coverage of House floor proceedings on another channel. C-SPAN also televises important committee hearings in both houses. Each house also transmits its televised proceedings directly to congressional offices.

Current Services Estimates—Executive branch estimates of the anticipated costs of federal programs and operations for the next and future fiscal years at existing levels of service and assuming no new initiatives or changes in existing law. The president submits these estimates to Congress with the annual budget and includes an explanation of the underlying economic and policy assumptions on which they are based, such as anticipated rates of inflation, real economic growth and unemployment, plus program caseloads and pay increases.

Custody of the Papers—Possession of an engrossed measure and certain related basic documents that the two houses produce as they try to resolve their differences over the measure.

Dance of the Swans and the Ducks—A whimsical description of the gestures some members use in connection with a request for a recorded vote, especially in the House. When members want their colleagues to stand in support of the request, they move their hands and arms in a gentle upward motion resembling the beginning flight of a graceful swan. When they want their colleagues to remain seated to avoid such a vote, they move their hands and arms in a vigorous downward motion resembling a diving duck.

Dean—Within a state's delegation in the House of Representatives, the member with the longest continuous service.

Debate—In congressional parlance, speeches delivered during consideration of a measure, motion or other matter, as distinguished from speeches in other parliamentary situations, such as one-minute and special order speeches when no business is pending. Virtually all debate in the House of Representatives is under some kind of time limitation. Most debate in the Senate is unlimited; that is, a senator, once recognized, may speak for as long as he or she chooses, unless the Senate invokes cloture.

Debt Limit—The maximum amount of outstanding federal public debt permitted by law. The limit (or ceiling) covers virtually all debt incurred by the government except agency debt. Each congressional budget resolution sets forth the new debt limit that may be required under its provisions.

Deferral—An impoundment of funds for a specific period of time that may not extend beyond the fiscal year in which it is proposed. Under the Impoundment Control Act of 1974, the president must notify Congress that he is deferring the spending or obligation of funds provided by law for a project or activity. Congress can disapprove the deferral by legislation.

Deficit—The amount by which the government's outlays exceed its budget receipts for a given fiscal year. Both the president's budget and the annual congressional budget resolution provide estimates of the deficit or surplus for the upcoming and several future fiscal years.

Degrees of Amendment—Designations that indicate the relationships of amendments to the text of a measure and to each other. In general, an amendment offered directly to the text of a measure is an amendment in the first degree, and an amendment to that amendment is an amendment in the second degree. Both houses normally prohibit amendments in the third degree — that is, an amendment to an amendment to an amendment.

Delegate—A nonvoting member of the House of Representatives elected to a two-year term from the District of Columbia, the territory of Guam, the territory of the Virgin Islands or the territory of American Samoa. By law, delegates may not vote in the full House but they may participate in debate, offer motions (except to reconsider) and serve and vote on standing and select committees. On their committees, delegates possess the same powers and privileges as other members and the Speaker may appoint them to appropriate conference committees and select committees.

Denounce—A formal action that condemns a member for misbehavior; considered by some experts to be equivalent to censure. (See Censure.)

Dilatory Tactics—Procedural actions intended to delay or prevent action by a house or a committee. They include, among others, offering numerous motions, demanding quorum calls and recorded votes at every opportunity, making numerous points of order and parliamentary inquiries and speaking as long as the applicable rules permit. The Senate rules permit a battery of dilatory tactics, especially lengthy speeches, except under cloture. In the House, possible dilatory tactics are more limited. Speeches are always subject to time limits and debate-ending motions. Moreover, a House rule instructs the Speaker not to entertain dilatory motions and lets the Speaker decide whether a motion is dilatory. However, the Speaker may not override the constitutional right of a member to demand the yeas and nays, and in practice usually waits for a point of order before exercising that authority. (See Cloture.)

Discharge a Committee—Remove a measure from a committee to which it has been referred in order to make it available for floor consideration. Noncontroversial measures are often discharged by unanimous consent. However, because congressional committees have no obligation to report measures referred to them, each house has procedures to extract controversial measures from recalcitrant committees. Six discharge procedures are available in the House of Representatives. The

Senate uses a motion to discharge, which is usually converted into a discharge resolution.

District Office—Representatives maintain one or more offices in their districts for the purpose of assisting and communicating with constituents. The costs of maintaining these offices are paid from members' official allowances. Senators can use the official expense allowance to rent offices in their home state, subject to a funding formula based on their state's population and other factors.

District Work Period—The House term for a scheduled congressional recess during which members may visit their districts and conduct constituency business.

Division Vote—A vote in which the chair first counts those in favor of a proposition and then those opposed to it, with no record made of how each member votes. In the Senate, the chair may count raised hands or ask senators to stand, whereas the House requires members to stand; hence, often called a standing vote. Committees in both houses ordinarily use a show of hands. A division usually occurs after a voice vote and may be demanded by any member or ordered by the chair if there is any doubt about the outcome of the voice vote. The demand for a division can also come before a voice vote. In the Senate, the demand must come before the result of a voice vote is announced. It may be made after a voice vote announcement in the House, but only if no intervening business has transpired and only if the member was standing and seeking recognition at the time of the announcement. A demand for the yeas and nays or, in the House, for a recorded vote, takes precedence over a division vote.

Doorkeeper of the House—A former officer of the House of Representatives who was responsible for enforcing the rules prohibiting unauthorized persons from entering the chamber when the House is in session. The doorkeeper was usually the candidate of the majority party. In 1995 the office was abolished and its functions transferred to the sergeant at arms.

Effective Dates—Provisions of an act that specify when the entire act or individual provisions in it become effective as law. Most acts become effective on the date of enactment, but it is sometimes necessary or prudent to delay the effective dates of some provisions.

Electronic Voting—Since 1973 the House has used an electronic voting system to record the yeas and nays and to conduct recorded votes. Members vote by inserting their voting cards in one of the boxes at several locations in the chamber. They are given at least fifteen minutes to vote. When several votes occur immediately after each other, the Speaker may reduce the voting time to five minutes on the second and subsequent votes. The Speaker may allow additional time on each vote but may also close a vote at any time after the minimum time has expired. Members can change their votes at any time before the Speaker announces the result. The House also uses the electronic system for quorum calls. While a vote is in progress, a large panel above the Speaker's desk displays how each member has voted. Smaller panels on either side of the chamber display running totals of the votes and the time remaining. The Senate does not have electronic voting.

Enacting Clause—The opening language of each bill, beginning "Be it enacted by the Senate and House of Representatives of the United States of America in Congress assembled..." This language gives legal force to measures approved by Congress and signed by the president or enacted over the president's veto. A successful motion to strike it from a bill kills the entire measure.

Engrossed Bill—The official copy of a bill or joint resolution as passed by one chamber, including the text as amended by floor action and certified by the clerk of the House or the secretary of the Senate (as appropriate). Amendments by one house to a measure or amendments of the other also are engrossed. House engrossed documents are printed on blue paper; the Senate's are printed on white paper.

Enrolled Bill—The final official copy of a bill or joint resolution passed in identical form by both houses. An enrolled bill is printed on parchment. After it is certified by the chief officer of the house in which it originated and signed by the House Speaker and the Senate president pro tempore, the measure is sent to the White House for the president's signature.

Entitlement Program—A federal program under which individuals, businesses or units of government that meet the requirements or qualifications established by law are entitled to receive certain payments if they seek such payments. Major examples include Social Security, Medicare, Medicaid, unemployment insurance and military and federal civilian pensions. Congress cannot control their expenditures by refusing to appropriate the sums necessary to fund them because the government is legally obligated to pay eligible recipients the amounts to which the law entitles them.

Equality of the Houses—A component of the Constitution's emphasis on checks and balances under which each house is given essentially equal status in the enactment of legislation and in the relations and negotiations between the two houses. Although the House of Representatives initiates revenue and appropriation measures, the Senate has the right to amend them. Either house may initiate any other type of legislation, and neither can force the other to agree to, or even act on, its measures. Moreover, each house has a potential veto over the other because legislation requires agreement by both. Similarly, in a conference to resolve their differences on a measure, each house casts one vote, as determined by a majority of its conferees. In most other national bicameral legislatures, the powers of one house are markedly greater than those of the other.

Ethics Rules—Several rules or standing orders in each house that mandate certain standards of conduct for members and congressional employees in finance, employment, franking and other areas. The Senate Permanent Select Committee on Ethics and the House Committee on Standards of Official Conduct investigate alleged violations of conduct and recommend appropriate actions to their respective houses.

Exclusive Committee—(1) Under the rules of the Republican Conference and House Democratic Caucus, a standing committee whose members usually cannot serve on any other standing committee. As of 2000 the Appropriations, Energy and Commerce (beginning in the 105th Congress), Ways and Means and Rules Committees were designated as exclusive committees. (2) Under the rules of the two party conferences in the Senate, a standing committee whose members may not simultaneously serve on any other exclusive committee.

Executive Calendar—The Senate's calendar for committee reports on its executive business, namely treaties and nominations. The calendar numbers indicate the order in which items were referred to the calendar but have no bearing on when or if the Senate will consider them. The Senate, by motion or unanimous consent, resolves itself into executive session to consider them.

Executive Document—A document, usually a treaty, sent by the president to the Senate for approval. It is referred to a committee in the same manner as other measures. Resolutions to ratify treaties have their own "treaty document" numbers. For example, the first treaty submitted in the 106th Congress would be "Treaty Doc 106-1."

Executive Order—A unilateral proclamation by the president that has a policy-making or legislative impact. Members of Congress have challenged some executive orders on the grounds that they usurped the authority of the legislative branch. Although the Supreme Court has ruled that a particular order exceeded the president's authority, it has upheld others as falling within the president's general constitutional powers.

Executive Privilege—The assertion that presidents have the right to withhold certain information from Congress. Presidents have based their claim on (1) the constitutional separation of powers; (2) the need for secrecy in military and diplomatic affairs; (3) the need to protect individuals from unfavorable publicity; (4) the need to safeguard the confidential exchange of ideas in the executive branch; and (5) the need to protect individuals who provide confidential advice to the president.

Executive Session—(1) A Senate meeting devoted to the consideration of treaties or nominations. Normally, the Senate meets in legislative session; it resolves itself into executive session, by motion or by unanimous consent, to deal with its executive business. It also keeps a separate Journal for executive sessions. Executive sessions are usually open to the public, but the Senate may choose to close them.

Expulsion—A member's removal from office by a two-thirds vote of his or her house; the supermajority is required by the Constitution. It is the most severe and most rarely used sanction a house can invoke against a member. Although the Constitution provides no explicit grounds for expulsion, the courts have ruled that it may be applied only for misconduct during a member's term of office, not for conduct before the member's election. Generally, neither house will consider expulsion of a member convicted of a crime until the judicial processes have been exhausted. At that stage, members sometimes resign rather than face expulsion. In 1977 the House adopted a rule urging members convicted of certain crimes to voluntarily abstain from voting or participating in other legislative business.

Extensions of Remarks—An appendix to the daily Congressional Record that consists primarily of miscellaneous extraneous material submitted by members. It often includes members' statements not delivered on the floor, newspaper articles and editorials, praise for a member's constituents and noteworthy letters received by a member, among other material. Representatives supply the bulk of this material; senators submit very little. "Extensions of Remarks" pages are separately numbered, and each number is preceded by the letter "E." Materials may be placed in the Extensions of Remarks section only by unanimous consent. Usually, one member of each party makes the request each day on behalf of his or her party colleagues after the House has completed its legislative business of the day.

Federal Debt—The total amount of monies borrowed and not yet repaid by the federal government. Federal debt consists of public debt and agency debt. Public debt is the portion of the federal debt borrowed by the Treasury or the Federal Financing Bank directly from the public or from another federal fund or account. For example, the Treasury regularly borrows money from the Social Security trust fund. Public debt accounts for about 99 percent of the federal debt. Agency debt refers to the debt incurred by federal agencies such as the Export-Import Bank but excluding the Treasury and the Federal Financing Bank, which are authorized by law to borrow funds from the public or from another government fund or account.

Filibuster—The use of obstructive and time-consuming parliamentary tactics by one member or a minority of members to delay, modify or defeat proposed legislation or rules changes. Filibusters are also sometimes used to delay urgently needed measures to force the body to accept other legislation. The Senate's rules permitting unlimited debate and the extraordinary majority it requires to impose cloture make filibustering particularly effective in that chamber. Under the stricter rules of the House, filibusters in that body are short-lived and therefore ineffective and rarely attempted.

Fiscal Year—The federal government's annual accounting period. It begins Oct. 1 and ends on the following Sept. 30. A fiscal year is designated by the calendar year in which it ends and is often referred to as FY. Thus, fiscal year 1998 began Oct. 1, 1997, ended Sept. 30, 1998, and is called FY98. In theory, Congress is supposed to complete action on all budgetary measures applying to a fiscal year before that year begins. It rarely does so.

Five-Minute Rule—A House rule that limits debate on an amendment offered in Committee of the Whole to five minutes for its sponsor and five minutes for an opponent. In practice, the committee routinely permits longer debate by two devices: the offering of pro forma amendments, each debatable for five minutes, and unanimous consent for a member to speak longer than five minutes. Consequently, debate on an amendment sometimes continues for hours. At any time after the first ten minutes, however, the committee may shut off debate immediately or by a specified time, either by unanimous consent or by majority vote on a nondebatable motion. The motion, which dates from 1847, is also used in the House as in Committee of the Whole, where debate also may be shut off by a motion for the previous question.

Floor—The ground level of the House or Senate chamber where members sit and the houses conduct their business. When members are attending a meeting of their house they are said to be on the floor. Floor action refers to the procedural actions taken during floor consideration such as deciding on motions, taking up measures, amending them and voting.

Floor Manager—A majority party member responsible for guiding a measure through its floor consideration in a house and for devising the political and procedural strategies that might be required to get it passed. The presiding officer gives the floor manager priority recognition to debate, offer amendments, oppose amendments and make crucial procedural motions.

Frank—Informally, members' legal right to send official mail postage free under their signatures; often called the franking privilege. Technically, it is the autographic or facsimile signature used on envelopes instead of stamps that permits members and certain congressional officers to send their official mail free of charge. The franking privilege has been authorized by law since the first Congress, except for a few months in 1873. Congress reimburses the U.S. Postal Service for the franked mail it handles.

Function or Functional Category—A broad category of national need and spending of budgetary significance. A category provides an accounting method for allocating and keeping track of budgetary resources and expenditures for that function because it includes all budget accounts related to the function's subject or purpose such as agriculture, administration of justice, commerce and housing and energy. Functions do not necessarily correspond with appropriations acts or with the budgets of individual agencies. As of 2000 there were twenty functional categories, each divided into a number of subfunctions.

Gag Rule—A pejorative term for any type of special rule reported by the House Rules Committee that proposes to prohibit amendments to a measure or only permits amendments offered by the reporting committee.

Galleries—The balconies overlooking each chamber from which the public, news media, staff and others may observe floor proceedings.

General Appropriation Bill—A term applied to each of the thirteen annual bills that provide funds for most federal agencies and programs and also to the supplemental appropriation bills that contain appropriations for more than one agency or program.

Germaneness—The requirement that an amendment be closely related — in terms of subject or purpose, for example — to the text it proposes to amend. A House rule requires that all amendments be germane. In the Senate, only amendments offered to general appropriation bills and budget measures or proposed under cloture must be germane.

Germaneness rules can be waived by suspension of the rules in both houses, by unanimous consent agreements in the Senate and by special rules from the Rules Committee in the House. Moreover, presiding officers usually do not enforce germaneness rules on their own initiative; therefore, a nongermane amendment can be adopted if no member raises a point of order against it. Under cloture in the Senate, however, the chair may take the initiative to rule amendments out of order as not being germane, without a point of order being made. All House debate must be germane except during general debate in the Committee of the Whole, but special rules invariably require that such debate be "confined to the bill." The Senate requires germane debate only during the first three hours of each daily session. Under the precedents of both houses, an amendment can be relevant but not necessarily germane. A crucial factor in determining germaneness in the House is how the subject of a measure or matter is defined. For example, the subject of a measure authorizing construction of a naval vessel is defined as being the construction of a single vessel; therefore, an amendment to authorize an additional vessel is not germane.

Gerrymandering—The manipulation of legislative district boundaries to benefit a particular party, politician or minority group. The term originated in 1812 when the Massachusetts legislature redrew the lines of state legislative districts to favor the party of Gov. Elbridge Gerry, and some critics said one district looked like a salamander. (See also Congressional District; Redistricting.)

Government Accountability Office (GAO)—A congressional support agency, often referred to as the investigative arm of Congress. It evaluates and audits federal agencies and programs in the United States and abroad on its initiative or at the request of congressional committees or members.

Gramm-Rudman-Hollings Act of 1985—Common name for the Balanced Budget and Emergency Deficit Control Act of 1985, which established new budget procedures intended to balance the federal budget by fiscal year 1991. (The timetable subsequently was extended and then deleted.) The act's chief sponsors were senators Phil Gramm (R-Texas), Warren Rudman (R-N.H.) Ernest Hollings (D-S.C.).

Grandfather Clause—A provision in a measure, law or rule that exempts an individual, entity or a defined category of individuals or entities from complying with a new policy or restriction. For example, a bill that would raise taxes on persons who reach the age of sixty-five after a certain date inherently grandfathers out those who are sixty-five before that date. Similarly, a Senate rule limiting senators to two major committee assignments also grandfathers some senators who were sitting on a third major committee before a specified date.

Grants-in-Aid—Payments by the federal government to state and local governments to help provide for assistance programs or public services.

Hearing—Committee or subcommittee meetings to receive testimony on proposed legislation during investigations or for oversight purposes. Relatively few bills are important enough to justify formal hearings. Witnesses often include experts, government officials, spokespersons for interested groups, officials of the General Accounting Office and members of Congress.

Hold—A senator's request that his or her party leaders delay floor consideration of certain legislation or presidential nominations. The majority leader usually honors a hold for a reasonable period of time, especially if its purpose is to assure the senator that the matter will not be called up during his or her absence or to give the senator time to gather necessary information.

Hold (or Have) the Floor—A member's right to speak without interruption, unless he or she violates a rule, after recognition by the presiding officer. At the member's discretion, he or she may yield to another member for a question in the Senate or for a question or statement in the

House, but may reclaim the floor at any time.

Hold-Harmless Clause—In legislation providing a new formula for allocating federal funds, a clause to ensure that recipients of those funds do not receive less in a future year than they did in the current year if the new formula would result in a reduction for them. Similar to a grandfather clause, it has been used most frequently to soften the impact of sudden reductions in federal grants. (See Grandfather Clause.)

Hopper—A box on the clerk's desk in the House chamber into which members deposit bills and resolutions to introduce them. In House jargon, to drop a bill in the hopper is to introduce it.

Hour Rule—A House rule that permits members, when recognized, to hold the floor in debate for no more than one hour each. The majority party member customarily yields one-half the time to a minority member. Although the hour rule applies to general debate in Committee of the Whole as well as in the House, special rules routinely vary the length of time for such debate and its control to fit the circumstances of particular measures.

House As In Committee of the Whole—A hybrid combination of procedures from the general rules of the House and from the rules of the Committee of the Whole, sometimes used to expedite consideration of a measure on the floor.

House Calendar—The calendar reserved for all public bills and resolutions that do not raise revenue or directly or indirectly appropriate money or property when they are favorably reported by House committees.

House Manual—A commonly used title for the handbook of the rules of the House of Representatives, published in each Congress. Its official title is Constitution, Jefferson's Manual and Rules of the House of Representatives.

House of Representatives—The house of Congress in which states are represented roughly in proportion to their populations, but every state is guaranteed at least one representative. By law, the number of voting representatives is fixed at 435. Four delegates and one resident commissioner also serve in the House; they may vote in their committees but not on the House floor. Although the House and Senate have equal legislative power, the Constitution gives the House sole authority to originate revenue measures. The House also claims the right to originate appropriation measures, a claim the Senate disputes in theory but concedes in practice. The House has the sole power to impeach, and it elects the president when no candidate has received a majority of the electoral votes. It is sometimes referred to as the lower body.

Immunity—(1) Members' constitutional protection from lawsuits and arrest in connection with their legislative duties. They may not be tried for libel or slander for anything they say on the floor of a house or in committee. Nor may they be arrested while attending sessions of their houses or when traveling to or from sessions of Congress, except when charged with treason, a felony or a breach of the peace. (2) In the case of a witness before a committee, a grant of protection from prosecution based on that person's testimony to the committee. It is used to compel witnesses to testify who would otherwise refuse to do so on the constitutional ground of possible selfincrimination. Under such a grant, none of a witness's testimony may be used against him or her in a court proceeding except in a prosecution for perjury or for giving a false statement to Congress. (See also Contempt of Congress.)

Impeachment—The first step to remove the president, vice president or other federal civil officers from office and to disqualify them from any future federal office "of honor, Trust or Profit." An impeachment is a formal charge of treason, bribery or "other high Crimes and Misdemeanors." The House has the sole power of impeachment and the Senate the sole power of trying the charges and convicting. The House impeaches by a simple majority vote; conviction requires a two-thirds vote of all senators present.

Impeachment Trial, Removal and Disqualification—The Senate conducts an impeachment trial under a separate set of twenty-six rules that appears in the Senate Manual. Under the Constitution, the chief justice of the United States presides over trials of the president, but the vice president, the president pro tempore or any other senator may preside over the impeachment trial of another official.

The Constitution requires senators to take an oath for an impeachment trial. During the trial, senators may not engage in colloquies or participate in arguments, but they may submit questions in writing to House managers or defense counsel. After the trial concludes, the Senate votes separately on each article of impeachment without debate unless the Senate orders the doors closed for private discussions. During deliberations senators may speak no more than once on a question, not for more than ten minutes on an interlocutory question and not more than fifteen minutes on the final question. These rules may be set aside by unanimous consent or suspended on motion by a two-thirds vote.

The Senate's impeachment trial of President Clinton in 1999 was only the second such trial involving a president. It continued for five weeks, with the Senate voting not to convict on the two impeachment articles.

Senate impeachment rules allow the Senate, at its own discretion, to name a committee to hear evidence and conduct the trial, with all senators thereafter voting on the charges. The impeachment trials of three federal judges were conducted this way, and the Supreme Court upheld the validity of these rules in Nixon v. United States, 506 U.S. 224, 1993.

An official convicted on impeachment charges is removed from office immediately. However, the convicted official is not barred from holding a federal office in the future unless the Senate, after its conviction vote, also approves a resolution disqualifying the convicted official from future office. For example, federal judge Alcee L. Hastings was impeached and convicted in 1989, but the Senate did not vote to bar him from office in the future. In 1992 Hastings was elected to the House of Representatives, and no challenge was raised against seating him when he took the oath of office in 1993.

Impoundment—An executive branch action or inaction that delays or withholds the expenditure or obligation of budget authority provided by law. The Impoundment Control Act of 1974 classifies impoundments as either deferrals or rescissions, requires the president to notify Congress about all such actions and gives Congress authority to approve or reject them.

Inspector General (IG) In the House of Representatives—A position established with the passage of the House Administrative Reform Resolution of 1992. The duties of the office have been revised several times and are now contained in House Rule II. The inspector general (IG), who is subject to the policy direction and oversight of the Committee on House Administration, is appointed for a Congress jointly by the Speaker and the majority and minority leaders of the House. The IG communicates the results of audits to the House officers or officials who were the subjects of the audits and suggests appropriate corrective measures. The IG submits a report of each audit to the Speaker, the majority and minority leaders and the chairman and ranking minority member of the House Administration Committee; notifies these five members in the case of any financial irregularity discovered; and reports to the Committee on Standards of Official Conduct on possible violations of House rules or any applicable law by any House member, officer or employee. The IG's office also has certain duties to audit various financial operations of the House that had previously been performed by the General Accounting Office.

Instruct Conferees—A formal action by a house urging its conferees to uphold a particular position on a measure in conference. The instruc-

tion may be to insist on certain provisions in the measure as passed by that house or to accept a provision in the version passed by the other house. Instructions to conferees are not binding because the primary responsibility of conferees is to reach agreement on a measure and neither House can compel the other to accept particular provisions or positions.

Investigative Power—The authority of Congress and its committees to pursue investigations, upheld by the Supreme Court but limited to matters related to, and in furtherance of, a legitimate task of the Congress. Standing committees in both houses are permanently authorized to investigate matters within their jurisdictions. Major investigations are sometimes conducted by temporary select, special or joint committees established by resolutions for that purpose.

Some rules of the House provide certain safeguards for witnesses and others during investigative hearings. These permit counsel to accompany witnesses, require that each witness receive a copy of the committee's rules and order the committee to go into closed session if it believes the testimony to be heard might defame, degrade or incriminate any person. The committee may subsequently decide to hear such testimony in open session. The Senate has no rules of this kind.

Item Veto—Item veto authority, which is available to most state governors, allows governors to eliminate or reduce items in legislative measures presented for their signature without vetoing the entire measure and sign the rest into law. A similar authority was briefly granted to the U.S. president under the Line Item Veto Act of 1996. According to the majority opinion of the Supreme Court in its 1998 decision overturning that law, a constitutional amendment would be necessary to give the president such item veto authority.

Jefferson's Manual—Short title of Jefferson's Manual of Parliamentary Practice, prepared by Thomas Jefferson for his guidance when he was president of the Senate from 1797 to 1801. Although it reflects English parliamentary practice in his day, many procedures in both houses of Congress are still rooted in its basic precepts. Under a House rule adopted in 1837, the manual's provisions govern House procedures when applicable and when they are not inconsistent with its standing rules and orders. The Senate, however, has never officially acknowledged it as a direct authority for its legislative procedure.

Johnson Rule—A policy instituted in 1953 under which all Democratic senators are assigned to one major committee before any Democrat is assigned to two. The Johnson Rule is named after its author, Sen. Lyndon B. Johnson, D-Texas, then the Senate's Democratic leader. Senate Republicans adopted a similar policy soon thereafter.

Joint Committee—A committee composed of members selected from each house. The functions of most joint committees involve investigation, research or oversight of agencies closely related to Congress. Permanent joint committees, created by statute, are sometimes called standing joint committees. Once quite numerous, only four joint committees remained as of 2002: Joint Economic, Joint Taxation, Joint Library and Joint Printing. None has authority to report legislation.

Joint Resolution—A legislative measure that Congress uses for purposes other than general legislation. Similar to a bill, it has the force of law when passed by both houses and either approved by the president or passed over the president's veto. Unlike a bill, a joint resolution enacted into law is not called an act; it retains its original title. Most often, joint resolutions deal with such relatively limited matters as the correction of errors in existing law, continuing appropriations, a single appropriation or the establishment of permanent joint committees. Unlike bills, however, joint resolutions also are used to propose constitutional amendments; these do not require the president's signature and become effective only when ratified by three-fourths of the states. The House designates joint resolutions as H.J. Res., the Senate as S.J. Res. Each house numbers its joint resolutions consecutively in the order of introduction during a two-year Congress.

Joint Session—Informally, any combined meeting of the Senate and the House. Technically, a joint session is a combined meeting to count the electoral votes for president and vice president or to hear a presidential address, such as the State of the Union message; any other formal combined gathering of both houses is a joint meeting. Joint sessions are authorized by concurrent resolutions and are held in the House chamber, because of its larger seating capacity. Although the president of the Senate and the Speaker sit side by side at the Speaker's desk during combined meetings, the former presides over the electoral count and the latter presides on all other occasions and introduces the president or other guest speaker. The president and other guests may address a joint session or meeting only by invitation.

Joint Sponsorship—Two or more members sponsoring the same measure.

Journal—The official record of House or Senate actions, including every motion offered, every vote cast, amendments agreed to, quorum calls and so forth. Unlike the Congressional Record, it does not provide reports of speeches, debates, statements and the like. The Constitution requires each house to maintain a Journal and to publish it periodically.

Junket—A member's trip at government expense, especially abroad, ostensibly on official business but, it is often alleged, for pleasure.

Killer Amendment—An amendment that, if agreed to, might lead to the defeat of the measure it amends, either in the house in which the amendment is offered or at some later stage of the legislative process. Members sometimes deliberately offer or vote for such an amendment in the expectation that it will undermine support for the measure in Congress or increase the likelihood that the president will veto it.

King of the Mountain (or Hill) Rule—(See Queen of the Hill Rule.)

LA—(See Legislative Assistant.)

Lame Duck—Jargon for a member who has not been reelected, or did not seek reelection, and is serving the balance of his or her term.

Lame Duck Session—A session of a Congress held after the election for the succeeding Congress, so-called after the lame duck members still serving.

Last Train Out—Colloquial name for last must-pass bill of a session of Congress.

Law—An act of Congress that has been signed by the president, passed over the president's veto or allowed to become law without the president's signature.

Lay on the Table—A motion to dispose of a pending proposition immediately, finally and adversely; that is, to kill it without a direct vote on its substance. Often simply called a motion to table, it is not debatable and is adopted by majority vote or without objection. It is a highly privileged motion, taking precedence over all others except the motion to adjourn in the House and all but three additional motions in the Senate. It can kill a bill or resolution, an amendment, another motion, an appeal or virtually any other matter.

Tabling an amendment also tables the measure to which the amendment is pending in the House, but not in the Senate. The House does not allow the motion against the motion to recommit, in Committee of the Whole, and in some other situations. In the Senate it is the only permissible motion that immediately ends debate on a proposition, but only to kill it.

(The) Leadership—Usually, a reference to the majority and minority leaders of the Senate or to the Speaker and minority leader of the House. The term sometimes includes the majority leader in the House and the majority and minority whips in each house and, at other times, other party officials as well.

Legislation—(1) A synonym for legislative measures: bills and joint resolutions. (2) Provisions in such measures or in substantive amendments offered to them. (3) In some contexts, provisions that change existing substantive or authorizing law, rather than provisions that make appropriations.

Legislation on an Appropriation Bill—A common reference to provisions changing existing law that appear in, or are offered as amendments to, a general appropriation bill. A House rule prohibits the inclusion of such provisions in general appropriation bills unless they retrench expenditures. An analogous Senate rule permits points of order against amendments to a general appropriation bill that propose general legislation.

Legislative Assistant (LA)—A member's staff person responsible for monitoring and preparing legislation on particular subjects and for advising the member on them; commonly referred to as an LA.

Legislative Day—The day that begins when a house meets after an adjournment and ends when it next adjourns. Because the House of Representatives normally adjourns at the end of a daily session, its legislative and calendar days usually coincide. The Senate, however, frequently recesses at the end of a daily session, and its legislative day may extend over several calendar days, weeks or months. Among other uses, this technicality permits the Senate to save time by circumventing its morning hour, a procedure required at the beginning of every legislative day.

Legislative History—(1) A chronological list of actions taken on a measure during its progress through the legislative process. (2) The official documents relating to a measure, the entries in the Journals of the two houses on that measure and the Congressional Record text of its consideration in both houses. The documents include all committee reports and the conference report and joint explanatory statement, if any. Courts and affected federal agencies study a measure's legislative history for congressional intent about its purpose and interpretation.

Legislative Process—(1) Narrowly, the stages in the enactment of a law from introduction to final disposition. An introduced measure that becomes law typically travels through reference to committee; committee and subcommittee consideration; report to the chamber; floor consideration; amendment; passage; engrossment; messaging to the other house; similar steps in that house, including floor amendment of the measure; return of the measure to the first house; consideration of amendments between the houses or a conference to resolve their differences; approval of the conference report by both houses; enrollment; approval by the president or override of the president's veto; and deposit with the Archivist of the United States. (2) Broadly, the political, lobbying and other factors that affect or influence the process of enacting laws.

Legislative Veto—A procedure, declared unconstitutional in 1983, that allowed Congress or one of its houses to nullify certain actions of the president, executive branch agencies or independent agencies. Sometimes called congressional vetoes or congressional disapprovals. Following the Supreme Court's 1983 decision, Congress amended several legislative veto statutes to require enactment of joint resolutions, which are subject to presidential veto, for nullifying executive branch actions.

Limitation on a General Appropriation Bill—Language that prohibits expenditures for part of an authorized purpose from funds provided in a general appropriation bill. Precedents require that the language be phrased in the negative: that none of the funds provided in a pending appropriation bill shall be used for a specified authorized activity. Limitations in general appropriation bills are permitted on the grounds that Congress can refuse to fund authorized programs and, therefore, can refuse to fund any part of them as long as the prohibition does not change existing law. House precedents have established that a limitation does not change existing law if it does not impose additional duties or burdens on executive branch officials, interfere with their discretionary authority or require them to make judgments or determinations not required by existing law. The proliferation of limitation amendments in the 1970s and early 1980s prompted the House to adopt a rule in 1983 making it more difficult for members to offer them. The rule bans such amendments during the reading of an appropriation bill for amendments, unless they are specifically authorized in existing law. Other limitations may be offered after the reading, but the Committee of the Whole can foreclose them by adopting a motion to rise and report the bill back to the House. In 1995 the rule was amended to allow the motion to rise and report to be made only by the majority leader or his or her designee. The House Appropriations Committee, however, can include limitation provisions in the bills it reports.

Line Item—An amount in an appropriation measure. It can refer to a single appropriation account or to separate amounts within the account. In the congressional budget process, the term usually refers to assumptions about the funding of particular programs or accounts that underlie the broad functional amounts in a budget resolution. These assumptions are discussed in the reports accompanying each resolution and are not binding.

Line-Item Veto—(See Item Veto.)

Line Item Veto Act of 1996—A law, in effect only from January 1997 until June 1998, that granted the president authority intended to be functionally equivalent to an item veto, by amending the Impoundment Control Act of 1974 to incorporate an approach known as enhanced rescision. Key provisions established a new procedure that permitted the president to cancel amounts of new discretionary appropriations (budget authority), new items of direct spending (entitlements) or certain limited tax benefits. It also required the president to notify Congress of the cancellation in a special message within five calendar days after signing the measure. The cancellation would become permanent unless legislation disapproving it was enacted within thirty days. On June 25, 1998, in Clinton v. City of New York the Supreme Court held the Line Item Veto Act unconstitutional, on the grounds that its cancellation provisions violated the presentment clause in Article I, clause 7, of the Constitution.

Live Pair—A voluntary and informal agreement between two members on opposite sides of an issue, one of whom is absent for a recorded vote, under which the member who is present withholds or withdraws his or her vote to offset the failure to vote by the member who is absent. Usually the member in attendance announces that he or she has a live pair, states how each would have voted and votes "present." In the House, under a rules change enacted in the 106th Congress, a live pair is only permitted on the rare occasions when electronic voting is not used.

Live Quorum—In the Senate, a quorum call to which senators are expected to respond. Senators usually suggest the absence of a quorum, not to force a quorum to appear, but to provide a pause in the proceedings during which senators can engage in private discussions or wait for a senator to come to the floor. A senator desiring a live quorum usually announces his or her intention, giving fair warning that there will be an objection to any unanimous consent request that the quorum call be dispensed with before it is completed.

Loan Guarantee—A statutory commitment by the federal government to pay part or all of a loan's principal and interest to a lender or the holder of a security in case the borrower defaults.

Lobby—To try to persuade members of Congress to propose, pass, modify or defeat proposed legislation or to change or repeal existing laws. Lobbyists attempt to promote their preferences or those of a group, organization or industry. Originally the term referred to persons frequenting the lobbies or corridors of legislative chambers in order to speak to lawmakers. In a general sense, lobbying includes not only direct contact with members but also indirect attempts to influence them, such as writing to them or persuading others to write or visit them, attempting to mold public opinion toward a desired legislative goal by various means and contributing or arranging for contributions to members' election campaigns. The right to lobby stems from the First Amendment to the Constitution, which bans laws that abridge the right of the people to petition the government for a redress of grievances.

Lobbying Disclosure Act of 1995—The principal statute requiring disclosure of — and also, to a degree, circumscribing — the activities of lobbyists. In general, it requires lobbyists who spend more than 20 percent of their time on lobbying activities to register and make semiannual reports of their activities to the clerk of the House and the secretary of the Senate, although the law provides for a number of exemptions. Among the statute's prohibitions, lobbyists are not allowed to make contributions to the legal defense fund of a member or high government official or to reimburse for official travel. Civil penalties for failure to comply may include fines of up to $50,000. The act does not include grassroots lobbying in its definition of lobbying activities.

The act amends several other lobby laws, notably the Foreign Agents Registration Act (FARA), so that lobbyists can submit a single filing. Since the measure was enacted, the number of lobby registrations has risen from about 12,000 to more than 20,000. In 1998 expenditures on federal lobbying, as disclosed under the Lobbying Disclosure Act, totaled $1.42 billion. The 1995 act supersedes the 1946 Federal Regulation of Lobbying Act, which was repealed in Section 11 of the 1995 Act.

Logrolling—Jargon for a legislative tactic or bargaining strategy in which members try to build support for their legislation by promising to support legislation desired by other members or by accepting amendments they hope will induce their colleagues to vote for their bill.

Lower Body—A way to refer to the House of Representatives, which is considered pejorative by House members.

Mace—The symbol of the office of the House sergeant at arms. Under the direction of the Speaker, the sergeant at arms is responsible for preserving order on the House floor by holding up the mace in front of an unruly member, or by carrying the mace up and down the aisles to quell boisterous behavior. When the House is in session, the mace sits on a pedestal at the Speaker's right; when the House is in Committee of the Whole, it is moved to a lower pedestal. The mace is forty-six inches high and consists of thirteen ebony rods bound in silver and topped by a silver globe with a silver eagle, wings outstretched, perched on it.

Majority Leader—The majority party's chief floor spokesperson, elected by that party's caucus — sometimes called floor leader. In the Senate, the majority leader also develops the party's political and procedural strategy, usually in collaboration with other party officials and committee chairmen. The majority leader negotiates the Senate's agenda and committee ratios with the minority leader and usually calls up measures for floor action. The chamber traditionally concedes to the majority leader the right to determine the days on which it will meet and the hours at which it will convene and adjourn. In the House, the majority leader is the Speaker's deputy and heir apparent and helps plan the floor agenda and the party's legislative strategy and often speaks for the party leadership in debate.

Managers—(1) The official title of members appointed to a conference committee, commonly called conferees. The ranking majority and minority managers for each house also manage floor consideration of the committee's conference report. (2) The members who manage the initial floor consideration of a measure. (3) The official title of House members appointed to present impeachment articles to the Senate and to act as prosecutors on behalf of the House during the Senate trial of the impeached person.

Mandatory Appropriations—Amounts that Congress must appropriate annually because it has no discretion over them unless it first amends existing substantive law. Certain entitlement programs, for example, require annual appropriations.

Markup—A meeting or series of meetings by a committee or subcommittee during which members mark up a measure by offering, debating and voting on amendments to it.

Means-Tested Programs—Programs that provide benefits or services to low-income individuals who meet a test of need. Most are entitlement programs, such as Medicaid, food stamps and Supplementary Security Income. A few—for example, subsidized housing and various social services—are funded through discretionary appropriations.

Members' Allowances—Official expenses that are paid for or for which members are reimbursed by their houses. Among these are the costs of office space in congressional buildings and in their home states or districts; office equipment and supplies; postage-free mailings (the franking privilege); a set number of trips to and from home states or districts, as well as travel elsewhere on official business; telephone and other telecommunications services; and staff salaries.

Member's Staff—The personal staff to which a member is entitled. The House sets a maximum number of staff and a monetary allowance for each member. The Senate does not set a maximum staff level, but it does set a monetary allowance for each member. In each house, the staff allowance is included with office expenses allowances and official mail allowances in a consolidated allowance. Representatives and senators can spend as much money in their consolidated allowances for staff, office expenses or official mail, as long as they do not exceed the monetary value of the three allowances combined. This provides members with flexibility in operating their offices.

Method of Equal Proportions—The mathematical formula used since 1950 to determine how the 435 seats in the House of Representatives should be distributed among the fifty states in the apportionment following each decennial census. It minimizes as much as possible the proportional difference between the average district population in any two states. Because the Constitution guarantees each state at least one representative, fifty seats are automatically apportioned. The formula calculates priority numbers for each state, assigns the first of the 385 remaining seats to the state with the highest priority number, the second to the state with the next highest number and so on until all seats are distributed. (See Apportionment.)

Midterm Election—The general election for members of Congress that occurs in November of the second year in a presidential term.

Minority Leader—The minority party's leader and chief floor spokesman, elected by the party caucus; sometimes called minority floor leader. With the assistance of other party officials and the ranking minority members of committees, the minority leader devises the party's political and procedural strategy.

Minority Staff—Employees who assist the minority party members of a committee. Most committees hire separate majority and minority party staffs but they also may hire nonpartisan staff. Senate rules state that a committee's staff must reflect the relative number of its majority and minority party committee members, and the rules guarantee the minority at least one-third of the funds available for hiring partisan staff. In the House, each committee is authorized thirty professional staff, and the minority members of most committees may select up to ten of these staff

(subject to full committee approval). Under House rules, the minority party is to be "treated fairly" in the apportionment of additional staff resources. Each House committee determines the portion of its additional staff it allocates to the minority; some committees allocate one-third; and others allot less.

Modified Rule—A special rule from the House Rules Committee that permits only certain amendments to be offered to a measure during its floor consideration or that bans certain specified amendments or amendments on certain subjects.

Morning Business—In the Senate, routine business that is to be transacted at the beginning of the morning hour. The business consists, first, of laying before the Senate, and referring to committees, matters such as messages from the president and the House, federal agency reports and unreferred petitions, memorials, bills and joint resolutions. Next, senators may present additional petitions and memorials. Then committees may present their reports, after which senators may introduce bills and resolutions. Finally, resolutions coming over from a previous day are taken up for consideration. In practice, the Senate adopts standing orders that permit senators to introduce measures and file reports at any time, but only if there has been a morning business period on that day. Because the Senate often remains in the same legislative day for several days, weeks or months at a time, it orders a morning business period almost every calendar day for the convenience of senators who wish to introduce measures or make reports.

Morning Hour—A two-hour period at the beginning of a new legislative day during which the Senate is supposed to conduct routine business, call the calendar on Mondays and deal with other matters described in a Senate rule. In practice, the morning hour very rarely, if ever, occurs, in part because the Senate frequently recesses, rather than adjourns, at the end of a daily session. Therefore the rule does not apply when the senate next meets. The Senate's rules reserve the first hour of the morning for morning business. After the completion of morning business, or at the end of the first hour, the rules permit a motion to proceed to the consideration of a measure on the calendar out of its regular order (except on Mondays). Because that normally debatable motion is not debatable if offered during the morning hour, the majority leader may, but rarely does, use this procedure in anticipating a filibuster on the motion to proceed. If the Senate agrees to the motion, it can consider the measure until the end of the morning hour, and if there is no unfinished business from the previous day it can continue considering it after the morning hour. But if there is unfinished business, a motion to continue consideration is necessary, and that motion is debatable.

Motion—A formal proposal for a procedural action, such as to consider, to amend, to lay on the table, to reconsider, to recess or to adjourn. It has been estimated that at least eighty-five motions are possible under various circumstances in the House of Representatives, somewhat fewer in the Senate. Not all motions are created equal; some are privileged or preferential and enjoy priority over others. Some motions are debatable, amendable or divisible, while others are not.

Multiple and Sequential Referrals—The practice of referring a measure to two or more committees for concurrent consideration (multiple referral) or successively to several committees in sequence (sequential referral). A measure may also be divided into several parts, with each referred to a different committee or to several committees sequentially (split referral). In theory this gives all committees that have jurisdiction over parts of a measure the opportunity to consider and report on them.

Before 1975, House precedents banned such referrals. A 1975 rule required the Speaker to make concurrent and sequential referrals "to the maximum extent feasible." On sequential referrals, the Speaker could set deadlines for reporting the measure. The Speaker ruled that this provision authorized him to discharge a committee from further consideration of a measure and place it on the appropriate calendar of the House if the committee fails to meet the Speaker's deadline. The Speaker also used combinations of concurrent and sequential referrals. In 1995 joint referrals were prohibited. Now each measure is referred to a primary committee and also may be referred, either concurrently or sequentially, to one or more other committees, but usually only for consideration of portions of the measure that fall within the jurisdiction of each of those other committees.

In the Senate, before 1977 concurrent and sequential referrals were permitted only by unanimous consent. In that year, a rule authorized a privileged motion for such a referral if offered jointly by the majority and minority leaders. Debate on the motion and all amendments to it is limited to two hours. The motion may set deadlines for reporting and provide for discharging the committees involved if they fail to meet the deadlines. To date, this procedure has never been invoked; multiple referrals in the Senate continue to be made by unanimous consent.

Multiyear Appropriation—An appropriation that remains available for spending or obligation for more than one fiscal year; the exact period of time is specified in the act making the appropriation.

Multiyear Authorization—(1) Legislation that authorizes the existence or continuation of an agency, program or activity for more than one fiscal year. (2) Legislation that authorizes appropriations for an agency, program or activity for more than one fiscal year.

Nomination—A proposed presidential appointment to a federal office submitted to the Senate for confirmation. Approval is by majority vote. The Constitution explicitly requires confirmation for ambassadors, consuls, "public Ministers" (department heads) and Supreme Court justices. By law, other federal judges, all military promotions of officers and many high-level civilian officials must be confirmed.

Oath of Office—Upon taking office, members of Congress must swear or affirm that they will "support and defend the Constitution...against all enemies, foreign and domestic," that they will "bear true faith and allegiance" to the Constitution, that they take the obligation "freely, without any mental reservation or purpose of evasion," and that they will "well and faithfully discharge the duties" of their office. The oath is required by the Constitution, and the wording is prescribed by a statute. All House members must take the oath at the beginning of each new Congress. Usually, the member with the longest continuous service in the House swears in the Speaker, who then swears in the other members. The president of the Senate or a surrogate administers the oath to newly elected or reelected senators.

Obligation—A binding agreement by a government agency to pay for goods, products, services, studies and the like, either immediately or in the future. When an agency enters into such an agreement, it incurs an obligation. As the agency makes the required payments, it liquidates the obligation. Appropriation laws usually make funds available for obligation for one or more fiscal years but do not require agencies to spend their funds during those specific years. The actual outlays can occur years after the appropriation is obligated, as with a contract for construction of a submarine that may provide for payment to be made when it is delivered in the future. Such obligated funds are often said to be "in the pipeline." Under these circumstances, an agency's outlays in a particular year can come from appropriations obligated in previous years as well as from its current-year appropriation. Consequently, the money Congress appropriates for a fiscal year does not equal the total amount of appropriated money the government will actually spend in that year.

Off-Budget Entities—Specific federal entities whose budget authority, outlays and receipts are excluded by law from the calculation of budg-

et totals, although they are part of government spending and income. As of early 2001, these included the Social Security trust funds (Federal Old-Age and Survivors Insurance Fund and the Federal Disability Insurance Trust Fund) and the Postal Service. Government-sponsored enterprises are also excluded from the budget because they are considered private rather than public organizations.

Office of Management and Budget (OMB)—A unit in the Executive Office of the President, reconstituted in 1970 from the former Bureau of the Budget. The Office of Management and Budget (OMB) assists the president in preparing the budget and in formulating the government's fiscal program. The OMB also plays a central role in supervising and controlling implementation of the budget, pursuant to provisions in appropriations laws, the Budget Enforcement Act and other statutes. In addition to these budgetary functions, the OMB has various management duties, including those performed through its three statutory offices: Federal Financial Management, Federal Procurement Policy and Information and Regulatory Affairs.

Officers of Congress—The Constitution refers to the Speaker of the House and the president of the Senate as officers and declares that each house "shall chuse" its "other Officers," but it does not name them or indicate how they should be selected. A House rule refers to its clerk, sergeant at arms and chaplain as officers. Officers are not named in the Senate's rules, but Riddick's Senate Procedure lists the president pro tempore, secretary of the Senate, sergeant at arms, chaplain and the secretaries for the majority and minority parties as officers. A few appointed officials are sometimes referred to as officers, including the parliamentarians and the legislative counsels. The House elects its officers by resolution at the beginning of each Congress. The Senate also elects its officers, but once elected Senate officers serve from Congress to Congress until their successors are chosen.

Omnibus Bill—A measure that combines the provisions of several disparate subjects into a single and often lengthy bill.

One-Minute Speeches—Addresses by House members that can be on any subject but are limited to one minute. They are usually permitted at the beginning of a daily session after the chaplain's prayer, the pledge of allegiance and approval of the Journal. They are a customary practice, not a right granted by rule. Consequently, recognition for one-minute speeches requires unanimous consent and is entirely within the Speaker's discretion. The Speaker sometimes refuses to permit them when the House has a heavy legislative schedule or limits or postpones them until a later time of the day.

Open Rule—A special rule from the House Rules Committee that permits members to offer as many floor amendments as they wish as long as the amendments are germane and do not violate other House rules.

Order of Business (House)—The sequence of events prescribed by a House rule during the meeting of the House on a new legislative day that is supposed to take place, also called the general order of business. The sequence consists of (1) the chaplain's prayer; (2) reading and approval of the Journal; (3) the pledge of allegiance; (4) correction of the reference of public bills to committee; (5) disposal of business on the Speaker's table; (6) unfinished business; (7) the morning hour call of committees and consideration of their bills; (8) motions to go into Committee of the Whole; and (9) orders of the day. In practice, the House never fully complies with this rule. Instead, the items of business that follow the pledge of allegiance are supplanted by any special orders of business that are in order on that day (for example, conference reports; the corrections, discharge or private calendars; or motions to suspend the rules) and by other privileged business (for example, general appropriation bills and special rules) or measures made in order by special rules or unanimous consent. The regular order of business is also modified by unanimous consent practices and orders that govern recognition for one-minute speeches (which date from 1937) and for morning-hour debates, begun in 1994. By this combination of an order of business with privileged interruptions, the House gives precedence to certain categories of important legislation, brings to the floor other major legislation from its calendars in any order it chooses and provides expeditious processing for minor and noncontroversial measures.

Order of Business (Senate)—The sequence of events at the beginning of a new legislative day, as prescribed by Senate rules and standing orders. The sequence consists of (1) the chaplain's prayer; (2) the pledge of allegiance; (3) the designation of a temporary presiding officer if any; (4) Journal reading and approval; (5) recognition of the majority and minority leaders or their designees under the standing order; (6) morning business in the morning hour; (7) call of the calendar during the morning hour (largely obsolete); and (8) unfinished business from the previous session day.

Organization of Congress—The actions each house takes at the beginning of a Congress that are necessary to its operations. These include swearing in newly elected members, notifying the president that a quorum of each house is present, making committee assignments and fixing the hour for daily meetings. Because the House of Representatives is not a continuing body, it must also elect its Speaker and other officers and adopt its rules.

Original Bill—(1) A measure drafted by a committee and introduced by its chairman or another designated member when the committee reports the measure to its house. Unlike a clean bill, it is not referred back to the committee after introduction. The Senate permits all its legislative committees to report original bills. In the House, this authority is referred to in the rules as the "right to report at any time," and five committees (Appropriations, Budget, House Administration, Rules and Standards of Official Conduct) have such authority under circumstances specified in House Rule XIII, clause 5.

(2) In the House, special rules reported by the Rules Committee often propose that an amendment in the nature of a substitute be considered as an original bill for purposes of amendment, meaning that the substitute, as with a bill, may be amended in two degrees. Without that requirement, the substitute may only be amended in one further degree. In the Senate, an amendment in the nature of a substitute automatically is open to two degrees of amendment, as is the original text of the bill, if the substitute is offered when no other amendment is pending.

Original Jurisdiction—The authority of certain committees to originate a measure and report it to the chamber. For example, general appropriation bills reported by the House Appropriations Committee are original bills, and special rules reported by the House Rules Committee are original resolutions.

Other Body—A commonly used reference to a house by a member of the other house. Congressional comity discourages members from directly naming the other house during debate.

Outlays—Amounts of government spending. They consist of payments, usually by check or in cash, to liquidate obligations incurred in prior fiscal years as well as in the current year, including the net lending of funds under budget authority. In federal budget accounting, net outlays are calculated by subtracting the amounts of refunds and various kinds of reimbursements to the government from actual spending.

Override a Veto—Congressional enactment of a measure over the president's veto. A veto override requires a recorded two-thirds vote of those voting in each house, a quorum being present. Because the president must return the vetoed measure to its house of origin, that house votes first, but neither house is required to attempt an override, whether imme-

diately or at all. If an override attempt fails in the house of origin, the veto stands and the measure dies.

Oversight—Congressional review of the way in which federal agencies implement laws to ensure that they are carrying out the intent of Congress and to inquire into the efficiency of the implementation and the effectiveness of the law. The Legislative Reorganization Act of 1946 defined oversight as the function of exercising continuous watchfulness over the execution of the laws by the executive branch.

Oxford-Style Debate—The House held three Oxford-style debates in 1994, modeled after the famous debating format favored by the Oxford Union in Great Britain. Neither chamber has held Oxford-style debates since then. The Oxford-style debates aired nationally over C-SPAN television and National Public Radio. The organized event featured eight participants divided evenly into two teams, one team representing the Democrats (then holding the majority in the chamber) and the other the Republicans. Both teams argued a single question chosen well ahead of the event. A moderator regulated the debate, and began it by stating the resolution at issue. The order of the speakers alternated by team, with a debater for the affirmative speaking first and a debater for the opposing team offering a rebuttal. The rest of the speakers alternated in kind until all gained the chance to speak.

Parliamentarian—The official advisor to the presiding officer in each house on questions of procedure. The parliamentarian and his or her assistants also answer procedural questions from members and congressional staff, refer measures to committees on behalf of the presiding officer and maintain compilations of the precedents. The House parliamentarian revises the House Manual at the beginning of every Congress and usually reviews special rules before the Rules Committee reports them to the House. Either a parliamentarian or an assistant is always present and near the podium during sessions of each house.

Party Caucus—Generic term for each party's official organization in each house. Only House Democrats officially call their organization a caucus. House and Senate Republicans and Senate Democrats call their organizations conferences. The party caucuses elect their leaders, approve committee assignments and chairmanships (or ranking minority members, if the party is in the minority), establish party committees and study groups and discuss party and legislative policies. On rare occasions, they have stripped members of committee seniority or expelled them from the caucus for party disloyalty.

Pay-as-You-Go (PAYGO)—A provision first instituted under the Budget Enforcement Act of 1990 that applies to legislation enacted before Oct. 1, 2002. It requires that the cumulative effect of legislation concerning either revenues or direct spending should not result in a net negative impact on the budget. If legislation does provide for an increase in spending or decrease in revenues, that effect is supposed to be offset by legislated spending reductions or revenue increases. If Congress fails to enact the appropriate offsets, the act requires presidential sequestration of sufficient offsetting amounts in specific direct spending accounts. Congress and the president can circumvent this requirement if both agree that an emergency requires a particular action or if a law is enacted declaring that deteriorated economic circumstances make it necessary to suspend the requirement.

Permanent Appropriation—An appropriation that remains continuously available, without current action or renewal by Congress, under the terms of a previously enacted authorization or appropriation law. One such appropriation provides for payment of interest on the public debt and another the salaries of members of Congress.

Permanent Authorization—An authorization without a time limit. It usually does not specify any limit on the funds that may be appropriated for the agency, program or activity that it authorizes, leaving such amounts to the discretion of the appropriations committees and the two houses.

Permanent Staff—Term used formerly for committee staff authorized by law, who were funded through a permanent authorization and also called statutory staff. Most committees were authorized thirty permanent staff members. Most committees also were permitted additional staff, often called investigative staff, who were authorized by annual or biennial funding resolutions. The Senate eliminated the primary distinction between statutory and investigative staff in 1981. The House eliminated the distinction in 1995 by requiring that funding resolutions authorize money to hire both types of staff.

Personally Obnoxious (or Objectionable)—A characterization a senator sometimes applies to a president's nominee for a federal office in that senator's state to justify his or her opposition to the nomination.

Pocket Veto—The indirect veto of a bill as a result of the president withholding approval of it until after Congress has adjourned sine die. A bill the president does not sign but does not formally veto while Congress is in session automatically becomes a law ten days (excluding Sundays) after it is received. But if Congress adjourns its annual session during that ten-day period the measure dies even if the president does not formally veto it.

Point of Order—A parliamentary term used in committee and on the floor to object to an alleged violation of a rule and to demand that the chair enforce the rule. The point of order immediately halts the proceedings until the chair decides whether the contention is valid.

Pork or Pork Barrel Legislation—Pejorative terms for federal appropriations, bills or policies that provide funds to benefit a legislator's district or state, with the implication that the legislator presses for enactment of such benefits to ingratiate himself or herself with constituents rather than on the basis of an impartial, objective assessment of need or merit. The terms are often applied to such benefits as new parks, post offices, dams, canals, bridges, roads, water projects, sewage treatment plants and public works of any kind, as well as demonstration projects, research grants and relocation of government facilities. Funds released by the president for various kinds of benefits or government contracts approved by him allegedly for political purposes are also sometimes referred to as pork.

Postcloture Filibuster—A filibuster conducted after the Senate invokes cloture. It employs an array of procedural tactics rather than lengthy speeches to delay final action. The Senate curtailed the postcloture filibuster's effectiveness by closing a variety of loopholes in the cloture rule in 1979 and 1986.

Power of the Purse—A reference to the constitutional power Congress has over legislation to raise revenue and appropriate monies from the Treasury. Article I, Section 8 states that Congress "shall have Power To lay and collect Taxes, Duties, Imposts and Excises, [and] to pay the Debts." Section 9 declares: "No Money shall be drawn from the Treasury, but in Consequence of Appropriations made by Law."

Preamble—Introductory language describing the reasons for and intent of a measure, sometimes called a whereas clause. It occasionally appears in joint, concurrent and simple resolutions but rarely in bills.

Precedent—A previous ruling on a parliamentary matter or a long-standing practice or custom of a house. Precedents serve to control arbitrary rulings and serve as the common law of a house.

President of the Senate—One constitutional role of the vice president is serving as the presiding officer of the Senate, or president of the Senate. The Constitution permits the vice president to cast a vote in the Senate only to break a tie, but the vice president is not required to do so.

President Pro Tempore—Under the Constitution, an officer elected by the Senate to preside over it during the absence of the vice president of the United States. Often referred to as the "pro tem," this senator is usually a member of the majority party with the longest continuous service in the chamber and also, by virtue of seniority, a committee chairman. When attending to committee and other duties the president pro tempore appoints other senators to preside.

Presiding Officer—In a formal meeting, the individual authorized to maintain order and decorum, recognize members to speak or offer motions and apply and interpret the chamber's rules, precedents and practices. The Speaker of the House and the president of the Senate are the chief presiding officers in their respective houses.

Previous Question—A nondebatable motion which, when agreed to by majority vote, usually cuts off further debate, prevents the offering of additional amendments and brings the pending matter to an immediate vote. It is a major debate-limiting device in the House; it is not permitted in Committee of the Whole in the House or in the Senate.

Private Bill—A bill that applies to one or more specified persons, corporations, institutions or other entities, usually to grant relief when no other legal remedy is available to them. Many private bills deal with claims against the federal government, immigration and naturalization cases and land titles.

Private Calendar—Commonly used title for a calendar in the House reserved for private bills and resolutions favorably reported by committees. The private calendar is officially called the Calendar of the Committee of the Whole House.

Private Law—A private bill enacted into law. Private laws are numbered in the same fashion as public laws.

Privilege—An attribute of a motion, measure, report, question or proposition that gives it priority status for consideration. Privileged motions and motions to bring up privileged questions are not debatable.

Privilege of the Floor—In addition to the members of a house, certain individuals are admitted to its floor while it is in session. The rules of the two houses differ somewhat but both extend the privilege to the president and vice president, Supreme Court justices, cabinet members, state governors, former members of that house, members of the other house, certain officers and officials of Congress, certain staff of that house in the discharge of official duties and the chamber's former parliamentarians. They also allow access to a limited number of committee and members' staff when their presence is necessary.

Pro Forma Amendment—In the House, an amendment that ostensibly proposes to change a measure or another amendment by moving "to strike the last word" or "to strike the requisite number of words." A member offers it not to make any actual change in the measure or amendment but only to obtain time for debate.

Pro Tem—A common reference to the president pro tempore of the Senate or, occasionally, to a Speaker pro tempore. (See President Pro Tempore; Speaker Pro Tempore.)

Procedures—The methods of conducting business in a deliberative body. The procedures of each house are governed first by applicable provisions of the Constitution, and then by its standing rules and orders, precedents, traditional practices and any statutory rules that apply to it. The authority of the houses to adopt rules in addition to those specified in the Constitution is derived from Article I, Section 5, clause 2, of the Constitution, which states: "Each House may determine the Rules of its Proceedings...." By rule, the House of Representatives also follows the procedures in Jefferson's Manual that are not inconsistent with its standing rules and orders. Many Senate procedures also conform with Jefferson's provisions, but by practice rather than by rule. At the beginning of each Congress, the House uses procedures in general parliamentary law until it adopts its standing rules.

Proxy Voting—The practice of permitting a member to cast the vote of an absent colleague in addition to his or her own vote. Proxy voting is prohibited on the floors of the House and Senate, but the Senate permits its committees to authorize proxy voting, and most do. In 1995, House rules were changed to prohibit proxy voting in committee.

Public Bill—A bill dealing with general legislative matters having national applicability or applying to the federal government or to a class of persons, groups or organizations.

Public Debt—Federal government debt incurred by the Treasury or the Federal Financing Bank by the sale of securities to the public or borrowings from a federal fund or account.

Public Law—A public bill or joint resolution enacted into law. It is cited by the letters "PL" followed by a hyphenated number. The digits before the hyphen indicate the number of the Congress in which it was enacted; the digits after the hyphen indicate its position in the numerical sequence of public measures that became law during that Congress. For example, the Budget Enforcement Act of 1990 became PL 101-508 because it was the 508th measure in that sequence for the 101st Congress. (See also Private Law.)

Qualification (of Members)—The Constitution requires members of the House of Representatives to be twenty-five years of age at the time their terms begin. They must have been citizens of the United States for seven years before that date and, when elected, must be "Inhabitant[s]" of the state from which they were elected. There is no constitutional requirement that they reside in the districts they represent. Senators are required to be thirty years of age at the time their terms begin. They must have been citizens of the United States for nine years before that date and, when elected, must be "Inhabitant[s]" of the states in which they were elected. The "Inhabitant" qualification is broadly interpreted, and in modern times a candidate's declaration of state residence has generally been accepted as meeting the constitutional requirement.

Queen of the Hill Rule—A special rule from the House Rules Committee that permits votes on a series of amendments, especially complete substitutes for a measure, in a specified order, but directs that the amendment receiving the greatest number of votes shall be the winning one. This kind of rule permits the House to vote directly on a variety of alternatives to a measure. In doing so, it sets aside the precedent that once an amendment has been adopted, no further amendments may be offered to the text it has amended. Under an earlier practice, the Rules Committee reported "king of the hill" rules under which there also could be votes on a series of amendments, again in a specified order. If more than one of the amendments was adopted under this kind of rule, it was the last amendment to receive a majority vote that was considered as having been finally adopted, whether or not it had received the greatest number of votes.

Quorum—The minimum number of members required to be present for the transaction of business. Under the Constitution, a quorum in each house is a majority of its members: 218 in the House and 51 in the Senate when there are no vacancies. By House rule, a quorum in Committee of the Whole is 100. In practice, both houses usually assume a quorum is present even if it is not, unless a member makes a point of no quorum in the House or suggests the absence of a quorum in the Senate. Consequently, each house transacts much of its business, and even passes bills, when only a few members are present. For House and Senate committees, chamber rules allow a minimum quorum of one-third of a committee's members to conduct most types of business.

Quorum Call—A procedure for determining whether a quorum is present in a chamber. In the Senate, a clerk calls the roll (roster) of senators. The House usually employs its electronic voting system.

Ramseyer Rule—A House rule that requires a committee's report on a bill or joint resolution to show the changes the measure, and any committee amendments to it, would make in existing law. The rule requires the report to present the text of any statutory provision that would be repealed and a comparative print showing, through typographical devices such as stricken-through type or italics, other changes that would be made in existing law. The rule, adopted in 1929, is named after its sponsor, Rep. Christian W. Ramseyer, R-Iowa. The Senate's analogous rule is called the Cordon Rule.

Rank or Ranking—A member's position on the list of his or her party's members on a committee or subcommittee. When first assigned to a committee, a member is usually placed at the bottom of the list, then moves up as those above leave the committee. On subcommittees, however, a member's rank may not have anything to do with the length of his or her service on it.

Ranking Member—(1) Most often a reference to the minority member with the highest ranking on a committee or subcommittee. (2) A reference to the majority member next in rank to the chairman or to the highest ranking majority member present at a committee or subcommittee meeting.

Ratification—(1) The president's formal act of promulgating a treaty after the Senate has approved it. The resolution of ratification agreed to by the Senate is the procedural vehicle by which the Senate gives its consent to ratification. (2) A state legislature's act in approving a proposed constitutional amendment. Such an amendment becomes effective when ratified by three-fourths of the states.

Reapportionment—(See Apportionment.)

Recess—(1) A temporary interruption or suspension of a meeting of a chamber or committee. Unlike an adjournment, a recess does not end a legislative day. Because the Senate often recesses from one calendar day to another, its legislative day may extend over several calendar days, weeks or even months. (2) A period of adjournment for more than three days to a day certain, especially over a holiday or in August during odd-numbered years.

Recess Appointment—A presidential appointment to a vacant federal position made after the Senate has adjourned sine die or has adjourned or recessed for more than thirty days. If the president submits the recess appointee's nomination during the next session of the Senate, that individual can continue to serve until the end of the session even though the Senate might have rejected the nomination. When appointed to a vacancy that existed thirty days before the end of the last Senate session, a recess appointee is not paid until confirmed.

Recommit—To send a measure back to the committee that reported it; sometimes called a straight motion to recommit to distinguish it from a motion to recommit with instructions. A successful motion to recommit kills the measure unless it is accompanied by instructions.

Recommit a Conference Report—To return a conference report to the conference committee for renegotiation of some or all of its agreements. A motion to recommit may be offered with or without instructions.

Recommit with Instructions—To send a measure back to a committee with instructions to take some action on it. Invariably in the House and often in the Senate, when the motion recommits to a standing committee, the instructions require the committee to report the measure "forthwith" with specified amendments.

Reconciliation—A procedure for changing existing revenue and spending laws to bring total federal revenues and spending within the limits established in a budget resolution. Congress has applied reconciliation chiefly to revenues and mandatory spending programs, especially entitlements. Discretionary spending is controlled through annual appropriation bills.

Recorded Vote—(1) Generally, any vote in which members are recorded by name for or against a measure; also called a record vote or roll-call vote. The only recorded vote in the Senate is a vote by the yeas and nays and is commonly called a roll-call vote. (2) Technically, a recorded vote is one demanded in the House of Representatives and supported by at least one-fifth of a quorum (forty-four members) in the House sitting as the House or at least twenty-five members in Committee of the Whole.

Recorded Vote by Clerks—A voting procedure in the House where members pass through the appropriate "aye" or "no" aisle in the chamber and cast their votes by depositing a signed green (yea) or red (no) card in a ballot box. These votes are tabulated by clerks and reported to the chair. The electronic voting system is much more convenient and has largely supplanted this procedure. (See Committee of the Whole; Recorded Vote; Teller Vote.)

Redistricting—The redrawing of congressional district boundaries within a state after a decennial census. Redistricting may be required to equalize district populations or to accommodate an increase or decrease in the number of a state's House seats that might have resulted from the decennial apportionment. The state governments determine the district lines. (See Apportionment; Congressional District; Gerrymandering.)

Referral—The assignment of a measure to committee for consideration. Under a House rule, the Speaker can refuse to refer a measure if the Speaker believes it is "of an obscene or insulting character."

Report—(1) As a verb, a committee is said to report when it submits a measure or other document to its parent chamber. (2) A clerk is said to report when he or she reads a measure's title, text or the text of an amendment to the body at the direction of the chair. (3) As a noun, a committee document that accompanies a reported measure. It describes the measure, the committee's views on it, its costs and the changes it proposes to make in existing law; it also includes certain impact statements. (4) A committee document submitted to its parent chamber that describes the results of an investigation or other study or provides information it is required to provide by rule or law.

Representative—An elected and duly sworn member of the House of Representatives who is entitled to vote in the chamber. The Constitution requires that a representative be at least twenty-five years old, a citizen of the United States for at least seven years and an inhabitant of the state from which he or she is elected. Customarily, the member resides in the district he or she represents. Representatives are elected in even-numbered years to two-year terms that begin the following January.

Reprimand—A formal condemnation of a member for misbehavior, considered a milder reproof than censure. The House of Representatives first used it in 1976. The Senate first used it in 1991. (See also Censure; Code of Official Conduct; Denounce; Ethics Rules; Expulsion; Seniority Loss.)

Rescission—A provision of law that repeals previously enacted budget authority in whole or in part. Under the Impoundment Control Act of 1974, the president can impound such funds by sending a message to Congress requesting one or more rescissions and the reasons for doing so. If Congress does not pass a rescission bill for the programs requested by the president within forty-five days of continuous session after receiving the message, the president must make the funds available for obligation and expenditure. If the president does not, the comptroller general of the United States is authorized to bring suit to compel the release of those funds. A rescission bill may rescind all, part or none of an amount proposed by

the president, and may rescind funds the president has not impounded.

Reserving the Right To Object—Members' declaration that at some indefinite future time they may object to a unanimous consent request. It is an attempt to circumvent the requirement that members may prevent such an action only by objecting immediately after it is proposed.

Resident Commissioner from Puerto Rico—A nonvoting member of the House of Representatives, elected to a four-year term. The resident commissioner has the same status and privileges as delegates. Like the delegates, the resident commissioner may not vote in the House or Committee of the Whole.

Resolution—(1) A simple resolution; that is, a nonlegislative measure effective only in the house in which it is proposed and not requiring concurrence by the other chamber or approval by the president. Simple resolutions are designated H. Res. in the House and S. Res. in the Senate. Simple resolutions express nonbinding opinions on policies or issues or deal with the internal affairs or prerogatives of a house. (2) Any type of resolution: simple, concurrent or joint. (See Concurrent Resolution; Joint Resolution.)

Resolution of Inquiry—A resolution usually simple rather than concurrent calling on the president or the head of an executive agency to provide specific information or papers to one or both houses.

Resolution of Ratification—The Senate vehicle for agreeing to a treaty. The constitutionally mandated vote of two-thirds of the senators present and voting applies to the adoption of this resolution. However, it may also contain amendments, reservations, declarations or understandings that the Senate had previously added to it by majority vote.

Revenue Legislation—Measures that levy new taxes or tariffs or change existing ones. Under Article I, Section 7, clause 1 of the Constitution, the House of Representatives originates federal revenue measures, but the Senate can propose amendments to them. The House Ways and Means Committee and the Senate Finance Committee have jurisdiction over such measures, with a few minor exceptions.

Revise and Extend One's Remarks—A unanimous consent request to publish in the Congressional Record a statement a member did not deliver on the floor, a longer statement than the one made on the floor or miscellaneous extraneous material.

Revolving Fund—A trust fund or account whose income remains available to finance its continuing operations without any fiscal year limitation.

Rider—Congressional slang for an amendment unrelated or extraneous to the subject matter of the measure to which it is attached. Riders often contain proposals that are less likely to become law on their own merits as separate bills, either because of opposition in the committee of jurisdiction, resistance in the other house or the probability of a presidential veto. Riders are more common in the Senate.

Roll Call—A call of the roll to determine whether a quorum is present, to establish a quorum or to vote on a question. Usually, the House uses its electronic voting system for a roll call. The Senate does not have an electronic voting system; its roll is always called by a clerk.

Rule—(1) A permanent regulation that a house adopts to govern its conduct of business, its procedures, its internal organization, behavior of its members, regulation of its facilities, duties of an officer or some other subject it chooses to govern in that form. (2) In the House, a privileged simple resolution reported by the Rules Committee that provides methods and conditions for floor consideration of a measure or, rarely, several measures.

Rule Twenty-Two—A common reference to the Senate's cloture rule. (See Cloture)

Second-Degree Amendment—An amendment to an amendment in the first degree. It is usually a perfecting amendment.

Secretary of the Senate—The chief financial, administrative and legislative officer of the Senate. Elected by resolution or order of the Senate, the secretary is invariably the candidate of the majority party and usually chosen by the majority leader. In the absence of the vice president and pending the election of a president pro tempore, the secretary presides over the Senate. The secretary is subject to policy direction and oversight by the Senate Committee on Rules and Administration. The secretary manages a wide range of functions that support the administrative operations of the Senate as an organization as well as those functions necessary to its legislative process, including record keeping, document management, certifications, housekeeping services, administration of oaths and lobbyist registrations. The secretary is responsible for accounting for all funds appropriated to the Senate and conducts audits of Senate financial activities. On a semiannual basis the secretary issues the Report of the Secretary of the Senate, a compilation of Senate expenditures.

Section—A subdivision of a bill or statute. By law, a section must be numbered and, as nearly as possible, contain "a single proposition of enactment."

Select or Special Committee—A committee established by a resolution in either house for a special purpose and, usually, for a limited time. Most select and special committees are assigned specific investigations or studies but are not authorized to report measures to their chambers. However, both houses have created several permanent select and special committees and have given legislative reporting authority to a few of them: the Ethics Committee in the Senate and the Intelligence Committees in both houses. There is no substantive difference between a select and a special committee; they are so called depending simply on whether the resolution creating the committee calls it one or the other.

Senate—The house of Congress in which each state is represented by two senators; each senator has one vote. Article V of the Constitution declares that "No State, without its Consent, shall be deprived of its equal Suffrage in the Senate." The Constitution also gives the Senate equal legislative power with the House of Representatives. Although the Senate is prohibited from originating revenue measures, and as a matter of practice it does not originate appropriation measures, it can amend both. Only the Senate can give or withhold consent to treaties and nominations from the president. It also acts as a court to try impeachments by the House and elects the vice president when no candidate receives a majority of the electoral votes. It is often referred to as "the upper body," but not by members of the House.

Senate Manual—The handbook of the Senate's standing rules and orders and the laws and other regulations that apply to the Senate, usually published once each Congress.

Senator—A duly sworn elected or appointed member of the Senate. The Constitution requires that a senator be at least thirty years old, a citizen of the United States for at least nine years and an inhabitant of the state from which he or she is elected. Senators are usually elected in even-numbered years to six-year terms that begin the following January. When a vacancy occurs before the end of a term, the state governor can appoint a replacement to fill the position until a successor is chosen at the state's next general election or, if specified under state law, the next feasible date for such an election, to serve the remainder of the term. Until the Seventeenth Amendment was ratified in 1913, senators were chosen by their state legislatures.

Senatorial Courtesy—The Senate's practice of declining to confirm a presidential nominee for an office in the state of a senator of the president's party unless that senator approves.

Seniority—The priority, precedence or status accorded members according to the length of their continuous service in a house or on a committee.

Seniority Loss—A type of punishment that reduces a member's seniority on his or her committees, including the loss of chairmanships. Party caucuses in both houses have occasionally imposed such punishment on their members, for example, for publicly supporting candidates of the other party.

Seniority Rule—The customary practice, rather than a rule, of assigning the chairmanship of a committee to the majority party member who has served on the committee for the longest continuous period of time.

Seniority System—A collection of long-standing customary practices under which members with longer continuous service than their colleagues in their house or on their committees receive various kinds of preferential treatment. Although some of the practices are no longer as rigidly observed as in the past, they still pervade the organization and procedures of Congress.

Sequestration—A procedure for canceling budgetary resources — that is, money available for obligation or spending — to enforce budget limitations established in law. Sequestered funds are no longer available for obligation or expenditure.

Sergeant at Arms—The officer in each house responsible for maintaining order, security and decorum in its wing of the Capitol, including the chamber and its galleries. Although elected by their respective houses, both sergeants at arms are invariably the candidates of the majority party.

Session—(1) The annual series of meetings of a Congress. Under the Constitution, Congress must assemble at least once a year at noon on Jan. 3 unless it appoints a different day by law. (2) The special meetings of Congress or of one house convened by the president, called a special session. (3) A house is said to be in session during the period of a day when it is meeting.

Severability (or Separability) Clause—Language stating that if any particular provisions of a measure are declared invalid by the courts the remaining provisions shall remain in effect.

Sine Die—Without fixing a day for a future meeting. An adjournment sine die signifies the end of an annual or special session of Congress.

Slip Law—The first official publication of a measure that has become law. It is published separately in unbound, single-sheet form or pamphlet form. A slip law usually is available two or three days after the date of the law's enactment.

Speaker—The presiding officer of the House of Representatives and the leader of its majority party. The Speaker is selected by the majority party and formally elected by the House at the beginning of each Congress. Although the Constitution does not require the Speaker to be a member of the House, in fact, all Speakers have been members.

Speaker Pro Tempore—A member of the House who is designated as the temporary presiding officer by the Speaker or elected by the House to that position during the Speaker's absence.

Speaker's Vote—The Speaker is not required to vote, and the Speaker's name is not called on a roll-call vote unless so requested. Usually, the Speaker votes either to create a tie vote, and thereby defeat a proposal or to break a tie in favor of a proposal. Occasionally, the Speaker also votes to emphasize the importance of a matter.

Special Session—A session of Congress convened by the president, under his constitutional authority, after Congress has adjourned sine die at the end of a regular session. (See Adjournment Sine Die; Session.)

Spending Authority—The technical term for backdoor spending. The Congressional Budget Act of 1974 defines it as borrowing authority, contract authority and entitlement authority for which appropriation acts do not provide budget authority in advance. Under the Budget Act, legislation that provides new spending authority may not be considered unless it provides that the authority shall be effective only to the extent or in such amounts as provided in an appropriation act.

Spending Cap—The statutory limit for a fiscal year on the amount of new budget authority and outlays allowed for discretionary spending. The Budget Enforcement Act of 1997 requires a sequester if the cap is exceeded.

Split Referral—A measure divided into two or more parts, with each part referred to a different committee.

Sponsor—The principal proponent and introducer of a measure or an amendment.

Staff Director—The most frequently used title for the head of staff of a committee or subcommittee. On some committees, that person is called chief of staff, clerk, chief clerk, chief counsel, general counsel or executive director. The head of a committee's minority staff is usually called minority staff director.

Standing Committee—A permanent committee established by a House or Senate standing rule or standing order. The rule also describes the subject areas on which the committee may report bills and resolutions and conduct oversight. Most introduced measures must be referred to one or more standing committees according to their jurisdictions.

Standing Order—A continuing regulation or directive that has the force and effect of a rule, but is not incorporated into the standing rules. The Senate's numerous standing orders, like its standing rules, continue from Congress to Congress unless changed or the order states otherwise. The House uses relatively few standing orders, and those it adopts expire at the end of a session of Congress.

Standing Rules—The rules of the Senate that continue from one Congress to the next and the rules of the House of Representatives that it adopts at the beginning of each new Congress.

Standing Vote—An alternative and informal term for a division vote, during which members in favor of a proposal and then members opposed stand and are counted by the chair.

Star Print—A reprint of a bill, resolution, amendment or committee report correcting technical or substantive errors in a previous printing; so called because of the small black star that appears on the front page or cover.

State of the Union Message—A presidential message to Congress under the constitutional directive that the president shall "from time to time give to the Congress Information of the State of the Union, and recommend to their Consideration such Measures as he shall judge necessary and expedient." Customarily, the president sends an annual State of the Union message to Congress, usually late in January.

Statutes at Large—A chronological arrangement of the laws enacted in each session of Congress. Though indexed, the laws are not arranged by subject matter nor is there an indication of how they affect or change previously enacted laws. The volumes are numbered by Congress, and the laws are cited by their volume and page number. The Gramm-Rudman-Hollings Act, for example, appears as 99 Stat. 1037.

Straw Vote Prohibition—Under a House precedent, a member who has the floor during debate may not conduct a straw vote or otherwise ask for a show of support for a proposition. Only the chair may put a question to a vote.

Strike From the *Record*—Expunge objectionable remarks from the Congressional Record, after a member's words have been taken down on a point of order.

Subcommittee—A panel of committee members assigned a portion of the committee's jurisdiction or other functions. On legislative committees, subcommittees hold hearings, mark up legislation and report measures to their full committee for further action; they cannot report directly to the chamber. A subcommittee's party composition usually reflects the ratio on its parent committee.

Subpoena Power—The authority granted to committees by the rules of their respective houses to issue legal orders requiring individuals to appear and testify, or to produce documents pertinent to the committee's functions, or both. Persons who do not comply with subpoenas can be cited for contempt of Congress and prosecuted.

Subsidy—Generally, a payment or benefit made by the federal government for which no current repayment is required. Subsidy payments may be designed to support the conduct of an economic enterprise or activity, such as ship operations, or to support certain market prices, as in the case of farm subsidies.

Sunset Legislation—A term sometimes applied to laws authorizing the existence of agencies or programs that expire annually or at the end of some other specified period of time. One of the purposes of setting specific expiration dates for agencies and programs is to encourage the committees with jurisdiction over them to determine whether they should be continued or terminated.

Sunshine Rules—Rules requiring open committee hearings and business meetings, including markup sessions, in both houses, and also open conference committee meetings. However, all may be closed under certain circumstances and using certain procedures required by the rules.

Supermajority—A term sometimes used for a vote on a matter that requires approval by more than a simple majority of those members present and voting; also referred to as extraordinary majority.

Supplemental Appropriation Bill—A measure providing appropriations for use in the current fiscal year, in addition to those already provided in annual general appropriation bills. Supplemental appropriations are often for unforeseen emergencies.

Suspension of the Rules (House)—An expeditious procedure for passing relatively noncontroversial or emergency measures by a two-thirds vote of those members voting, a quorum being present.

Suspension of the Rules (Senate)—A procedure to set aside one or more of the Senate's rules; it is used infrequently, and then most often to suspend the rule banning legislative amendments to appropriation bills.

Task Force—A title sometimes given to a panel of members assigned to a special project, study or investigation. Ordinarily, these groups do not have authority to report measures to their respective houses.

Tax Expenditure—Loosely, a tax exemption or advantage, sometimes called an incentive or loophole; technically, a loss of governmental tax revenue attributable to some provision of federal tax laws that allows a special exclusion, exemption or deduction from gross income or that provides a special credit, preferential tax rate or deferral of tax liability.

Televised Proceedings—Television and radio coverage of the floor proceedings of the House of Representatives has been available since 1979 and of the Senate since 1986. They are broadcast over a coaxial cable system to all congressional offices and to some congressional agencies on channels reserved for that purpose. Coverage is also available free of charge to commercial and public television and radio broadcasters. The Cable-Satellite Public Affairs Network (C-SPAN) carries gavel-to-gavel coverage of both houses.

Teller Vote—A voting procedure, formerly used in the House, in which members cast their votes by passing through the center aisle to be counted, but not recorded by name, by a member from each party appointed by the chair. The House deleted the procedure from its rules in 1993, but during floor discussion of the deletion a leading member stated that a teller vote would still be available in the event of a breakdown of the electronic voting system.

Third-Degree Amendment—An amendment to a second-degree amendment. Both houses prohibit such amendments.

Third Reading—A required reading to a chamber of a bill or joint resolution by title only before the vote on passage. In modern practice, it has merely become a pro forma step.

Three-Day Rule—(1) In the House, a measure cannot be considered until the third calendar day on which the committee report has been available. (2) In the House, a conference report cannot be considered until the third calendar day on which its text has been available in the Congressional Record. (3) In the House, a general appropriation bill cannot be considered until the third calendar day on which printed hearings on the bill have been available. (4) In the Senate, when a committee votes to report a measure, a committee member is entitled to three calendar days within which to submit separate views for inclusion in the committee report. (In House committees, a member is entitled to two calendar days for this purpose, after the day on which the committee votes to report.) (5) In both houses, a majority of a committee's members may call a special meeting of the committee if its chairman fails to do so within three calendar days after three or more of the members, acting jointly, formally request such a meeting.

In calculating such periods, the House omits holiday and weekend days on which it does not meet. The Senate makes no such exclusion.

Tie Vote—When the votes for and against a proposition are equal, it loses. The president of the Senate may cast a vote only to break a tie. Because the Speaker is invariably a member of the House, the Speaker is entitled to vote but usually does not. The Speaker may choose to do so to break, or create, a tie vote.

Title—(1) A major subdivision of a bill or act, designated by a roman numeral and usually containing legislative provisions on the same general subject. Titles are sometimes divided into subtitles as well as sections. (2) The official name of a bill or act, also called a caption or long title. (3) Some bills also have short titles that appear in the sentence immediately following the enacting clause. (4) Popular titles are the unofficial names given to some bills or acts by common usage. For example, the Balanced Budget and Emergency Deficit Control Act of 1985 (short title) is almost invariably referred to as Gramm-Rudman (popular title). In other cases, significant legislation is popularly referred to by its title number (see definition (1) above). For example, the federal legislation that requires equality of funding for women's and men's sports in educational institutions that receive federal funds is popularly called Title IX.

Track System—An occasional Senate practice that expedites legislation by dividing a day's session into two or more specific time periods, commonly called tracks, each reserved for consideration of a different measure.

Transfer Payment—A federal government payment to which individuals or organizations are entitled under law and for which no goods or services are required in return. Payments include welfare and Social Security benefits, unemployment insurance, government pensions and veterans benefits.

Treaty—A formal document containing an agreement between two or more sovereign nations. The Constitution authorizes the president to make treaties, but the president must submit them to the Senate for its approval by a two-thirds vote of the senators present. Under the Senate's rules, that vote actually occurs on a resolution of ratification. Although the Constitution does not give the House a direct role in approving treaties, that body has sometimes insisted that a revenue treaty is an invasion of its prerogatives. In any case, the House may significantly affect the application of a treaty by its equal role in enacting legislation to implement the treaty.

Trust Funds—Special accounts in the Treasury that receive earmarked taxes or other kinds of revenue collections, such as user fees, and from which payments are made for special purposes or to recipients who meet the requirements of the trust funds as established by law. Of the more than 150 federal government trust funds, several finance major entitlement programs, such as Social Security, Medicare and retired federal employees' pensions. Others fund infrastructure construction and improvements, such as highways and airports.

Unanimous Consent—Without an objection by any member. A unanimous consent request asks permission, explicitly or implicitly, to set aside one or more rules. Both houses and their committees frequently use such requests to expedite their proceedings.

Uncontrollable Expenditures—A frequently used term for federal expenditures that are mandatory under existing law and therefore cannot be controlled by the president or Congress without a change in the existing law. Uncontrollable expenditures include spending required under entitlement programs and also fixed costs, such as interest on the public debt and outlays to pay for prior-year obligations. In recent years, uncontrollables have accounted for approximately three-quarters of federal spending in each fiscal year.

Unfunded Mandate—Generally, any provision in federal law or regulation that imposes a duty or obligation on a state or local government or private sector entity without providing the necessary funds to comply. The Unfunded Mandates Reform Act of 1995 amended the Congressional Budget Act of 1974 to provide a mechanism for the control of new unfunded mandates.

Union Calendar—A calendar of the House of Representatives for bills and resolutions favorably reported by committees that raise revenue or directly or indirectly appropriate money or property. In addition to appropriation bills, measures that authorize expenditures are also placed on this calendar. The calendar's full title is the Calendar of the Committee of the Whole House on the State of the Union.

Upper Body—A common reference to the Senate, but not used by members of the House.

U.S. Code—Popular title for the United States Code: Containing the General and Permanent Laws of the United States in Force on.... It is a consolidation and partial codification of the general and permanent laws of the United States arranged by subject under 50 titles. The first six titles deal with general or political subjects, the other forty-four with subjects ranging from agriculture to war, alphabetically arranged. A supplement is published after each session of Congress, and the entire Code is revised every six years.

User Fee—A fee charged to users of goods or services provided by the federal government. When Congress levies or authorizes such fees, it determines whether the revenues should go into the general collections of the Treasury or be available for expenditure by the agency that provides the goods or services.

Veto—The president's disapproval of a legislative measure passed by Congress. The president returns the measure to the house in which it originated without his signature but with a veto message stating his objections to it. When Congress is in session, the president must veto a bill within ten days, excluding Sundays, after the president has received it; otherwise it becomes law without his signature. The ten-day clock begins to run at midnight following his receipt of the bill. (See also Committee Veto; Item Veto; Line Item Veto Act of 1996; Override a Veto; Pocket Veto.)

Voice Vote—A method of voting in which members who favor a question answer aye in chorus, after which those opposed answer no in chorus, and the chair decides which position prevails.

Voting—Members vote in three ways on the floor: (1) by shouting "aye" or "no" on voice votes; (2) by standing for or against on division votes; and (3) on recorded votes (including the yeas and nays), by answering "aye" or "no" when their names are called or, in the House, by recording their votes through the electronic voting system.

War Powers Resolution of 1973—An act that requires the president "in every possible instance" to consult Congress before committing U.S. forces to ongoing or imminent hostilities. If the president commits them to a combat situation without congressional consultation, the president must notify Congress within forty-eight hours. Unless Congress declares war or otherwise authorizes the operation to continue, the forces must be withdrawn within sixty or ninety days, depending on certain conditions. No president has ever acknowledged the constitutionality of the resolution.

Well—The sunken, level, open space between members' seats and the podium at the front of each chamber. House members usually address their chamber from their party's lectern in the well on its side of the aisle. Senators usually speak at their assigned desks.

Whip—The majority or minority party member in each house who acts as assistant leader, helps plan and marshal support for party strategies, encourages party discipline and advises his or her leader on how colleagues intend to vote on the floor. In the Senate, the Republican whip's official title is assistant leader.

Yeas and Nays—A vote in which members usually respond "aye" or "no" (despite the official title of the vote) on a question when their names are called in alphabetical order. The Constitution requires the yeas and nays when a demand for it is supported by one-fifth of the members present, and it also requires an automatic yea-and-nay vote on overriding a veto. Senate precedents require the support of at least one-fifth of a quorum, a minimum of eleven members with the present membership of 100.

Congressional Information on the Internet

A huge array of congressional information is available for free at Internet sites operated by the federal government, colleges and universities and commercial firms. The sites offer the full text of bills introduced in the House and Senate, voting records, campaign finance information, transcripts of selected congressional hearings, investigative reports and much more.

THOMAS

The most important site for congressional information is THOMAS (*http://thomas.loc.gov*), which is named for Thomas Jefferson and operated by the Library of Congress. THOMAS' highlight is its databases containing the full text of all bills introduced in Congress since 1989, the full text of the *Congressional Record* since 1989 and the status and summary information for all bills introduced since 1973.

THOMAS also offers special links to bills that have received or are expected to receive floor action during the current week and newsworthy bills that are pending or that have recently been approved. Finally, THOMAS has selected committee reports, answers to frequently asked questions about accessing congressional information, publications titled *How Our Laws Are Made* and *Enactment of a Law* and links to lots of other congressional Web sites.

House of Representatives

The U.S. House of Representatives site (*http://www.house. gov*) offers the schedule of bills, resolutions and other legislative issues the House will consider in the current week. It also has updates about current proceedings on the House floor and a list of the next day's meeting of House committees. Other highlights include a database that helps users identify their representative, a directory of House members and committees, the House ethics manual, links to Web pages maintained by House members and committees, a calendar of congressional primary dates and candidate-filing deadlines for ballot access, the full text of all amendments to the Constitution that have been ratified and those that have been proposed but not ratified and lots of information about Washington, D.C., for visitors.

Another key House site is The Office of the Clerk On-line Information Center (*http://clerk.house.gov*), which has records of all roll-call votes taken since 1990. The votes are recorded by bill, so it is a lengthy process to compile a particular representative's voting record. The site also has lists of committee assignments, a telephone directory for members and committees, mailing label templates for members and committees, rules of the current Congress, election statistics from 1920 to the present, biographies of Speakers of the House, biographies of women who have served since 1917 and a virtual tour of the House Chamber.

One of the more interesting House sites is operated by the Subcommittee on Rules and Organization of the House Committee on Rules (*http://www.house.gov/rules/crs_reports. htm*). Its highlight is dozens of Congressional Research Service reports about the legislative process. Some of the available titles include *Legislative Research in Congressional Offices: A Primer, How to Follow Current Federal Legislation and Regulations; Investigative Oversight: An Introduction to the Law, Practice and Procedure of Congressional Inquiry;* and *Presidential Vetoes 1789 – Present: A Summary Overview.*

Senate

At least in the Internet world, the Senate is not as active as the House. Its main Web site (*http://www.senate.gov*) has records of all roll-call votes taken since 1989 (arranged by bill), brief descriptions of all bills and joint resolutions introduced in the Senate during the past week and a calendar of upcoming committee hearings. The site also provides the standing rules of the Senate, a directory of senators and their committee assignments, lists of nominations that the president has submitted to the Senate for approval, links to Web pages operated by senators and committees and a virtual tour of the Senate.

Information about the membership, jurisdiction and rules of each congressional committee is available at the U.S. Government Printing Office site (*http://www.access.gpo.gov/congress/ index.html*). It also has transcripts of selected congressional hearings, the full text of selected House and Senate reports and the House and Senate rules manuals.

General Reference

The Government Accountability Office, the investigative arm of Congress, operates a site (*http://www.gao.gov*) that provides the full text of its reports from 1975 to the present. The reports cover a wide range of topics: aviation safety, combating terrorism, counternarcotics efforts in Mexico, defense contracting, electronic warfare, food assistance programs, Gulf War illness, health insurance, illegal aliens, information technology, long-term care, mass transit, Medicare, military readiness, money laundering, national parks, nuclear waste, organ donation and student loan defaults, among others.

The GAO Daybook is an excellent current awareness tool. This electronic mailing list distributes a daily list of reports and testimony released by the GAO. Subscriptions are available by sending an e-mail message to *majordomo@www.gao.gov*, and in the message area typing "subscribe daybook" (without the quotation marks).

Current budget and economic projections are provided at the Congressional Budget Office Web site (*http://www.cbo.gov*). The site also has reports about the economic and budget outlook for the next decade, the president's budget proposals, federal civilian employment, Social Security privatization, tax reform, water use conflicts in the West, marriage and the federal income tax and the role of foreign aid in development, among other topics. Other highlights include monthly budget updates, historical budget data, cost estimates for bills reported by congressional committees and transcripts of congressional testimony by CBO officials.

Campaign Finance

Several Internet sites provide detailed campaign finance data for congressional elections. The official site is operated by the Federal Election Commission (*http://www.fec.gov*), which regulates political spending. The site's highlight is its database of campaign reports filed from May 1996 to the present by House and presidential candidates, political action committees and political party committees. Senate reports are not included because they are filed with the Secretary of the Senate. The reports in the FEC's database are scanned images of paper reports filed with the commission.

The FEC site also has summary financial data for House and Senate candidates in the current election cycle, abstracts of court decisions pertaining to federal election law from 1976 to 1997, a graph showing the number of political action committees in existence each year from 1974 to the present and a directory of national and state agencies that are responsible for releasing information about campaign financing, candidates on the ballot, election results, lobbying and other issues. Another useful feature is a collection of brochures about federal election law, public funding of presidential elections, the ban on contributions by foreign nationals, independent expenditures supporting or opposing a candidate for federal office, contribution limits, filing a complaint, researching public records at the FEC and other topics. Finally, the site provides the FEC's legislative recommendations, its annual report, a report about its first twenty years in existence, the FEC's monthly newsletter, several reports about voter registration, election results for the most recent presidential and congressional elections and campaign guides for corporations and labor organizations, congressional candidates and committees, political party committees and nonconnected committees.

The best online source for campaign finance data is Political Money Line (*http://www.tray.com*). The site's searchable databases provide extensive itemized information about receipts and expenditures by federal candidates and political action committees from 1980 to the present. The data, which are obtained from the FEC, are quite detailed. For example, for candidates contribu-

tions can be searched by Zip Code. The site also has lists of the top political action committees in various categories, lists of the top contributors from each state and much more.

Another interesting site is the American University Campaign Finance Web site (*http://www1.soc.american.edu/campfin/index. cfm*), which is operated by the American University School of Communication. It provides electronic files from the FEC that have been reformatted in .dbf format so they can be used in database programs such as Paradox, Access and FoxPro. The files contain data on PAC, committee and individual contributions to individual congressional candidates.

More campaign finance data is available from the Center for Responsive Politics (*http://www.opensecrets.org*), a public interest organization. The center provides a list of all "soft money" donations to political parties of $100,000 or more in the current election cycle and data about "leadership" political action committees associated with individual politicians. Other databases at the site provide information about travel expenses that House members received from private sources for attending meetings and other events, activities of registered federal lobbyists and activities of foreign agents who are registered in the United States.

Index

Abortion, 64, 80-81
Abramoff, Jack
  lobbying scandal, 37, 40, 49, 54, 69, 76
  scandal and American Indians, 42-44
Abt Associates Inc., 30
Abu Ghraib prison, 72
ACLU. *See* American Civil Liberties Union (ACLU)
ACTFU. *See* All China Federation of Trade Unions (ACFTU)
Addington, David H., 23
Adler, Prudence, 19
"Advice and Consent: The Politics of Judicial Appointments" (Segal), 83
Advisory Panel on Federal Tax Reform, 114
Aetna, 105
Afghanistan (war), 25
AFL-CIO, 6-7
Akin, Todd (R-Mo.), 68
Albright, Madeleine, 96
Alito, Samuel A., Jr., 12, 76, 80, 81, 82-84
All, David, 54
All China Federation of Trade Unions (ACFTU), 6-7
Allen, Ron, 42, 44
al Qaeda, 21, 23, 48, 65
  prisoners, 72-73
Altria Group Inc., 88
American Beverage Association, 92
American Board of Internal Medicine, 103
American Civil Liberties Union (ACLU), 15, 23, 73
American Enterprise Institute, 33, 65, 103
American Indians, 42-44
  "State of Indian Nations" speech, 43
American Institute of Certified Public Accountants, 116
American Medical Association, 54
American Online, 14
Americans for Tax Reform, 8, 63, 110
Americans with Disabilities Act, 90
American Tort Reform Association, 87
America Online, 104
Anders, Christopher E., 73
Anti-Terror Law (2001), 16
Antos, Joseph, 103, 106
Arctic National Wildlife Refuge, 28, 68, 76
Arkansas healthy habits program, 91
ARKids First, 91
Armey, Dick, 45, 47, 48
Armstrong, Jerome, 54
Ashcroft, John, 26, 83
Association of Research Libraries, 19
AT&T Corp., 24
Ayotte v. Planned Parenthood of Northern New England, 81

Baker, Ross K., 26
Baker, Stewart, 97, 98
Balkin, Jack M., 13
Bankruptcy law, 63
Bankston, Kevin, 17-18
Banzhaf, John F., III, 89-90, 91
Barr, Bob, 52
Barrow, John (D-Ga.), 41
Baucus, Max (D-Mont.), 83

Bauer, Gary L., 108
Bayer AG, 96
Bayh, Evan (D-Ind.), 97
Bean, Melissa (D-Ill.), 41
Beaver, Diane, 23
Bennett, Robert F. (R-Utah), 6, 51
Berman, Howard L. (D-Calif.), 12
Berry, Marion (D-Ark.), 4, 9
Biden, Joseph R., Jr. (D-Del.), 65, 72-75
Bilbray, Brian P., 41
Binder, Sarah, 67
BIPAC. *See* Business Industry Political Action Committee (BIPAC)
Blackmun, Harry, 81
Blank, Paul, 10
Blogging, 54, 56, 58
Blunt, Roy (R-Mo.), 9, 31, 49, 69
Boehlert, Sherwood (R-N.Y.), 49, 68
Boehner, John A. (R-Ohio), 46, 47, 48, 49, 51, 52, 54
Bolger, Glen, 63
Bolton, John R., 64
Bonacich, Edna, 7
Bonjean, Ron, 52
Boozman, John (R-Ark.), 5
Bork, Robert H., 82, 83
Boswell, Leonard L. (D-Iowa), 41
Bowman, Karlyn, 65
Bradley, Curtis A., 22
Brady, David, 47
Brandeis, Louis D., 80
Breaux, John B. (D-La.), 114
"Bridges to Excellence" program, 103
Brookings Institution, 67
Brown, Sherrod (D-Ohio), 40
Brownback, Sam (R-Kan.), 64, 112
Brown v. Board of Education, 81
Buchanan, Patrick, 112
Budget, federal
  and social programs, 27-31
  targets for spending cuts, 31
Buffet, Warren, 8
Bullock, Charles, 48
Bumpers, Dale, 4
Bureau of Economic Analysis, 94
Burns, Conrad (R-Mont.), 36, 40
Burns, Max, 41
Burns International, 95
Busby, Francine, 41
Bush, George W.
  election of, 48, 49
  on energy, 77, 78
  and executive authority, 21-26
  on health care, 77, 78, 100-106
  on Hurricane Katrina, 79
  on immigration, 107, 113
  impeachment possibility, 26
  influence on 2006 elections, 36
  and Iraq War, 70-75
  on NSA eavesdropping, 14, 18
  and public opinion polls, 46
  and Republican Party, 50
  on social programs and budget, 27-31
  on Social Security, 52
  speech to Detroit Economic Club, 27, 30
  State of the Union address (2006), 76-79

  on taxes, 114
  on torture of prisoners, 72
Bush, Jeb, 105
Business Industry Political Action Committee (BIPAC), 57, 58, 59
Business Roundtable, 54, 57, 103
Butler, Stuart M., 102, 105
Bybee, Jay S., 23
Byrd, Robert C. (D-W.Va.), 51

CAFTA. *See* Central American Free Trade Agreement (CAFTA)
Cain, Bruce, 39
Call, Amy, 68
Campbell, John, 38
Campbell Soup, 89
Canner, Steve, 99
Cantor, Eric (R-Va.), 31
Cantwell, Maria (D-Wash.), 40
Carl Buddig & Co., 89
Carlyle Group, 98
Carmona, Richard H., 87
Carnegie, Andrew, 96
Carnivore (software), 19
Carper, Thomas R. (D-Del.), 68
Case, Steve, 104
Casey, Bob, 37, 40
Casey, Greg, 57, 59
Castellari, John, 57
Castle, Michael N. (R-Del.), 28, 52, 68
Catholic Church, 108
Cato Institute, 8, 117
CDC. *See* Centers for Disease Control and Prevention (CDC)
Center for Constitutional Rights, 24
Center for Consumer Freedom, 89
Center for Democracy and Citizenship, 26
Center for Democracy and Technology, 14, 17
Center for International Security Studies, 97
Center for Legal and Judicial Studies, 33
Center for Science in the Public Interest (CSPI), 87, 89
Center for Strategic and International Studies, 71, 97
Center on Budget and Policy Priorities, 28
Centers for Disease Control and Prevention (CDC), 88, 90
Central American Free Trade Agreement (CAFTA), 57, 62, 63, 67, 69
CFIUS. *See* Committee on Foreign Investment in the United States (CFIUS)
Chafee, Lincoln (R-R.I.), 40, 68, 69
Chamber of Commerce. *See* U.S. Chamber of Commerce
Chambliss, Saxby (R-Ga.), 22
Chemerinsky, Erwin, 81
Cheney, Dick, 21, 23, 46, 48, 51, 62
Chertoff, Michael, 79
Chevron Corp., 98
Chickasaw Nation, 42
Child Online Protection Act (1998), 17
China National Offshore Oil Corp., 95, 98
Civil Rights Act (1866), 12
Civil War, 22
Clean Air Act, 64
Cleary, Pat, 56

Clinton, Bill
    health and weight issues, 91
    and health care, 101, 106
    judicial nominations, 82, 83
    on NAFTA, 38
    presidency and impeachment of, 47, 48
    on Wal-Mart, 9
Clinton, Hillary Rodham (D-N.Y.), 97, 111
Club for Growth, 46
Coburn, Tom (R-Okla.), 113
Coca-Cola Co., 87, 89, 115
Cochran, Thad (R-Miss.), 29
CocoaVia, 92
Codey, Richard J., 41
"Colbert Report," 54
Cole, Tom (R-Okla.), 42
Coleman, Norm (R-Minn.), 97
Collins, Mac, 41
Collins, Susan (R-Maine), 68, 80
Comey, James, 26
Commerce Department, 94
Committee on Foreign Investment in the
    United States (CFIUS), 96, 97, 99
Common Cause, 10
Commonwealth Fund, 104
Community Bankers of America, 9
Community Development Work Study
    Program, 31
Conant, Alex, 32
Coney, Lillie, 57
Congress
    approval ratings poll, 36
    and blogging, 54
    e-mail to, 58
    on immigration policy, 107-113
    and Iraq War, 70-75
    and partisanship, 66-69
    plans for 2006, 62-65
    on port security conflict, 96, 97-99
    and Republican dominance, 45-52
    on State of the Union address, 77
Congressional Management Foundation, 58, 59
"Congressional Politics of Immigration
    Reform" (Gimpel), 109
Congressional Review Act, 9
ConnectYourCare Inc., 105
Conrad, Kent (D-N.D.), 68
Conservative Political Action Committee, 111
Consumer Product Safety Commission, 32, 33
"Contract With America," 38, 46, 47, 48-49
Cook, Rhodes, 38
Cordesman, Anthony H., 71, 74-75
Cornyn, John (R-Texas), 13, 33, 109, 113
Corporate America, investment in, 93-99
Corzine, Jon, 41
Couch v. United States, 16
Council on Foundations, 8
Craig, Larry E. (R-Idaho), 33
CSPI. See Center for Science in the Public
    Interest (CSPI)
Culpepper, Lee, 2, 5, 7, 11
Cunningham, Bryan, 22-23, 25
Cunningham, Randy "Duke," 39, 40, 78
Cuno, Charlotte, 115

"The Daily Show," 29
DaimlerChrysler, 95, 115
Dallas-Ft. Worth International, 55
Darr, Carol, 58
Davis, Richard, 82

Davis, Thomas M., III (R-Va.), 40, 79
Daynard, Richard A., 90
Dayton, Mark (D-Minn.), 41
Deal, Nathan (R-Ga.), 12, 13
Dean, Howard, 55
Defense Production Act (1950), 97
DeLauro, Rosa (D-Conn.), 9, 10, 11
DeLay, Tom (R-Texas)
    ethics scandal, 62, 76
    and GOP majority, 45-46
    timeline, 46-49
    and partisan politics, 67
    resignation of, 39, 40
    and Wal-Mart lobbying, 4
Deloitte Center for Health Solutions, 102
Democracy 21, 55
Democracy Data & Communications, 57, 59
Democrats
    and 2006 midterm elections, 36-41
    on immigration policy, 112-113
    and judicial nominations, 82-84
    response to State of the Union, 76
    and partisanship, 66-69
Dempsey, James, 14, 17
DeSipio, Louis, 38
Detainee rights, 72-73
Detroit Economic Club, 30
DeWine, Mike (R-Ohio), 26, 40, 69, 70
Dingell, John D. (D-Mich.), 32
Dinh, Viet, 23
Dobson, James, 108
Dole, Bob, 47, 51, 90
Domenici, Pete B. (R-N.M.), 77
Domestic spying, 21-26
    opinion polls on, 22
Dongen, Dirk Van, 54-55
DP World, 96, 97, 99
Drug Enforcement Agency, 19
Duane Reade pharmacies, 104
Duffy, Trent, 26
DuPont Co., 96

Eastman, John C., 12-13
Edelman Public Relations, 56
Education and the Workforce Committee
    (House), 28
Edwards, Chris, 117
Edwards, Mickey, 21, 22
Ekern, Anne, 18
Elections, 2006 midterm
    opinion polls on, 37, 40
Electronic Communications Privacy Act
    (1986), 15, 16, 18
Electronic Frontier Foundation, 17, 24
Electronic Privacy Information Center, 24-25, 57
Elk, John, 13
Elk v. Wilkins, 13
Ellsworth, Brad, 41
Ence, Ron, 3, 9
Erickson, Markham, 17
Even Start, 27-31
Extend Benefits LLC, 105

Fairchild Semiconductor Corp., 93
Family Research Council, 44
Farrell, Diane, 41
FBI. See Federal Bureau of Investigation (FBI)
FDA. See Food and Drug Administration
    (FDA)
Federal Aviation Administration, 49

Federal Bureau of Investigation (FBI), 19
Federal Communications Commission
    and internet wiretapping, 19
Federal Deposit Insurance Corporation, 5
Federal government
    relations with states, 32-33
Federal Motor Carrier Safety Administration, 10
Feinstein, Dianne (D-Calif.), 113
Financial Services Roundtable, 58, 59
First Amendment, 24
FISA. See Foreign Intelligence Surveillance Act
    (FISA)
Fitch, Brad, 58
527 organizations, 46
Flake, Jeff (R-Ariz.), 24, 52
Focus on the Family, 108
Foley, Mark (R-Fla.), 13
Foley, Thomas S., 46
Food and Drug Administration (FDA), 32-33
Food court, 87
Food industry
    and obesity, 87-92
Ford, Harold E., Jr. (D-Tenn.), 40, 69
Foreign Intelligence Surveillance Act (FISA),
    21-22, 23
    and the Constitution, 24-25
Fortas, Abe, 83
Fourteenth Amendment, 12-13
Fourth Amendment, 18, 24
    and the internet, 15
Francona, Rick, 75
Frank, Barney (R-Mass.), 9
Freedom of Information Act, 24-25
Freiwald, Susan, 19
Frist, Bill (R-Tenn.)
    and 2006 elections, 36-37, 40
    on gay marriage, 79
    and GOP majority timeline, 49
    on immigration policy, 107, 109-110
    as majority leader, 50-51, 68, 77

Gale, William G., 117
Gallagher, Janne, 8
"Gang of 14" (Senate), 24
Gang of Seven, 46
GAO. See Government Accountability Office
    (GAO)
Garcia, Joe, 43
Garrow, David J., 81
Gates, Bill, 8
Gates Foundation, 8
Gaziano, Todd, 33
General Electric Capital Corp., 11
General Electric Co., 103
General Mills, 89
Geneva Conventions, 72
Gerberding, Julie L., 90
Gerlach, Jim (R-Pa.), 41
Ghazal, Maria, 103
Gidari, Albert, 19
Gilchrest, Wayne T. (R-Md.), 68
Gilchrist, Jim, 38
Giles, Jason, 43
Gillibrand, Kirsten, 41
Gimpel, James, 109
Gingrich, Newt, 45, 46, 47, 48
Ginsburg, Ruth Bader, 83, 84
Global Crossing Ltd., 98
"God Save this Honorable Court" (Tribe), 83
Goeas, Ed, 62, 64, 65

Gonzalez, Alberto R., 23, 26
Goodling, Bill, 28, 29
Goodling Institute for Research in Family
    Literacy, 29, 31
Goodman, Susan, 54
Google Inc., 15, 17, 18, 19
Gould, Lewis L., 50
Government Accountability Office (GAO), 79,
    97
Graham, Edward M., 93-94
Graham, Lindsey (R-S.C.), 23, 72-73, 83, 112
Gramm, Phil (R-Texas), 116
Grassley, Charles E. (R-Iowa), 59, 76
Grass-roots organizing, 53-55, 57
Green, John, 108
Greenberger, Marcia, 84
Gregg, Judd (R-N.H.), 51
Greve, Michael, 33
Grocery Manufacturers Association, 92
Grossman, Andrew, 10
Guantánamo Bay prisoners, 21, 72-73

Hackett, Paul, 41
Hagel, Chuck (R-Neb.), 75
Hamdi, Yaser, 73
Hamdi v. Rumsfeld, 22
Harjo, Suzan Shown, 43
Harkin, Tom (D-Iowa), 90
Hart-Scott-Rodino antitrust law (1976), 99
Hastert, J. Dennis (R-Ill.), 37, 45, 47, 48, 50, 52
Hayden, Michael V., 23
Haynes, William, 23
Hayworth, J.D. (R-Ariz.), 107
Head Start, 28
Health care, 100-106
    Bush on, 77, 78
    hospital pricing, 103
    and pay-for-performance care, 104-105
Health insurance companies, 101
Health reimbursement accounts (HRAs), 102
Health savings accounts (HSAs), 102-103
Healthy Communities Access Program, 31
HEB groceries, 104
Heritage Foundation, 8, 33, 102
Herzlinger, Regina E., 103
Hill, Baron P., 41
Hinderaker, John, 54
Holmes, Josh, 38
Homeland Security, Dept. of, 97
Honda, 95
Hoover Institution, 46, 47
HOPE VI program, 28, 31
Hostettler, John (R-Ind.), 41
House Immigration Reform Caucus, 111
Howard, Jerry, 115
Hoyer, Steny H. (D-Md.), 68
Hubbard, Al, 102
Huckabee, Mike, 90-91
Hunter, Duncan (R-Calif.), 97
Hurricane Katrina, 62
    emergency monetary relief, 63, 64
    rebuilding, 38, 76
    response investigation, 79
Hussein, Saddam, 73
Hutchison Whampoa Ltd., 98
Hwang, Jenny, 108

IBM, 98
IBM Corp., 98
Immigration, 107-113

reform, 64
and the 14th Amendment, 12-13
Inc. (magazine), 57
Independent Community Bankers
    of America, 3
Indian Country Today (newspaper), 43
Industrial Revolution, 94, 96
Inslee, Jay (D-Wash.), 14
Institute for International Economics, 94
Institute for Politics, Democracy & the
    Internet, 58
Institute of Medicine, 88
Internal Revenue Service, 10, 115
Internet
    blogging, 54, 56
    dial-up vs. broadband, 17, 18
    and grass-roots organizing, 57
    IP addresses, 19
    and libraries, 19
    privacy, 14-19
    and search engines, 17-18
    and spam filters, 58
    and web-based initiatives, 53-55
Intuit Inc., 105
Investments, foreign, 93-99
iPod, 38
Iraq War, 25, 47
    and possibility of civil war, 74
    support from Congress, 70-75
Islam
    and prejudice against, 99
    riots after cartoon publication, 26
    sectarian violence in Iraq, 72-73, 74

Jack in the Box, 89
Jackson, Robert H., 22-23, 72-73
Jacobs, Lawrence, 46, 52
Jacobson, Michael, 90
Jamestown S'Klallam Tribe, 42
Japan Inc., 93
Jefferson, William J. (D-La.), 79
Jeffords, James M. (I-Vt.), 41, 48
Jindal, Bobby (R-La.), 69
Jochum, Rita Lari, 59
Johnson, Jacqueline, 43, 44
Johnson, Lyndon B., 83
Johnson, Nancy L. (R-Conn.), 68
Josten, Bruce, 54
Judicial filibuster, 82
Justice Department, 15, 17, 19

Kaine, Timothy, 41
    Democratic response to State of the Union,
    76-78
Kean, Tom, Jr., 40
Keating, David, 46
Keck, Beth, 8
Keller, William, 97, 99
Kellogg Co., 87, 89
Kennedy, Anthony M., 81
Kennedy, Edward M. (D-Mass.), 107, 110-111,
    112-113
Kerry, John (D-Mass.), 18, 37, 68
KeySpan Corp., 95
Kies, Kenneth, 117
Kilgore, Jerry, 41
King, Peter T. (R-N.Y.), 96
Kingston, Jack, 54
Kirk, Mark Steven (R-Ill.), 68
Klain, Ron, 104

Klein, Ron, 41
Koch, George W., 4, 7
Kofinis, Chris, 4
Kogan, Richard, 28
Korean War, 24
Kosovo (war), 25
Kraft Foods Inc., 88, 89, 92
Krempasky, Mike, 56
"K Street" project, 45
Kurdish Pesh Merga, 74
Kyl, Jon (R-Ariz.), 113

Labor Department
    Wage and Hour Division, 10
Laffey, Stephen, 40
Laird v. Tatum, 25
Lamberti, Jeff, 41
Land, Richard, 108
Landrieu, Mary L. (D-La.), 51, 68
La Raza Unida, 113
Lautenberg, Frank R. (D-N.J.), 96
Leach, Jim (R-Iowa), 6, 9
Leahy, Patrick J. (D-Vt.), 15, 23, 83
Leapfrog Group, 104
Leavitt, Michael O., 32
Lenovo Group LTD., 98
Lewinsky, Monica, 48
Lewis, James, 97
Lezy, Norm, 4
Libby, I. Lewis "Scooter," 23
Lieberman, Joseph I. (D-Conn.), 112
Li Jianming, 7
Lincoln, Blanche (D-Ark.), 4
Lindquist, Stefanie, 84
Livingston, Robert L., 48
Lockheed Corp., 98
Lockheed-Martin, 97
Lott, Trent (R-Miss.), 4, 47, 49, 51
Love Field (Dallas, TX), 53
LTV Corp., 98
Lumbee Indian tribe, 42
Lumenos Inc., 100, 101, 105
Lungren, Dan (R-Calif.), 25, 110
Lynch, Dotty, 37-38

Mack, Connie (R-Fla.), 114
Mack, David, 71-72, 74, 75
Madigan, Edward, 46
Madrid, Patricia, 18, 41
Mann, Thomas E., 75
Manson, Marshall, 56
Marchick, David, 94, 96, 98
Markey, Edward J. (D-Mass.), 18
Marshall, Jim (D-Ga.), 41
Marshall, Thurgood, 81, 83
Mars Inc., 92
Martinez, Mel (R-Fla.), 109, 110
Martin Marietta Corp., 98
Maryland Legislature
    on Wal-Mart and health care, 11
Maskrey, Judy, 59
Massachusetts Supreme Judicial Court, 89
McAdams, John, 56
McCain, John (R-Ariz.)
    anti-torture amendment, 72-73
    on detainee abuse, 65, 72-73
    on illegal immigration, 107, 110-113
McCain-Kennedy immigration proposal, 110,
    112-113
McCaskill, Claire, 40

McConnell, Mitch (R-Ky.), 50-51
McConnon, B.R., 57, 59
McDermott, Jim (D-Wash.), 67
McDonald's Corp., 89-92
McGavick, Mike, 40
McHenry, Patrick T. (R-N.C.), 69
McKay, Christie, 29, 30, 31
McKinsey and Co., 103
McNulty, James, 95
McSweeney, David, 41
Medicaid and Medicare
    and budget cuts, 28
    and changing healthcare system, 105
    coverage of Viagra, 31
    drug law, 106
    expansion of, 46
    and obesity, 87
Melancon, Charlie (D-La.), 41
Menendez, Robert (D-N.J.), 40, 97
Merrill, Thomas W., 3
Microsoft Corp., 4
Microsoft MSN, 17, 18
Miers, Harriet, 82, 83
Miller, Bill, 57, 58
Minnis, Peggy A., 31
MinuteClinic, 105
Minuteman Project, 38, 110, 111
Mitsubishi, 93, 98
Mollohan, Alan B. (D-W.Va.), 40
Morgan, Lance, 8
Motor Vehicle Safety Act, 33
MoveOn.org, 55
Mulligan, Deirdre, 17, 19
Murphy, Lois, 41
Murtha, John P. (D-Pa.), 65, 75

Nader, Ralph, 115
Nadler, Jerrold (D-N.Y.), 24
NAFTA. See North American Free Trade
    Agreement (NAFTA)
NAM. See National Association of
    Manufacturers (NAM)
National Association of Evangelicals, 108
National Association of Home Builders, 115
National Association of Manufacturers
    (NAM), 56
National Association of Wholesaler-
    Distributors, 55
National Center for Family Literacy, 29
National Conference on State Legislatures, 32
National Congress of American Indians, 42,
    43-44
National Council of La Raza, 29
National Economic Council, 102
National Even Start Association, 29
National Foreign Trade Council, 98
National Governors Association (NGA), 90-91,
    115
National Grid, 95
National Highway Traffic and Safety
    Administration (NHTSA), 32-33
National Hispanic Christian Leadership
    Conference, 108
National Indian Gaming Association, 42
National Indian Gaming Commission, 42
National Labor Relations Board, 42
National Partnership for Women & Families, 10
National Republican Committee
    and iPods, 38
National Republican Congressional

Committee, 40
National Republican Senatorial Committee, 40
National Restaurant Association, 5, 87, 92
National Security Agency (NSA)
    and domestic spying, 18, 21-26
    unauthorized spying, 65
National Security Council, 24
National Women's Law Center, 84
Nelson, Ben (D-Neb.), 68, 83, 113
Nelson, Glen, 105
NetCoalition, 17
Ney, Bob (R-Ohio), 40
NGA. See National Governor's Association
    (NGA)
NHTSA. See National Highway Traffic and
    Safety Administration (NHTSA)
"No Child Left Behind," 49
Norquist, Grover, 63-64, 110, 112
North American Free Trade Agreement
    (NAFTA), 38
NSA. See National Security Agency (NSA)
Nussle, Jim (R-Iowa), 46

Obama, Barack (D-Ill.), 79, 112
Oberstar, James L. (D-Minn.), 10
Obesity, 86-92
Ochsenschlager, Tom, 116, 117
O'Connor, Sandra Day, 80-81, 84
Office of Management and Budget (OMB), 30,
    32
Office of Thrift Supervision, 6
Oklahoma City bombing, 97
OMB. See Office of Management and Budget
    (OMB)
    1-800-Schedule, 105
Opinion polling, 38, 40
Opthalmologists, activism of, 54

PacifiCare Health System, 105
Packwood, Bob, 115, 116, 117
Padilla, José, 73
PART. See Program Assessment Rating Tool
    (PART)
Partisan politics, 66-69
Patraeus, David, 26
Patriot Act, 69, 76, 97
    extension of, 62, 64
    and federal budget, 28
    and internet privacy, 19
    and pen register data, 19
Payne v. Tennessee, 80-81
Pelosi, Nancy (D-Calif.), 54, 67, 69
People for the Ethical Treatment
    of Animals, 89
PepsiCo Inc., 87, 89, 92
Perkins, Tony, 44
Persian Gulf War, 25
Pew Hispanic Center
    study on labor and illegal immigrants, 110
Pew Research Center for the People & the Press
    report on religion and immigration, 108
Philip Morris USA, 88, 89
Pinkerton's Inc., 95
Pinkham, Doug, 54, 59
Pitney, Jack, 110, 111
Planned Parenthood of Southeastern Pa. v. Casey, 81
Platts, Todd R. (R-Pa.), 29, 31
Plessy v. Ferguson, 81
Plyer v. Doe, 13
Pollack, Kenneth M., 74

Portman, Rob, 41
Port security conflict, 96, 97-99
Powell, Colin L., 104
PPG Industries, 55, 58, 59
Price Waterhouse, 117
Prisoner abuse, 72-73
Procter & Gamble, 104
Program Assessment Rating Tool (PART), 30
Project HOPE, 104
Prosperity Project, 58
Pryce, Deborah (R-Ohio), 63-65
Pryor, Mark (D-Ark.), 58
Public Affairs Council, 54, 59
Public Citizen, 33

Quan, Katie, 6

Radio Act (1927), 96
Raines, Franklin, 104
Rasul, Shafiq, 73
Rasul v. Bush, 73
Reagan, Ronald, 33, 117
Rebovich, David, 37
Redi Clinic, 104-105
RedState.org, 56
Regula, Ralph (R-Ohio), 28-29, 30
Rehnquist, William H., 80-81
Reid, Harry (D-Nev.), 78, 113
Reinhardt, Uwe E., 101
Reinsch, William, 98, 99
Religious groups
    on immigration, 108
Republicans
    and 2006 midterm elections, 36-41
    and Bush, 26
    "Contract With America," 38
    Gang of Seven, 46
    and immigration policy, 107-113
    "Revolution" of 1994, 45
Republican Study Committee, 52
Revolutionary War, 22
Revolution LLC, 104, 105
Reynolds, Thomas M. (R-N.Y.), 40
Ridgway, Matthew B., 97
Roach, Eric, 41
Roberts, John G., Jr., 64, 80-81, 82-84
Roberts, Pat (R-Kan.), 22
Rockefeller Center, 93, 98
Rodriguez, Samuel, Jr., 108
Roe v. Wade, 64, 80-81, 84
Rogers, Mike (R-Mich.), 44
Romero, Anthony, 23
Romero, Craig, 41
Roosevelt, Franklin D., 22
Rotenberg, Marc, 19
Rothrock, Aubrey, III, 8
Rove, Karl, 29, 31, 111
Rowe, Jack, 105
Rudalevige, Andrew, 48
Rudy, Tony, 40
Rural Housing and Economic Development
    program, 31
Rutledge, John, 83

Safe and Drug-Free Shools program, 31
Salazar, Ken (D-Colo.), 83
Salvation Army, 4
Same-sex marriage, 64
Sam's Club, 105
Sanders, Bernard (I-Vt.), 41

San Juan Pueblo, 43
Santorum, Rick (R-Pa.), 37, 46, 69, 79
Sapp, Carolyn, 10
Sara Lee, 89
Sarbanes, Paul S. (D-Md.), 41
Scalia, Antonin, 81, 83
Scanlon, Michael, 40
Schiavo, Terri, 62, 107
Schlafly, Phyllis, 108
Schumer, Charles E. (D-N.Y.), 12, 84, 93
Schwartz, Victor, 87-89, 90-92
Schwarzenegger, Arnold, 92
Scott, H. Lee, Jr., 4
Securitas Security Services USA Inc., 95
Sefl, Tracy, 10
Segal, Jeffrey A., 83-84
Senate. *See* Congress
Sensenbrenner, F. James, Jr. (R-Wisc.), 13, 26
September 11, 2001, terrorist attacks, 48, 97
Service Employees International Union, 6, 10, 56
Sessions, Jeff (R-Ala.), 113
setlovefree.com, 53
Shadegg, John (R-Ariz.), 49
Shailor, Barbara, 6-7
Shapiro, Rick, 55, 58
Shaw, E. Clay, Jr. (R-Fla.), 41
Shays, Christopher (R-Conn.), 41, 68
Shelby, Richard C. (R-Ala.), 96
Shell Oil, 95
Sherman, Chris, 17, 18
Shiite Badr militias, 74
Shopfloor.org, 56
Sierra Club, 10
Sifry, David, 56
Silliman, Scott L., 26, 72
Simmons, Rob (R-Conn.), 31
Simpson, Alan K., 47, 109, 110-111, 112
Skaggs, David, 26
Smith v. Maryland, 16
Snowe, Olympia J. (R-Maine), 29, 31, 68
Social Security overhaul, 62
Sodexho, 93, 95
Sodrel, Mike (R-Ind.), 41
Souter, David H., 84
Southern Baptists, 108
Southwest Airlines, 53-54, 55
Specter, Arlen (R-Pa.), 18, 22, 23, 26, 29, 65, 80, 87
Spellings, Margaret, 31
Stanley, Jay, 15, 18
Stanton, John, 90, 92
"State of Indian Nations" speech, 43
Steele, Michael, 40
Sterling Drug Inc., 96
Stern, Andrew J., 6

Steuerle, Eugene, 116
Strasburg, Gale, 92
Subway, 87, 92
Sullivan, John (R-Okla.), 59
Sunrise Research Corp., 115
Sununu, John E. (R-N.H.), 19
Supreme Court
    on abortion, 80-81
    confirmation hearings, 82-84
    on detainee rights, 72-73
    and precedents, 80-81
Sweeney, John E. (R-N.Y.), 41
Synergy Partners Inc., 29

Talent, Jim (R-Mo.), 40, 69
Talley, Kevin, 29
Tancredo, Tom (R-Colo.), 107, 111-112
Tate, Powell, 8
Taxes
    cuts, 63
    state of in America, 114-117
    states and corporations, 115
Taylor, Wendy, 59
Teamsters, 115
Technorati.com, 56
Terrorist attacks, 97
Thomas, Clarence, 81, 83
Thompson, Joe, 91
Thomson CSF, 98
Thompson, Kevin, 115
Thurmond, Strom, 49, 51
Tooke, Chip, 101
Toronto-Dominion Bank, 6
Towns, Edolphus (D-N.Y.), 67
Toyota, 95
Trading with the Enemy Act, 96
Transportation Department, 10
Tribe, Laurence H., 82
Truman, Harry S, 22, 72
Trust for America's Health, 91
Tushnet, Mark, 25

United Arab Emirates
    and U.S. port operations, 51, 97-98
United States v. Miller, 16
United States v. Wong Kim Ark, 13
Unocal Corp., 95, 98
Urban Institute, 116
U.S. Chamber of Commerce, 10, 54, 55, 57, 58, 59, 63, 87, 89, 113
"U.S. National Security and Foreign Direct Investment" (Graham and Marchick), 94
U.S. Steel, 96
Utah bank charter
    and Wal-Mart, 11

Utah industrial loan company (ILC), 7, 9
Verizon Corp., 104
Veterans Affairs, Dept. of, 54, 59
VetsCoalition.org, 59
Viacom Inc., 87
Vietnam War, 24
Vitter, David (R-La.), 79

Wake Up Wal-Mart, 4, 11
Walker, David M., 79
"Wal-Mart: The High Cost of Low Price" (film), 3, 11
Wal-Mart Stores Inc., 3-11
    and walk-in clinics, 104-105
    and web attacks, 56
Wal-Mart vs. Women, 10
Wal-Mart Watch, 11, 56
Walton, Helen, 8
Walton, John, 8
Walton, Rob, 8
Walton, Sam, 3, 4, 8
Walton Family Foundation, 8
War, declaration of, 24-25
Warner, John W. (R-Va.), 24
Warner, Mark, 41
War Powers Act, 24
Warren, Earl, 81
Washington, George, 83
Watts, J.C., 48
Webb, Matthew, 89
Web logs. *See* blogging
WebMD, 105
WellPoint/Anthem, 101
Wells Fargo, 95
Wendy's, 91
Wertheimer, Fred, 55, 58
Whalen, Bill, 46
White, Byron R., 81
Whittington, Keith, 84
Wilensky, Gail R., 104
Wilkins, David, 42, 44
Wilson, Heather A. (R-N.M.), 18, 24, 26, 30, 41
Wilson, Woodrow, 96
Winborn, Erik, 4, 9
Wiretapping Act (1968), 16, 18
Wong Kim Ark, 13
World Relief, 108
World Trade Center bombings, 97
World War II, 24
Wright, Jim, 46

Yahoo, 14, 17, 18
Yoo, John C., 21, 23, 26
Youngstown Sheet and Tube Co. v. Sawyer, 22